'Indicting the 45th President is a compelling and incisive examination of the unprecedented crimes of, and threats posed by, Donald Trump. In meticulous detail Gregg Barak explores a multifaceted web of white-collar, corporate, and state crimes and sheds light on the formidable obstacles faced by those seeking to hold Trump and his associates responsible for their actions. With insightful analysis, the book offers a fierce critique of the current state of U.S. constitutional democracy and proposes a vision for a reformed and improved democratic system. This timely and incisive work serves as a clarion call and constitutes a vital contribution to the ongoing discussion on the fragility of democracy in the face of the unscrupulous use of power.'

**Isabel Schoultz,** *Associate Professor in Sociology of Law,*
*Lund University, Sweden*

'Gregg Barak engenders fear, loathing and perhaps hope through his consistent insight via command of detail as he forensically interrogates how Teflon Don and his sycophantic entourage across politics, law, media and militarizing civil society have embraced immorality, duplicity, corruption and naked authoritarianism to plunge the U.S. democratic system into unprecedented crisis. Brilliantly traversing the legal travails of Trump – through the unprecedented lawsuits including "hush money" payments, the mishandling of government documents, obstruction of justice, criminal contempt and, last but hardly least, the January 6th Insurrection – Indicting the 45th President is a must read for scholars and defenders of social justice. It presents the most stark yet thoroughly analytical of warnings about the contours and dimensions of the current and present danger to American democracy – while at the same time provides the reader with the hope of a re-framed democratic vision for all Americans. A monumental achievement.'

**Steve Tombs,** *Emeritus Professor of Criminology,*
*The Open University, UK*

'Criminologist Barak's previous book detailed the numerous crimes former President Donald Trump committed prior to, during, and after his presidency. This second book confronts Trump's use of power, privilege, and wealth to evade the law. As an examination of our failure to control crimes of the powerful, this thoroughly researched window into the 45th President's litany of escapes from justice is ultimately a warning about the weakness of American democracy and the vulnerability of constitutional rights in the face of autocratic tribalist ideology empowered by privilege. His solution is to reform the political system to make America fully democratic. Barak's political criminology is a must-read expose of what is wrong with power politics and what needs to be done to fix it.'

**Stuart Henry,** *Professor Emeritus, School of Public Affairs,*
*San Diego State University, USA*

T0373548

'This is yet another compelling book by Gregg Barak, a luminary in our international criminological community. He shows us that our research may not change the world, but it does change the way we look at it. Indicting the 45th President should be required reading for anyone wanting to understand the relationships between law, politics, and criminal justice.'

**Vincenzo Ruggiero,** *Professor of Sociology, Middlesex University, London, England*

'Gregg Barak's second book on Donald Trump provides an astute analysis of the social, political, mediatic, and judicial contexts that contribute to our understanding of how an ex-president became the defendant in an unprecedented number of lawsuits. With clear, straightforward language, Barak scrutinizes the world of post-truths and conspiratorial theories rooted in the histories of racism, misogyny, and xenophobia. At the same time, he demonstrates why building a better democracy depends on holding Trump accountable for his crimes and establishing social justice for all. I believe Barak's reflections on democracy are relevant wherever political candidates and "authoritarian strongmen" intend to rise as salvationist alternatives of power. I further believe that Barak's book not only exposes the weaknesses of American democracy, but it also shares the types of reforms and changes of the law and the U.S. constitution that would ameliorate these adverse conditions.'

**Marília de Nardin Budó,** *Professor of Criminology, Federal University of Santa Catalina, Brazil*

' "The Truth is Stranger than Fiction" is the title of a 1915 short film about fraud and criminal behavior and aptly describes the antics of Donald Trump. Barak's interdisciplinary venture into the dystopian Trumpian world is a story, like many crime movies and books, that even Lee Child and Tom Clancy would find unbelievable as a plot line. This seminal work offers a sometimes blunt but accurate portrayal of a misogynistic white-collar criminal and notorious mob boss. Barak explores the illegal and unethical behavior of a man who has engaged in misdeeds that stem from narcissistic self-interests. This book, one among thousands, stands out by detailing the unique and insightful criminological, psychological, sociological, legal, and theoretical explanations of an unstable fraudster who attempted to destroy the ideals of democracy.'

**Mary Dodge,** *Professor of Criminology & Criminal Justice, University of Colorado Denver, USA*

# INDICTING THE 45TH PRESIDENT

*Indicting the 45th President* is a sequel to *Criminology on Trump* in real time, continuing the criminological investigation into the former US president. Developing and expanding on the themes of family dynamics, deviance, deception, dishonesty, and the weaponization of the law, this book offers the next chapter on the world's most successful outlaw.

In this new book, Gregg Barak considers the campaigns and policies, the corruption, the state-organized abuses of power and obstructions of justice, the pardons, the failed insurrection, the prosecutions, the indictment of Trump and the politics of punishment as these revolve around the Trumpian character and social structures that encourage such crimes of the powerful. Barak also thoroughly addresses the threat to American Democracy, critiques the current state of the U.S. constitutional system, and proposes reforms to enhance justice for all in the United States.

Another accessible and compelling read, this is essential reading for all those engaged with state and white-collar crime in the context of power and privilege, and those seeking a criminological understanding of Trump's evasion of law and justice.

**Gregg Barak** is an American criminologist, academic, and author. He is Emeritus Professor of criminology and criminal justice at Eastern Michigan University.

# Crimes of the Powerful

Crimes of the Powerful encompasses the harmful, injurious, and victimizing behaviors perpetrated by privately or publicly operated businesses, corporations, and organizations as well as the state mediated administrative, legalistic, and political responses to these crimes.

The series draws attention to the commonalities of the theories, practices, and controls of the crimes of the powerful. It focuses on the overlapping spheres and inter-related worlds of a wide array of existing and recently developing areas of social, historical, and behavioral inquiry into the wrongdoings of multinational organizations, nation-states, stateless regimes, illegal networks, financialization, globalization, and securitization.

These examinations of the crimes of the powerful straddle a variety of related disciplines and areas of academic interest, including studies in criminology and criminal justice; law and human rights; conflict, peace, and security; economic change, environmental decay, and global sustainability.

**Criminology on Trump**
*Gregg Barak*

**Indicting the 45th President**
Boss Trump, the GOP, and What We Can Do About the Threat to American Democracy
*Gregg Barak*

For more information about this series, please visit: www.routledge.com/Crimes-of-the-Powerful/book-series/COTP

# INDICTING THE 45TH PRESIDENT

Boss Trump, the GOP, and What We Can Do About the Threat to American Democracy

*Gregg Barak*

LONDON AND NEW YORK

Designed cover image: © Jane Rosenburg

First published 2024
by Routledge
4 Park Square, Milton Park, Abingdon, Oxon OX14 4RN

and by Routledge
605 Third Avenue, New York, NY 10158

*Routledge is an imprint of the Taylor & Francis Group, an informa business*

© 2024 Gregg Barak

The right of Gregg Barak to be identified as author of this work has been
asserted in accordance with sections 77 and 78 of the Copyright, Designs and
Patents Act 1988.

*British Library Cataloguing-in-Publication Data*
A catalogue record for this book is available from the British Library

ISBN: 978-1-032-48021-3 (hbk)
ISBN: 978-1-032-45477-1 (pbk)
ISBN: 978-1-003-39066-4 (ebk)

DOI: 10.4324/9781003390664

Typeset in Sabon
by Newgen Publishing UK

*For the 1st Amendment and the 4th Estate without which I could not have told this story. There are too many political, legal, cultural, and historical writers or commentators to identify here. So shout out to four unusual suspects to hold accountable for my radically exacting discourse: Jamelle Bouie, Chauncey DeVega, Joyce Vance, and Andrew Weissmann.*

# CONTENTS

# ABOUT THE AUTHOR

**Gregg Barak** is an American criminologist, academic, and author. He is Emeritus Professor of criminology and criminal justice at Eastern Michigan University, a former visiting distinguished professor in the College of Justice & Safety at Eastern Kentucky University, and a 2017 Fulbright Scholar at the School of Law, Pontificia Universidade Catholica, Porto Alegre, Brazil. Barak is the author and editor of more than 20 books, including the award-winning titles *Gimme Shelter: A Social History of Homelessness in Contemporary America* (1991), *Theft of a Nation: Wall Street Looting and Federal Regulatory Colluding* (2012), *Unchecked Corporate Power: Why the Crimes of Multinational Corporations Are Routinized Away and What We Can Do About It* (2017), and *Criminology on Trump* (2022). The Academy of Criminal Justice Sciences Fellow was also the recent Co-founder and former North American Editor of the *Journal of White Collar and Corporate Crime*. Barak is also a contributing writer for *Salon* and *The Crime Report*.

# PREFACE

*Criminology on Trump* was an examination of one of the world's most successful outlaws, Donald J. Trump. Over the course of five decades, Trump had been accused of sexual assault, tax evasion, money laundering, non-payment of employees, and the defrauding of tenants, customers, contractors, investors, bankers, attorneys, and charities. Along the way Trump owned at least 20 different businesses that went "belly up" and six times he filed for Chapter 11 bankruptcy. Nevertheless, Trump managed to amass power alongside of much of the wealth that his father had made and passed along to him between 1949 and 1999. In a few words, Trump was never the self-made "art of the deal" billionaire that he professed to be.

Similarly, Trump's political success had nothing whatsoever to do with his understanding of domestic or international affairs. Nor did Trump win the 2016 race for the presidency based on his expertise in business, finance, or real estate. Rather, Trump's rise to the pinnacle of power and his ability to retain power even after losing the 2020 presidential election and his failed coup two months later came from his expertise as a con artist. And his uncanny ability to double down over and over on obvious lies of deception and to get away with it for a myriad of reasons that will be accounted for throughout *Indicting the 45ᵗʰ President*. Much of the empowerment of Donald J. Trump (DJT) came from his understanding of the usefulness of tabloid journalism, branding, social media, and labelling combined with the talent to nurture his celebrityhood as the host for more than a decade of the acclaimed TV series *The Apprentice* with the slogan "You're Fired!." Finally, the extent of Trump's political power was fully realized because the former president was operating more like a criminal or an organized gangster than as a public servant or someone who had taken an oath to uphold the US Constitution and defend the nation.

In a nutshell, the power of Trump has come from his shrewd salesmanship and hustler like abilities to alter social reality for millions of people – even though the majority of people know that there is not a grain of truth to any of the lies that he and his allies are always spreading – mostly because this fairy tale of a nightmare and Trump as their redeeming savior is what his QAnon adherents and Make America Great Again (MAGA) base of supporters have been praying for. Trump's "art of the steal" and his skillful gaslighting can also be described as the convoluted attractiveness of the art of a barker's con *à la* P.T. Barnum. The American showman, businessman, and politician best remembered for founding the Barnum & Bailey Circus and promoting celebrated hoaxes.

In my first account of Trump's lawlessness, I explained how the fraudulent behavior of the Houdini of white-collar crime escaped the clutches of the long arm of the law with only some minor scratches. And without one criminal indictment. I described how the racketeer-in-chief used his four years in the White House to broaden his financial schemes of corruption. I also revealed how Trump expanded his criminal enterprise by monetizing the powers of the presidency for the benefit of himself, the Trump Organization, and his children. Falling in line and conforming with other scams and rackets from a lifelong pattern of mixing legitimate and illegitimate business transactions.

Throughout the reign of Trump, his administrative teams sought to deconstruct and to weaponize the nation-state apparatus including such workplaces as the Environmental Protection Agency, the Consumer Protection Agency, and the Department of Justice. The politicalization of the Department of Justice (DOJ) by Trump with the cooperation of his third Attorney General Bill Barr was blatant and over-the-top corruption and interference in the administration of criminal justice. The two men went so far as to not only delay the release of the Mueller Report so they could spin the findings about the Russian interference in the 2016 presidential election, but they also appointed the hard-nosed prosecutor John H. Durham as a Special Counsel to discover any wrongdoing during the Russian investigation as evidence of a "deep state" conspiracy by either intelligence or law enforcement to go after and sink Donald Trump.

The political differences between the 2016 and the 2024 presidential races are at least four. First, Russia had not invaded Ukraine. Second, Trump had not taken a neutral position in the Russian-Ukraine War claiming that if he was elected, he could resolve the crisis and stop the killing in 24 hours. Third, President Putin had become fully public with his support of Donald Trump for 2024 by the publication of Russia's expanded list of sanctioned Americans on May 19, 2023. Many of those persons singled out for travel and financial restrictions were seen as adversaries or enemies of Trump. Among those included were Letitia James, the state attorney general of New York who had sued Trump for alleged fraud, Special Prosecutor Jack Smith who was investigating three different yet not unrelated Trumpian criminal matters, and Brad Raffensperger, the Georgia secretary of state who recorded rebuffing Trump's repeated attempts to reverse the outcome of the Georgia presidential election in 2020.[1] Fourth and not least of all was another warning from the Department of Homeland Security (DHS) about the potential for violence leading up to the 2024 election because of the heightened intersection of disinformation and hate.[2]

According to the National Terrorism Advisory System bulletin posted on May 24, 2023, potential targets of this violence included the Capitol's critical infrastructure, faith-based institutions, government facilities, and marginal communities. Other potential victims of violence include school children, racial and ethnic minorities, the LGBTQ+ community, law enforcement, and government personnel. These domestic terrorist assaults of the past and present, and presumably the future, have been motivated by perceptions of "rigged" 2020 and 2024 presidential elections, legislative and judicial decisions, and last but not least by racial and sexual animosity. These potential domestic terrorists are constituted mostly by home grown extremists, white hetero-exclusionists, and by those inspired by illiberal, autocratic, or fascist ideologies.[3]

During the time between the Mueller Investigation in 2016 and the release of the Durham final report in May 2023 revealing that his inquiry had failed to find any wrongdoing in the origins of the Russian investigation, two of its "field investigators," Rudy Giuliani and Bill Barr while on assignment in Italy to discover evidence of persecution or witch-hunting, did manage to gather some other worthy tips that apparently connected Trump to some unrelated criminality. Not surprisingly, Durham never bothered to follow up on this information preferring instead to "deep six" any incriminating evidence about the then president.[4] When Durham delivered his report after four years nearly twice as long as the Mueller investigation took, he thanked President Biden's Attorney General Merritt Garland for his continued support of an independent investigation into the investigation that had once before been investigated by the Inspector General doing what inspector general do, once again to the chagrin of Trump and his actual weaponization of the US Department of Justice.[5]

Less than two years after being sworn into office, Boss Trump armed with the help of a handful of billionaires, the Fox News corporation, his devoted MAGA base, and such media platforms as Twitter, Facebook, and YouTube took control of the Republican Party. After his re-election loss to Joe Biden by more than 7 million votes, #45 spent his final days in office not as a lame duck about to hand over the keys of the White House to occupant #46. Instead, the soon to be former president was preoccupied with resisting his electoral defeat by any means necessary. This included the orchestration of bogus lawsuits, government officials, political hacks, and fake electors to overturn a totally fair presidential election and to interfere with the congressional certification of President-elect Joe Biden on January 6, 2021.

The final report of the House Select Committee was released to the public in December 2022 with hundreds of recorded transcripts, testimony from 1000+ witnesses, and mountains of incriminating evidence. The 800-page volume documented Trump's intentional assault on the rule of law and US democracy. This in-depth story was about how Trump, humiliated by his loss to Sleepy Joe and lusting to hold on to political power, conspired with his band of Republican consiglieres to defraud the American people and, if they could, take back and overturn the 2020 presidential election. One of the forwards to the four published editions of the House text was written by *The New Yorker* magazine's David Remnick. Remnick captures the essence of the person who should by most accounts go down in US history as Public Enemy No. 1:

> In his career as a New York real-estate shyster and tabloid denizen, then as the forty-fifth President of the United States, Trump has been the most transparent of public figures. He does little to conceal his most distinctive characteristics: his racism, misogyny, dishonesty, narcissism, incompetence, cruelty, instability, and corruption. And yet what has kept Trump afloat for so long, what has helped him evade ruin and prosecution, is perhaps his most salient quality: he is shameless. That is the never-apologize-never-explain core of him. Trump is hardly the first dishonest President, the first incurious President, the first liar. But he is the most shameless. His contrition is impossible to conceive.[6]

No question that Trump's shamelessness in addition to his vibrant sociopathic personality were key attributes that well served the former president over the course of his life. However, what prevented Trump from evading prosecution and ruin all these years is captured in the various struggles to impeach or to criminalize the former president. Namely, Trump's abilities to corral and maximize economic and political power, on the one hand, and, on the other hand, his mobster-like tendencies to corrupt, to fix, to resist, and to intimidate not only ordinary people, politicians, victims, witnesses, and jurors, but also the law enforcement community.

Speaking to reporters on March 13, 2023, aboard Trump Air Force One on his way to Davenport, Iowa, the 2024 presidential candidate was rebuking his former Vice President Mike Pence for a speech that he gave the night before at the white-tie Gridiron dinner in DC. Pence's gaffe had been to state that Trump should be held accountable for the events of January 6. As usual Trump must always blame others for his crimes saying au contraire, "don't blame me, blame Mike. It was all his fault." Trump continued, "Had he sent the votes back to the legislatures, they wouldn't have had a problem with Jan. 6, so in many ways you can blame him." Trump was referring to Pence's refusal to lawlessly reject the electoral college votes in Congress as the lame duck president had wanted him to do. Trump tersely explained: "Had he sent them back to Pennsylvania, Georgia, Arizona…I believe, number one, you would have had a different outcome. But I also believe you wouldn't have had 'Jan. 6' as we call it."[7]

What distinguishes *Criminology on Trump* and its sequel *Indicting the 45th President* from the more than 7000 books on Trump, including those serious works from the fields of journalism, business, law, political science, and psychology, is these are the only two books written from the perspectives of a criminologist grounded in the operations of social control and the etiology of crime, including the moving human parts of white-collar, organizational, political, and governmental criminality. Since the early 1970s my criminological "beat" has primarily revolved around the contradictory conditions of the crimes of the powerful and the crimes of the powerless as these classes of perpetrators experience selective enforcement and differential application of the law.

The luxury or privilege of not being concerned about certain laws and their consequences belongs "to the rich and powerful, and to others who believe that because of their skin color, gender or other types of [advantage] are immune from the perils that may terrify others." Conversely, everyday people especially "the poor, the working class, Black and brown folks, a large majority of women, LGBTQ people and members of other vulnerable and disadvantaged communities do not have the privilege of ignoring" the law or thinking that it does not apply to them.[8] One constant in the differential administration of criminal justice is that ordinary persons without privilege are criminally indicted every day without unreasonable delays. Their criminal charges are not subject to prosecutorial obsession over whether a conviction beyond a reasonable doubt can be absolutely secured by a jury of their peers before indictments are brought forth.

Moreover, the crimes of the powerful are not common offenses committed by ordinary people nor are they typically delt with as matters of criminal law. Rather, these are elite offenses committed by persons who use their privileged statuses and economic wealth to accomplish crime and to resist crime control. Structurally, these elite or privileged conflicts with the law are normally not subject to criminal sanctions or the loss of liberty. They are usually responding to civil liabilities and compensatory damages. Unlike the offenses of the powerless that are only subject to criminal sanctions, the offenses of the powerful are subject to civil, criminal, and administrative laws.

Because of these intersecting legal arrangements of accountability, Wall Street institutions and securities financiers,[9] multinational corporations and their bosses,[10] or wealthy and corrupt former presidents for that matter will often remain for very long periods of time – if not indefinitely – beyond incrimination. Think of Too Big to Fail, Big Tobacco, Big Chemical, Big Oil, Big Pharma, and so on. As an informal rule, only on those exceptional occasions where there has been enough social pressure brought to bear on both the contradictions of these crimes and harms of the powerful, as well as on the legitimation of the "wheels of justice," built up over many years, sometimes for decades, are these offenders no longer above the law and held criminally accountable for what generally represents a fraction of the harms or injuries that they have wreaked.

Ergo, the myth that no persons or corporations are above the law has little to do with the workings of law enforcement in the United States, or elsewhere for that matter. *Special treatment* of privileged people, especially those who have reached the pinnacles of economic power and political authority are often held unaccountable for their criminal misdeeds. In the spring of 2023, former head US Attorney for the Southern District of Alabama Joyce Vance wrote about US Supreme Court Justice Clarence Thomas in the context of the legal difficulties of suing Fox News and the Trump Organization. When Thomas' conflicts of interest and alleged criminal conduct had become a judicial scandal, and after Chief Justice John Roberts had declined an invitation to testify before the US Congress about SCOTUS' lack of a judicial code of ethics or oversight, the distinguished law professor and MSNBC contributor underscored that "much of what we are experiencing comes down to a single flaw in our system: high-level officials are not held to the same standards of accountability that the rest of us are."[11] Or as George W. Bush's ethics czar Richard Painter stated on MSMBC's The ReidOut on May 4, 2023, Justice Thomas has clearly violated the ethics regulations of the Supreme Court of the United States (SCOTUS) as well as the law and should be impeached by the US Congress and removed from the court at a minimum.

When it comes to the normalization of crime and criminalization, the powerful and privileged have always had institutionalized advantages, and the powerless and oppressed have always had institutionalized disadvantages.[12] These inequities or biases in the substantive laws have also over time been processed through the discretionary formalities and informalities of the procedural law. From this perspective of justice evolution, the variance in the accountability and management of criminals and the distinct systems of social control in play should be viewed legalistically – conforming with the state definitions of harm and injury – and extra-legalistically – conforming with the ideologically informed practices of law enforcement. In other words, when it comes to specific laws and the different institutionalized relations of resolving conflicts and administering justice, people's choices of crime and their forms of social control are not the same or equal.

Structurally, the crimes of people are mostly shaped by their differential access to legal and illegal opportunities and the types of punishments they receive are mostly shaped by the intersections of their socioeconomic statutes and the substantive laws they break. For example, rich people do not hold up 7-Elevens for a few hundred dollars a heist and poor people do not price fix for hundreds of millions of dollars looted over time and space. And law enforcement does not care as much about capitalists' thefts as it does about workers thefts even though the costs of the former are 100 times more than the costs of the latter. This corporeality is also evidenced by finite resources and the allocation of an overabundance of money spent for policing "street" crimes as compared with an underabundance of money spent for policing "suite" crimes.

Legal myths aside, before becoming president-elect in 2016, Donald Trump, his organization, businesses, and employees at every level of government were subject to a range of legal probes. Here is a timeline of those investigations between 1973 and 2016:

1973: Trump Organization sued by the federal government for housing discrimination.
1978: Trump Organization accused of violating consent decree.
1979: Trump allegedly investigated for bribery.
1980: Trump subpoenaed in relation to an FBI investigation of corruption at the Trump Tower construction site.
1987: The Federal Trade Commission asks the Justice Department to prosecute Trump.
1988: The US Attorney's Office investigates Trump's role in the sale of two apartments to an alleged member of the mob.
1990: The Security and Exchange Commission reportedly investigated Trump's stock dealings.
1991: A Trump casino admits breaking the law by having Fred Trump buy uncashed chips and the Trump Plaza fined for discrimination.
1992: Congressional investigators link Trump businesses to Asian organized crime interests.
2000: The state of Texas investigates Trump University.
2011: Trump settles with Trump Soho buyers after a criminal investigation into sales of the property was opened.
2013: The state of New York files a civil fraud lawsuit against Trump University.
2016: The state of New York investigates the Trump Foundation and it pays a fine for making an improper political contribution.[13]

Prior to Trump becoming President, the matter of criminally indicting him had always begged the question: "How many years of accumulated lawlessness and abuse of power would it take before the criminal law would, if ever, catch up with Teflon Don?" The answer had been more than 40 years and counting. After Trump became the former President of the United States (POTUS), the question was reframed:

How long would it take a twice impeached Commander-in-Chief undergoing countless criminal investigations, including pilfering classified documents from the United States and trying to steal a presidential election from the American people, to be charged and held accountable for these serious felony crimes?

The answer to the first part of this question came on April 4, 2023, when Trump was arraigned in Manhattan and charged by the people of New York with 34 counts of falsifying business records related to violations of election and tax laws used to cover up hush money payments made to suppress two of his extramarital sexual liaisons from becoming public knowledge during the 2016 race for the presidency. When the commission of those fraudulent crimes first occurred, such knowledge of them may very well have tipped the scales and prevented Trump from narrowly winning the presidency. The answer to the second part of this question will not be fully known until after the 2024 election and Trump's upcoming criminal trials are concluded, assuming that they do indeed materialize. Before either the elections or the trials occur, however, as a result of the rulings by Colorado (judicially) and Maine (administratively) to disqualify Trump from running in their respective states for the 2024 presidency based on their interpretations of Section 3 of the 14th Amendment – "No person shall…hold any office, civil or military, under the United States, or any State, who have previously taken an oath … as an officer of the United States … to support the Constitution of the United States" and who has also "engaged in insurrection or rebellion against the same, or given aid or comfort to the enemies thereof" – the US Court will have to weigh in on this section that should really be a no brainer for any layperson let alone for any member of the highest court. Moreover, a super majority of Constitutional experts agree, whether they are liberal or conservative and even if they prefer politically that the voters would decide, that Trump should be disqualified from running for any office.

So it will be interesting to see at this historical moment with the Court's credibility at an all-time low whether the originalist and textualist majority as they refer to themselves would dare rule against one of the most cherished amendments to the US Constitution. And, if they rule against the 14th Amendment and do not disqualify Trump, how they will rationalize their decision to normalize insurrections led by the POTUS as "no big deal" the same as Trump and the Republican majority has been doing for more than three years. It will also be interesting to see how long it takes this reactionary Supreme Court to render its opinion compared to how long it took the only other SCOTUS rulings when the future of the POTUS was on the line. As in the cases of Richard Nixon's Watergate and cover up in 1974 and the Gore v. Bush presidential election in 2000 when it only took weeks in the former case and only days in the latter case.

The answer to another intriguing historical presidential question will have to wait at least until after the impending criminal trials of Donald Trump and the 2024 and 2028 presidential elections to evaluate whether the failed insurrectionist was indeed the worst and most influential President of all time. The only other real contender for the title was another one term President James Buchanan (1857–1861) who has arguably held the title up to now.

While both Buchanan and Trump acted against the democratic interests of the United States in the case of the latter by interfering for example in presidential State elections, it remains to be seen if Buchanan's betrayal to country and people was more egregious and consequential than Trump's failed treasonous and seditious behavior. Trump too was certainly a racially charged President, hesitating to condemn white supremacy and citizen militancy, while advancing discriminatory policies as POTUS and after leaving office. On the other hand, Buchanan was a pro-slavery Democrat, supported the Dred Scott Supreme Court decision which held that the US Constitution did not extend the rights of American citizenship to people of Black African descent. He pressured Kansas to adopt a pro-slavery constitution and even endorsed the secession of the Southern states that led to the formation of the Confederacy and the Civil War.

*Indicting the 45th President: Boss Trump, the GOP, and What We Can Do About the Threat to American Democracy* picks up where *Criminology on Trump* left off and it takes us as far as early 2024 where Trump and his team of lawyers have been successfully "running out the clock" or delaying the commencement of his four criminal trials as the GOP primaries have begun and the November presidential election is rapidly approaching.

On the very same day as the assault on the Capitol a leadership group consisting of the 117th bicameral Gang of Eight still in shock came together with the unanimity of country over party to draw up papers to both impeach and convict the treasonous Insurrectionist-in-Chief.[14] Unfortunately, "democracy over ideology" was only temporary as the Republican leadership wasted little time before capitulating to Boss Trump. This was especially true of House Minority Leader Kevin McCarthy (R-CA) who performed a 180 and flew down to Mar-a-Lago to cower before Trump. From that moment forward, Kevin had his viral selfie with the Boss and his ticket punched to become the House Majority leader when the time would come two years later. Unceremoniously, the Grand Old Party (GOP) had also sealed a deal with the diabolical former president to defend his Big Lie about a rigged election and to weaponize legislature committees as much as possible to harass and bully those persons of law enforcement who were investigating and prosecuting Trump. Likewise, the Republican Party had promised to ignore the events leading up to the violent assault on the Capitol and to whitewash the day of January 6 as much as possible from the annals of American history.

In a nutshell, *Indicting the 45th President* is the story of the struggle between the rule of law, due process, and free elections for all to uphold the belief that no person is above the law, not even the POTUS versus Boss Trump, the Republican Party, and their corrupt powers to vandalize the federal republic and to suppress or further restrict the democratic-constitutional rights of the people. The draconian legal stances of the GOP were politically solidified on February 13, 2021, when all but seven Republican US senators voted not to convict the twice impeached 45th president for High Crimes and Misdemeanors. The politicalization of these impeachment decisions and the "jury nullification" exercised by the GOP for the second time in 13 months served not only to justify Trumpian misbehavior and to facilitate authoritarianism, but also to accelerate the anti-democratic agenda of the Republican Party. This also allowed Trump and his technocratic adept minions to continue with their fraudulent fundraising to the tune of $250 million dollars based on January 6 alone.

These adjudicative failures of the "separations of powers" or the "balance of powers" to defer to the rule of law rather than to the rule of force were not without their damaging after-effects. The political chaos and harm that ensued from not having impeached the disgraceful Trump from the body politic only served to invigorate a constitutional crisis in the democratic republic. The "get out of jail" passes levied by the GOP were not without terrible losses for the American people as these only permitted the Trumpian cancer to further metastasize. Without the excision of Trump from the body politic or absence, any legal accountability for him from the Republican praetorians, the GOP's selective, authoritarian, and anti-democratic agenda remains active in every red state across America.

The ongoing lies and bombastic speech of Trump and his allies, for example, as laid out in Chapter 1 of this book became scenarios of what is known as stochastic terror. Or the "idea that even if people in power don't specifically call their followers to violence," by engaging in the rhetoric of violence "as a legitimate tactic or by demonizing a political enemy on a platform capable of reaching millions of people, one of those millions will be inspired to violent action."[15] Moreover, the numerous bird calls for violence by Trump and his sycophants as well as their hate filled ethnic, gender, and misogynous words have too often been responsible for the precipitous escalation in racially and sexually motivated violence against nonwhites, Muslims, Jews, Asians, Latin Americans, and members of the LGBQT+ community.

On November 8, 2022, only after Trump announced his presidential candidacy for 2024, did Attorney General Merrick Garland finally get around to appointing Jack Smith as Special Counsel to oversee what had seemed up to that point to be two rather trepid federal investigations under way.[16] One month later on December 6, 2022, a jury in Manhattan found the Trump Organization and its CFO Allen Weisselberg guilty of 17 counts of criminal tax fraud and of falsifying business records. Remarkably, the principal owner of this close-knit business enterprise was not even charged in the lawsuit. By the end of 2022 and the beginning of 2023, other investigations, likely indictments, and eventual criminal trials involving Trump, his adult children, and their associates were all slowly working their ways to the legal surface.[17] Less than six months later on May 9, 2023, a jury of his peers, six men and three women, found Trump liable in a civil lawsuit for sexually abusing but not raping E. Jean Carroll and awarded her $5 million in damages.

Maureen Dowd mentioned in a column one week after the second criminal indictment of Trump that for years she had earlier tried to "fathom Hamlet's motives, state of mind, family web, obsessions" as a revenge play. Now like the rest of us, she found herself in "another revenge play about a rotten kingdom." As a criminologist who began observing Trump's public behavior in the 1980s and seriously study "everything" about the person since he announced his candidacy for the presidency in 2015, I can totally relate to Dowd when she writes:

> The man who dumbed down the office of the presidency is a less gratifying subject than the smarty-pants doomed prince. Hamlet is transcendent, while Trump is merely transgressive. But we can't shuffle off the mortal coil of Trump. He has burrowed, tick-like, into the national bloodstream, causing all kinds of septic responses.[18]

By the fall of 2022, I had been writing commentaries about the appropriateness of using the Racketeer Influenced and Corruption Organization laws, federal or state, to prosecute Donald Trump and his interconnected rings of loosely organized political actors as a criminal enterprise whose participants had been conspiring in a slew of political-economic rackets against American democracy as well as the rule of law. Juristically, Trump's coup plots had all been premeditated, organized, multitiered, and multifaceted. In real time, his failed insurrection involved a series of overlapping and cascading conspiracies whose "tentacles [had] included numerous Republican officials, right-wing paramilitaries, media propagandists, private funders, interest groups, think tanks, and other agents."[19] I was suggesting that these disparate and yet inter-related lawless offenses pertaining to the myriad of ongoing and concurrent investigations of the multiplicity of crimes perpetrated by Trump and his political associates to undermine constitutional democracy could be amalgamated and prosecuted together as a classic "hub and spoke" or multi-prong criminal conspiracy under RICO.

Salon
**Prosecuting Boss Trump: Build a RICO case against his
entire criminal empire**
Donald Trump has run a criminal enterprise for more than 40 years.
We can't allow him to get away with any of it.
September 27, 2022[20]

**By Gregg Barak**
Even folks who support Donald Trump might agree that the former president is a con artist, a master gaslighter and a shrewd racketeer. As I argue in my book "Criminology on Trump," the Houdini of white-collar crime and founder and

CEO of the Trump Organization has effectively operated a criminal enterprise, beginning in 1980. He did so for the next 36 years before being elected President in November 2016. Throughout his presidency and afterward, Trump continued running, and even expanding, his criminal enterprise.

Trump's lifetime as an outlaw and a racketeer may finally be coming to an end after more than four decades of eluding the criminal law. He is currently encircled by at least six or seven significant civil or criminal investigations. Most legal scholars or former US prosecutors will likely approach these white-collar, corporate, and state crimes evidently committed by Trump and his associates as disparate and unrelated litigating conflicts.

I would contend, however, that when Trump's fraudulent behavior is seen through the lenses of racketeering and the vantage point of a criminal enterprise, all his offenses or violations, whether civil or criminal, could be legally brought together and prosecuted under RICO, the Racketeer Influenced and Corrupt Organizations Act.

Just as Trump and his allies could be prosecuted for sedition, obstruction of justice and election racketeering, in a classic "hub and spoke" multi-pronged criminal conspiracy, the illegal activities at issue in each of these individual investigations or lawsuits can be viewed over time as spokes of the same criminal enterprise.

Trump is an outlaw, and I mean that literally. He habitually breaks laws of all kinds while remaining a free person. Trump is also a special type of outlaw because he has no moral compass and no loyalty to anyone besides himself. In fact, he thinks and acts as an authentic sociopath.

Trump is not an outlaw out of negligence, incompetence, or ignorance of the illegalities of the marketplace, the civil and criminal laws, or the Constitution of the United States. Quite the contrary. Trump knows the subtle differences between what is lawfully right and what is unlawfully wrong. Even more important, Trump is an expert on criminal intent – and the lack thereof.

Moreover, Trump knows all about plausible deniability and has nurtured the idea that throughout his activities he was allegedly following or deferring to other people, such as lawyers, accountants, and appraisers. He also appreciates that the legal system is fluid in both theory and practice and is subject to valuation and interpretation. Finally, Trump understands that the administration of justice is malleable and subject to a high degree of internal and external discretionary power.

As a racketeer or mobster, Trump has always intermingled his legitimate affairs of business with the illegitimate affairs of organized crime. As he told a panel at the Museum of Television and Radio in Los Angeles in 2004, shortly after he signed his first contract to do "The Apprentice," he had been reluctant to sign on with the reality TV show because of all the mobsters that frequent his place of work: "I [didn't] want to have cameras all over my office, dealing with contractors, politicians, mobsters and everyone else I have to deal with in my business." More than a decade later as a presidential candidate, in one of his moments of public candor, he responded to a question about his friends in organized crime, "Winners team up with mobsters, losers don't."

Days after Donald Trump became the President-elect in 2016, without any admission of wrongdoing, he settled three civil lawsuits against the defunct Trump University for $25 million, two from California and one from New York, which had been folded into one class-action lawsuit.

One year after the Trump University settlement was approved by the court overseeing the Southern District of New York, Trump was ordered by the New York Supreme Court in November 2019 to pay "$2 million in damages for improperly using charitable assets to intervene in the 2016 presidential primaries and further his own political interests." That award was part of New York Attorney General Letitia James' lawsuit against the Donald J. Trump Foundation and its directors – Trump himself and his three adult children, Donald, Jr., Ivanka, and Eric.

As part of that settlement, the Trump Foundation was shut down and the funds that were illegally misused had to be restored. The foundation and its directors agreed to multiple stipulations in order to resolve the remaining claims in the lawsuit. Among these, Trump admitted to personally misusing funds at the Trump Foundation, and his adult children were subject to mandatory training requirements. Finally, if the Trump Organization tried to start a new charity, Trump agreed to restrictions on future charitable services and to ongoing reporting to the attorney general's office.

Flash forward from there to the 220-page complaint in the fraud lawsuit filed by James against Trump and those same three adult children last week in state Supreme Court. Trump is accused of padding his net worth by some $2 billion, and James is seeking at least $250 million in damages, the estimated value derived from the alleged fraud between 2010 and 2021.

Compared to $250 million, the Trump University and Trump Foundation fraud lawsuits now seem like chump change – especially because the resolution of this lawsuit may well mean the demise of the Trump Organization. Among other sanctions, James wants the Trump Organization to be placed under a stewardship and not to engage in any commercial real estate acquisitions for five years. She is also asking the court to ban Trump, Donald, Jr., Ivanka, and Eric from ever again running a company based in New York.

When we recently learned that James' office had "rebuffed an offer" from Trump's attorneys to settle this civil lawsuit, I wanted to know – and still want to know – how much Trump was willing to pay (or do) to make the case go away, especially knowing that losing the case could mean the end of his family business.

At her news conference last Wednesday, James explained that the investigation not only "revealed that Donald Trump engaged in years of illegal conduct to inflate his worth, to deceive banks and the people of the great state of New York" but also uncovered evidence of potential criminal violations, including insurance, bank, and tax fraud. James has shared her findings with both the IRS and the Southern District, where these cases could be pursued as criminal rather than civil matters.

Meanwhile, from the big-picture criminological perspective, we also know the Justice Department has been investigating the fraudulent Save America PAC – Trump's main fundraising vehicle since he lost the 2020 election – which promotes baseless assertions about election fraud, and also played a role in trying to overturn the election and instigating the January 6 assault on the Capitol.

There are also the ongoing DOJ criminal investigations into Trump's seditious conspiracy and obstruction of justice related to the fake electors scheme and failed coup that followed the 2020 election, as well as the stolen or "borrowed" classified documents recovered from Mar-a-Lago this summer.

As I opined in the Miami Herald last Wednesday, "When it comes to prosecuting Trump, it's not a matter of 'if,' but 'when'" the various lawsuits will materialize, and specifically what crimes he will be prosecuted for. After all, the racketeer in chief has literally engaged in decades of lawlessness and hundreds of potential violations spanning the years before, during, and after his presidency.

Before the June and July select committee hearings on January 6, and the subsequent scandal that emerged surrounding the classified documents found at Mar-a-Lago, I was concerned that Trump would once again most likely escape criminal prosecution. But once it became obvious that the DOJ almost certainly could not refrain from prosecuting the former president for his obvious crimes, secondary concerns kicked in.

I suspect we may see a hierarchy of discretionary prosecutions established, where the DOJ chooses to settle for one prosecution amid the myriad of possibilities, allowing Trump to escape accountability for most of his crimes. Even worse, there's the possibility that Trump would cut a deal to avoid any criminal trials and imprisonment.

In calling for the use of RICO to prosecute Boss Trump and his affiliated supporters for the crimes of the January 6th assault on the Capitol, I was in the company of Constitutional scholar Laurence Tribe from Harvard Law School and my Substack mentor Joyce Vance on all things legal. There was also the aborted state racketeering RICO case against the former president that was revealed when Carey Dunne and Mark Pomerantz resigned from the Manhattan district attorney's office in January 2022.[21] By March 2023, when the 34 felony charges were brought by Bragg, RICO was not among them. On the other hand, among the many criminal charges laid out against Trump and his allies in Fulton County, Georgia the RICO statutes of that state were central and made the number of indictments, charges, and counts possible.

On April 24, 2023, in a letter to Sheriff Patrick Labat, the Fulton County District Attorney Fani Willis announced to the world that she was likely to bring forth multiple indictments sometime between July 11 and September 1, 2023.

> In the near future, I will announce charging decisions resulting from the investigation my office has been conducting into possible criminal interference in the administration of Georgia's 2020 General Elections. I am providing this letter to bring to your attention the need for heightened security and preparedness in coming months due to this pending announcement.

In the context of the numerous threats that Alvin Bragg in NYC and she in Fulton County as well as others had already received, Willis continued:

> Open-source intelligence has indicated the announcement of the decisions in this case may provoke a significant public reaction. We have seen in recent years that some may go outside of public expressions of opinion that are protected by the First Amendment to engage in acts of violence that will endanger the safety of our community. As leaders, it is incumbent upon up to prepare.[22]

Well prepared and secured against the possibility of violence that did not materialize around this or the three previous indictments of Trump and his allies.

Back in May 2022, when a judge had empaneled a special grand jury to hear testimony in the case, according to *The Atlanta Journal-Constitutional* reporters Hallerman and Rankin: "Snipers patrolled nearby rooftops as helicopters circled overhead. Law Enforcement also deployed a SWAT team to protect jurors as they returned to their cars at the end of the day." Six months after that, "before jurors interviewed Michael Flynn, Trump's former national security adviser, they assigned heavily armed officers to guard the courthouse steps and brought in a bomb-sniffing dog."[23] DA Willis finished her letter by saying, "Please accept this correspondence as notice to allow you sufficient time to prepare the Sheriff's Office and coordinate with local, state and federal agencies to ensure that our law enforcement community is ready to protect the public."[24]

The original 1970 federal RICO Act had focused on the relationship between corrupt politicians, local and state governments, and syndicated criminals. From its origins, this law understood that interacting groups and organized activities could concurrently be engaged in both illicit and licit purposes. Unlike other criminal prosecutorial laws, the objective of RICO statutes was to attack the organized relations of those politicos and/or criminals who had joined forces to collaborate on the commission of various scams or rackets as part of a "criminal enterprise." Whether all the conspiring participants ever communicated directly with one another is not relevant because RICO statutes do not require direct communications between individuals to establish a conspiracy to commit certain crimes such as obstruction of justice.

On May 4, 2023, after a four-month trial of the Proud Boys, several members were convicted of crimes for their roles on January 6. Leader Enrique Tarrio who was not physically present on that infamous day and Ethan Nordean, Joseph Biggs, and Zachery Rehl who were present were all found guilty of seditious conspiracy and multiple other crimes including the obstruction of government proceedings to interfere with the certification of the electoral college tabulation of votes. However, Dominic Pezzola one of those charged with seditious conspiracy was found not guilty of that charge though he was found guilty of the other criminal charges.

Similarly, back in January 2023 Elmer Stewart Rhodes III, the 2009 founder and leader of the Oath Keepers – a far right, anti-government group – and Kelly Meggs, the leader of the Florida chapter of this organization were both found guilty of seditious conspiracy and other crimes related to the breach of the Capitol. Rhodes received a sentence of 18 years in prison. Judge Amit P. Mehta had this to say to the recipient of the first punishment to be handed down for the crime of seditious conspiracy: "You sir, present an ongoing threat and a peril to this country, to the republic and the very fabric of our democracy." Mehta also pointed out that Rhodes had been continuing to spread conspiracy theories and violent rhetoric in interviews from behind bars. The judge predicted, "The moment you are released you will be prepared to take up arms against your government."[25]

Using RICO to link the convictions of the Proud Boys and/or the Oath Keepers to Trump and his inner circle of seditious conspirators as part of one grand seditious conspiracy on January 6 would require at least one person, such as the "dirty trickster" Roger Stone, Ali Alexander, or Alex Jones, to have been in communication between the three groups of seditious conspirators. This "motley crew" of potential conspirators have denied any wrongdoing and they have not at least so far been charged in connection with the insurrection. However, their presence along with Rudy Giuliani and others camped out in Washington at the Willard Hotel "war room" in the days before the Capitol assault and their checking out from the hotel as the conflagration began, along with many of their incriminating public statements provide Special Prosecutor Jack Smith and his team of investigators with the predication to explore the possible, if not, probable connections between these various groups of conspirators to at least collectively act to interfere with the certification of the electoral college vote, if not to engage with Trump in the crime of seditious conspiracy. As it turned out no seditious conspiracy or inciting a riot were leveled at the two conspiracies to overturn the 2020 election.

Historically, RICO has been used to dismantle ethnically organized criminal groups. In the United States, RICO has not been used traditionally to prosecute elite political conspiracies. Only in the last decade has RICO begun to be used to prosecute "respectable" white-collar criminals like Donald Trump. Previously, RICO statutes were not employed to go after high-profile political racketeers, such as Chicago's father and son Mayors Richard J. Daley and Richard M. Daley after four decades of governmental corruption between them, or the former corrupt Maryland Governor and Nixon's Vice President Spiro Agnew who had been forced to resign from the latter.[26]

Agnew avoided impeachment or indictment for his crimes by resigning. More importantly, Richard M. Nixon resigned as President on August 8, 1974, because of the botched break-in at the Democratic National Committee headquarters located on the sixth floor of the Watergate Hotel and Office complex in Washington, DC. Exactly one month later Nixon was pardoned by his successor Gerald Ford before he could be criminally charged for what his subordinates were found guilty of and went to prison for. To avoid criminal prosecution for his myriad of crimes especially those on January 6 Trump did no such thing. On the contrary, Teflon Don was hoping that he would once again escape culpability for his illegal ways of taking care of business. Trump was also betting that sectors within both political parties would exert enough pressure on "the powers that be" not to indict him for different but related reasons such as setting the precedent that presidents or former presidents are truly above the law.

Trump may have won that bet had he only disappeared from the political scene never to be heard from again and were it not for the fact that predictable Trump had to naturally "triple dog dare" the government not to indict America's outlaw-in-chief. Seriously though, in the face of all of the accumulating evidence of his civil and criminal wrongdoings, ongoing lies and denials of the legitimacy of President Biden, and his announcement to the chagrin of 72% of US voters, including most Republicans, that he was running for the presidency for a third straight time. Eventually, Trump gave the US Department of Justice no other choice but to criminally indict him for matters of a failed insurrection, stolen classified documents, and fraudulent fundraising.

Much of this second book addresses the unprecedented crimes presented by a lawless habitual offender and former president as well as the obstacles of holding Trump and his economic and political allies accountable for a myriad of white-collar, corporate, and state crimes related to the multi-prong conspiracy to overturn the results of the 2020 presidential election that when not successful culminated in the January 6th assault on the Capitol. Based on little more than Boss Trump's fanatical obsession with keeping the power of POTUS, his chronic lying, and complete control of the Republican Party, these adversarial contests over criminal accountability were finally coming to the state courts of New York and Georgia as well as to the federal district courts of Florida and the District of Columbia.

No longer was the body politic merely privy to High Crimes and Misdemeanors for which President Trump could have twice been immediately fired as the Commander-in-Chief and banned from the presidency for the rest of his life. In other words, had Trump not escaped the sanctions of impeachment first in 2020 and again in 2021, I believe that Trump would have kept his "squeaky clean" records of lawlessness and never having been indicted let alone convicted of any criminal law. Instead, Americans watched as Trump continued to raise the legal and political stakes compelling the once reluctant state and federal prosecutors to indict him for all types of criminal acts that are all subject to long terms in prison. These crimes have included seditious conspiracy, defrauding the United States, espionage, obstruction of justice, and wire fraud. Whether Trump is acquitted or convicted of these political crimes, his indictments and prosecutions cannot be disconnected from the constitutional and democratic crises revolving around the numerous efforts by the Republicans to defend the naked lawlessness of Trump, the duplicity of the Republican leadership to overturn the 2020 presidential election, and the nascent authoritarian movement in this country.

The adversarial struggle to bring Boss Trump and his conspirators to some kind of accountability has been playing out within a hostile environment of tribalism reinforced by the political arrangements of US democracy. This tribalism allows for the examination of the strengths and the weaknesses of the democratic representative system of the federal republic of the United States. In turn, such an examination allows for any of us in the constitutional peanut gallery to propose ideas, initiatives, and projects to tend to and to hopefully fix what has been afflicting our constitutional body politic for far too long. The objective being not only to save our existing democratic arrangements from current rife and authoritarian threat, but also to amend and expand these democratic arrangements not only in government, but also throughout the commonwealth. In the workplace, in the community, and in the home by way of establishing a new majoritarian form of governing to augment the existing consensus form of governing. My contention is that a more inclusive democracy can be created by reconstituting some of the democratic power directly to the people. This would be in addition to the indirect representative power of the people. Together, such power in the hands of the people could ameliorate the fundamental contradictions between capitalist legality for the powerful and economic liberty for the powerless. In turn, these enhancements in democratic rule could reduce the social and political alienation experienced by most Americans whether they are Democrats, Republicans, or Independents.

Admittedly, the direct power of the people has never been a popular idea with most of the members elected to the US Congress regardless of political party. The bipartisan preference has always been for the people to have indirect rather than direct power through their representatives. As far back as the 1787 Constitutional Convention in Philadelphia, there was widespread agreement among the framers, whether they were Federalists like Alexander Hamilton, John Jay, and James Madison or Anti-Federalists like Thomas Jefferson, Patrick Henry, and Samuel Adams that democracy would be a far cry from one person, one vote. Initially o*f, by, and for the people* pertained indirectly only to white, propertied men. Over the course of the next 200 years, the right to vote not without much resistance was gradually extended to all people 18 years or older. To this very day, ordinary people have not possessed the right to vote up or down on any policies that become federal laws as they are entitled to do so under many state constitutions. In opposition to a representative form of government and its "antidemocratic" view of one person, one vote, like more than a few political scientists, I am arguing for direct people power as a means of exchanging an experimental "tyranny of a minority" for an experimental "tyranny of a majority."

As John Adams wrote in a 1780 letter to Jonathan Jackson, a federalist New England lawyer who was best known for a pamphlet he wrote critiquing the Philadelphia Constitution as excessively democratic: "There is nothing that I dread So much, as a Division of the Republick into two great Parties, each arranged under its Leader, and concerting Measures in opposition to each other." Similarly, in his 1796 farewell address, George Washington warned that "the alternate domination of one faction over another, sharpened by the spirit of revenge, natural to party dissension, which in different ages and countries has perpetuated the most horrid enormities, is itself a frightful despotism."[27] Flashing forward to today, the political tribalism that Adams dreaded is very much alive and not well. It is still embodied by bipartisan Republicans and Democrats that still prefer consensus minority representative rule over direct majority rule of the people even though for the past three decades, this tyranny of minority rule has been increasingly partisan, dysfunctional, and destructive of the body politics. In short, into its third century the existing US political system is clearly not working as effectively as it could be and is presently knee-deep in an existential crisis that threatens without hyperbole the very survival of American democracy.

Three years after the failed insurrection, the American people find themselves suffering from factionalism or hyper-partisanship and the tyranny of minority rule where alleged bipartisan agreement, let alone, shared empathy on any of the issues of our time has become annoyingly verboten.

In part, this is because of several procedural and substantive rules inside and outside of the US Congress. Most notoriously are the filibustering and supermajorities in the US Senate that all too often strangle proactive legislation for the benefit of most people as well as for the general welfare of the commonwealth. These "antidemocratic" mechanisms of governing are also supported by the counter-majoritarian and unfair aspects of the rules of American democracy like the Electoral College (EC) and political gerrymandering. Moreover, in red states across the country from Ohio to Florida to Arkansas to North Carolina to Montana, the GOP controlled state legislatures and supreme courts are doing everything in their power to advance new rules and measures to secure minority rule over majority rule, such as raising the percentages of votes for the passage of statewide ballot initiatives or referendums on popular concerns like the reproductive freedom of women from simple majorities to supermajorities. The Republicans are also trying to create mini electoral colleges statewide as another means for stopping the will of the people.

On April 28, 2023, a newly elected Republican majority of the North Carolina Supreme Court reversed an earlier ruling that voting maps drawn after the 2020 population census were in violation of the state constitution because they amounted to political gerrymandering. On the same day, former Attorney General Eric Holder appointed by President Obama issued a statement on the matter. He warned Americans of what was at stake should voting districts remain in the hands of partisan politicians and not in the hands of, for example, elected boards of nonpartisan citizens as one alternative operating in several states like Michigan. The AG stated that this "shameful, delegitimizing decision to allow the unjust, blatant manipulation of North Carolina's voting districts was not a function of legal principle, it was a function of political, personnel and partisan opportunism. Neither the map nor the law have changed...only the makeup of the majority of the North Carolina Supreme Court has changed. History will not be kind to this court's majority" and the state's highest tribunal will "forever be stained for irreparably harming" its "legitimacy and reputation."[28] Fortunately, for now while leaving the door open in the future, the 6-3 Supreme Court decision rejected the "independent state theory" ruling against Republicans fighting for a congressional district map that would have favored GOP candidates. And more importantly would have given state legislatures unchecked control over federal elections and restricting the power of state courts to review certain election laws.

As a contrarian of political science I am arguing from a "pure" democratic perspective that the time has come for the United States to upgrade from a "tyranny of the minority" that the GOP is doubling down on to a "tyranny of the majority" of the people that Democrats should all be supporting. If this daunting transformation of our political system could be realized to expand the democratic rights of the people and their capacities to cogovern, then not unlike the Second American Revolution that abolished chattel slavery and expanded the franchise, a Third American Revolution could abolish the EC, *Citizens United*, supermajorities, filibusters, and other anti-democratic rules of governing. Coupled with a direct form of, by, and for the people democracy to buttress at the federal level, these legal reforms would represent the kinds of political change necessary to bring our body politic that much closer to realizing its dream of a "perfect union." These changes would also push back against the regressive, exclusive, and anti-democratic agendas of the Republican Party that are threatening American democracy.

## Notes

1 Peter Baker. 2023. Russia's latest sanctions on U.S. officials turn to Trump enemies. *The New York Times*. May 21. www.nytimes.com/2023/05/21/world/europe/rus sia-sanctions-trump.html

2 Julia Ainsley. 2023. DHS warns of attacks against government buildings, minority groups ahead of 2024 election. *NBC News*. May 24. www.nbcnews.com/politics/ dhs-warns-attacks-government-buildings-minority-groups-ahead-2024-elec

3 National Terrorism Advisory System Bulletin. 2023. Summary of terrorism-related threat to the United States. *Homeland Security*. May 24. www.dhs.gov/ ntas/advisory/national-terrorism-advisory-system-bulletin-may-24-2023

4 Charlie Savage, Glenn Thrush, Adam Goldman and Katie Benner. 2023. In final report, Trump-era special counsel denounces Russia investigation. *The New York Times*. May 15. www.nytimes.com/2023/05/15/us/politics/trump-russia-invest igation-durham.html

5 See Report on matters related to intelligence activities and investigations arising out of the 2016 presidential campaigns, submitted by Special Counsel John H. Durham pursuant to *28 C.F.R. § 600.8(c)* May 12. Washington, DC.

6 David Remnick. 2022. The devastating new history of the January 6th insurrection. *The New Yorker*. December 22. www.newyorker.com/news/american-chronicles/ the-devastating-new-history-of-the-january-sixth-insurrection

7 Isaac Arnsdorf and Maeve Reston. 2023. Trump claims violence he inspired on Jan. 6 was Pence's fault. *Washington Post*. March 13. www.washingtonpost.com/ politics/2023/03/13/trump-pence-iowa/

8 Chauncey DeVega. 2022. The Trump paradox: America is sick of this guy – but we can't afford to turn away. *Salon*. December 13. www.salon.com/2022/12/13/ the-paradox-america-is-sick-of-this-guy--but-we-cant-afford-to-turn-away/

9 Gregg Barak. 2012. *Theft of a Nation: Wall Street Looting and Federal Regulatory Colluding*. New York: Rowman & Littlefield.

10 Gregg Barak. 2017. *Unchecked Corporate Power: Why the Crimes of Multinational Corporations Are Routinized Away and What We Can Do About It*. London and New York: Rutledge.

11 Joyce Vance. 2023. The week ahead. *Civil Discourse with Joyce Vance*. April 16. https://joycevance.substack.com/p/the-week-ahead

12 Donald Black. 1976/2010. *The Behavior of Law*. Bingley: Emerald Group Publishing Limited.

13 Philip Bump. 2016. A quick review of 40 years of investigations into Donald Trump and his businesses. *The Washington Post*. October 31. www.washingtonpost.com/news/the-fix/wp/2016/10/31/a-quick-review-of-40-years-of-investigations-into-donald-trumps-businesses/

14 Rachel Bade and Karoun Demirjian. 2022. *Unchecked: The Untold Story Behind Congress's Botched Impeachments of Donald Trump*. New York: HarperCollins.

15 Ellen Ioanes. 2022. An atmosphere of violence: Stochastic terror in American politics. *Vox*. November 5. www.vox.com/2022/11/5/23441858/violence-stochastic-terror-american-politics-trump-pelosi

16 U.S. Department of Justice, Office of Public Affairs. 2022. Appointment of special counsel. November 18. www.justice.gov/opa/pr/appointment-special-counsel-0

17 Ankush Khardori. 2022. Where does Trump's legal ride end? *The New York Times*. November 20. Sunday Opinion, pp. 6–7.

18 Maureen Dowd. 2023. To jail or not to jail. *The New York Times*. June 18. Sunday Opinion, p. 3.

19 Chauncey DeVega. 2022. Longtime federal prosecutor says the evidence is 'conclusive' – but Trump may not end up in jail. *Salon*, October 17. www.rawstory.com/longtime-federal-prosecutor-says-the-evidence-is-conclusive-but-trump-may-not-end-up-in-jail/

20 www.salon.com/2022/09/27/prosecuting-boss-trump-build-a-rico-case-against-his-entire-criminal-empire. See also, Gregg Barak. The final 187 minutes of a 'multi-prong' criminal conspiracy. *The Crime Report*. July 22. https://thecrimereport.org/2022/07/22/the-final-187-minutes-of-a-multi-prong-criminal-conspiracy

21 Mark Pomerantz. 2023. *People vs. Donald Trump: An Inside Account*. New York: Simon & Schuster.

22 Quoted in Tamar Hallerman and Bill Rankin. 2023. EXCLUSIVE: DA says indictment announcement coming this summer in Trump probe. *The Atlantic Journal-Constitution*. April 24. www.ajc.com/politics/trump-probe-da-urges-law-enforcement-to-prep-for-indictments-this-summer

23 Hallerman and Rankin. 2023.

24 Quoted in Hallerman and Rankin. 2023.

25 Spencer S. Hsu, Rachel Weiner and Tom Jackman. 2023. Oath Keepers leader Rhodes sentenced to 18 years for Jan. 6 seditious conspiracy. *The Washington Post*. May 25. www.washingtonpost.com/dc-md-va/2023/05/25/oath-keepers-sentencing-seditious-conspiracy-jan6

26 Agnew had been operating a criminal enterprise since he was elected Baltimore County Executive in 1962 and throughout his administration as governor of Maryland when elected in 1966 until he became the vice president in 1968, and after that until he was forced to resign as VP in 1973. At the time, he was being investigated by the US. Attorney for the District of Maryland on suspicions of criminal conspiracy, bribery, extortion, and tax fraud. Agnew pleaded *nolo contendere* to one felony charge of tax evasion and resigned from office.

27 Quoted in Russ Feingold and Peter Prendiville. 2022. *The Constitution in Jeopardy: An Unprecedented Effort to Rewrite Our Fundamental Law and What We Can Do About It*. New York: Public Affairs, p. 160.

28 Quoted in Joyce Vance. 2023. The North Carolina Supreme Court signs off on a political gerrymander. *Civil Discourse*. April 28. https://joycevance.substack.com/p/the-north-carolina-supreme-court

# INTRODUCTION

## Defending Crimes, Incendiary Rhetoric, and the Big Lie

Donald Trump's Big Lie that the election was stolen and his "onslaught of falsehoods about the November [2020] election misled millions of Americans, undermined faith in the electoral system, sparked a deadly riot" – and by February 6, 2021, had already cost the US taxpayer $519 million and was still growing. Those costs had "mounted daily as government agencies at all levels" had

> been forced to devote public funds to respond to actions taken by Trump and his supporters…The expenditures include legal fees prompted by dozens of fruitless lawsuits, enhanced security in respond to death threats against poll workers, and costly repairs needed after the Jan. 6 insurrection at the Capitol.[1]

In a similar vein, Special Counsel Jack Smith's two investigations of the former president cost $9.2 million in the first five months after he was tapped in November 2022 by Attorney General Merrick Garland to take charge of the Department of Justice's ongoing Trump-related investigations.[2] At this rate, it will cost the taxpayer $25 million a year. A total of $1.9 million of those expenditures were paid to US Marshalls to protect Mr. Smith and his family as well as other investigators who have faced threats after Boss Trump and his fellow thugs singled them out on social media. Some have called this a "Trump Tax" referring to the government having "to expend disproportionate time and energy on the former president and defending themselves against his unfounded claims that they are persecuting him at the expense of public safety."[3] On the other hand, Trump's legal expenditures for the first six months of 2023 came to $16 million, paid by the Save

DOI: 10.4324/9781003390664-1

America super Political Action Committee (PAC).[4] All of which means that Trump's political supporters were paying more money to defend Trump than the taxpayers or the people were paying to prosecute him and his fellow criminals.

By the end of 2022, Donald Trump was facing 19 civil and criminal cases. According to an online analytical forum, JustSecurity.org, there were "an additional 10 pending cases at various stages in state and federal courts that were targeting Trump allies in right-wing media and propaganda fronts."[5] Everywhere the former president was trying to look away from, attorneys – civil and criminal – seemed to be hard at work breathing down his or the necks of law violating associates (see Figure 0.1). At a video hearing on May 23, 2023, before Judge Juan Merchan in the Manhattan "hush money" case to agree to the terms of a protective order, he was sitting at a table next to his attorney Todd Blanche, looking dejected and scowling, an American flag is draped behind him.

Judge Merchan confirmed that Trump was free to talk about the lawsuit and that his First Amendment rights were not being restrained in any way. Immediately following the hearing, Trump posted @realDonaldTrump:

> Just had New York County Supreme Court hearing where I believe my First Amendment Rights, "Freedom of Speech," have been violated, and they forced upon me a trial date of March 25th, right in the middle of Primary season. Very unfair, but this is exactly what the Radical Left Democrats wanted. It's called ELECTION INTERFERENCE, and nothing like this has ever happened in our Country before!!!

**FIGURE 0.1**   Various pending Trump prosecutions and lawsuits.

*Source:* Adapted from *Andrea Mitchell Reports*, MSNBC. May 23, 2023.

Off point, Trump was correct about the unprecedented nature of the lawlessness of a former president and leading 2024 Grand Old Party (GOP) presidential candidate. Concerning the matter of "protective orders," criminal legal expert Joyce Vance wrote the next day that judges are typically patient with criminal defendants because they "don't want to do anything that could lead to a conviction being reversed on appeal." And with "lots of lawsuits against him in progress simultaneously and the prospects of more indictments to come, judges will have to use the tools at their disposal wisely to ensure that justice is done."[6]

Trump was publicly maintaining that there was nothing to any of these cases as in the earlier Russian investigation or the two impeachment trials. These current investigations and lawsuits surrounding the most litigious person in American history were all unfounded as well. Most of them were either fraudulent hoaxes, partisan witch hunts, or conspiracy offshoots of a "deep state" out to get him. Always the aggrieved victim and the revengeful warrior, Trump was once again struggling to escape from these allegedly politically motivated offenses and the forthcoming criminal indictments.[7] After his first federal indictment, Trump was twisting this message a bit, "In the end, they're not coming after me. They're coming after you – and I'm just standing in their way."[8] Echoing himself from the 2020 re-election campaign where he was messaging that "I'm the only thing standing between the American Dream and total anarchy, madness, and chaos."[9]

Soon after the 2022 midterms and by the time Trump announced his 2024 candidacy for the GOP a few weeks later, Republicans were making the scale of the federal investigations of Mr. Trump and his associates an issue in itself. For example, on July 12, 2023, during a contentious House Judiciary Committee, Republicans bombarded FBI Director Christopher A. Wray, a Trump appointee, "with criticisms about his role in investigating" the former president, "efforts to address extremist violence and the bureau's electronic surveillance practices." Led by committee chairman, Rep Jim Jordan of Ohio, the committee Republicans

> treated Mr. Wray as if he were a hostile witness – repeatedly interrupting his attempts to answer their rapid-fire queries with shouted rebuttals. Most sought to portray the nation's premier law enforcement agency, and Mr. Wray…as a political tool of the Democrats.[10]

They also suggested that they "might block the reauthorization of warrantless surveillance program used to investigate several people suspected of involvement in the Jan. 6 breach or oppose funding for the bureau's new headquarters."[11]

At the start of 2023 criminologists and non-criminologists alike were asking themselves three related questions pertaining to the former president and announced presidential candidate for 2024: Would Teflon Don once more escape the clutches of the long arm of the law? Would the former president be indicted and prosecuted for a slew of crimes, including those committed against the US Constitution and the rule of law? If indicted, would Trump be held liable for his acts of lawlessness committed before, during, and after his presidency or would he be exonerated by a jury of his peers? These and other related questions pertaining to a lawless businessman and entertainment celebrity turned President of the United States (POTUS) and corrupting political entrepreneur have certainly provided high drama and tension in a world of integrated entertainment, politics, and sports. However, politics as entertainment or sport should not be the objects of electoral politics.[12] Then again throughout US history there have been more than a few "outlaws" and "lawmen" who had become folk icons capturing the fictional and nonfictional American imaginations.

These populist or people's outlaws like Billy the Kidd, Jesse James, Butch Cassidy, John Wesley Hardin, Bonnie and Clyde, or D.B. Cooper and lawmen like Wild Bill Hickok, Wyatt Earp, Elliott Ness, and J. Edgar Hoover were from mid-19th to end of the mid-20th century and these criminals and crime-fighters all had a "fanbase" not unlike like Donald Trump. While there are similarities in the anomic social psychology of their fanbases and Trump's, there are also differences between those iconic outlaws or lawmen and Teflon Don – notably having been a twice impeached as well as criminally indicted former president. Most importantly, only the former Commander-in-Chief became a revolutionary out to destroy the old liberal democratic order and to establish a new authoritarian regime. The other outlaws and lawmen were far more parochial and narrower in their scope of lawless or lawful activities. They were for the most part either breaking or defending laws designed to control the crimes of the powerless. These outlaws and lawmen were more or less all playing by the established rules or norms of the constitutional legal game unlike Trump who is on a self-aggrandizing mission to destroy them.

With the exception of FBI Director Hoover who like Trump was also weaponizing law enforcement and the Department of Justice for their own power, the other folk heroes or anti-heroes were not engaged in efforts to overturn the American system and its institutions for any other reasons than to avoid legal accountability and/or to use their abuse of authority for nothing other than enhancing their individual power at the expense of everyone else. Unlike Trump, most of these other icons were not also in the business of messaging and shaping their own stories. When they did engage in "self-promotion," there was no social media available to exploit for the taking. In the case of Trump, he and his ideological allies Steve Bannon and Steve Miller as far back as his first presidential campaign in 2016 were busy shaping their deep state and persecution narrative in defense of the politically incorrect, anti-woke and make America racist. sexist, homophobic, and nativistic again.

By his first impeachment in 2020, this anti-democratic narrative had already taken control of the Republican party. This narrative only became stronger after losing the "stolen" presidential election in 2020, the failed coup and assault on the Capitol on January 6, and the second impeachment trial one month later. So entrenched had Trump's nonsensical and crazy narrative become that with each new indictment it offers more "proof" of its absurd delusion. Regardless of the facts and the law, the sentiments behind Trump's undying support will not significantly change unless or until after the lawless former president begins to be convicted for his alleged crimes of corruption and racketeering committed before, during, and after his presidency.

In the meantime, while Trump was busy distorting his first classified documents criminal indictment, a number of former members of the Trump administration were coming out publicly and denouncing Trump. Most notably among those Johnny-come-lately "never Trumpers" were former Secretary of State Mark Esper and former Attorney General Bill Barr. On State of the Union Esper told CNN's Jake Tapper that the former president should not be trusted with national secrets: "It's just irresponsible action that places our service members at risk, places our national security at risk" and "I think this process needs to play out and people held to account, the president held to account."[13] Also making the media circuits was the hypocrite Barr who should have been impeached for his weaponization of the Department of Justice (DOJ) and collusion with the former president who during his tenure wanted to have his proverbial "cake and eat it too." Speaking on CBS' Face the Nation he said that he did not believe that Trump should continue to be the Republican standard-bearer because of his reckless conduct and his efforts to overturn the 2020 election: "He will always put his own interests and gratifying his own ego ahead of everything else, including the country's interests."[14] At the same time, because of Trump's supposed previous persecution by the government Barr was still defending their unseemly interventionist actions on behalf of Trump and against his adversaries up and until the January 6 assault on the Capitol.[15]

After Trump in June 2023 was criminally indicted in Florida for not returning classified documents including nuclear secrets, most experts were saying that the criminalizing of a former president in the middle of the 2024 presidential campaign "could further undermine confidence in democratic principles and institutions of government."[16] As this *Washington Post* article reported:

America's institutions have been attacked repeatedly over the past half-dozen years, thanks principally to the conduct and actions of Donald Trump. The next 18 months could further undermine confidence in democracy and the rule of law as the former president seeks a return to the White House while defending himself against federal and state criminal charges.[17]

Regardless of the outcome of the 2024 presidential election, how could it be otherwise with the lawless and anti-democratic track record of the former president and his Republican party?

Likewise, many scholars and political strategists understood that should Trump escape justice once again and not be criminally convicted, the Democrats would be disappointed with the outcome of the jury system but not with their relative trust of governmental and democratic institutions, separating the administration of justice and the crimes of the powerful from their contempt for and distrust of the anti-democratic and authoritarian Trump and his minions. Conversely, these political observers also knew that should Trump not be elected again in 2024 whether he was still facing criminal adjudication or had already been convicted and imprisoned, most Republicans would erroneously continue to distrust their government and the democratic-constitutional system. This dystopian reality was succeeding primarily because Trump and company had already successfully brainwashed their followers with a perpetual flow of disinformation, creative grifting, and habitual lying.

While virtually no political strategists, Democratic or Republican, were giving Trump any chance of defeating President Biden in a head-to-head contest even with the electoral college bias in the former president's favor, there were several announced third-party or independent candidates that could possibly tip the election in favor of Trump. More significantly there was an attempt by No Labels, an American political organization funded by non-transparent dark money that allegedly supports centrism and bipartisanship seeking a presidential-vice presidential ticket of potential candidates like Democratic (in name only) Senator Joe Manchin from West Virginia and former Republican Maryland Governor Larry Hogan. Ostensibly nonpartisan this advocacy group according to Mother Jones has also been helping a firm to raise money for election deniers, MAGA Republicans, and the radical Trump right.[18] In short, this is really nothing more than an organized effort to cipher off votes from Joe Biden in order to bring back the Racketeer-in-Chief to the White House.

CFO Allen Weisselberg pleaded guilty to 15 criminal counts including tax fraud, grand larceny, and conspiracy along with comptroller Jeffrey McConney on December 6, 2022. Meanwhile, the former president was not charged on any of these crooked accounting counts. Anyone unfamiliar with the modus operandi of Donald Trump should have learned a valuable lesson about loyalty in Trumpworld. Weisselberg, a 40-year-long Trump employee, did not "flip" or "rat" out Boss Trump as a witness for the prosecution.

Instead, he was fined and jailed for four months at Rikers Island. During the same criminal case, two of the Trump Organization entities – the Trump Corporation and the Trump Payroll Corporation – were found guilty by a jury of all 17 criminal counts charged, including a scheme to defraud, conspiracy, criminal tax fraud, and falsifying business records.[19]

Another valuable Trump loyalty lesson was learned when the contents of a trove of exchanged text messages that former White House chief of staff Mark Meadows had turned over to the January 6 House Committee back in early 2021 became public. When these texts were released a month after the November 8, 2022, midterm elections, they revealed the extensive plotting efforts that ensued between Meadows and 34 Republican lawmakers to overturn and steal the election from president-elect Joe Biden.[20] The messages included "at least 364 texts from members of Congress to Meadows and at least 95 messages from Meadows to the lawmakers." This very real conspiracy as contrasted with the numerous fake conspiracies propagated by Trumpism included high-profile Republicans like US Senator Ted Cruz of Texas and House Representatives Jim Jordan of Ohio and Mo Brooks of Alabama. Brooks has been described by longtime Trump adviser Jason Miller "as the 'ringleader' of the effort to block the certification of the election results."[21]

Moreover, on February 17, 2023, we learned that Special Counsel Jack Smith was engaging with several of Trump's high-ranking praetorian elite guard who were all resisting subpoenas to testify as witnesses and/or targets of the January 6th and Mar-a-Lago criminal investigations. Smith had "at least eight ongoing secret battles before Chief Judge Beryl Howell of the U.S. District Court and the judges of the Circuit Court of Appeals in Washington."[22] The former Vice President Mike Pence was a key witness in the former investigation because he had refused to go along with Trump's plot not to certify the 2020 election on January 6. At the time, Pence had already published a book about the Capitol assault and had designs on a 2024 run for the GOP nomination for presidency. He was also refusing to appear before the grand jury and was prepared to take his appeal all the way to the US Supreme Court. Before following up on his threats to appeal, Pence agreed to talk with Smith and his team of lawyers, answering questions and testifying for some five and a half hours before a grand jury on April 28, 2023. It was further disclosed over that weekend that Smith had expanded his January 6 and Mar-a-Lago investigations

> to determine whether Mr. Trump and his aides violated federal wire fraud statutes as they raised as much as $250 million through a political action committee by saying they needed the money to fight to reverse election fraud even though they had been told repeatedly that there was no evidence to back up those fraud claims.[23]

On another related criminal investigation, the Fulton County District Attorney Fani Willis had subpoenaed 75 witnesses. Among these were 16 prominent Republicans including Georgia Party Chairman David Shafer for their roles in falsely claiming that they were "duly elected and qualified electors" for Trump. Also subpoenaed was Rudy Giuliana as well as Mark Meadows, former Assistant Attorney General Jeffrey Clark, and Trump's constitutional lawyer and professor of law John Eastman. These alleged co-conspirators for both January 6th and the fake elector scheme involving six states had each appealed unsuccessfully not to testify before the Fulton County grand jury.[24]

During the runup to the 2022 midterm elections, Trump was crisscrossing the country campaigning on behalf of his election denying candidates and for his MAGA believing base that Trump had, indeed, not lost the election without some kind of foul play. Altogether there were 299 GOP election deniers running for national, state, and local office. At those rallies in mostly high-profile closely contested state races for the presidency, Trump's rambling speeches usually lasted between 75 and 95 minutes having little to do with any substantive issues or his endorsed candidates. And everything to do with Trump's victimization and personal grievances. In true Trumpian form, he was perpetually demonizing opponents, circulating conspiracy theories, using incendiary rhetoric, and dispensing disinformation. All consumed as "red meat" for his MAGA base and most Republicans as well. For example, at his Thursday rally in Sioux City, Iowa, on November 3 and his Saturday rally in Latrobe, Pennsylvania, on November 5, three days prior to the November 8th midterm elections, his respective speeches at the two rallies "contained at least 58 false or misleading statements" and "at least another 24 distinct falsehoods."[25]

After the terrible underperformance of the GOP and the high-profile election denying candidates backed by Trump lost and buttressed by the January 6 House Hearings throughout the summer of 2022, it seemed as though Trump was losing control over the news cycles as he had owned them ever since he won the GOP nomination for president in 2016.[26] At least for a short period of time – about 100 days – the loss of his former bully pulpits offline and online had seemed to critically weaken his ability to shape the political narrative. Several data points from Google analytics and cable television beginning in 2022 were telling the story.

For example, the Google search interest index reflects a volume of searches. For Donald Trump searches peaked after he won his first term in office, precipitously dropped after he lost his bid for a second term in office, rose to about half of what its peak had once been and by November of 2022 had leveled off to where they had been before he announced in 2015. At the time of Trump's announcement for the 2024 presidential nomination on November 16, 2022, a Google search volume for Donald J. Trump (DJT),

Taylor Swift, and the World Cup in the United States revealed that the mad rush for Swift tickets was a tad less interesting than Trump's announcement, both barely registering compared to the World Cup.[27]

Cable TV coverage was even more revealing of the disinterest in Trump or his candidacy for 2024. Throughout the summer and fall of 2022 Trump tried to garner media attention by repeatedly teasing that he would run again in 2024, and then he announced his candidacy on November 16. In the months before he announced, Trump was "often ignored or hit with tough coverage."[28] Fox News, his former propaganda machine, rarely talked about the former president. MSNBC, the so-called progressive hub on cable news, covered him negatively during the House Hearings and after the FBI searched Mar-a-Lago for the stolen classified documents. In response to CNN's more "balanced" as well as negative cable news coverage, Trump filed two "I am not Hitler" defamation lawsuits against CNN. The first lawsuit in early December and after it was tossed out, a second lawsuit on December 30, 2022.[29] He also filed another defamation suit against *The Washington Post* for hundreds of millions of dollars that was dismissed as well. Even Trump's announcement speech failed to acquire much coverage. In fact, MSNBC did not bother to broadcast his announcement and Fox News after initially tuning into Trump's announcement cut away from his live remarks shortly after he began rambling on during the 1-hour-plus speech.

Not to be deterred Trump's inflammatory utterances and bogus lawsuits "kept on keeping on," such as his defamation lawsuit filed against his former fixer Michael Cohen for $450 million after the plaintiff-in-chief was indicted by the Manhattan district attorney on 34 felony counts in April 2023. At this point in time, during the rape-defamation federal civil trial in Manhattan filed by E. Jean Carroll against Trump where he chose not to appear or put on any kind of defense, US District Judge Lewis Kaplan had warned Trump and his attorneys about "potential liability" should Trump continue with his inflammatory remarks on social media or elsewhere about Carroll.[30] The day before Trump was found liable for battery and defamation and ordered to pay Carroll $5 million in damages on May 8, Judge Juan Merchan presiding over Trump's first criminal indictment of any kind, over hush money, prohibited Trump from posting evidence on social media, agreeing with a motion by Manhattan District Attorney Alvin Bragg.

Once again, Trump was grabbing political reporters by their prefrontal cortex and directing their coverage to his political narrative. In fact, by the time of the settlement against Fox News – the largest in defamation history – for $787.5 million in damages for the first of a litany of defamation lawsuits with Dominion and other plaintiffs such as the global voting machine company Smartmatic as well as a Fox News producer Abby Grossman. And before the firing of Tucker Carlson on April 29 because of something that Tucker had written about being a white supremacist and worrying about enjoying a video of white racist violence against a Black man, Fox News already had the Trump propaganda machine of disinformation back up and running.

However, by this point in time, 2024 candidate Trump no longer necessarily needed the propaganda assistance of Fox News as both his narrative and Trumpism were being covered as politically newsworthy. The executive editor of Salon, Andrew O'Hehir, had characterized the repackaging of Republican "know-nothingism" to Republican "know-everythingism" as key to legitimating the messaging of "isolationism, nativism, mythic and sentimental individualism, an ingrained and unquestioned ideology of white supremacy and male supremacy, a generalized mistrust of all large institutions, all centers of power and all forms of academic or professional expertise."[31]

At CNN coverage was not propagandistic. However, it was "business as usual" at least from the perspective of Trump controlling the political narrative of deception. During his stay in the White House, the network that had previously undergone a mutually antagonistic relationship with Trump announced on May 2nd that Trump would be participating in a CNN presidential town hall on May 10th in New Hampshire. Trump alone would be taking questions from allegedly New Hampshire Republicans and undeclared voters planning to vote in the 2024 GOP presidential primary.[32] As it turned out, there were plenty of GOP officials from other states in attendance. And the handful of questions posed from the audience came from those individuals who had voted for Trump in 2020, some of whom even worked on his previous campaign. The event aired at 8:00 p.m. prime time, lasted 70 minutes less two commercial interruptions of relief for all, but the MAGA packed audience loved and ate up every pathological statement that flowed seamlessly from Trump. The town hall or more accurately Trump rally was held at St. Anselm College and moderated by Kaitlan Collins one of the anchors from "CNN This Morning" who on the fly did an excellent job of pushing back on Trump's litany of lies. From start to finish Trump continually steamrolled over her to the absolute joy of the sycophants in attendance. Here is a sampling of Trump's comments during the town hall highlighted by MSNBC on "Morning Joe" the next day, May 11, 2023:

- Continued attacks on 2020 election, calling it a "shame" and "rigged"
- Said E. Jean Carrol's civil rape case was a "fake story" and referred to her as a "whack job" [though a jury of six men and three women found him liable for sexual abuse, defamation, and awarded her $5 million one day earlier]
- Called Moderator Kaitlan Collins a "nasty person"
- Complimented Russian President Vladimir Putin, calling him a "smart guy," refused to side with Ukraine

- Defended keeping classified documents at Mar-a-Lago, said he had "every right to do it"
- Pushed Republicans to default if they don't get "massive cuts" on the debt ceiling deal
- Said he was "inclined to pardon some January 5th rioters

What Trump was peddling on CNN to his conned consumers was essentially the same old pack of disinformation, hatred, and nonsense that he was propagating in 2016, 2018, 2020, 2022, and now in 2024.

During the 2022 midterm elections, most of Trump's stump speeches for other political candidates including those rallies on September 3 in Pennsylvania, September 17 in Ohio, September 23 in North Carolina, October 1 in Michigan, and October 9 in Nevada were the exact same ones that Trump had been giving since the early summer when the FBI executed a search warrant at his Mar-a-Lago home and country club in Palm Beach, Florida. By Labor Day, Trump was finishing off his thematic orations by painting dystopian portraits of a broken United States that only he could restore to its former greatness. Often playing in the background of these events was QAnon like melodic-orchestral music featuring swelling strings, gentle bell tones, and brooding piano harmonies.[33]

Let us in some detail take the rally in Robstown, Texas, on October 22 to illustrate.[34] Before landing in his freshly painted Boeing 757 named "Trump Air Force One," he flew over the crowd as Trump does whenever the venue allows. As the crowd waits in anticipation for the "savior" to take the stage, the music includes three of Trump's favorite theme songs: Andrew Lloyd Webber's "Memory" from the musical Cats, Elvis Pressley's "Suspicious Minds," and "Real American," which was wrestler Hulk Hogan's entrance song. Wearing a sport jacket, white shirt, no tie, and a red MAGA hat Trump opened his remarks as he often does, "Let's have a little fun."

What did Trump have to celebrate about? Three days earlier a released Monmouth University Poll taken after the January 6 House Select Committee had completed its next to last public hearing in October had revealed that just 27% of all Americans and only 17% of Republicans were even tuning in to the televised hearings. Forty percent of Americans believed that Trump should be criminally charged. Thirty-six percent believed that he was directly responsible for the Capitol assault. A mere 8% of those hearing viewers had changed their minds in the affirmative direction of Trump's responsibility and most of those persons were Democrats. At the same time, 60% of those surveyed thought that the recently subpoenaed Trump should have to testify, and if testifying, 77% thought he should do so publicly.

Other Monmouth poll findings included: 26% thought that the House investigation of the January 6 incident had helped to strengthen American democracy, 35% thought democracy had been weakened, and 33% thought it had had no impact. As for the presence of the former president in the future of American politics – even after the classified documents caper at Mar-a-Lago was exposed – 50% thought Trump posed no danger while 47% thought he did. All in all, Patrick Murray, the director of the independent Monmouth University Polling Institute had this to say: "If anything, the House hearings seem to have driven Republicans further into the Trump camp."[35] That was certainly the case after his first criminal indictment when he stretched his lead significantly further over Florida Governor Ron DeSantis the only other GOP candidate for the nomination polling in double figures.

In any case, the former president began his Texas rally appearance in late October by praising Texas Governor Greg Abbott, Lt. Gov. Dan Patrick, and Attorney General Ken Paxton. For the record, Patrick and Paxton unsuccessfully sued to challenge the 2020 presidential election results in four states that did not include Texas. The *Houston Chronicle* reported that "Trump said Paxton would have figured out the voter fraud in about two minutes if he was his AG." The newspaper also pointed out that in 2021 Paxton's staff had "spent 20,000 hours looking for 2020 voter fraud and did not uncover anything beyond isolated incidents."[36] There were many different explanations for those casted votes. While the fraudulent votes were bipartisan, most came from registered Republicans.[37] It is not at all difficult to understand why Trump was so keen on the embattled attorney general in the runup to the 2022 midterm elections: "Paxton has been mired in scandal and served under a cloud of criminal charges for most of his tenure as the state's top lawyer."[38]

Serving in his third term as AG, Paxton had previously "initiated lawsuits that overturned or blocked major Biden and Obama administrative policies, particularly on immigration."[39] Paxton's "crowning achievement" perhaps was his unprecedented impeachment as a state attorney general in Texas on May 27, 2023.[40] After a couple days of preparation and more than 2 hours of debate, an overwhelming majority of the members of the Texas House voted to impeach the state attorney general, 121–3. Paxton called the vote, "illegal, unethical, and profoundly unjust."[41] The Texas Senate on September 16 acquitted the AG of 16 articles of impeachment alleging corruption and bribery.

On Friday the day before the impeachment vote, the comfortably elected three-term attorney general made a rare appearance before assembled reporters to criticize the process, saying that the impeachment was being organized by the Democrats and liberal Republicans. He had also stated that these "corrupt politicians in the Texas House are demonstrating that blind loyalty to Speaker Dade Phelan," also a Republican, were "showcasing their absolute contempt for the electoral process."[42] Trump immediately blasted the impeachment proceedings as an attempt "to unseat 'the most hard working and effective' attorney general and thwart 'the large number of American Patriots' who had voted for Paxon." Trump also called Governor Abbott "missing in action" and he wanted to know from his Truth Social network followers, "What is our Country coming to?"[43] Two days later @ realDonaldTrump, the Insurrectionist-in-Chief partially answered his own question when he posted:

> Happy Memorial Day to all, but especially to those who gave the ultimate sacrifice for the country they love, and to those in line of a very different but equally dangerous fire, stopping the threats of the terrorists, misfits and lunatic thugs who are working feverishly from within to overturn and destroy our once great country, which has never been in a greater peril than it is right now. We must stop the communists, Marxists and fascist "pigs" at every turn and make American great again.

Back at the Texas rally before the 2022 midterms, Trump next called out former Rep. Beto O'Rourke (D-TX) who was challenging Abbott for governor for being a "flake" and then labeled House Speaker Nancy Pelosi (D-CA) "crazy." That was all he had to say about any Texas contests for political office as he quickly pivoted to talking about his two favorite subjects, himself and his bogus complaints about murderers, rapists, migrants, far-left lunatics, the liberal media, woke censorship, the Russian hoax, the Pulitzer Prize, and the Black Lives Matter cities of Detroit, Philadelphia, and Atlanta.[44]

Naturally, Trump complained about the House Select Committee investigating the January 6 attack on the US Capitol and the subpoena he had received from the committee the day before laying out one dozen of his crimes. Trump repeated lines from a 14-page letter he issued to the Select Committee when he had first learned of the forthcoming subpoena on October 13th. Trump referred to the committee members as "highly partisan political Hacks and Thugs whose sole function is to destroy the lives of hard-working Patriots." He called the investigation a "Charade and Witch Hunt" and that the committee members were corrupt for not investigating the "massive Election Fraud."[45] Shaking his head from side to side and using one of his favorite refrains, "Oh, these crooked people, these crooked people. They are so terrible." As usual, he then pointed out that he had run twice for president and had won both times.

Trump also suggested that *Politico*'s Josh Gerstein and Alexander Ward be forced to reveal who leaked Justice Samuel Alito's draft of the opinion overturning *Roe vs. Wade*. Without data or evidence of any kind, Trump also falsely claimed that Mexico was the most dangerous country in the world,[46] and that on average each drug dealer kills some 500 people. Then he preceded to call for their executions,[47] aware that his base had been upset with him for signing the "liberal" and bipartisan First Step Act (2018) into law. A highly touted federal prison reform act, the first of its kind in more than a decade, meant to enhance the lives of inmates. It was not only poorly rolled out and never fully implemented by the Trump administration, but by the end of 2022, the legislation had yet to yield any improvement in federal prison conditions or to have reduced prisoner recidivism.[48]

From the same weekend there was the Sunday lead story in *The New York Times* entitled: "Trump Backers Use 'Devil Terms' to Rally Voters."[49] This article focused on how incendiary rhetoric was fueling polarization in America. The authors had analyzed more than 3.7 million tweets, Facebook ads, newsletters, and congressional speeches. Among their findings, they underscored that at the "forefront of this polarization are Republicans who voted to reject the Electoral College results that cemented Mr. Trump's defeat last year." Tweets from nine of those congressional representatives were also highlighted on the front-page of *The NY Times* as follows:

**Mary Miller,** June 25, 2022: We will never surrender our country to the Democrats, the Marxists, and the Hate-America leftists who want to destroy this country.

**Kevin McCarthy,** January 26, 2021: Just look at the first week of the Biden Administration. It's been America last and China first.

**Barry Moore,** July 30, 2021: Pelosi is no longer a benevolent dictator – she's a tyrant.

**Lauren Boebert,** June 29, 2022: Democrats hate Voter ID because it makes it harder for them to cheat. Democrats hate free speech because it makes it harder for them to lie. Democrats hate the Second Amendment because it makes it harder for them to steal your liberty.

**Mo Brooks,** May 14, 2021: Never have I feared so much for America's future. American-hating Socialists seek to upend the American way of life based on liberty and freedom and replace it with dictatorial government that controls every aspect of our lives.

**Louie Gohmert,** December 9, 2021: The January 6 commission has become an out-of-control political tool for the Democratic vigilantes to target their opponents. We're going to need a select committee to investigate the civil rights abuses of the commission.

**Ronny Jackson,** April 15, 2021: Make no mistake about it, the most radical anti-American leftists in Congress are in control. If you have a Democrat representing you, you MUST stand up to America's LAST Marxists that are radically and systematically DESTROYING our country.

**Madison Cawthorn,** April 5, 2021: AOC's top congressional priorities: (1) Photoshoots; (2) Virtue Signaling; and (3) Destroying America.

**Pat Fallon,** June 21, 2021: Joe Biden needs to take a cognitive test. Now.

As part of The ReAwaken America Tour, a cabal of election deniers, QAnon proponents, and "right-wing cuckoo birds" had come together that same weekend for a two-day event. Held in Pennsylvania at Spooky Nook Sports, ReAwaken America has been described as part of a Christian crusade. It has also been characterized as a dangerous mix of misinformation, nationalism, and divisive political rhetoric. A long list of speakers at the event included such "luminaries" as Eric Trump, Roger Stone, Ret. General Michael Flynn, pillow guy Mike Lindell, and Doug Mastriano, the Pennsylvania GOP gubernatorial candidate for 2022.[50] The opening prayer set the zeitgeist for the event: "God, open the eyes of Pres Trump's understanding, that he will know how to implement divine intervention. And that you will not surround him with RINO trash, in the name of Jesus." Conspiratorial discourse peppered throughout the two days included "everything from McDonald's being part of the 'deep state' to 'demonic satellites' controlling the voting system in the United States."[51]

A Friday night highlight was when Eric called his father from the stage and played the audio into a mic for all to hear. The audience was going wild as the two men chatted: "So dad, you have an amazing crowd here in Pennsylvania." As he held up his phone for everyone to scream into, Trump can be heard saying from the small speaker of Eric's phone:

Wonderful son who's treated everyone fantastically. He works so hard. He's such a great guy. We love you all and we'll be back doing things... we're going to bring this country back. Our country's never been in such bad shape as it is now. I just wanna thank everybody and please treat my boy good because he's a great one.[52]

Moments before Eric had been handed the mic from Mastriano's self-proclaimed prophet, Julie Green, who was accompanying him everywhere he went on the campaign trail. Green claimed among other things that God would be executing political figures "for their planned pandemic, shortages, inflation, mandates and for stealing an election." She was at the event to personally deliver a message from God who had told her, "You can't stop my son, who is the rightful president." On the campaign circuit some of her other revelations and conspiracy theories included: Pelosi "loves to drink little children's blood"; the government is conducting "human sacrifices"; and that President Joe Biden was "secretly dead" and being played by a "Hollywood actor."[53]

Trump may be from the theater of the absurd, but he is not crazy. While the 45th President of the United States (POTUS) could very well be diagnosed as a sociopath, he is a far cry from certifiable insanity. For the record, Trump does not believe in any of the nonsense circulating among his cult followers or political supporters any more than he thinks the election was stolen from him. He is simply perpetuating and exploiting whatever gobbledygook is out there as Trump also believes that delusions are made for suckers and other losers not for fantasizing winners like himself. Whereas the former president may not be clinically nuts or deluded, he is a verifiable con man, grifter, and fraudster. Trump is also a habitual liar and cheat as well a geriatric bully. Armed with his indefatigable ego and highly insecure narcissistic personality, the "very stable genius" as he has referred to himself had indeed become the United States' authoritarian strongman that he always wanted to become.[54] Finally, as a long time racist, misogynist, and wannabe autocrat with guidance from Steve Bannon and Stephen Miller, he learned about The Great Replacement conspiracy and tapped into the history of white nationalism and Christian hegemony in America.[55]

Flash forward seven months later and once again without attending the ReAwaken America two-day event at the Trump National Doral Miami hotel and resort, he was calling in to legitimate the traveling roadshow touring America as part of his Trumpian campaign efforts for the presidency in 2024.[56] This time Trump was letting people know that his old buddy Lt. General Michael Flynn, founder of Stop the Steal and co-founder of ReAwaken America, would be returning to Washington should he be elected president for a "third time." For those who may not know or recall, Flynn was Trump's first national security adviser who had to leave the White House after a couple of months in office, and he was convicted of lying in relation to Russian interference with the 2016 presidential election. He was later pardoned by Trump as were several others in Trump's first campaign who were also involved in crimes prosecuted by Special Counsel Robert Mueller.

As part of the introduction to his interview with Adam Hochschild two weeks before the 2022 midterm elections, Chauncey DeVega had captured contemporary history and the orange man:

> America and many other parts of the world are under siege by illiberal forces that are seeking to end democracy under the banner of right-wing populism and other authoritarian visions. Such forces are old and new at the same time.
>
> In the United States and many other parts of the world, right-wing street thugs and paramilitaries have staged marches and engaged in acts of violence against their "enemies" – which include Black and brown people, immigrants of all races, LGBTQ people, liberals and "socialists," Jewish people, Muslims and other targeted groups – as part of a reactionary revolutionary project to enforce "tradition" and "conservative" values and return their societies to a mythic past of "greatness" and "unity."
>
> It is clear that Donald Trump still aspires to be an authoritarian strongman and fascist, looking to some of the worst such leaders in history

as his role models. To that point, Trump's coup attempt on Jan. 6 had echoes of Adolf Hitler's Beer Hall putsch and Reichstag fire [in 1923], both of which preceded the Nazi Seizure of power.[57]

Hitler was arrested several days later and after a 24-day trial was found guilty of treason and sentenced to five years in Landsberg prison. He was released after nine months. However, that had been enough time for him to pen a draft of his highly influential *Mein Kampf*. More than two and a half years after January 6, Trump had not yet been arrested and charged with crimes for that infamous day.

Not until June 19, 2023, did we learn that the FBI had resisted opening a probe into Trump's role in January 6 for a variety of reasons prominent among those was that Attorney General Merritt Garland did not want to appear "political" like his predecessor Bill Barr had been as a willing until he wasn't stooge of Trump's. It was more than a year after January 6 and not before the House Subcommittee had delivered its 800-page investigation to the DOJ, and the world had already been privy to the insurrectionary behavior of the former president and his conspiring allies vis-à-vis eight publicly televised hearings before prosecutors, and the FBI would jointly commence a probe of actions directed from the White House to try to steal the election. "Even then, the FBI stopped short of identifying the former president as a focus of that investigation," even though everyone had known from January 6th that the then president at a minimum had obstructed justice.[58]

Similarly, justice officials had also quashed an early plan to create a task force to focus on people in Trump's "orbit" like Mark Meadows, Rudi Giuliana, John Eastman, and those like Roger Stone who had been camped out at the Willard Hotel "war room" in the days leading up to the assault on the Capitol.[59] The DOJ was also reluctant and dragged its feet in the Mar-a-Lago classified documents case because it was more afraid of the consequences of pursuing a former president for seditious conspiracy than it was afraid of the consequences of not doing so. Eventually, thanks to the brilliant work of the House Subcommittee, the compelling investigative journalism by the fourth estate, and Trump having announced in November 2022 he was once again running for president in 2024 that Attorney General Garland was left with no choice but to appoint Special Prosecutor Jack Smith. Something Garland should have done with respect to both January 6th and the fake elector scam involving seven swing states to overturn the Biden election some 22 months before.

A couple of weeks after his lackluster announcement that he was running for a third time had laid an egg, and because nobody seemed to care anymore and most GOP leaders were privately wishing that Trump would simply disappear, on December 3, 2022, Trump reverted to his political playbook of "shock and awe" as a means of gathering attention. At the end of what had been a terrible week for Trump, he had to say anything to distract from and/or to change the conversation, the crazier usually the better. What with the conviction of two Oath Keepers for seditious conspiracy and the 11th Circuit US Court of Appeals reversal of a judge's appointment of an independent arbiter to vet the seized classified documents from Mar-a-Lago, Trump was doubling down on his anti-democratic rhetoric. Always working hard on his counterfactual and fictional narratives the former president over that weekend on his Truth Social platform was offering up such criticisms as: "The world is laughing at the United States of America and its corrupt and rigged Presidential Election of 2020!" And in all caps, "UNPRECEDENTED FRAUD REQUIRES UNPRECEDENTED CURE." His cure would require "the termination of all rules, regulations, and articles, even those found in the Constitution."[60] Crazy, desperate, or gaslighter? If crazy does not mean to imply insanity in the legal sense, then all three apply.

Less than 48 hours later, Trump was trying to soften or walk back what the world had already read from his Truth Social posts.

The Fake News is actually trying to convince the American People that I said I wanted to "terminate" the Constitution. This is simply more DISINFORMATION & LIES, just like RUSSIA, RUSSIA, RUSSIA, and all of their other HOAXES & SCAMS.

Trump continued:

What I said was that when there is "MASSIVE & WIDESPREAD FRAUD & DECEPTION," as had been irrefutably proven in the 2020 Presidential Election, steps much be immediately taken to RIGHT THE WRONG. Only FOOLS would disagree with that and accept STOLEN ELECTIONS. MAGA![61]

In the late spring the indictment walls were beginning to close in on Trump and he was having a terrible first week of May 2023. What with the wrapping up of the E. Jean Carroll rape and defamation trial where Trump did not have the testicles to make a court appearance or put on an affirmative defense. With eight of the accused fake Trump electors in Georgia agreeing to take immunity deals from DA Willis, and with the seditious conspiracy convictions of four leaders of the Proud Boys on Thursday, Trump took to his Truth Social account in the wee hours of Saturday morning to lash out at Jack Smith. The Special Counsel had been interviewing key witnesses surrounding Trump's stolen classified documents recovered by the FBI at Mar-a-Lago. In classic Trumpian projection, he was employing his ju-jitsu style of rhetoric to slam others for falsely doing precisely what Trump has been, in fact, doing. For example, @realDonaldTrump:

The Special "Prosecutor," Jack Smith, who is harassing, threatening, and terrorizing people who work for me, probably illegally, and totally at odds with the way Crooked Joe Biden is being treated, will no longer be known as the Special "Prosecutor," but rather, the Special "Persecutor." He is a Trump Hating SLIMEBALL who is going far beyond the original instructions of the Department of Injustice. The Witch Hunt continues, as it always will, with the Radical Left, Country Destroying, Lunatics![62]

This unadulterated poppycock is classic Trump that critics and supporters alike have all come to know as the authentic outlaw-in-chief. Loathed by the former, admired by the latter, and enjoyed by all in America as a tragic figure in a dramatic political comedy. While Trump may have temporarily lost some of his former political traction, Trumpism and defending the insurrection remained the top priority of the GOP controlled 118th House agenda. On January 10, 2023, the very first full day of actual work under the Republican Speaker Keven McCarthy, half the time was spent pandering to the insurrectionist-in-chief. The other half of their time was spent politicizing several oversight activities and establishing along party lines three highly contested investigative subcommittees. The most controversial was the formation of the Select Subcommittee on the Weaponization of the Federal Government. Trumpian insurrectionists and legislators were now leading weaponizing investigations much in the spirit of Trump and AG Barr, trying to interfere with and to obstruct the numerous investigations into the former president as well as themselves for, among other things, weaponizing the Justice Department.

The incoming chairman of the Judiciary Committee was Representative Jim Jordan (R-OH), a stanch ally of Trump who blew off a subpoena to testify about his own conspiratorial role in the failed coup before the January 6 House Select Committee. He became the chair of the subcommittee on weaponization. Talk about the "pot calling the kettle black" or "the fox guarding the hen house." Jordan had been deeply involved in Trump's efforts to overturn the 2020 election. He had already spent months investigating what he claimed was a bias in federal law enforcement against conservatives. His intention was "to use his gavel and subpoena power to escalate and expand the inquiry" of conspiracy theories to include searching for evidence that federal workers had become political agents on behalf of the Democrats. Jordan was immediately demanding documents about ongoing criminal investigations so that among other things, he could have access to the evidence against himself and his co-conspirators.[63] Naturally, the DOJ would never release those documents as Jordan knew full well. These demands were nothing more than Kabuki theater and performance politics serving to undermine American democracy. Fortunately, after five months and several hearings, they had failed miserably to accomplish anything except to look stupid as they say because all they had was a nothing burger without any condiments or evidence of any kind for their various conspiracy theories about a "deep state" out to get Trump.

Even more disturbing and harmful to the rule of law and democracy was the more than inappropriate reactions of powerful Republicans mostly from the US House of Representatives. Responding prematurely to a Trump posting from his Truth Social platform on March 18, 2023, that he was going to be arrested and indicted on Tuesday, March 21, by Manhattan District Attorney Alvin Bragg which did not materialize. Within hours of Trump's "tweet" the head toady and House Speaker Kevin McCarthy had directed House committees to investigate Bragg and his investigation of the former president, claiming that what had not yet even occurred would be "an outrageous abuse of power by a radical DA who lets violent criminals walk as he pursues political vengeance against President Trump." Other politicos sucking up to the Boss, chiming in about the weaponization of justice in America, and trying to defend or whitewash the myriad of crimes committed by Trump included: Representative Chip Roy (R-Texas), Senator J.D. Vance (R-Ohio), and to a lesser degree former Vice President Mike Pence.[64] As Kurt Bardella, a former senior advisor to Republicans on the House Oversight Committee had opined: "The United States Congress has no legitimate reason to meddle in an active investigation by a New York prosecutor. It's a flagrant abuse of power that establishes a dangerous precedent threatening to upend the justice system."[65]

Of course, there was no risk whatsoever that Bragg would give the House of Representatives the time of day when it comes to complying with their absurd requests. In an email to his staff following McCarthy's statement and Trump's posted threats to his very life, the Manhattan DA wrote that his office would "not tolerate attempts to intimidate our office or threaten the rule of law in New York."[66] Bragg further stated that in coordination with the New York City Police Department that his office would "ensure that any specific or credible threats against the office will be fully investigated."[67] That was before he had received two personal death threats in the mail with harmless white powder.[68] As Bardella concluded after supplying countless examples of GOP corruption and lawlessness:

> Evidently, if you are a Republican seeking high office, criminal conduct is no disqualification; it's verging on a prerequisite. Turning the House of Representatives into a glorified conspiracy to obstruct justice is the latest manifestation of the party's enthusiastic embrace of organized crime.[69]

Trump's use and abuse of the DOJ while he was president surpassed anything that President "tricky dicky" Richard Nixon could ever have dreamed about. And in trying to "de-weaponize" the Justice Department as a former president vis-à-vis the Select Subcommittee on the Weaponization of the Federal Governance was an unprecedented "obstruction of justice" by the GOP even though their work was failing to score any real wins. By May 2023, Republican politicians including Congresswoman Marjorie Taylor Green and Senator Chuck Grassley, as well as Fox News host Sean Hannity, were accusing President Biden of bribery when he was vice-president even though Republican Senator Josh Hawley had acknowledged that nobody had seen any evidence. Nevertheless, Grassley and Republican Representative James Comer issued a subpoena for records that they believed may contain evidence of a scheme. The White House dismissed the accusations as unfounded and motivated by political bias. Nevertheless, after 11 months of investigating without any evidence the House on December 13, 2023 authorized an impeachment inquiry into President Biden, with every Republican voting for and every Democrat voting against. Meanwhile, Green was now calling for the impeachment of Biden as other Republicans had been doing since he became president on January 20, 2021. This form of GOP representative governance had been circulating the body politic since the 2018 midterm elections. This authoritarian approach to representative democracy has been inflicting all voters with a congressional dystopia, an Orwellian nightmare, and a post-Trump anti-democratic movement in America. In the more recent past, this resurgent civic disease or illness in American politics could be traced back to the racist backlash from the 2008 election and 2012 re-election of President Barack Hussein Obama.

The roots of this contemporary anti-democratic and authoritarian movement were also conjoined with those Republicans that have been enamored with the "Unitary Executive" theory of power. Like two-time US Attorney General Barr who has "always believed that those post-Watergate reforms were foolishly restrictive and unrealistic but they worried that the silly voters would react badly to blatantly hackish partisanship so they've always kept up the pretense of an independent Justice Department."[70] At the same time, while both parties over the years have complained about politicized Justice Departments, the Republicans have made it clear that they don't even believe in the concept of an independent justice department. And that they prefer for the DOJ to operate as a part of the Presidential Cabinet – at least when the GOP holds the power of the executive branch. Now that Trump has broken all the norms and rules so transparently and unashamedly, he has made hackish partisanship fashionable if not acceptable to the American people. As Heather Digby Parton has argued, the Republicans plan to capitalize on Trump's criminality for decades to come. In this sense, Trump has become a human smokescreen for the GOP:

> The fact is that the Republican Party's alleged hostility to the "Deep State" is nothing more than a set-up to co-opt state power for themselves. They're

chafed under the rules and regulations that preclude them from behaving like crooks and liars such as Richard Nixon and Donald Trump for the last 50 years. They don't want to get rid of the "Deep State," they just want to get rid of all the impediments to using it the way they believe it's meant to be used: against their political enemies. Trump's flagrant criminality has perversely given them exactly the excuse they need to do it.[71]

In different words, while it may still have been the Trumpian Republican party after the criminal indictments in 2023, the Boss' days of hegemonic control of the party had already peaked though it may not have seemed so during the GOP primaries, and his days of omnipotent power were coming to an end especially after his upcoming 2024 defeat. In the meanwhile, and to the very end of Trumpism, the former president's corruption and even his campaigning as an indicted or convicted criminal in 2024 would become a very useful tool for the GOP leadership who, despite the perplexity over whether "to pardon" or "not to pardon" the former president by the other GOP candidates for the 2024 presidential nomination, are also not unlike the Democratic leadership. In the sense that they are all praying for criminal convictions and the incarceration of the 45th President so that once free of the corrupting and disrupting Trump each of the two partisan parties can move on with their fundamentally different political agendas.

At Trump's first official 2024 campaign rally in Waco, Texas, on March 25, 2023, vendors were selling T-shirt, hats, and flags with slogans such as "FREE TRUMP" and "[EXPLETIVE] BIDEN." When the former president took the stage, the big screen behind him was playing video of the January 6 assault on the Capitol as Trump with hand over heart pledged allegiance to the United States as a jailhouse recording of the January 6 choir of patriotic "political prisoners" sang in the background. Among the notable themes of the evening were Democratic abuse of power, prosecutorial misconduct, and the politicalization of injustice. The likely GOP presidential candidate for the 2024 nomination spent his 90 minutes vacillating between being a savior and being a victim though always promising retribution for himself and pardons for the January 6 "hostages."

For example, "We've been fighting for seven years…standing up to the Marxists, the socialists, the stupid warmongers…the fake news media… They don't want to tell the truth, that's why they're going down the tubes. America is awful and elections are rigged." Only Trump can "save America" even as he's "persecuted with investigations." The ex-president also slammed President Biden and his administration as "one of those depraved" chapters in American history. "Straight out of a Stalinist Russia horror show. A banana republic, that's what we've become" as he vowed that when the 2024 election is over, "I will be the president of the United States [and] you will be vindicated and proud."[72] Sociologist Philip Gorski, co-author of *The*

*Flag and the Cross: White Christian Nationalism and the Threat to American Democracy* (2022) has described Trump's role in the dark and dystopian imagery as "positing himself as the long arm of the Lord, the long arm of divine vengeance."[73]

Most significantly is that the leading GOP presidential contender and presumed 2024 nominee's end-of-the-world framing of his political campaign was not only connecting with religious audiences, but it was also meshing well with QAnon conspiracy adherents. By the spring of 2023, these apocalyptic story lines were "having something of a secular, post-pandemic cultural moment as well – including in hit shows such as HBO's 'The Last of Us'."[74] More ominously for those who take Trump seriously, such apocalyptic pronouncements were giving them licenses for violence because "gee whiz folks" everything else depends on it especially when you cannot obtain it lawfully or constitutionally.

In the polarized, fractured, and profit-driven communications world of social media, those people like Donald Trump that we think of as authentic and down to earth are merely those who have learned to exploit the transactional constructions of narrative rhetoric.[75] For example, in the middle of the Dominion Voting Systems' $1.6 billion defamation lawsuit against Rupert Murdoch and his right-wing propaganda machine working on behalf of the former president, its resident pluto-populist multimillionaire Tucker Carlson provided selective footage of January 6 on his March 6, 2023, evening show shared with him by House Speaker McCarthy as a "day in the park" of sightseeing visitors at the Capitol. That was after a "trove of text messages, emails, and other material from Fox News executives and on-air personalities were made public" that had revealed among other things that Carlson passionately hated the then-president and called him a "demonic" force.[76]

The cherry picked clips taken from some 41,000 hours of video shared with Carlson by the House Speaker were another feeble attempt to whitewash the violent and failed insurrection. These clips were ridiculous on their face and had proved nothing.[77] And yet, on Truth Social Trump was thanking Carlson and Murdoch for perpetuating the Big Lies even though neither man believed them. Trump was also calling for the prosecution of the January 6 House Select Committee members for treason. Trump has a long history of accusing other folks of treason including President Barack Obama, House Speaker Nancy Pelosi, and director of the FBI James Comey.[78] Echoing the former president's call for the death of the nation's top general, Trump supporters at Iowa rallies were calling out Gen. Mark Milley's "treason" for his phone call to reassure China in the aftermath of the storming of the Capitol.

While Carlson's public-relations gambit was a quasi-immediate failure – with several prominent Republicans such as Senate Minority Leader Mitch McConnel and his colleague from Utah Senator Mitt Romney weighing in against the false narrative – Trump who had been vowing retribution and reprisals only two days before at the annual Conservative Political Action Conference in Maryland[79] was polling among New Hampshire Republican voters for the 2024 presidential nomination at 58% followed by Ron DeSantis at 17%, Nikki Haley at 6%, and Mike Pence at 4%.[80] Meanwhile, the cult of the January 6 martyrs was alive and well at CPAC: "J6ERS POLITICAL PRISONERS AND LOST LOVED ONES YOU ARE NOT ALONE!"[81] In fact, Marjorie Taylor Greene (R-GA) working with the House Oversight Committee Chair James Comer (R-KY) was busy organizing a trip that occurred on March 24, 2023, for members of Congress to visit the Washington, DC jail in support of those January 6 defendants who were still being held in pre-trial detention.[82]

The rest of *Indicting the 45th President* is divided into three parts. Part I, An Absence of Bipartisanism, consists of four chapters that describe the US democratic system in bipartisan crisis as evidenced by the partisan struggle for political power fueled by Boss Trump and the code of immorality, fraudulent duplicity, corrupting authority, and a Republican party bent on contracting freedom for all but white heterosexual men. Chapter 1, Conspiracy Theories and Mediated Memes in a World of Post-Truth America, is framed within the context of the wave of defamatory claims and litigation seeking accountability from those individuals or media that were spreading lies depicting the 2020 presidential election as stolen. By using the assault on the House Speaker's husband, ballot drop boxes, kitty litter stalls in school bathrooms, and the Club Q Massacre as illustrations of socially mediated politics and hate speech, connections are made between GOP campaign strategies and the whitewashing of crimes, intimidation, violence, victim scapegoating, and discriminatory legislation across red state America.

Chapter 2, Scaremongering, Party Politics, and the Crisis in US Democracy, begins during the Reconstruction Era following the Civil War with an historical overview of frightening or fear-inducing stereotypes of racial, religious, and political identities that were used to motivate or stimulate grievance and revenge up through the emergence of the Cold War following WWII at the height of McCarthyism. This is shadowed by a debunking of the bipartisan myths about law and order as well as about crime and crime control from the 1940s through the 2022 midterm elections. A critique of limitless campaign spending and partisan politics is then presented as a rationale for publicly financed elections. Next, the dynamics of the 118th Congress are explored to foreshadow the next Trumpian White House with or without the Corruptor-in-Chief should that materialize in 2024 or 2028. The chapter finishes with an outline of the unfinished business of American democracy.

Chapter 3, Oligarchy, Kleptocracy, and the Maestro of Looting, revolves around styles of corruption in relation to money laundering, global investment, and offshore capital not as in parking money outside the United States to avoid taxes as in a Caribbean Island, Panama City, Switzerland, or elsewhere in the world. Rather, these forms of corruption have to do with groups of lawyers in places like Nevada, North Dakota, and Delaware that have legalized the art of the anonymous shell company residing in the United States. The chapter begins by laying out the similar backgrounds and inherited real estate wealth of Donald Trump and his son-in-law Jared Kushner, as well as their corresponding access to different international oligarchies and kleptocracies in Russia, Ukraine, Israel, and Saudi Arabia. Next, there is an in-depth discussion of "influence market corruption" characteristic of developed nations to distinguish it from the more commonly known forms of corruption associated with developing and/or autocratic nations. The chapter also expands upon the themes and examples of stocking the swamp, paying to play, and anti-democratic corruption for profit that I examined in *Criminology on Trump*. The chapter then pivots to Trump's fraudulent taxes, the weaponization of the Department of Justice, and the cultural fabrication of "anti-corruption" as an instrument of political exploitation.

Chapter 4, On the Divided House Select Committee Investigation of the Capitol Assault, offers an overview of the televised hearings and a condensed version of the Final Report of the Select Committee including its findings, summaries, appendices, recommendations, witness transcripts, and footnotes. The volume of material evidence secured by the Committee about the January 6 insurrection far exceeded everyone's imagination and provided the DOJ not only with a roadmap and a blueprint for prosecutorial investigation but also with a powerful kick on the backside to "get on the cases" of the most important political crimes in US history and to bring all those persons responsible to accountability and criminal justice for all. This was due to the skill and diligence of the committee members, its staff of some one hundred people, and the hiring of the producer and former president of ABC News division James Goldston to choregraph a multi-mediated series of very captivating hearings.

Part II, Indicting Donald Trump for Vandalizing the Federal Republic, consists of four chapters that highlight the criminal charges against as well as the pre-indictment, pre-trial public, and legal strategies of the unprecedented lawsuits against a former president of the United States. Chapter 5, The People of the State of New York v. Donald J. Trump, lays out the charges in Trump's criminal indictment in April 2023 in Manhattan for "hush money" payments. I do so by sharing five real time commentaries of mine. Three of these were written for *The Crime Report* and two for *Salon*. They were published before, during, and after Trump's very first criminal indictment ever to foreshadow what could be expected with respect to the subsequent criminal indictments and from defendant Trump and his team of lawyers.

Chapter 6, The Mar-a-Lago Classified Documents Caper, begins by sharing a Mar-a-Lago Prosecution Memo written by a team of lawyers more than six months before the US Special Prosecutor Jack Smith completed his investigation. The Memo concluded that based on the publicly available evidence at that time that a powerful case existed against Trump for the mishandling of government documents, obstruction of justice, and criminal contempt. The chapter then turns to the timeline and the 20-month-long struggle of the National Archives and the Federal Bureau of Investigation to retrieve the classified documents from Trump's Mar-a-Lago home and country club, the mountain of incriminating evidence that had become known by May 2023. Also included was speculation about the possibility of charges involving the Espionage Act and finally to an overview of the charges that were rendered on June 8, 2023.

Chapter 7, The People of Fulton County, Georgia v. Donald J. Trump et al, frames this indictment in the context of what Trump and his attorneys would not stoop to in order to disrupt, stymie, or avert investigations and potential indictments. The chapter discusses the back-and-forth between the two legal teams, the grand jury, the bench, and the wider community. These included the security precautions that District Attorney Fani Willis deemed necessary as well as her legal fight not to be disqualified from overseeing the case that all occurred in the runup to the indictments that finally came on August 14, 2023, after two and a half years of serious and complicated investigation across several states from Arizona to Pennsylvania. Followed by a detailing of the charges and the accused defendants.

Chapter 8, Trump's Conspiracies to Overturn the 2020 Election that Led to the January 6th Assault on the Capitol, begins with the acknowledgment that a number of Trump attorneys and former aids, including Vice President Mike Pence, would eventually testify before a grand jury investigation. Some of those witnesses and/or co-conspirators began testifying around Labor Day 2022, more than two months before the appointment of Special Prosecutor Jack Smith. In early 2023, there were two shots in the arm buttressing the strength of the case against Trump and his allies. One from US District Judge Amit P. Mehta who refused to dismiss three lawsuits seeking damages from Trump for physical and emotional injuries that occurred on January 6. The other was from US District Judge David O. Carter who had determined while addressing the issues of privileged emails between Trump and his lawyers that based on the preponderance of the evidence it was "more likely than not" that Trump had engaged in federal crimes. Lastly, the chapter turns to an overview of the indictments of the three conspiracies and obstruction of justice charges against the soul defendant Donald J. Trump and six uncharged and unidentified co-conspirators on August 1, 2023.

Part III, Liberty, Justice, and American Democracy, consists of two chapters that taken together first provides a critique of the existing US constitutional democracy and second "what needs to be done" to establish a reformed, an amended, and a new and improved constitutional democracy. Chapter 9, American Mythology, Bipartisan Alienation, and Partisan Politics, opens with an overview of the Racketeer-Influenced and Corrupt Organization statutes as a means of demystifying the study of crime and criminal justice in the United States. It then turns to a discussion of politics as a blending of "logos" and "mythos" and to differences between these in a post-modern world. The chapter also provides a review of the bipartisan myths surrounding US democracy, followed by an examination of the economic social history behind the bipolar myths of American exceptionalism. Next, the chapter describes two decades of rising partisan antipathy by way of exit polls from the 2016 and the 2020 presidential elections as well as from the 2018 and the 2022 midterm elections as a means of tracking the similarities and dissimilarities of the two major political parties in this nation. The chapter finishes with a riff on partisan power, the alt-right political agenda, and the threat to American democracy.

Chapter 10, Tyranny of a Minority or Tyranny of a Majority, brings together the thematic arguments that surround the case for a new democracy in the United States. By first summarizing why the existing ideals of a representative democracy have fallen short, and second why the fruition of the Bill of Rights depends upon the establishment of and incorporation of economic rights for all Americans. Next, the chapter presents a new democratic vision based on human equity and social justice. The chapter also provides concrete reforms for overcoming the economic and political obstacles to justice for all and for amending the US Constitution to become more of a pure or a direct democracy rather than a representative or indirect democracy. Finally, it ends with a citizens' agenda for a democratic civil society.

## A Preparatory Postscript to Trumpian America

When the baneful saga of Donald Trump finally comes to a long overdue ending, his legacy, if the GOP can survive his political debacle and being on the wrong side of history, will include a party that rejects American constitutionalism, is about deconstructing the state or emptying out as much as possible the executive branch, the Department of Justice, the Environmental Protection Agency, the Consumer Protection Agency, and so on by swapping in or substituting ideological true believers for those professional experts and public servants who have taken an oath to the US Constitution. This preoccupation of Trump to clear out and not clean up the Department of Justice which had been investigating and has indicted and will shortly be prosecuting the former president for his smorgasbord of political crimes and his desire to dissolve almost 50 years of an "independent" attorney general with a reconstituted and weaponized AG as in the case of his "fixer" Bill Barr, for example, has also become a preoccupation of the Republican Party who are now about defunding the FBI.

In other words, it is not only whether Trump is elected president again in 2024 but also about other Republicans such as Florida Governor Ron DeSantis or former Vice President Mike Pence who saved US democracy at the critical moment. If not in 2024, then in 2028, these Republicans would like nothing better than to perpetuate Trumpism without Trump. In a similar vein, the nationalist and so-called populist conservatives have grown increasingly "enthusiastic about using the state to enforce a particular social order" as in the decisions of the alt-right SCOTUS. The Republican Party has also "begun to take on the values and attitudes of the smalltime capitalist and the family firm." In many ways, this is simply Republican "business as usual" as "business owners have always been a critical part of state and local Republican politics."[83] Afterall, the nation's state legislatures and county boards of supervisors have always been full of family-owned businesses from car dealerships to food franchises and from construction companies to landscaping businesses. Among those elements that distinguish these closely held models of ownership from multinational corporations are the degrees to which these businesses are understood to be extensions of the business owners that appear to exercise total authority over their places of production so long as their employees have not organized and established a union.

As Jamelle Bouie has concluded,

If the nature of our work shapes our values – if the habits of mind we cultivate on the job extend to our lives beyond it – then someone in a position of total control over a closely held business like, say, the Trump empire might bring those attitudes, those habits and pathologies, to political office.[84]

That was the case in spades with respect to Donald Trump where there was no separation between the POTUS and the Trump Organization. Moreover, as the Republican Party came to wrap itself around the lawless and fraudulent Trump, and as the GOP came to shape itself around the Trump persona, it also adopted his anomic and nihilistic world view, and the ideology of a crime boss. No longer content to run government for businesses' sake, the Republican Party as with Trump now want to run the government as though it was their very own privately owned enterprise. However, this "doesn't mean greater efficiency or responsiveness or whatever else most people associate with private industry, it means instead, government as the fief of a small-business tyrant."[85]

The current struggle between democratic and anti-democratic forces in the context of revolutions and civil wars – ours and other nation's – takes us to the heart of the matter in America as analyzed by biologist and climatologist turned political historian, Peter Turchin, in his recently published *End Times: Elites, Counter-Elites, and the Path of Political Disintegration* that addresses the iron laws of oligarchy and wealth pumps that always take from the poorest and the masses in order to giveth to the richest persons and corporations. A historical situation in which the United States has found itself since President Ronald Reagan took office in 1980. In a nutshell, this contemporary crisis in government is about intra-elite competition and conflict on the one hand, and about the weakened legitimacy of the state, its laws, and institutions, on the other hand, as both of these political conditions are exacerbated by the economic conditions of elite overproduction and popular immiseration. Fortunately, the "reintegration" of these types of political-economic crises have been repaired in America's past. We too can incorporate those temporary remedies from the past. However, going forward I am arguing that to be most effective against the fight for authoritarianism and to preclude the next cycle of institutional *crisis* from happening again, we must also transform our present constitutional democracy from a "tyranny of the minority" to a "tyranny of the majority."

## Notes

1  Toluse Olorunnipa and Michelle Ye Hee Lee. 2021. Trump's lie that the election was stolen has cost $519 million (and counting) as taxpayers fund enhanced security, legal fees, property repairs and more. *The Washington Post*. February 6. www.washingtonpost.com/politics/interactive/2021/cost-trump-election-fraud

2  Robert Legare. 2023. Trump special counsel investigations cost over $9 million in first five months. *CBS News*. July 7. www.cbsnews.com/news/trump-special-coun sel-probes-cost-over-9-million-in-the-first-five-months

3  Glenn Thrush and Adman Goldman, Ben Protess and Alan Feuer. 2023. As inquiries compound, justice system pours resources into scrutinizing Trump. *The New York Times*. July 23. www.nytimes.com/2023/07/23/us/politics/trump-inv estigations-jack-smith-justice-department.html

4  Shane Goldmacher and Maggie Haberman. 2023. As legal fees mount, Trump steers donations into PAC that has covered them. *The New York Times*. June 25. www.nytimes.com/2023/06/25/us/politics/trump-donations-legal-fees.html

5  Steven Rosenfeld. 2022. Accountability looms for media outfits that spread lies about 2020 election. *The Nation Memo*. November 12. www.nationalmemo.com/ lawsuits-against-election-lies

6  Joyce Vance. 2023. Today in America: Trump can't help himself. *Civil Discourse*. May 24. https://joycevance.substack.com/p/today-in-america-trump-cant-help

7  Was Trump speaking the truth? After all, regardless of Trump's lifetime of fraud and lawlessness, he had never been personally convicted, or even indicted, of a single solitary crime before 2023. Civilly, both he and the Trump COrganization had been sued numerous times over five decades for fraudulent activities losing such high-profile cases as those involving Trump University and the Trump Foundation. As for the Trump Organization, it's the very first criminal indictment came on July 30, 2021, in Manhattan, NY, for operating a 15-year-long fraudulent tax scheme. After a six-week criminal trial, a jury verdict on December 6, 2022, convicted the family-run business and Trump Organization of all 17 criminal charges brought forth by the prosecution. Miraculously, Trump was not even charged with one of those crimes even though his signatures appeared on some of the incriminating evidence.

8 Matt Dixon. 2023. Trump delivers post-indictment speech: 'They're coming after you'. *CNBC.* June 10. www.cnbc.com/2023/06/10/trump-set-to-deliver-fiery-post-indictment-speech-theyre-coming-after-you

9 The Hill. 2020. @thehill. August 21, 1:29 P.M. https://twitter.com/thehill/status/1296862045783171077

10 Adam Goldman and Glenn Thrush. 2023. House republicans criticize F.B.I. in contentious hearing. *The New York Times.* July 12 www.nytimes.com/2023/07/12/us/politics/christopher-wray-fbi-house-judiciary-committee.html

11 Thrush et al. 2023.

12 As Jim Geraghty wrote in a *Washington Post* opinion piece, January 4, 2023:

> Getting a lot more Americans *interested* in politics is not the same as getting a lot more Americans *knowledgeable* about the workings of democracy or government. It has brought the worldview associated with sports-talk radio to politics; you've got a team and you want that team to win, and the other team is always the worst, and the refs are always unfairly treating your side. Heaven forbid you concede that the other team played a better game.

As proof of American ignorance, Geraghty continues: "People complain that government isn't doing what they want it to do, without caring to examine the document that lays out what the government can and cannot do." And finally. "It's as though Americans have taken a shiny new federal government out of a gaudily wrapped box and are trying to make it work without bothering to read the instruction manual." www.washingtonpost.com/opinions/2023/01/04/mtv-rock-the-vote-politics-entertainment/

13 Jasmine Wright and Aileen Graef. 2023. Trump should not be trusted with national secrets if charges prove true, his ex-Defense secretary says. *CNN Politics.* June. 18. www.cnn.com/2023/06/18/politics/trump-national-secrets-mark-esper-cnntv/index.html

14 Robert Klemko and Mariana Alfaro. 2023. Barr slams Trump's defense in documents case as 'absurd' and 'wacky'. *The Washington Post.* June. 18. www.washingtonpost.com/politics/2023/06/18/trump-indictment-bill-barr

15 Ximena Bustillo. 2022. Barr calls Trump's fraud claims 'detached from reality' in Jan. 6 panel testimony. *NPR.* June 13. www.npr.org/2022/06/13/1104634760/barr-trump-detached-from-reality-jan-6

16 Dan Balz and Ann E. Marrow. 2023. The collision of former president Donald Trump's criminal indictment with the presidential campaign could further undermine confidence in democratic principles and institutions of government, experts say. *The Washington Post.* June 17. www.washingtonpost.com/national-security/2023/06/17/trump-indictment-candidacy-democracy-institutions

17 Ibid.

18 David Corn. 2023. No labels is helping a firm that raises money for right-wing extremists. *Mother Jones.* June 14. www.motherjones.com/politics/2023/06/no-labels-is-helping-a-firm-that-raises-money-for-right-wing-extremists-anedot

19 Shayna Jacobs. 2022. Trump organization convicted in N.Y. criminal tax fraud trial. *The Washington Post.* December 6. www.washingtonpost.com/national-security/2022/12/06/trump-organization-guilty-tax-fraud/

20 Hunter Walker, Josh Kovensky and Emine Yucel. 2022. Mark Meadows exchanged texts with 34 members of Congress about plans to overturn the 2020 election.

*Talking Points Memo*. December 12. https://talkingpointsmemo.com/feature/mark-meadows-exchanged-texts-with-34-members-of-congress-about-plans-to-overturn-the-2020-election

21 Igor Derysh. 2022. "Our last hope is Marshall Law!": Leaked Mark Meadows texts reveal secret GOP Jan. 6 plotting. *Salon*. December 13. www.salon.com/2022/12/13/our-last-hope-is-marshall-law-leaked-mark-meadows-texts-reveal-secret-jan-6-plotting/

22 Philip Allen LaCovara, and Dennis Aftergut. 2023. Special counsel Jack Smith and the Subpoena Battles. *The Bulwark*. February 17. www.thebulwark.com/special-counsel-jack-smith-and-the-subpoena-battles/

23 Maggie Haberman, Alan Feuer and Jonathan Swan. 2023. Prosecutors in Jan. 6 case step up inquiry into Trump fund-raising. *The New York Times*. April 28 and May 1. www.nytimes.com/2023/04/28/us/politics/jan-6-prosecutors-trump-fund-raising.html

24 Lucian K. Truscott IV. 2023. A cover-up fit for a coup: Georgia grand jury says witnesses in Trump probe lied. *Salon*. February 18. www.salon.com/2023/02/18/a-cover-up-for-a-coup-georgia-grand-jury-says-witnesses-in-probe-lied/

25 Isaac Arnsdorf. 2022. In speeches, Trump uses dozens of lies, exaggerations to draw contrast with Biden. *The Washington Post*. November 7. www.washingtonpost.com/politics/2022/11/07/trump-falsehoods-lies-speeches/

26 David Byler. 2022. Donald Trump is begging for attention. Nobody cares. *The Washington Post*. December 7. www.washingtonpost.com/opinions/2022/12/07/donald-trump-2024-stunts-attention/

27 Ibid.

28 Ibid.

29 Jose Pagliery. 2023. Lawsuit reveals Trump can't stand being compared to Hitler. *Daily Beast*. January 10. www.thedailybeast.com/lawsuit-reveals-trump-cant-stand-being-compared-to-hitler

30 Adam Klasfeld. 2023. Trump's latest Truth Social posts swiping at E. Jean Carroll mid-trial could spark 'potential" liability,' judge warns. *Law & Crime*. April 26th. https://lawandcrime.com/live-trials/e-jean-carroll-rape-suit/trumps-latest-truth-social-posts-swiping-at-e-jean-carroll-mid-trial-could-spark-potential-liability-judge-warns/

31 Andrew O'Hehir. 2023. "Dark Brandon Tonight": Joe Biden, Tucker Carlson and the lure of the unsayable. *Salon*. April 30. www.salon.com/2023/04/30/dark-brandon-tonight-joe-biden-tucker-carlson-and-the-lure-of-the-unsayable

32 CNN Staff. 2023. Trump to appear at CNN town hall in New Hamsphire. *CNN Politics*. May 2. www.cnn.com/2023/05/01/politics/donald-trump-town-hall/index.html

33 Isaac Arnsdorf, Josh Dawsey and Michel Scherer. 2022. How a Trump soundtrack became a QAnon phenomenon. *The Washington Post*. September 23. www.washingtonpost.com/politics/2022/09/23/trump-qanon-song/

34 Bob Brigham. 2022. Trump tries to boost Texas GOP with rambling 105-minute rally speech. *Raw Story*. October 22. www.rawstory.com/trump-rally-robstown-texas/

35 Monmouth University Poll. 2022. Trump should testify to Jan. 6 Committee. October 19. www.monmouth.edu/polling-institute/reports/monmouthpoll_us_101922/

36 Jasper Scherer, Jeremy Wallace and Benjamin Wermund. 2022. Trump Texas rally: Trump takes jabs at Beto O'Rourke, says he'll 'probably' run again in 2024. *Houston Chronicle*. October 22. www.houstonchronicle.com/politics/texas/article/Trump-Texas-rally-live-updates-17525659.php?utm_campaign=socialflow&utm_source=twitter.com&utm_medium=referral

37 Christina. A. Cassidy. 2021. Far too little vote fraud to tip election to Trump, AP finds. *AP News*. December 14. https://apnews.com/article/voter-fraud-election-2020-joe-biden-donald-trump-7fcb6f134e528fee8237c7601db3328f

38 Carla Astudillo and Chris Essig. 2023. Ken Paxton was impeached by the Texas House. See how each representative voted. *The Texas Tribune*. May 27. www.texastribune.org/2023/05/27/ken-paxton-texas-house-impeachment-vote/

39 Zach Despart and James Barragan. 2023. Texas AG Ken Paxton impeached, suspended from duties; will face Senate trial. *The Texas Tribune*. May 27. www.texastribune.org/2023/05/27/ken-paxton-impeached-texas-attorney-general

40 Erin Douglas and Robert Downen. 2029. God, money and Dairy Queen: How Texas investigators secured the impeachment of attorney general Ken Paxton. *RawStory*. May 29. www.rawstory.com/god-money-and-dairy-queen-how-texas-house-investigators-secured-the-impeachment-of-attorney-general-ken-paxton

41 Quoted in Despart and Barragan. 2023.

42 Ibid.

43 Ibid.

44 Brigham. 2022.

45 Katherine Pompilio. 2022. Trump responds to Jan. 6 committee subpoena. *Lawfare*. October 14. www.lawfareblog.com/trump-responds-jan-6-committee-subpoena

46 According to Global World Peace index, Mexico is not even in the top 20 most dangerous countries.

47 It is worth noting that the international cocaine trafficker and three-time felon, Joseph Weichselbaum, was Trump's personal helicopter pilot in the 1980s and more recently was a lessee of one of Trump's luxury Manhattan apartments. See, David Cay Johnston. 2016. *The Making of Donald Trump*. New York: Melville House Publishing.

48 Ames Grawert and Patricia Richman. 2022. The first step act's prison reforms. *Brennan Center for Justice*. September 23. www.brennancenter.org/our-work/research-reports/first-step-acts-prison-reforms

49 Jennifer Valentino-DeVries and Steve Eder. 2022. Trump backers use 'Devil Terms' to rally voters. *The New York Times*. October 23. Front page.

50 Kelly McClure. 2022. The ReAwaken America Tour is The Warped Tour for right-wing cuckoo birds. *Salon*. October 22. www.salon.com/2022/10/22/the-reawaken-america-tour-is-the-warped-tour-for-right-wing-coo-coo-birds/

51 Zachary Petrizzo. 2022. Pro-Trump tour flies off the rails over 'demonic Satellites' and 'Deep State' McDonald's. *Daily Beast*. October 23. www.thedailybeast.com/pro-trump-reawaken-america-tour-flies-off-the-rails-over-demonic-satellites-and-deep-state-mcdonalds?via=newsletter&source=DDMorning

52 McClure. 2022.

53 Eric Hananoki. 2022. Doug Mastriano's campaign "prophet": Political executions are coming, Biden "is no longer alive," Pelosi drinks "children's blood." *Media Matters*. August 11. www.mediamatters.org/qanon-conspiracy-theory/doug-mastriano-campaign-prophet-julie-green-political-executions-are-coming

54 Gregg Barak. 2022. Donald Trump's life of crime: Most books are clueless – these five explain him best. *Salon*. October 5. www.salon.com/2022/10/05/donald-life-of-crime-most-books-are-clueless--these-five-explain-him-best/

55 ADL. 2021. "The Great Replacement:" An Explainer. April 19. www.adl.org/resources/backgrounders/the-great-replacement-an-explainer

56 Kelly Weill. 2023. Trump's call-in to far-right roadshow is red meat for Christian nationalists. *Daily Beast*. May 15. www.thedailybeast.com/trumps-call-in-to-michael-flynns-far-right-roadshow-is-red-meat-for-christian-nationalists

57 Chauncey DeVega. 2022. Adam Hochschild on history and the orange man: "We haven't had a figure exactly like him before." *Salon*. October 24. www.salon.com/2022/10/24/adam-hochschild-on-history-and-the-orange-man-we-havent-had-a-figure-exactly-like-him-before/

58 Carol D. Leonnig and Aaron C. Davis. 2023. FBI resisted opening probe into Trump's role in Jan. for more than a year. *The Washington Post*. June 19. www.washingtonpost.com/investigations/2023/06/19/fbi-resisted-opening-probe-into-trumps-role-jan-6-more-than-year

59 Jacqueline Alemany, Emma Brown, Tom Hamburger and Jon Swaine. 2021. Ahead of Jan. 6, Willard hotel in downtown D.C. was a Trump team 'command center' for effort to deny Biden the presidency. *The Washington Post*. October 23. www.washingtonpost.com/investigations/willard-trump-eastman-giuliani-bannon/2021

60 Brad Reed. 2022. Trump doubles down on calls to 'terminate' Constitution in furious all-caps Truth Social post. *Raw Story*. December 3. www.rawstory.com/trump-coup-2658827194/

61 Dessi Gomez. 2022. Trump tries to walk back his call to suspend the constitution as 'Fake News,' 'Disinformation & Lies'. *The Wrap*. December 5. www.thewrap.com/donald-trump-constitution-termination-truth-social-response/

62 https://truthsocial.com/@realDonaldTrump/posts/110319745806723101

63 Luke Broadwater and Catie Edmondson. 2023. Divided house approves G.O.P. inquiry into 'Weaponization' of government *The New York Time*. January 10. www.nytimes.com/2023/01/10/us/politics/house-republican-committee-weaponization-government.html

64 Giselle Ruhiyyih Ewing. 2023. McCarthy calls for House investigations as Republicans slam potential Trump indictment. *Politico*. March 18. www.politico.com/news/2023/03/18/republicans-trump-indictment-mccarthy-00087741

65 Kurt Bardella. 2023. Kevin McCarthy's Republicans have a clear stance on Trump's alleged crimes: They support them. *Los Angeles Times*. March 21. www.latimes.com/opinion/story/2023-03-21/kevin-mccarthy-republicans-trump-indictment

66 Mark Morales and Artemis Moshtaghian. 2023. Manhattan DA says his office won't tolerate 'attempts to intimidate' following Trump posts. *CNN Politics*. March 19. www.cnn.com/2023/03/19/politics/new-york-security-trump-bragg/index.html

67 Ibid.

68 Nikki McCann Ramirez. 2023. Alvin Bragg received death threat, white power. *Rolling Stone*. March 24. www.rollingstone.com/politics/politics-news/death-threat-white-powder-alvin-bragg-1234703578/

69 Bardella. 2023.

70 Heather Digby Parton. 2023. Republicans plan to capitalize on Trump's criminality for decades. *Salon*. June 16. www.salon.com/2023/06/16/plan-to-capitalize-on-criminality-for-decades
71 Ibid.
72 Quoted in Nicole Russell. 2023. Trump's kickoff rally speech in Waco: Half whining victim, half pompous overpromising. *The Sacramento Bee*. March 25. www.sacbee.com/opinion/the-point/article273602305.html
73 Quoted in Karen Tumulty. 2023. Donald Trump is promising the apocalypse. *The Washington Post*. March 28. www.washingtonpost.com/opinions/2023/03/28/trump-2024-battle-apocalypse-rhetoric/
74 Tumulty. 2023.
75 Emily Hund. 2023. *The Influencer Industry: The Quest for Authenticity on Social Media*. Princeton, NJ: Princeton University Press.
76 Oliver Darcy, Jon Passantino et al. 2023. Fox Chairman Rupert Murdoch rejected election conspiracy theories, dominion lawsuits documents show. *CNN*. March 7. www.cnn.com/2023/03/07/media/fox-news-dominion-lawsuit/index.html
77 Tom Nichols. 2023. The January 6 whitewash will backfire. *The Atlantic*. March 7. www.theatlantic.com/newsletters/archive/2023/03/jan-6-carlson-mccarthy/673312/
78 Steve Benen. 2023. Trump wants January 6 committee members to be charged with 'treason'. March 8.
79 Maggie Haberman and Shame Goldmacher. 2023. Trump, Vowing 'Retribution,' foretells a second term of spite. *The New York Times*. March 7. www.nytimes.com/2023/03/07/us/politics/trump-2024-president.html
80 Emerson Poll of 384 Republican Voters. 2023. Reported on "Good Moring Joe." *MSNBC*. March 8. www.msnbc.com/rachel-maddow-show/maddowblog/trump-wants-jan-6-committee-members-charged-treason
81 Laura Jedeed. 2023. The cult of the January 6 martyrs. *The New Republic*. March 6. https://newrepublic.com/article/170991/cpac-january-6-riot-prisoners
82 Emily Brooks and Mychael Schnell. 2023. House GOP organizing trip to see jailed Jan. 6 defendants, led by Marjorie Taylor Greene. *The Hill*. March 8. https://thehill.com/homenews/house/3890426-house-gop-organizing-trip-to-see-jailed-jan-6-defendants-led-by-marjorie-taylor-greene/
83 Jamelle Bouie. 2023. Trump believes the presidency is his. *The New York Times*. June 25. Sunday Opinion, p. 3.
84 Ibid.
85 Ibid.

# PART I
# An Absence of Bipartisanism

# 1

# CONSPIRACY THEORIES AND MEDIATED MEMES IN A WORLD OF POST-TRUTH AMERICA

By the time the 2022 midterm elections were over, there was already a "wave of litigation seeking accountability from media purveyors" who had been spreading "smears and lies that falsely depicted the 2020 presidential election as 'stolen'." Those lawsuits that were either heading toward trial or settlement may be viewed as augmenting the many high-profile investigations and prosecutions seeking accountability from Donald Trump, his administration, as well as campaign aides for pursuing courses of action to overturn the 2020 presidential election. Each of the low-profile lawsuits was alleging that "media-based provocateurs" were "smearing officials, local government workers, ordinary voters, and others by publishing false and defamatory claims about them," or additionally that their civil rights had been violated "by deploying illegal and violent tactics."[1] These lawsuits stand apart from the Dominion Voting Systems lawsuit filed by one of the United States' largest voting machinery makers who settled for $787.5 billion in compensation from Fox News for defaming its computer systems.[2] Nevertheless, Fox has not become more circumspect about the lies that it continues to broadcast to its moneymaking audience in light of at two upcoming civil defamation lawsuits, one filed in February 2021 by another election technology company, Smartmatic for $2.7 billion, and the other filed by Abby Grossberg a former Fox News producer in March 2023 who had worked with the hosts Maria Bartiromo and Tucker Carlson.[3]

Many of these lesser-known cases were being litigated with the assistance of Protect Democracy, a nonpartisan nonprofit organization that was formed in late 2016 with an urgent and explicit mission: "to prevent American democracy from declining into a more authoritarian form of government."[4] These media-centered lawsuits represent a spectrum of litigation seeking to discover evidence about the broad national conspiracy by Trump and his

DOI: 10.4324/9781003390664-3

allies to overturn the popular and Electoral College outcomes of 2020. Some of Protect Democracy's high-profile lawsuits included these four cases:

- A defamation lawsuit against Rudolph Giuliani in federal court brought by two former election workers in Fulton County, Georgia, Ruby Freeman and her daughter Shaye Moss, who testified before House Select Committee on January 6. In late October 2022, a judge denied Giuliani's motion to dismiss the case. Two months later a federal judge ordered the former prosecutor turn criminal to pay the plaintiffs $148 million; a few days later he filed for bankruptcy.
- A lawsuit against filmmaker Dinesh D'Souza, True the Vote, Salem Media, and others involved in the 2020 election conspiracy film, *2000 Mules*, for defamation and voter intimidation, on behalf of a Georgia man who was falsely accused of breaking the law in the movie and its related promotional materials.
- A voter intimidation lawsuit in Texas in response to an incident in 2020 where the "Texas Trump Train" – a caravan of Trump-supporting motor vehicles – tried to force a Joe Biden campaign bus off a highway at high speed. Discovery has been proceeding.
- A defamation lawsuit against Project Veritas, James O'Keefe, and Richard Hopkins, for spreading the lie after the 2020 election that the postmaster in Erie, Pennsylvania, was illegally backdating ballots at postal facilities. A state court denied motions to dismiss the case.

Nevertheless, each of these media-generated lawsuits had revolved around lies, disinformation, memes, conspiracy theories, and charges of defamation as part of what some have equated as a cultural need for 24/7 entertainment. A socially mediated situation that has "blurred the line between fiction and reality—on television, in American politics, and in our everyday lives."[5] And from the integrated terrains of cognitive psychology, linguistics, philosophy, literary, and film criticism, as well as neuroscience, it is argued that humans are hard-wired to absorb or accumulate facts and information, on the one hand, and to lose themselves in stories, fictional or nonfictional, on the other hand. Both as they choose sides and attune themselves to protagonists and antagonists playing out in books, big and small screens, and the contemporary political campaigns. Psychologist Richard Gerrig labeled this phenomenon "narrative transportation" whereby persons can become immersed in alternative worlds, stories, realities, or fictions that are capable of not only altering attitudes and beliefs, but also intentions and actions.[6] In the case of the latter, changing people's beliefs about normative institutions and actions is also referred to as "narrative persuasion." Something that the Trumpian Liar-in-Chief has habitually availed himself of during the course of his lifetime.

The problems of "truth" in the United States have also been magnified by the mass media's captivity to its own centrist ideology of journalist balance and neutrality that plays to the political status quo, which contributes further to the many issues of representative democracy, public policy, and the rule of law. John Stoehr argues that the nation's most lucrative media properties, in their coverage of the Democrats and the Republicans, and in their choices of "determining what's news, treat the parties, which they take to represent one-half of this country, as if they were equal in nature, theory and practice, though the differences are obvious." He continues that treating the two parties as equals is an act of "democratic politics, a way of persuading an audience to believe that a political worldview ('centrism')" whether it even politically exists as normative is not a "credible way to describe taking two things that are not the same and making them appear the same for the purpose of manufacturing, by comparison, an imaginative 'center'."[7]

More critically, Chauncey DeVega has argued that with a few notable exceptions the mainstream news media, the political elites, and the gatekeepers of "the approved public discourse cannot and will not admit the true nature of an epistemic crisis because to do so would challenge the legitimacy of their own authority and implicate them in the crisis itself."[8] DeVega points out that by early 2023 Trump was continuing "to stalk the nation while Ron DeSantis and the other Republican fascists [were] perfecting and expanding their campaign to kill the country's multiracial pluralistic democracy and turn it into a version of Viktor Orban's Hungary or Vladimir Putin's Russia," and what in effect should they succeed would become "an American Apartheid Christofascist plutocracy for the twenty-first century."[9] In the end, "the American news media as an industry will not consistently oppose Donald Trump or the larger 'conservative' movement because it needs to have access to those voices and personalities to make money."[10]

In the world of electronic or digital media – whether at work, in the classroom, eating a meal out, or during a sports competition – campaigns are all becoming performances and the voters are also performers, or at least participating fans taking part in the nation's political story lines. Going further, Megan Garber believes that we are living in an evolving metaverse of the future as she explains:

> Dystopias often share a common feature: Amusement, in their skewed worlds, becomes a means of captivity rather than escape. George Orwell's *1984* had the telescreen, a Ring-like device that surveilled and broadcast at the same time. The totalitarian regime of Ray Bradbury's *Fahrenheit 451* burned books, yet encouraged the watching of television. Aldous Huxley's *Brave New World* described the "feelies" – movies that, embracing the tactile as well as the visual, were "far more real than reality." In 1992, Neal Stephenson's sci-fi novel *Snow Crash* imagined a form of virtual entertainment so immersive that it would allow people, essentially, to live within it.[11]

Each of these writers warned that in the future we will all surrender to constant entertainment:

> We will become so distracted and dazed by our fictions that we'll lose our sense of what is real. We will make our escapes so comprehensive that we cannot free ourselves from them. The result will be a populace that forgets how to think, how to empathize with one another, even how to govern and be governed.[12]

Garber shares a story about the many responses to the Uvalde, Texas, massacre that Quinta Brunson, the star actor and creator of the ABC sitcom *Abbott Elementary*, received from her online followers about the killing of 19 children and two of their teachers in the spring of 2022. Brunson took to Twitter to write critically about the requests from her fans to write a school-shooting story line into her sitcom: "People are that deeply removed from demanding more from the politicians they've elected and are instead demanding 'entertainment'."[13] While Garber acknowledged Brunson's understandable frustration, her take was different: "...it's hard to blame the fans who, as they grieved a real shooting, sought comfort in a fictional one. They have been conditioned to expect that the news will instantaneously become [a soothing form of] entertainment."[14] Finally, online culture and news entertainment love those extremophilic influencers like Trump so long as they are perpetually pinballing from one fervor or passion to the next.[15]

In *Gonzo Governance: The Media Logic of Donald Trump* (2023), media connoisseur David Altheide argues that American democracy is in crisis because of what he refers to as the *gonzo governance* of US politics or the media-inspired fracturing of institutional norms and processes that has coincided with, if not been saturated by, the new digital ecology of communications. In various forms, the media has always played a significant role in presidential elections, but things were different in 2016 and 2020:

> Extensive use of digital media, including Facebook, Twitter, and other global digital platforms, made these elections personal, instantaneous, and visual. This was critical for hacking and manipulation of disinformation, as well as the widespread use of fake sites launched and massaged with algorithms and artificial intelligence. The dominant commercial interests supporting these platforms were easily aligned with propagandists' skills in mining users' data, preferences, emotions, and vulnerabilities to tailor messages and deliver concierge quality disinformation. This had consequences for both voters and candidates. But most importantly, this changing media landscape fractured significant democratic processes and institutions, pushing the United States toward a more autocratic approach to governance like those of so-called "illiberal democracies."[16]

Within the context of socially mediated politics and the era of Trumpian post-truth realities, the rest of this chapter examines the relationships between conspiracy theories, interacting memes, civil discourses, political campaigning, and policy agendas related to crime and justice.

## Conspiracy Theories and Mediated Memes

Conspiracy theories and mediated memes based on fictions, falsehoods, misinformation, and lies can prompt acts of violence that need to be disavowed, and in turn these are often disowned by more conspiracy theories that prompt more acts of violence. Within the context of these cyclical actions of violence and perpetual normalizing or downplaying of this contagious violence, a flood of more defensive misinformation and falsehoods metastasizes infecting factions of the body politic that have a need to deflect and/or suppress these social realities for whatever reasons.[17] Like in the case of the January 6 attack on the Capitol that was inspired by Trump's repeated lying about a "stolen" election that began months before the "rigged" election never happened. Less than two years later and one week before the 2022 midterm elections, there was another assault of Democratic House Speaker Nancy Pelosi's husband Paul that arose because of lies, conspiracy theories, and disinformation overload.

After the Republican leadership initially called Trump out for his failed coup, the GOP and their alt-right allies were quick to circle the wagons around Trump, playing down, denying, or inventing alternative stories for that insurrectionary day in American history.[18] As for their whitewashing conspiracy theories, these included blaming the insurrection first on Antifa and later the Federal Bureau of Investigation (FBI). Evidently, those fictions and other related conspiracies were believed by Paul Pelosi's attacker in the early morning hours of October 28, 2022. Much more on the attack and the workings of socially mediated politics in a few paragraphs, but first some background information on Trump's proclivities for violence linked to racism and weaponization.

Trump has always cultivated weapons of political cruelty, brutality, and violence. As far back as 1989 Trump took out full-page newspaper ads calling for the reinstatement of the death penalty in New York to be used on five wrongfully convicted Black men for the brutal rape of a Central Park jogger committed instead by a lone and non-related serial offender.[19] Trump's "enthusiasm for violence – including torture, extra-judicial murder and shooting of both migrants and protesters – has been a consistent theme of his politics."[20] For example, speaking to a group of supporters at Mar-a-Lago shortly after announcing his 2024 candidacy for the presidency in November 2022, Trump threatened that if elected, he "would send the military into American cities, even if local officials objected, and repeatedly stressed his eagerness for executing drug dealers and human traffickers after quick, summary trials."[21] By March 2023, on the campaign trail of grievance and revenge, Trump's new refrain became, "I'm your warrior, I am justice, I am retribution."

At the same time, there are other forms of political violence related to classes of scapegoats, mass psychology, and deference to authority as we learned from both Nazi Germany and the psychologist Stanley Milgram. Milgram's 1961 laboratory experiment at Yale University on student subjects who thought that they were applying electrical shocks to others taught us about the social relations of universal psychology, enigmatic leaders, the authoritarian personality, anticipatory obedience, and collective behavior. The conclusions reached were that even "normal" individuals are willing to harm or even kill others in the service of charismatic authority tied to new, noble, or mystical experiences. The diversity of Trump acolytes constituting the insurrectionists, election denialists, and deep state conspiracists that made up the backbone of the people who stormed the Capitol on January 6 also reinforces the findings of Milgram's "authoritarian personality."[22]

In the months before the San Francisco Bay area middle-aged man, David DePape, was arrested for attacking House Speaker Nancy Pelosi's husband in front of two cops with body cams running, he had published hundreds of posts supportive of fringe commentators and far-right personalities, mostly trolling Jews, Blacks, Democrats, the media, as well as transgender people. Dark and disturbing photos and videos or memes often appeared among his online posts. DePape published "a drawing of the Devil kneeling and asking a caricature of a Jewish person to teach him the arts of 'lying, deception, cheating, and incitement'." Several contained "lifelike images of rotting human flesh and blood, including a zombified Bill Gates and Hillary Clinton. Others depict[ed] headless bodies against bleak, dystopian landscapes."[23]

The self-described suicidal DePape also posted conspiracy theories on Facebook about COVID vaccines, the 2020 election, and the assault on the Capitol.[24] During his interrogation released to the public on January 2023, DePape confessed to the police about his attack and his motivation: "the person on TV lying every day was Pelosi" and the Democratic Party "are criminals" that "were submitting fake evidence to spy on rival campaigns" like Trump's and others; "it's an endless fucking crime spree…until they were able to steal the election."[25] Two days later as part of a live radio interview from jail, DePape apologized not for the attack on Paul Pelosi but for not being better prepared for his assault on their home.

Years before DePape had embraced the right-wing vilification, if not demonization, of Democrats that had become common tweeting fare among GOP election deniers running up to the 2022 midterms, he had "dabbled in fringe movements of all sorts, including those associated with nudism and the Green Party."[26] After his assault became public, within hours elected Republicans and Make America Great Again (MAGA) stars with millions of followers immediately reached back to portray DePape as a "leftist, hemp bracelet-peddling 'hippie,' perhaps part of a 'false flag' operation to blame the right for the assault."[27] A better alternative and unsubstantiated scenario were that the 42-year-old DePape and the 82-year-old Paul Pelosi had had a sexual affair that had gone wrong when the two men in fact had never met before the break-in. No matter, thanks to Eric Trump posting a picture of a man's white underwear with a hammer, the weapon used to fracture the skull of Pelosi, along with other high-profile figures such as Elon Musk tweeting misinformation from an unreliable source; these tweets went viral.

Only a few days before, the richest person in the world with 170 million online followers had purchased the social media platform for $44 billion.[28] Chief Twit as Elon refers to himself had tweeted the homosexual relationship was a possibility.[29] He quickly responded to the push back and worldwide negativity to his tweet, almost immediately deleting his tasteless tweet. Too late, it had already gained traction and, together with Eric's tweet, was being retweeted together and enjoyed by tens of millions of online followers. GOP officials were also joining in to spread the disinformation, which had become part of the Republican Party after January 6.

For example, alongside a photo of a distressed-looking Nancy Pelosi, Rep. Clay Higgins (R-La) tweeted, "That moment you realize the nudist hippie male prostitute LSD guy was the reason your husband didn't make it to your fundraiser."[30] Rep. Marjorie Taylor Green (R-GA) speaking to Trump supporters at a Sioux City, Iowa rally on November 3, 2022, perhaps had the "best" false narrative: "Paul Pelosi was brutally attacked by a drugged out illegal alien that should have been deported and Paul Pelosi should have been a gun owner and shot his attacker."[31] Through tweets, podcasts, and TV appearances, 2022 GOP candidates for office, plus 21 already elected Republican officeholders, and other prominent personalities had been identified by *The NYTimes* as disseminating misinformation or casting doubt on the Pelosi attack. Each implies that the "public had not been told the full story of what happened and, in some cases, spread theories that were unfounded."[32]

Conspiracy-driven online distractions like those circulating around DePape and Pelosi were falsely connected to GOP claims about rising violent crime rates across America that according to the FBI were mostly flat following the pandemic and leading up to the midterm elections.[33] At the same time, in defense of their authoritarian agenda and their twisted Second Amendment view of a constitutional "right to violence," Republican politicians were once again conspicuously silent about the dramatic alt-right hate crimes, the rise in school shootings as well as in domestic terrorism, and the escalating threats to governmental officials that had been rising every year since Trump was first inaugurated president in 2017.[34]

Meanwhile, the Republican Party of alleged "law and order" and "rigged elections" was busy giving backup and cover to the most powerful career criminal in America. Some other spreaders of misinformation and those casting doubt on the Pelosi attack included high-profile politicians like US Senator Ted Cruz of Texas, North Carolina Lt. Governor Mark Robinson, and Arizona State Senator Wendy Rogers. At the same time, there were prominent alt-right media personalities getting out the lies and false narratives including Glenn Beck, Tucker Carlson, and Megyn Kelly.

Other circulating myths heading into the 2022 midterms, from stolen elections to ballot drop box patrols to kitty litter boxes set out in school lavatories for student use, can also be linked to conspiracy theories and memes that became part of GOP online messaging, electoral strategies, and on-the-ground talking points. Let us first see how a network of ballot dropping box patrols or "mule watchers" evolved from an alt-right documentary film and memes from Truth Social (TS). Second, how gender identification and a very real worldwide subculture of mostly young people known as "furries" were combined with an urban myth of grooming children became part of a larger GOP disinformation campaign about "woke culture," which became the subject of a bomb threat on March 24, 2023, as hundreds of people were arriving for the Motor City Furry Convention at the Marriott Hotel in Ypsilanti, Michigan.[35]

### Mule Watching and Drop Boxes

On Wednesday night, October 26, 2022, NBC News counted at least nine people who were watching ballot drop boxes in Mesa, Arizona, "a small part of what has become a growing effort by some conservatives to monitor ballot drop boxes in the hope of catching election fraud." Some people have stood to watch at drop boxes wearing military-style fatigues and ski masks over their faces while armed and carrying weapons, including AK-47s, "prompting complaints to the Arizona secretary of state" for voter intimidation.[36] By October 24 the incumbent secretary of state Katie Hobbs and Democratic candidate for governor of Arizona had already referred six cases to both the state attorney general's office and the US Justice Department for further investigation.[37] Other voting fraud hunters were on drive by patrol slowly rolling their vehicles passed one of many ballot drop boxes collecting early votes for the midterm elections. One driver of a black jeep creeping along Cory Avenue who declined to give his name stated that "he hoped to catch someone dropping off '100 ballots or 50 ballots'." This drop box watcher was "part of a volunteer effort to stop a certain type of voter fraud that has captivated, even though there is no evidence of its actually happening."[38]

These voting drop box watchers had fallen victims to another bogus conspiracy. This one about "ballot mules" had been generated on the

Twitter-like platform TS, formed in 2021 after Trump was removed from Twitter for instigating an insurrection. TS is owned by the Trump Media & Technology Group. Both the company and Trump have been under federal investigation by US prosecutors for money laundering involving Putin's ally Aleksandr Smirnov.[39] Beginning in July 2022, folks on TS along with other right-wing platforms such as Parler and Rumble had been discussing fictious ballot mules who were secretly dropping off hundreds of fake ballots during the middle of the night at drop boxes or election sites nationwide. This conspiracy received its biggest boost from the 90-minute propagandistic film, *2000 Mules*.

Directed by ultra-conservative commentator Dinesh D'Souza, it was released on May 20, 2022. On May 31, one month before Arizona GOP gubernatorial candidate Kari Lake won the primary, the 2020 election denier told "viewers on a right-wing broadcast outlet ahead of a state Senate hearing that 'we will sleep by those drop boxes. I'm rolling out my sleeping bag'."[40] Teaming up with True the Vote, a Texas-based nonprofit right-wing conspiracy group that describes itself as protecting election integrity that had a history of investigating alleged voter fraud in Arizona, Georgia, Michigan, Pennsylvania, and Wisconsin – the five battleground states that Trump lost to Biden – D'Souza claims that the film proves widespread voter fraud in the 2020 presidential election. Reuters Fact Check examined the film and had found no evidence showing proof of voter fraud.[41]

Nevertheless, the idea of organized drop box watching caught on a month later in a series of posts on TS. First, an anonymous TS member with 96 followers recommended "tailgate parties" in a reply to Seth Keshel, a Trumpian influencer who blogs and gives public speeches about how the 2020 election was stolen. Keshel "retruthed" the post, which is TS' sharing function, to his over 50,000 followers on July 22, adding: "I also like this idea. All night patriot tailgate parties at EVERY DROP BOX in America'."[42]

Inspired by True the Vote, whose president Catherine Engelbrecht and former board member Gregg Phillips were taken into custody on November 1, 2022 "after defying a court order to reveal more details in a civil case about one of their controversial attempts to uncover supposed fraud in the 2020 election."[43] Clean Elections USA, "a grassroots organization committed to election integrity," was established in early summer 2022. Its purpose was to help coordinate the monitoring of voting drop boxes. Clean Elections has also pushed "mule parties" and "drop box tailgates" on TS. The former president's account had also shared posts by users advocating surveillance of drop boxes. From its description of Who We Are:

While there are many who say the 2020 election was the most secure in American history, we know this is far from the truth. Every legal vote must be counted and it is unacceptable when illegal votes are added to the mix. Each person, no matter to which party they belong, is disenfranchised when fraudulent votes are included in the final count.

According to research conducted by True the Vote, "Mules" were paid to go from drop box to drop box, often driving from one county to the next, to stuff what we can only assume were fraudulent mail-in ballots. 2000 Mules clearly illustrated that there was a coordinated effort to stuff ballot boxes in 2020. Our immediate and urgent mission is to prevent this from happening in 2022. We are asking every patriotic American citizen to join as we organize to safeguard our elections with a legal presence at every ballot box in each and every state that has them.[44]

The organization founded by Tulsa, Oklahoma minister Melody Jennings, a TS influencer, was sued the last week of October 2022 by the Arizona Alliance for Retired Americans and Voto Latino for engaging in "conduct that is clearly meant to intimidate."[45]

### Litter Boxes for Furry Kids

Furries are adults and children who constitute a subculture of people interested in the anthropomorphic attributes of animal characters exhibiting human intelligence, facial expressions, speaking, walking on two legs, riding a bike, shooting hoops, skateboarding, dressing up in costumes, and so on. Furries may adopt animal-like personas and engage in short-term roleplaying as anthropomorphized animal characters. While millions of furries in the world still identify as humans, there are always a few crazies out there. The term "furry fandom" refers to those communities of people who gather either on the internet and/or attend various furry conventions.[46]

The roots of furry fandom can be traced back to a genre of comic books that originated in the underground comix movement of the 1970s that depicted explicit sex and was consumed mostly by males. Subsequently, at a 1980 science fiction convention, the concept of the furry was born as part of a discussion of the anthropomorphic characters in science fiction novels. As early as 1983 the term "furry fandom" was being used in fanzines. The first furry convention was held at the Holiday Inn Bristol Plaza in Costa Mesa, California in 1989. Once the internet arrived, furries became accessible to the general population and the most popular means for furry fans to socialize where they may chat, dress up in animal costumes, role-play, and so on.[47]

Fast forwarding to the 2022 midterm elections, there were at least 20 GOP candidates and elected officials who had claimed that K–12 schools were "placing litter boxes on campus or making other accommodations for students who identify as cats." Every school district identified by those 20 candidates was reached out to by NBC News, and it was confirmed that these claims were untrue: "There was no evidence that any school has deployed litter boxes for students to use because they identify as cats." No matter, the claim had "taken on a life of its own among a growing number of Republicans, conservative influencers and political commentators."[48] In an episode of *The Joe Rogan Experience* podcast that aired on Spotify the first week of October 2022, host Rogan told former US Rep. Tulsi Gabbard that a litter box had been

> installed in a school that his friend's wife worked at for a girl who "identifies as an animal." A clip of the discussion quickly began to circulate on social media. Rogan did not name the school, and his publicist did not respond to a request for comment.[49]

Here are three other examples:

- At a luncheon for Republican women in Mesa Country, Colorado, Rep. Lauren Boebert (R) warned that educators "are putting litter boxes in schools for people who identify as cats."
- Minnesota GOP gubernatorial nominee Scott Jensen asked during a campaign stop, "Why do we have litter boxes in some of the school districts so kids can pee in them, because they identify as a furry."
- And during a legislative hearing in Tennessee, two Republican state lawmakers discussed the "growing crisis" of public schools providing litter boxes for children who identify as cats, and they claimed it was happening across the state.[50]

To folks not steeped in the culture wars over gender identity that have engulfed schools from across the nation, such claims may sound crazy and confusing. However, coming from high-profile GOP members, they sound authoritative and are used by some politicians to alarm people by saying this is where protections for Lesbian, Gay, Bisexual, Transgender, Queer (LGBTQ) students have led. As Joan Donovan, research director of the Shorenstein Center on Media, Politics and Public Policy at Harvard University and co-author of *Meme Wars: The Untold Story of the Online Battles Upending Democracy in America*, had this to say, "What's most provocative about this hoax is how it turns on two key wedge issues for conservatives: educational accommodations and gender nonconformity."[51] For example, after Gov. Ron DeSantis (R-FL) signed into law the Parental Rights in Education bill in March of 2022, banning teachers from instruction on "sexual orientation" or "gender identity" in elementary schools, popularly known as the "Don't Say Gay Bill," several GOP controlled states were considering similar bills.[52]

Like an old-fashioned "game of telephone" only faster, rumors circulate on social media with descriptions of friends of friends who supposedly saw these things firsthand. The rise of the rumor of a litter box for peeing students demonstrates "how quickly some elements of truth can be twisted and mashed up with fully debunked assertions to create a viral narrative amplified by prominent politicians and news commentators."[53] Fox News most notoriously had been used to spread baseless and/or misleading claims about transpeople. In the span of only three weeks, Fox aired 170 segments. Nadine Bridges, the executive director of One Colorado, an LGBTQ rights organization, when asked about the litter box rumors had this to say: "It's only used to kind of sensationalize untruth, and to harm our community, in particular our transgender, nonbinary and gender-expansive youth. Why would you attack our most vulnerable to get your point across, especially since the point is baseless?"[54] Reina Sultan has explained how TikTok became an anti-LGBTQ plus hate machine to own the liberals and to fuel unprovoked harassment against teachers, hospitals, small businesses, and more.[55]

Like the majorities of midterm voting, Americans in 2022 were not concerned with any threats posed by mules, furries, or groomers but with the millions of Trumpian election deniers and conspiracy consumers. This was especially the case for those subcultures of Trumpists inclusive of the MAGA base who were falsely identifying as revolutionary patriots of 1776, and not role-playing like the hundreds and sometimes thousands of people who annually come together to participate in Civil War reenactments portraying either Union or Confederate infantry, artillery, or cavalry forces. More significantly, are those elected Republicans masquerading as Congresspeople, engaging in false flag operations, and identifying with Boss Trump as one of his capos, consiglieres, and associates. Looping back the "same sort of right-wing conspiracy mongers who brought us litter boxes were getting to work inventing Pelosi attack conspiracies."[56]

## The Club Q Massacre and the New Culture of Lynching

Using the case of the Club Q Massacre in Colorado, where five persons were killed and many more were injured by a lone shooter, allows our examination to come full circle in the world of mediated politics and post-truthism in America. Club Q brings the necessary connections together between the practices of victim scapegoating, discriminatory violence, and harmful legislating contrary to the interests of the LGBTQ community. For example, the prohibition of public drag shows, the banning of trans youth from sports, and the restrictions on gender-affirming medical care in many red states like Arkansas, Iowa, Mississippi, South Dakota, Tennessee, Utah, and Kentucky. Similarly, there are those laws vilifying transgender children and their families, making it illegal in Florida and elsewhere for teachers to talk about gender identification or sexual orientation, K–12. Finally, these types of anti-gender and anti-health care laws force many "non-straight" people back into their gendered closets and many other trans youth to have to out themselves.

As Jeet Heer captures about gender and sexuality in his essay's subtitle for *The Nation*, "Homophobic violence is fueled by the extreme right's victim blaming."[57] On November 19, 2022, a gunman opened fire at Club Q, an LGBTQ nightclub in Colorado Springs, CO. Before the shooter, Anderson Lee Aldrich was brought down by patrons; he had killed 5 people and injured 25. Mass shootings, including those motivated by homophobia and transphobia, have become all too common in 21st-century America. Right-wing media coverage by the end of 2022 was reminiscent of the turn of the 20th-century media coverage calling out lynching as deplorable and intolerable yet blaming the root causes of the problem of lynching on Black people (i.e., there are too many cases where a white woman has been attacked by "a brute of a negro"). Those remarks were from an editorial page of *The Washington Progress* in 1920, a North Carolina newspaper that foreshadows the same type of blaming the victims that we witness from the alt-right today. As Sarah Churchwell argues in *Behold, America: The Entangled History of "America First" and "the American Dream"* (2018): Lynching was used to reinforce white supremacy. It may have been extra-legal, but it was used to uphold the racist status quo. Lynchings were not only about the physical acts of racist perpetrators, but they were also edicts of social violence servicing racists and racist interests for those who would not personally dirty their own hands.

What made the Club Q shooting in Colorado different from previous mass shootings was the way the extreme right reacted to the incident. Much of the right, moderate and extreme, had abandoned their customary calls for thoughts and prayers accompanied by their expressions of sympathy for the victims. Instead, while ignoring Aldrich's homophobic background and his father's relief to learn that his son was not gay or trans but preferably a mass killer as told to a CBS reporter, these shooting victims were now being blamed for their own deaths. Aldrich's father's bigoted scorn for the victims was echoed by one of Trump's many attorneys and several prominent figures on alt-right media platforms.

Jenna Ellis, a lawyer who has served as an advisor to Donald Trump, issued a statement about the Club Q shooting on Twitter, on November 23 from Los Angeles, CA:

> The people killed in the nightclub that night, there is no evidence that they were Christians. Assuming they have not accepted the truth and affirmed Christ as the lord of their life they are now reaping the consequences of eternal damnation.

Ellis became the fourth defendant to plead guilty in the Georgia RICO case on October 24, 2023, for the felony of aiding and abetting false statements and writings.

Host of the Daily Wire's *The Matt Walsh Show* attacked drag shows as the problem: "If it's causing this much chaos and violence, why do [they] insist on continuing to do it?"[58] Jaimee Michell, founder of an anti-trans group called Gays Against Groomers, was featured on Tucker Carlson's nightly show on Fox News. According to Mitchell,

> the tragedy that happened in Colorado Springs the other night was expected and predictable. We all within Gays Against Groomers saw this coming from a mile away. And sadly, I don't think it's gonna stop until we end this evil agenda that is attacking children.[59]

As Heer writes:

> In 21st-century America, the right-wing push to reinforce heteronormative cultural domination has both a legal side and an extrajudicial side. The legal side can be seen in the anti-gay and anti-trans laws passed by governors like Ron DeSantis of Florida and Greg Abbot of Texas. The illegal Side comes from hate crimes like the Club Q massacre. The right-wing media cheers on the legal side of the homophobic and transphobic push, while also whitewashing the hate crimes or using them as a pretext to blame the victim.[60]

Heer warns us about the emergence of this new culture of lynching:

> The victim blaming of Ellis, Walsh, and Michell should be seen as not just bigotry but also implicitly a threat. The right is trying to create a new lynching culture, with LGBTQ people as the target. The lynching culture of Jim Crow America has both a legal and an extrajudicial side. The legal side was all the laws that affirmed white supremacy. The extrajudicial side was the actual lynching, which was often winked at by the police and respectable society.[61]

In the world of cultural war conflicts, whether it's Governor DeSantis v. Disney Corporation over "wokeness" – what used to be referred to as "political correctness" – MAGA media personalities v. Bud Light or Target, the alt-right anti-woke crowd has been busy peddling "dangerous and misleading narratives about the LGBTQ+ community"[62] and "increasingly wielding heavy-handed tactics – including state power and violent threats – to block corporations from making their own decisions about how to adapt to social change."[63]

### A Postscript on Social Media and the Conspiratorial Insurrectionists in Suits

At least two basic things should always be remembered. It was unregulated and laissez-faire incorporated, for profit Twitter and Facebook that gave

Trump his insurrectionary free pass that resulted in the storming of the Capitol.[64] Without Trump and his use of social media, there never would have been a failed coup on January 6, 2021. While "thousands of deluded insurrectionists attacked the Capitol because of the lies spread by Trump and his acolytes," the "bigger problem was inside the ranks of Congress itself, as most House Republicans voted not to certify the election based on those debunked theories." These are the "conspiratorial insurrectionists in suits" that became in charge of the House of Representatives after the 2022 midterm elections. Consequently, governing in the House was put on hold for two years so the GOP could launch pointless investigations into COVID vaccines, deep-state cover-ups, weaponization, and the House Select Subcommittee on January 6.[65]

Led by several Congressional people like Jim Jordan of Ohio and Trump loyalists in his administration like Chief of Staff Mark Meadows who had all ignored their subpoenas from the Select Committee for their roles in trying to illegally overturn the 2020 election, these folks were now investigating the investigators of Trump such as Manhattan District Attorney who was the first prosecutor to indict Trump in April 2023. Of course, like Trump who is always weaponizing and projecting his lawlessness onto everyone else, these lackeys for Trump with the same kind of irony have been busy trying to weaponize the business of Congressional oversight. Another case of the Trumpian "obstruction of justice" pot calling the kettle black as in "witch hunt" my ass.

After purchasing Twitter one month earlier the world's richest person reinstated Trump's account that had been removed on January 7, 2021. On Twitter, Musk wrote: "The People have spoken. Trump will be reinstated. Vox Populi, Vox Dei." According to Merriam-Webster, it is a Latin phrase that literally means "voice of the people." Its English usage has now become "the opinion of the majority of the people." According to Musk, 15 million votes were logged in to answer his question should Trump be reinstated. Nearly 52% voted in favor.

The director of the Stanford Internet Observatory Alex Stamos thought that it was strange or "odd" that Musk, who had spent months complaining about Twitter's problem with bot accounts, would use a Twitter poll in which bots could be voting to decide the issue and then assume that the result "reflects some kind of legitimate 'voice of the people'," adding further, "It is definitely possible for small groups to create large numbers of accounts to manipulate features like polls."[66] In fact, in Michael Cohen's first book on Trump, *Disloyal*, he explains how Trump and company were doing precisely that when non-public polling in 2015 was occurring before he had announced his primary candidacy for the presidency in 2016.

Naturally, Trump's reinstatement to Twitter immediately raised questions among misinformation experts and pretty much everyone else. For example,

Joan Donovan, the research director at Harvard's Shorenstein Center on Media, Politics and Public Policy, had the following to say. Trump could once again make Twitter a "a hotbed of hate, harassment and incitement," should Trump revert to his old form, much as he has been doing on TS since its formation after he was removed from Twitter following his incitement of a failed insurrection.[67] By the spring of 2023 the Gaslighter-in-Chief had not returned to Twitter with a vengeance and evidently he had decided not to perhaps because his TS posts find their way to Twitter and pretty much everywhere else online. On the other hand, by the time of his first 2024 campaign rally in Waco, Texas, on March 25, 2023, Trump had returned with a vengeance to YouTube.

## Notes

1 Steven Rosenfeld. 2022. Accountability looms for media outfits that spread lies about 2020 election. *TheNationalMemo*. November 12. www.nationalmemo. com/lawsuits-against-election-lies

2 The rise in conspiracy theories, mediated memes, and social media cannot be separated from the dying businesses of mainstream news publications and the "heavily subsidized right-wing agitprop" that has been "filling the gap." See Eric Alterman. 2022. The journalism business is bad, but we'll miss it when it's gone. *Altercation*. December 16. https://americanprospect.bluelena.io/index.php?act ion=social&chash=231141b34c82aa95e48810a9d1b33a79.1815&s=6fc8cb022 385c549f0dadd0f0cd6fd54

3 As Jonathan V. Last asked the day after the announced settlement for *Bulwark+ The Triad* regarding The Two Big Lessons of Dominion v. Fox: "What is the difference between 'media' and 'propaganda'?" He responded: "A media outlet is an organization whose biases are constrained—either well or poorly—by self-imposed codes of conduct. A propaganda outlet is an organization whose pursuit of an agenda is constrained only by the law." Last concludes that Fox is a propaganda outlet even when releasing a statement to the world because there is no admission that anything they broadcast was untrue, no apologize for promoting lies, and a promise to return to business as usual. Here is Fox's full text:

> We are pleased to have reached a settlement of our dispute with Dominion Voting Systems. We acknowledge the Court's rulings finding certain claims about Dominion to be false. This settlement reflects FOX's continued commitment to the highest journalistic standards. We are hopeful that our decision to resolve this dispute with Dominion amicably, instead of the acrimony of a divisive trial, allows the country to move forward from these issues.
>
> (https://thetriad.thebulwark.com/p/the-two-big-lessons-of-dominion-fox)

4 Quoted in Rosenfeld. 2022.

5 Megan Garber, 2023. We've lost the plot. *The Atlantic*. January 30. www.theatlan tic.com/magazine/archive/2023/03/tv-politics-entertainment-metaverse/672773/

6 Richard J. Gerrig. 1993. *Experiencing narrative worlds: On the psychological activities of reading*. Yale University Press. *APA PsycNet* Abstract. https://psycnet. apa.org/record/1993-98290-000

7 John Stoehr. 2023. The radical political ideology no one talks about. January 30. www.rawstory.com/raw-investigates/the-radical-political-ideology-no-one-talks-about/

8 Chauncey DeVega. 2023. Too little, too late: Why the media goes missing when Republicans go on the offensive. *Salon*. March 7. www.salon.com/2023/03/07/too-little-too-late-why-the-media-goes-missing-when-go-on-the-offensive/

9 Ibid.

10 Ibid.

11 Garber. 2023.

12 Ibid.

13 Quoted in Ibid.

14 Garber. 2023.

15 Helen Lewis. 2023. The internet loves an extremophile. *The Atlantic*. January 31. www.theatlantic.com/ideas/archive/2023/01/internet-youtube-podcast-guru-influencers-andrew-tate/

16 David L. Altheide. 2023. *Gonzo Governance: The Media Logic of Donald Trump*. New York: Rutledge, p. xiv.

17 Gregg Barak. 2003. *Violence and Nonviolence: Pathways to Understanding*. Thousand Oaks, CA: Sage Publications. See also, James Gilligan, M.D. 1997. *Violence: Reflections on a National Epidemic*. New York: Vintage Books.

18 Luke Broadwater. 2021. Republicans rewrite history of the Capitol riot, hampering an inquiry. *The New York Times*. May 18. www.nytimes.com/2021/05/13/us/politics/republicans-capitol-riot.html

19 Known as The Central Park Five.

20 Charlie Sykes. 2023. Trump's 2024 MAGA litmus test. *MSNBC*. January. 29. www.msnbc.com/opinion/msnbc-opinion/trump-vs-desantis-2024-republican-litmus-test-brutality-rcna67979

21 Ibid.

22 Alan Charles Elms and Stanley Milgram. 1966. Personality characteristics associated with obedience and defiance toward authoritative command. *Journal of Experimental Research in Personality*, 1(4): 282–289.

23 Aaron C. David and Dalton Bennett. 2022. Alleged assailant filled blog with delusional thoughts in days before Pelosi attack. *The Washington Post*. October 29. www.washingtonpost.com/investigations/2022/10/29/david-depape-blog-pelosi-fairies/

24 Casey Tolan, Curt Devine, Daniel A. Medina and Majlie de Puy Kamp. 2022. *CNN*. October 28. www.cnn.com/2022/10/28/politics/pelosi-attack-suspect-conspiracy-theories-invs

25 KTVU Staff. 2023. Paul Pelosi attack: David DePape interrogation recording released. *FOX 7 Austin*. January 27. www.rawstory.com/raw-investigates/the-radical-political-ideology-no-one-talks-about/

26 Hannah Allam and Squad Mekhennet. 2022. Accused Pelosi attacker's history shows blurry line of radicalization. *The Washington Post*. October 31. www.washingtonpost.com/national-security/2022/10/31/david-depape-pelosi-online-radicalization/

27 KTVU Staff. 2023.

28 Isaac Stanley-Beker. 2022. Elon Musk, right-wing figures push misinformation about Pelosi attack. *The Washington Post*. October 30. www.washingtonpost.com/politics/2022/10/30/paul-pelosi-attack-misinformation-elon-musk/

29 As David Frum wrote in an essay for *The Atlantic* about why he logged off Twitter,

> I saw Musk's now-infamous tweet about Paul Pelosi. He responded to a tweet from Hillary Clinton by sharing a link to a fake news story about Pelosi from a notoriously untrustworthy source – an outlet that had reported in 2016 that Clinton had died and that Democrats had replaced her on the campaign trail with a body double.
>
> (www.theatlantic.com/ideas/archive/2022/11/elon-musk-twitter-takeover-changes/671980/)

30 Allam and Mekhennet. 2022.

31 David Badash, The New Civil Rights Movement. 2022. Watch: Marjorie Taylor Green says Pau Pelosi is to blame for his near-fatal assault as he arrives home from hospital. *Raw Story*. November 4. www.rawstory.com/watch-marjorie-tay lor-greene-says-paul-pelosi-is-to-blame-for-his-near-fatal-as-he-arrives-home-from-hospital/

32 Annie Karni, Malika Khurana, and Stuart A. Thompson. 2022. How republicans fed a misinformation loop about the Pelosi attack. *The New York Times*. November 5. www.nytimes.com/interactive/2022/11/05/us/politics/pelosi-attack-misinfo-republican-politicians.html

33 Details are in Chapter 2.

34 SPLC. 2022. *The Year in Hate & Extremism in 2021 and Hate and Extremism in 2022*. Montgomery: Southern Poverty Law Center.

35 Fox 2 Staff. 2023. Motor City Furry Con evacuated after reported bomb threat in Ypsilanti. *Fox 2 Detroit*. March 24. www.fox2detroit.com/news/motor-city-furry-con-evacuated-after-reported-bomb-threat-in-ypsilanti

36 Vaughn Hillyard and Ben Collins. 2022. How 'mule watchers' evolved from a truth social meme into a ballot drop box patrol. *NBC News*. October 28. www.nbcnews.com/tech/internet/mule-watchers-evolved-truth-social-meme-ballot-drop-box-patrol-rcna54406. See also Reuters Fact Check, 2022. Fact-Check-Does '2000 Mules' provide evidence of voter fraud in the 2020 U.S. presidential election? *Reuters*. May 27. www.reuters.com/article/factcheck-usa-mules/fact-check-does-2000-mules-provide-evidence-of-voter-fraud-in-the-2020-u-s-presi dential-election-idUSL2N2XJ0OQ

37 Zoe Richards. 2022. Top Arizona election official refers more cases of potential voter intimation to law enforcement. *NBC News*. October 24. www.nbcnews.com/politics/2022-election/top-arizona-election-official-refers-cases-potential-voter-intimidatio-rcna53817

38 Hillyard and Collins. 2022.

39 Travis Gettys. 2023. Trump Media under investigation for Russian money laundering: Report. *Raw Story*. March 15. www.rawstory.com/trump-money-lau ndering/

40 Hillyard and Collins. 2022.

41 Reuters Fact Check. 2022. Fact Check-Does '2000 Mules' provide evidence of voter fraud in the 2020 U.S. presidential election? May 27. www.reuters.com/arti cle/factcheck-usa-mules/fact-check-does-2000-mules-provide-evidence-of-voter-fraud-in-the-2020-u-s-presidential-election-idUSL2N2XJ0OQ

42 Hillyard and Collins. 2022.

43 Paul P. Murphy. 2022. Leaders of right-wing election conspiracy group jailed after being found in contempt of court. *CNN Politics*. November 1. www.cnn.com/2022/11/01/politics/true-the-vote-leaders-jail-contempt-of-court

44 Clean Elections USA, N.D. https://cleanelectionsusa.org/. Error messages for this website as the data could not be verified.

45 Rebecca Shabad. 2022. Retiree, Latino organizations sue group, alleging voter intimidation in Arizona. *NBC News*. October 25. www.nbcnews.com/politics/2022-election/retiree-latino-organizations-sue-group-alleged-voter-intimidation-ariz-rcna53887

46 Courtney N. Plante, Stephen Reysen, Sharon E. Roberts, Kathleen C. Gerbasi. 2016. *Fur Science: A Summary of Five Years of Research from the International Anthropomorphic Research Project*. Waterloo: Furscience.

47 Rob Staeger, *Wayne Suburban*. 2001. Invasion of the furries. *Furry Fandom Infocenter*. July 26. www.furryfandom.info/invasion-furries-furry-fandom.htm

48 Tyler Kingkade, Ben Goggin, Ben Collins and Brandy Zadrozny. 2022. How an urban myth about litter boxes in schools became a GOP talking point. *Today.com*. October 15. www.today.com/news/news/urban-myth-litter-boxes-schools-became-gop-talking-point-rcna52401

49 Ibid.

50 Quoted in Ibid.

51 Ibid.

52 Kyle Morris. 2022. Not just Florida: States weigh bills banning gender ID and sexual orientation instruction. *Fox News*. April 1. www.foxnews.com/politics/states-weigh-measures-preventing-gender-identity-sexual-orientation-discussions-schools

53 James Factora. 2022. Conservatives are obsessed with this lie about students identifying as furries. *them*. October 5. www.them.us/story/conservatives-obsessed-furries-lie-lgbtq-students

54 Quoted in Kingkade et al. (2022).

55 Reina Sultan. 2022. How libs of TikTok became an anti-LGHTQ+ hate machine. *them*. September 10. www.them.us/story/libs-of-tik-tok-twitter-facebook-instagram-explained-childrens-hospitals-grooming

56 Dana Milbank. 2022. Here's what Paul Pelosi has in common with litter boxes. *The Washington Post*. November 2. www.washingtonpost.com/opinions/2022/11/02/paul-pelosi-litter-box-conspiracy-republicans/

57 Jeet Heer. 2022. The Club Q massacre and the new culture of lynching. *The Nation*. November 28. www.thenation.com/article/society/club-q-shooting.lynching/?utm_source=Sailthru&utm_medium=email&utm_campaign=Daily%2011.28.2022&utm_term=daily

58 Media Matters Staff. 2022. Matt Walsh blames victims of anti-LGBTQ violence in wake of mass shooting in Colorado Springs. *Media Matters*. November 22. www.mediamatters.org/matt-walsh/matt-walsh-blames-victims-anti-lgbtq-violence-wake-mass-shooting-colorado-springs

59 David Neiwert. 2022. The right's stochastic pundits warn of more violence if LGBTQ community doesn't stop 'grooming'. *Daily Kos*. November 23. www.dailykos.com/stories/2022/11/23/2138098/-The-right-s-stochastic-pundits-warn-of-more-violence-if-LGBTQ-community-doesn-t-stop-grooming

60 Heer. 2022.

61 Ibid.

62 Justin Baragona. 2023. MAGA media runs wild with BS claim of 'Tuck-Friendly' target kidswear. *Daily Beast*. May 23. www.thedailybeast.com/maga-media-runs-wild-with-bs-claim-of-tuck-friendly-target-kidswear

63 Greg Sargent. 2023. Target's surrender to MAGA rage shows how anti-wokeness really works. *The Washington Post*. May 25. www.washingtonpost.com/opini ons/2023/05/25/target-pulls-lgbtq-clothing-right-wing-maga

64 Steve Kovach. 2021. Trump got a free pass from Twitter and Facebook, and the result was a storming of the Capitol. *CNBC*. January 7. www.cnbc.com/2021/01/ 07/facebook-twitter-fueled-trumps-conspiracies-resulting-in-violence.html

65 Brian Klass. 2023. Asymmetrical conspiracism is hurting democracy. *The Atlantic*. January 17. www.theatlantic.com/ideas/archive/2023/01/conspiratorial-thinking- polarization-america-united-kingdom/672726/

66 Quoted in Ryan Mac and Kellen Browning. 2022. Elon Musk reinstates Trump's Twitter account. *The New York Times*. November 19. www.nytimes.com/2022/ 11/19/technology/trump-twitter-musk.html

67 Quoted in Ibid.

# 2

# SCAREMONGERING, PARTY POLITICS, AND THE CRISIS IN US DEMOCRACY

Scaremongering and fearmongering about religious, sexual, and ethnic identities have always been a vital component of scapegoat politics and worldwide grievances. In the United States, where fearmongering has often been joined by targeted or discriminatory violence, these patterned behavioral interactions are as American as Fourth of July parades. Whether locally or nationally, to varying degrees the combination of verbal and physical intimidation has been propagated by politicians, political parties, and governmental agencies. Fearmongering and fear-inducing grievances about freed Black people and white abolitionists during the Reconstruction Era announced by Abraham Lincoln's Emancipation Proclamation on New Year's Day, 1863, and following the end of the Civil War resonated with the Confederate portion of the body politic. Ergo, there was the passage of the Black codes in nearly all the Southern states designed to limit the freedom of African Americans and to ensure cheap labor by broadly drawn vagrancy statutes that facilitated local authorities arresting freedpeople and subjecting them to involuntary labor.

Succeeding the Russian Revolution of 1917 and nearing the end of WWI, and again after WWII, there was widespread fearmongering concerning the threats of communists, anarchists, and socialists. During the first Red Scare (1917–1920), Congress passed the Espionage Act of 1917 and the anti-anarchist Sedition Act of 1918. Both were signed into law by President Woodrow Wilson (1913–1921). The seditionist act went so far as to criminalize language that was deemed to be disloyal to the US government, making it a crime to "willfully utter, write, or publish any disloyal, profane, scurrilous, or abusive language about the form of the Government of the United States." During the Progressive Era (1900–1920), several states, including Idaho, California, Kansas, and Ohio, enacted criminal syndicalism laws that

DOI: 10.4324/9781003390664-4

were seldom enforced. These laws prohibited advocating "crime, sabotage, violence or other unlawful methods of terrorism as a means of accomplishing industrial or political reform."[1] In between the two Red Scares, there was the Roaring Twenties, the 1929 Crash and the Great Depression. There was also leading up to World War II as Rachel Maddow delineates in *Prequel: An American Fight Against Fascism*, Henry Ford, Charles Lindbergh, and other right-wing connivers trying to steer the US toward an alliance with the Nazis.

The second Red Scare (1950–1957) broke out during the early period of the Cold War when there were concerns about communist infiltration in the United States. Better known as the McCarthy Era or McCarthyism after its leading advocate Senator Joseph McCarthy (R-Wis) and his chief counsel Roy Cohn who Donald Trump would retain in 1973 on behalf of his father and himself to defend them from federal charges of discriminatory housing and rental practices. The McCarthy Era is remembered by the Hollywood Blacklists, the investigations of the House Un-American Activities Committee, and the televised hearings of suspected communists, Soviet spies, and leftist sympathizers who had allegedly infiltrated the federal government, the film industry, and prestige universities. One of the legacies of McCarthyism during the Trump era has been a weaponizing of law, politics, and culture, as well as the practices of making false, unfounded, and sensationalistic assertions.

Since the 1968 presidential campaign of Richard M. Nixon (1969–1974) and the days of President Ronald Reagan (1980–1988), the modern-day GOP as the alleged party of "law and order" has consistently engaged in grievance politics, fearmongering, and criminalizing the identities of nonwhite people. With the exceptions of the four presidential races of 2004, 2008, 2012, and 2020 whether street crime was high and rising as in the 1960s, 1980s and early 1990s, or was comparatively lower during the presidential races of 2000 and much lower by 2016, the Republican playbooks have always been about falsely depicting the Democratic Party as being "soft" on criminals and lenient on crime control. Despite the abundance of historical evidence to the contrary on both counts, these two mythic claims have stuck in the minds of Republicans and Democrats alike.

### The Myths of Partisan Crime Control

In the 2022 midterm elections, there "was a real anticipated fear/expectation that the crime rhetoric would take down the Democrats. But it didn't materialize."[2] Not only did the Red Wave not happen, but not since the 1986 midterm elections had the party not inside the White House performed as poorly. By habitually playing their racial crime cards, the Grand Old Party (GOP) has sustained the myth that they are the party that is "tough" on crime and that the Dems are the party that is "soft" on crime. These shared myths did not seem to have made a difference in the outcome of the 2022 elections. Historically, the falsehood that the GOP has been the party of "law and order" has worked primarily for two reasons.

First, both the Republicans and the Democrats have always reduced and equated the problem of crime to "street" crime while ignoring the problems of "suite" crime. Second, although the Democrats have periodically favored "best practices" criminal justice reform, for the past 50 years the two parties have both been tough on street crime when compared to the preventative crime policies and rehabilitative practices of the 1940s, 1950s, and 1960s.[3] This hyper-punitive reality of US criminal justice repression is evidenced by the two bipartisan and super majorities of Congress that passed the Comprehensive Crime Control Act of 1984 signed into law by Republican Ronald Reagan and the Violent Crime Control and Law Enforcement Act of 1994 signed into law by Democrat Bill Clinton.[4] Those draconian laws radically altered the directions of the enlightened crime control policies ushered into practice when Democratic President Lyndon Johnson signed into law the Omnibus Crime Control and Safe Streets Act of 1968.

Similar to the bipartisan strategies of crime control have been the bipartisan strategies of welfarism and immigration. From a criminogenic framework these policies are all catalysts of crimes and often counterproductive to their alleged goals. Since the mid-1990s immigration policy has been based on strategies of "prevention through deterrence." Making it more difficult to seek asylum or to separate family members, for example, would allegedly drive the number of immigrants seeking entrance to the US to decline. This kind of harmful and inhumane deterrence may be operative to a degree. At the same time, the reasons for people seeking emigration have not changed so the risks and costs of gaining entrance have had unintended consequences. They have been fomenting organized crime on the US-Mexican border. For organized crime groups operating along the 3,000-mile border, smuggling human cargo has become one of the most lucrative industries, up there with selling and buying drugs and weapons.

In related ways, these organized groups take advantage of the situation through the extortion of migrants as well as through targeted ransoms. Specifically, the US policies have pushed migrants to remain in other countries and as these strategies have relied on third countries like Mexico for enforcement, official corruption in those countries has expanded.[5] Meanwhile, the United States has done next to nothing to halt the flow of guns southward to meet Mexico demand. Likewise, Mexico has been doing little to halt the flow of opioids northward to meet US demand. The paradox here is that increased enforcement in either direction, or unilateral US intervention into Mexico to take out their criminal cartels as called for by Trump, DeSantis, Lindsey Graham, and other Republicans would only enhance the political power of criminals against the Mexican state.

Both the 1984 and the 1994 Crime Control laws are still in play today and are primarily responsible for our repressive systems of criminal justice and the abominable conditions of mass incarceration in America.[6] The rich body of empirical evidence over the past several decades has underscored the

United States' exceptional penchant for punitive punishment when compared to our own past practices or to those of other developed nations today:

> The imprisonment rate in the United States is approximately four times higher than the average rate in Europe, and nearly eight times higher than in the Netherlands and Germany. American prisons are estimated to hold 40% of individuals sentenced to life worldwide and 83% of those sentenced to Life Without the Possibility of Parole (LWOP). Data suggest that the average sentence length imposed in many U.S. states is more aligned with the criminal justice policies of less developed nations (Latin American countries specifically) than those of more industrialized countries.[7]

When it comes to mass shootings and killings with or without automatic weapons such as AK-47s and AR-15s, the United States is in a league of its own. By the third decade of the 21st century, mass shootings in the United States had become a daily affair. Gun violence had also become the number one killer of school-age children in this nation. According to Gun Violence Archive, an independent research and data collection organization, by May 8, 2023, there had been 199 mass shootings or about 1 every 16 hours, and more than 14,500 people had already died in the United States from gun violence in the first four months of the year.[8]

Anybody breathing knows that there is a deep partisan divide about gun violence and measures to reduce its frequency and occurrences in America. Not among the people of either political party affiliation, but among Democratic and Republican lawmakers. Democratic legislators would like to pass "common sense" gun reform favored by 80%–90% of all American voters depending on the particular measure.[9] Republican legislators, meanwhile, the so-called party of "law and order" or "tough on crime," are armed only with their prayers and condolences for the victims. They prefer to ignore or not prevent the epidemic of gun violence. Putting their heads in the sand and bowing to gun manufactures, they oppose virtually any gun legislation. However, they do support making the purchasing and open carrying of guns in public, even weapons of mass destruction like AR-15s less restrictive than in the past.

Consistent with George Orwell's dystopic novels, *Animal Farm and 1984*, the Republican leadership is busy reinforcing the killings of its own supporters as rates of homicide that are highest in Republican-controlled red states where gun legislation is most absent. These "shoot me in the face" politicians, who mostly defended Trump, attacked the judicial and jury system or remained silent after Trump was found liable for sexually abusing and defaming columnist E. Jean Carroll in May 2023. This is also the same "law and order" party that is now attacking the police, the military, the department of justice, and the rule of law while defending the former president's failed coup as well as an allegedly corrupt associate justice Clarence Thomas of the US Supreme Court "on the take" for millions of dollars' worth of gifts.

While the United States may still lead the developed world in gun deaths and be the most punitive nation when confronting street crimes the same cannot be said about suite crimes. Neither of the two parties with the exceptions of a few Democrats now and then in their rhetoric or practice has ever been anything but soft on white-collar and corporate crime. Since the days of the Savings and Loans looting at the end of the 1980s when more than 1,000 persons were criminally convicted, criminal prosecutions of financial offenders have been all but dormant in this country. Despite the escalation or ever-rising incidences of white-collar and corporate crime both at home and abroad, criminal prosecutions have been steadily declining.[10] After numerous corporate crime scandals – Enron, Arthur Anderson, WorldCom, Adelphia Communications, Tyco, and HealthSouth – broke publicly in quick succession and the discovery of the US Army and Central Intelligence Agency (CIA) series of human rights violations and war crimes against detainees in the Abu Ghraib prisons in Iraq came to global shame during the Republican watch of George W. Bush's first term, the Grand Old Party (GOP) went silent on the subject of crime during the 2004 presidential re-election campaign. After the financial markets imploded during Bush's second term in office due to institutional-wide securities frauds and regulatory colluding, the GOP was again silent about crime in the 2008 and 2012 elections.

Think of the 2008 Wall Street implosion. There were 10,000 financial securities fraudsters working the markets, millions of families who lost their mortgaged homes, dozens of Occupy Wall Street encampments across the country, and zero criminal prosecutions. As a critical Marxist-realist criminologist, I know that it has been the case that the crimes of capitalist accumulation are with rare exceptions beyond bourgeois incrimination. I also know that the crimes of the powerful especially those of corporate criminals are seldom subjects of the criminal law.[11] There is a much greater likelihood that the bourgeois legal state will pursue crimes by government employees and even political officials or those crimes against democracy and the rule of law, even by a former president of the United States who had heretofore becoming #45 never been held accountable for his white-collar or corporate criminality.

In the case of Wall Street, hundreds of looted billions, and the lack of any prosecutions was due, in part, to the Securities and Exchange Commission as well as the Federal Reserve System doing its best to normalize or rationalize away these illegal behaviors as something other than the securities criminal frauds that they were. Meanwhile, the DOJ took a "hands off" approach. President Obama and his Attorney General Eric Holder were talking about a financial crisis without the mention of criminality. In effect, giving the fraudulent looting of the Wall Street securities offenders a free pass, except for sanctioning once again the loan (bailout) of $700 billion at zero interest passed by a bipartisan Congress after two votes and signed into law by G.W. Bush.[12]

Full disclosure. The US House and Senate during Obama's first term with strong opposition from Republicans did manage to reign back in – the passage of the Wall Street Financial Reform and Consumer Protection Act of 2010 – some of those deregulated practices responsible, first, for the Savings and Loan debacle in the late 1980s and early 1990s, and second, for the Wall Street implosion in 2008. I am referring to the bipartisan Congresses beginning in the 1980s with President Reagan to erode the financial safeguards put in place after the Wall Street crash of 1929, and which culminated with the passage of the Gramm-Leach-Bliley Act signed into law by President Clinton in 1999 overturning the Glass-Steagall Act of 1933. Soon after Trump and the GOP majorities took power in 2017, they immediately cut the legs out from under the very successful Consumer Financial Protection Agency that had been holding financial interest rate inflaters accountable by making them reimburse their victimized consumers to the tune of more than $50 million in less than three years.

In the matter of political and governmental crime, the "law and order" Republicans have consistently been on the wrong side of the criminal law. Even putting aside Donald Trump's record-setting governmental corruption, obstruction of justice, and unprecedented insurrection, one must not forget the ongoing pattern of criminal actions by GOP Presidents and their administrations: Nixon and Watergate, Reagan and Irangate, G.W. Bush and Abu Ghraib. Although there was indeed accountability for the perpetrators of Watergate and Irangate as well as pardons for the two men at the top of those criminal pyramids, there were zero prosecutions or accountability for those responsible for Abu Ghraib and other crimes of war committed by President Bush, Vice President Dick Cheney, Secretary of Defense Donald Rumsfeld, or any of their four legal advisers.[13] Only military grunts serving as prison guards and carrying out direct orders were prosecuted and held to account for these crimes. One of the primary differences between Trump and his Republican predecessors is that the latter were covert about their lawlessness and criminality while the former president commits many of his violations in plain sight. Part of Trump's gaslighting brilliance has included his ability to get GOP power holders to either go along with his crimes as accomplishes or to look the other way as enablers of his crimes. All the time knowing that any disloyalty or crossing of Trump could result in a sentence of political exile as in the former Wyoming House of Representative member and power broker Liz Chaney.

During and after political electoral campaigns, despite the selective cherry picking about crime or the bipartisan agreements about crime control, there is almost always an absence of any tangible recognition of, let alone, mention or substantive public discussion about what can be done to control white-collar, corporate, or governmental crime – as if these crimes did not or do not exist. The normalization of these crimes of the powerful, the institutionalized under enforcement of their violations, and the invisible material reality that the number of corporate prosecutions of business criminals has been steadily declining every year since Bush II was re-elected in 2004. According to an analysis of Justice Department data by TRAC (Transactional Records Access Clearinghouse), a nonprofit data-gathering organization at Syracuse University, "business prosecutions fell to a record low in fiscal year 2022 even as there appeared to be no shortage of wrongdoing—from healthcare fraud to large-scale price fixing." For example, more than 4,000 federal white-collar prosecutions occurred that year. Of those, under 1% or only 31 of those defendants were businesses or corporate entities. This was "the lowest number of criminal prosecutions of business entities" since TRAC began tracking white-collar crime during the Reagan administration.[14]

### Spiral Spending and Partisan Politics

Political spending on federal elections has ballooned between 2000 and 2020 for several reasons including the innovation known as "joint fundraising committees" used by both political parties. In 2000 Congressional races spent a combined $2.9 billion. By 2020 that number had risen to $9.9 billion. Presidential races spent $2.4 billion in 2000. By 2020 that number had risen to $6.5 billion. While 55% of Republicans and 63% of Democrats say that "reducing influence of money in politics" should be a top concern for Congress, "wealthy contributors have been increasingly pumping cash into the political system – circumventing campaign finance laws in doing so."[15]

Federal and state spending on the 2022 midterms were the most expensive in history, topping $16.7 billion breaking the previous record of $13.7 billion. Adjusted for inflation, outside groups "spent about $1.9 billion to influence federal elections through Oct. 31, blowing past the 2018 midterm outside spending record of $1.6 billion." Total super Political Action Committee (PAC) spending has precipitously risen since SCOTUS decided *Citizens United* in 2010. Barred from formally coordinating with candidates, these PACS informally act as surrogates. Before *Citizens*, super PACS spent $63 million in 2010. Afterward, the number rose as follows: $345 million in 2014, $822 million in 2018, and $1.3 billion in 2022.[16]

Fueled by dark money and donations from deep-pocketed contributors, groups seeking to sway control of the US Senate were raking in the money. The biggest outside spenders were super PACs aligned with Republican and Democratic congressional leadership. Two Republican political action committees led the way in outside spending for federal races: The Senate

Leadership Fund and the Congressional Leadership Fund. The former a super PAC aligned with Senate Minority Leader Mitch McConnell, R-KY. It poured over $205 million into the midterms while backing Republicans running for Senate. The latter a hybrid PAC aligned with House Minority Leader Kevin McCarthy, R-CA. It spent more than $188 million.[17] On the other side of the isle, the Democratic-allied Senate Majority PAC "out raised its Republican counterpart in the first 19 days of October, $49 million to $26 million," according to the files with the Federal Election Commission.[18]

Clearly the obscenest and most wasted amount of money spent was on the Georgia US Senate race between incumbent Raphael Warnock (D), a highly competent and effective public servant, and his exceedingly flawed Republican challenger and newcomer to politics, Hershel Walker. A former star football player and buffoon of a candidate who spent most of his time on the campaign trail talking about werewolves, vampires,[19] and a bull ditching three cows that it had impregnated.[20] In their four-week Senate runoff election, more than $79 million was spent on TV ads alone. According to AdImpact, the total spending on televised advertisements for the two campaigns came to $335 million.[21] Their political contest should become the campaign poster for why there should be spending limits on privately financed elections if they are not eliminated altogether. And replaced with publicly financed elections that last no longer than 90 days. As Paul Waldman has written globally about campaign finance systems:

> Everyone must weigh two competing considerations. The first is the desire for elections that retain a reasonable amount of integrity, and are conducted in a manner that is, for lack of a better term, civilized. And the second is the principle of free speech, that a candidate for office should be able to say what he wants, as often as he wants, and spend as much as he wants doing it, even at the risk of corruption. In most other countries, they're decided that the first consideration is more important. In the U.S., [SCOTUS] decided that the second consideration is the one that matters.[22]

Federal candidates and political committees were on track for record 2022 midterm elections spending. Total federal elections were likely to exceed $9.3 billion, on track to surpass the inflation-adjusted 2018 midterm record of $7.1 billion.

> While OpenSecrets $9.3 billion estimate is slightly less than the $9.9 billion – adjusted for inflation – spent on U.S. congressional races in the 2020 election cycle, 2022 election spending was on pace to exceed the $8 billion in inflation-adjusted spending on congressional and presidential races during the 2016 election cycle.[23]

State-level candidates, party committees, and ballot measure committees were also on track to raise more than $7 billion during the 2022 election cycle exceeding the estimated $6.6 billion when adjusted for inflation. OpenSecrets Executive Director Sheila Krumholz has commented:

> Republicans and Democrats are engaged in an intensifying money race with polarization bringing more money than ever into our elections. State-level candidates vying to oversee future elections are seeing an especially noteworthy surge in funding, highlighting the public's concern with election integrity.

While Republican state-level candidates were projected to outraise Democratic candidates, parties of each affiliation raised in the low $400 million.[24]

Nearly two-thirds of the donations to US Senate candidates in the 2022 midterms came from out-of-state contributors reflecting an intense political tribalism in which the control of Congress has usurped the priority of local issues. A Bloomberg News analysis of Federal Election Committee showed that "Senate candidates got 64.8% of their donations from givers outside their home states from January 2021 through Sept. 30, 2022, up from 53.6% over the same period in the run-up to the 2018 midterms." During the same period the House campaigns "saw outside money increase to 43.5% of their hauls, up from 36.8%."[25]

More than 5% of election spending came from roughly 735 billionaires who had spent more than $880 million on the midterm elections.[26] The "100 largest donors" in the United States "collectively spent 60 percent more than *every small donor*" defined by those who gave $200 or less combined. Before *Citizens*, "small donors collectively outspent the 100 largest donors by a margin of more than three to one during the 2010 midterms."[27] By the 2022 federal midterms, billionaires had provided 15% of the funding. As the Brennan Center for Justice wrote:

> As a topline number, the political spending of billionaires is worrisome. But look at individual cases, and it only gets worse. In the primary alone, venture capitalist Peter Thiel spent $15 million supporting a single candidate, Ohio's new Senator-elect J.D. Vance. It isn't healthy for candidates across the political spectrum to owe so much to so few contributors. The U.S. government is not an investment vehicle for the ultra-wealthy. It's a problem we much address, sooner rather than later.[28]

Big money not only talks on TV where it facilitates falsehoods and misrepresentations, but it has also become a billion-dollar campaign effort embracing highly targeted audiences and a nearly rule-free digital world. For example, in the Pennsylvania race for US Senate between John Fetterman

(D) and Mehmet Oz (R), there was a barrage of online ads by a group of former members of Trump's inner circle, Citizens for Sanity. They had "targeted a demographic which was seminal in securing Joe Biden's victory in 2020: women over 25 in the suburbs of Philadelphia."[29] Running up to the midterm elections by way of YouTube and Google the "Fetterman loves criminals" ads appeared 6 million times over a ten-day period:

> The advert is in grainy black and white, with an edgy horror movie soundtrack. As gunfights erupt in the streets, the narrator announces in a gravely bass voice that John Fetterman, Democrat for a US Senate seat in Pennsylvania, "has a love affair with criminals."
>
> Fetterman has voted "over and over to release the state's most violent criminals, including murderers," the narrator says. If elected, he would "keep the drugs flowing, the killers killing, and the children dying."[30]

From the other side of the political spectrum comes another grainy black-and-white attack ad, titled Herschel Walker Can't Be Our Senator. This ad targeted women in Georgia where a run-off election was scheduled between Walker and incumbent Democratic Senator Raphael Warnock because the two were in a near statistical tie and neither candidate had received the 50% necessary by Georgia law to win the election, as the Libertarian candidate had received 2.1%. Not exactly a "tit for tat" attack ad but certainly an exaggeration of some facts as well as an omission of other damaging information to Walker. Referring to the former Georgian and National Football League (NFL) star running back, the ad begins: "Decades of violence against women. Guns. Razor blades. Choking. Stalking."[31] The add did not mention his out-of-wedlock estranged children nor that the avowed "prolife" candidate Walker had paid for at least one abortion for a former girlfriend.

Let us see how the GOP and Democratic parties did in the 2022 midterm elections when it came to telling truths, falsehoods, and disinformation with respect to the issues of "defunding" the police and abortion. Both parties often omit candidates' stated positions. Republicans have used "a variety of dishonest tactics to create the inaccurate impression that the Democratic candidates they are targeting support defunding police" that "means different things to different people."[32] Democrats are more about half-truths and distortions that have been misleading.

> Many of the Democratic ads accurately describe their Republican targets' strict anti-abortion positions. But some others employ slippery phrasing and the power of insinuation to promote the impression that certain Republican candidates have taken more aggressive anti-abortion stands than these candidates have.[33]

Here are examples from both parties.

Kevin Kiley, the Republican candidate for the House of Representatives in California's 3rd District, claimed of his Democratic opponent Kermit Jones: "If Pelosi has her way, Jones will join her defund the police." The on-screen text says, "PELOSI-JONES AGENDA: Defund the Police." Pure fiction. That was neither Pelosi nor Jones position. Back in February of 2020 Pelosi came out and stated that defunding the police was "not the position of the Democratic Party." During her tenure as House speaker under President Biden, the Democrats had passed policing reform legislation that provided additional funding to the police. Numerous Republican ads mischaracterized or falsely claimed that Democrats voted in Congress or state legislatives to defund. In another case of guilt by association from a super PAC called Moms for Safe Streets, an attack ad on Abigail Spanberger running for re-election in Virginia's 7th District claimed she joined Alexandria Ocasio-Cortez (AOC's) efforts to defund police. In reality, Spanberger, a former CIA officer and employee of the postal service's law enforcement arm, had been "one of the most vehement Democratic opponents of defunding the police." She had, in fact, supported a police reform bill that passed in 2021. While that law did not defund the police, it included various measures to try to improve police conduct.[34]

On the other side of the isle, an ad from the Democratic Congressional Campaign Committee claimed that "Ester Joy King even stands with Republicans who want a national abortion ban with no exceptions for rape or incest." This ad was released the day after a debate the night before when King stated that she was opposed to a federal abortion plan. While the ad was correct that "King describes herself as 'unapologetically pro-life' and that she praised the Supreme Court's decision overturning Roe v Wade," it did not mention that back in August King had also stated that she supported exceptions for rape, incest, and the life of the mother. An ad released in late September from a House Majority PAC targeted George Logan, the Republican candidate in Connecticut's 5th District. The attack ad claimed that Logan would help the Washington Republican leaders who were talking about a nationwide ban or abortion, including Connecticut. A week before the ad was released Logan had stated: "I don't support a national ban. I believe it should be up to the states. Right here in Connecticut, we have codified a woman's right to choose. That's what I support."[35]

Briefly for now. If we are to ever have free and fair elections, and a new and improved democracy to replace the hyperpartisan and polarized old democracy dependent primarily on money, money, and more money, then there are several reforms to our political system that are called for. These include but are not limited to abolishing the Electoral College, amending the constitutional amendment process, and rejecting the decision of the 2010 *Citizens United v. Federal Election Commission*. By passing federal and state laws to prohibit all private and corporate-funded elections and adopting some type of mandatory system of publicly funded elections.

While the Democrats would tend to support at least some of these reforms because these are in their party's interests, the Republicans would tend to oppose most of these reforms because these are not in their party's interests. One thing is certain as Marina Pino writing on behalf of the Brennan Center for Justice made clear on the eve of the 13th anniversary of the Supreme Court's *Citizens United* decision in 2023: Washington was shocked by two different campaign finance scandals. One for less than a million dollars involving the newly elected Rep. George Santos (R-NY) and the other for hundreds of millions of dollars involving the former FTX CEO Sam Bankman-Fried. Their "improprieties reveal the deficiencies throughout our campaign finance system that can be traced back – at least in part – to the Court's problematic jurisprudence."[36] The problem of "how truly ludicrous money in politics" has become runs much deeper and is even more daunting as Matt Lewis exposes in his latest book, *Filthy Rich Politicians*. Lewis explains how Americans could achieve accountability from their elected leaders by way of commonsense reforms. Unfortunately, many of the "ruling-class elites have a vested interest in rejecting the reforms" called for.[37] In the meanwhile, richer candidates from both major political parties get elected and these elected officials get richer the longer they stay in office. A Catch-22 situation if there ever was one.

### On the 2022 Midterms and Early in the 2024 Presidential Race

Echoing Marshall McLuhan's "the medium is the message," David Feldman has explained why the 2022 midterms were less about the voters and more about big business: "Consultants, radio stations, television networks, Google, Facebook, marketing executives and advertising agencies all earn millions taking a slice" of what constitutes about 5% of the $16.7 billion industry. He analogizes that in the same way that "television's message is watch more television," elections are about elections and the next election.

> That is the genius of Donald Trump. He totally gets this. Which is why Trump had made this election, and future elections, if we have any, about the election. Talk to any MAGA Republican, the only issue they're voting on is the election.[38]

Indeed, Trump, Trumpism, and the threat of the return of Trump like in 2020 became what the election was all about and that is precisely why he loss. Trump in combination with abortion made the difference, trumping all the other issues and bringing out the Democratic base and the young and first-time voters. The number of 2022 midterm voters surpassed the record setting 2018 midterms when Democrats retook the House in a blue tsunami. Trump also saddled the Republicans with some very weak and hand-picked candidates. For the first time ever in a midterm election, Independents voted by a few points more for the incumbent president's party and one with only a 42% approval rating. Historically, Independents would favor the out-of-power party by some ten points. When voting began in the 2022 midterms, the number one issue was voting for those candidates of one's party regardless of their resumes as most voters of either party agreed that this election was the most important midterm election in memory. Existential crisis or not, 90% of the registered voters of each political party voted straight party tickets. While many voters of both parties thought that democracy was on the ballot, 79% of all voters were feeling that things were in a state of chaos.[39]

Following the 2022 midterms, Chauncey DeVega interviewed Ian Bassin, co-founder and executive director of Protect Democracy, a nonpartisan nonprofit organization working to stop American democracy from declining into authoritarianism:

> The crisis of democracy that Donald Trump represents is part of a much larger global phenomenon that will not end anytime soon. The elections offered a strong sign of hope for American democracy – but Trump, the Republican fascists and their larger movement represent a base of many millions of voters, and they're not going away.[40]

Back on July 19, 2022, the Violence Prevention Research Program (VPRP) provided evidence for this reality when it released its findings from their online bilingual survey of 8,620 English and Spanish participants from May 13 to June 22. This was the first nationwide population-representative survey to explore personal willingness to engage in specific political violence scenarios.

"We expected the findings to be concerning, but these exceeded our worst expectations," stated lead author Garen Wintemute, an emergency department physician and director of VPRP and the California Firearms Violence Research Center at UC Davis.[41] The survey questions focused on three topics: (1) beliefs regarding democracy and the potential for violence in the United States; (2) beliefs regarding American society and institutions; and (3) support for and willingness to engage in violence, including political violence. Key findings included as follows:

- 67.2% perceive there is "a serious threat to our democracy."
- 50.1% agree that "in the next several years, there will be civil war in the United States."
- 42.4% agree that "having a strong leader for America is more important than having a democracy."

- 41.2% agree that "in America, native-born white people are being replaced by immigrants."
- 18.7% agree strongly or very strongly that violence or force is needed to "protect American democracy" when "elected leaders will not."

Among participants "who considered political violence to be at least sometimes justified to achieve a specific objective, 12.2% were willing to commit political violence 'to threaten or intimidate a person,' 10.4% 'to injure a person,' and 7.1% 'to kill a person'." Finally, among all survey participants,

> nearly 1 in 5 thought it was at least somewhat likely that within the next few years, in a situation where political violence was justified, "I will be armed with a gun." Four percent thought it at least somewhat likely that "I will shoot someone with a gun."[42]

With or without Donald Trump, DeVega unpacks the meaning of the 2022 midterms: "Democrats defied historic trends, conventional wisdom and the predictions of the Church of the Savvy and larger pundit class, and that in itself was remarkable." However, it is a

> mistake to view these midterm elections as a great victory for the Democratic Party and, by extension, democracy itself. This outcome, while unexpected by most observers, offers only a brief reprieve in what will likely be a decades-long fight against American neofascism.[43]

More expansively the federal republic of the United States of America has not been saved by the midterm elections as John Stoehr argues because this nation has never been one country. There is no united America per se so much as there are many Americas. Perhaps as many as 50 state-like countries not unlike nation-states in the European Union, residing inside of a "larger, overarching and made-up unit."[44] For more than two and one-third centuries, this federalism of states has been "held together loosely by a constitution" that "has been used to sow division as much as, or more than, to cement unity."[45] Moreover, there is less unity and more diversity among those red and blue designated states than most politicos contend. There are also purple states that exhibit the divisions within and between these divided states.

American disunity is reinforced or further aggravated by our existing (or unamended) constitutional system of a "tyranny by the minority." For example, though Americans are divided on their positions favoring or opposing abortion and/or the rights of girls and women to control their own reproductive capacities, people from either party overwhelmingly support reproductive freedom. Unfortunately, because of our nation's aversion to majority rule, nationalization, and the balance between federal and states' rights – not people's rights – those states as well as the supermajority of the nine justices of the US Supreme Court that have outlawed or restricted abortion can do so because our legal system is structured so they do not need to care what the majority of American people think about abortion, reproductive rights, or anything else for that matter. Even before the supermajority of six became a reality and *Roe* was overturned, the rightwing of the court had been busy "tearing up federal laws and court precedents" that had "in effect served as the glue that held the 50 states together as one."[46] Historically, there were the SCOTUS decisions that decided corporations were persons. More recently, there were the decisions of *Citizens United v. Federal Election Commission* (2010) and *Shelby County v. Holder* (2013). The original intent of the 14th Amendment has been so debaed or inverted that corporations are more protected by it than the people are.

The *Shelby* decision has turned out to be one of the great dividers and non-unifying decisions of our time. Before *Shelby* and since the passage of the Voting Rights Act (1965), those states with a history of racial animus in government policy had to get clearance from the Justice Department before they were allowed to change their election laws. The five-justice majority in Shelby had decided that these states were free of their former racial animus in contradiction to the repeated nearly unanimous votes by the US Congress. Since *Shelby*, Republican-controlled states across the country have "enacted laws that erode the power of racial minorities, deepened the white-power status quo, and have laid the foundation" for what some would argue are "becoming quasi-apartheid states organized to deprive majorities of their political power."[47]

During the 2022 midterm elections, the party of "law and order" was doing its best not only to deny a legitimate election, as well as a failed coup led by a former president, but they were also doing everything to overlook his four years of obstructing justice and weaponizing the Department of Justice (DOJ). According to an analysis by FiveThirtyEight, 60% of American voters had election deniers on their ballots. Think about 300 election deniers running for political office nationwide. More than half or 174 of them won if we could believe the former Liar-in-Chief. However, most of those were in uncontested or gerrymandered races. Moreover, in some of the key battleground states like Arizona, Nevada, Pennsylvania, and Michigan where I live, those candidates who peddled lies about a stolen election in 2020 were rejected. Many Democratic and Independent voters were also concerned that "Trump-backed Republican victories could give them enough power to hijack America's election machinery in future races, including the 2024 presidential contest."[48]

Many GOP candidates on the campaign trail were also denigrating the FBI, the Justice Department, and the imaginary "Deep State." Here is what candidate J.D. Vance running for the Ohio Senate who had flip-flopped on his opinion about the Nazi march in Charlottesville – once upon a time bashing Trump's response to the white supremacist rally and then subsequently referring to the event as a "ridiculous racial hoax"[49] – had to say about the "deconstruction of the administrative state" and controlling "elite culture" that he believed was corrupt, subversive, and malignant: "Rip out like a tumor the current American leadership class and then reinstall some sense of American political religion, some sense of shared values."[50] Vance went so far as to propose a "de-Nazification" program for purging liberals from government. Vance was the only one of ten candidates running for the US Senate and Governorships backed by Trump who won his election, defeating the moderate Democratic Representative Tim Ryan 53.3%–46.7%.

Since 2020, American fears and anxieties about being murdered, sexually assaulted, attacked in their cars or at home, and about their children being physically harmed while at school were all on the rise. And yet, as noted above property and violent street crimes based on FBI data were relatively moderate both preceding and during this period. For example, violence crime fell by an estimated 1% in 2021 led by an 8.9% drop in the robbery rate compared to 2020. Looking at murders, they showed a significant increase between 2019 and 2020, a smaller increase in 2021, and were declining in 2022.[51] Comparatively, murders during these years were about 50% lower in the aggregate than they had been in the late 1980s and early 1990s. What accounts for this disconnect between perceptions and reality?

According to a CNN analysis of AdImpact data in the first three weeks of October, the GOP spent $64.5 million on crime-focused ads, or one-quarter of their ad expenditures. Most of these ads were about the Democrats' allegedly defunding the police and trying to end cash bail for accused offenders. Sensing vulnerability in the public's imagination, if not in reality, the Democrats answered back by "dropping $58 million during the same period, accounting for 15% of their total ad spending."[52] In addition to the $5 million dollars spent daily on marketing "a fear of crime" in the run-up to the midterms, I would suggest that many of these tropes or perceptions of crime could be attributed to other things, such as too much television during the COVID lock down, saturated news coverage of the increasing numbers of daily mass shootings that represent between 1% and 2% of the overall gun shootings annually, and the spiraling rise in hate crimes that represent only a tiny fraction of everyday domestic violence in America.

Nevertheless, despite the elevated fears and anxieties about crime in general, most voters were more concerned about other issues. From the AP VoteCast exit polls conducted by Edison Research, the two most important issues were inflation (31%) and abortion (27%) by far as the next three important issues were crime and guns at 11% followed by immigration at 10%.[53] One of the takeaways of Insha Rahman of the Vera Institute of Justice was that "voters across the political spectrum [wanted] solutions, not scare tactics."[54] Scare tactics, however, is pretty much all the GOP has on a myriad of issues especially when compared to the efforts of Democrats.

In this regard, in his first 19 months in office, President Biden signed more executive orders and secured the appointment of more federal judges than any president in this century. In those same number of months Biden signed more productive bills into law than Trump did in four years or that Bush II and Obama did in eight years, including most notably the American Rescue Plan Act, the Infrastructure Investment and Jobs Act, and the Inflation Reduction Act. His administration also lowered the deficit by $1.75 trillion dollars during his first two years of office without GOP support except a minimal amount for infrastructure and chips manufacturing. By contrast the national debt rose almost $7.8 trillion during Trump's time in office, the third biggest increase, relative to the size of the economy, of any US president in history.[55]

In short, Biden delivered more on his campaign promises than any of his three predecessors combined and yet his approval ratings were subpar at best. By contrast, while the GOP is quite good at scare tactics and even better at opposing constructive legislative, they seldom have any ideas or policies, let alone, solutions when it comes to dealing with health care, climate change, crime and violence, the economy, or anything else for that matter. In different words, when it comes to "talking the talk" let alone "walking the walk," the GOP usually fails miserably. Unfortunately, these obvious realities do not seem to matter to the GOP electorate where hating the Democrats is "all you need." In fact, by the 2020 presidential campaign the Republicans had stopped "talking the talk" and did not even bother to come up with a platform for Trump to run on. Besides hate, Trump supporters were also voting for the con artist-in-chief because they liked his swagger, his unwokeness, and his uncanny ability to flip everybody off. In the 2022 midterms the Republicans were simply running on what they were against – most notably, truth, democracy, the rule of law, and pretty much everything the Democrats are for – rather than for any kind of constructive policy or agenda that they favored.

After a terrible midterm performance, much of the GOP, excluding the MAGA base, and even Fox News and the *New York Post* were beginning to take pot shots at Trump. The day after the election, the latter anointed the re-elected Florida Governor Ron DeSantis as "Defuture" of the party. On the day after that, Thursday, the newspaper had a caricature of Trumpty Dumpty sitting on a brick wall with the caption: "Don (who couldn't build a wall) had a great fall – can all the GOP's men put the party back together again?" In conjunction, those media outlets of the right-wing billionaire Rupert Murdoch, including Fox News, the *New York Post*, and *The Wall*

*Street Journal*, were getting behind an accompanying editorial penned by John Podhoretz.

> After three straight national tallies in which either he or his party or both were hammered by the national electorate, it's time for even his fans to accept the truth: Toxic Trump is the political equivalent of a can of Raid.

Podhoretz continued, "What Tuesday night's results suggest is that Trump is perhaps the most profound vote-repellant in modern American history. The surest way to lose in these midterms was to be a politician endorsed by Trump."[56] Even after Trump announced on November 16th his candidacy for the GOP presidential nomination for 2024, Republican operatives were keeping the former president away from the US Senate runoff election held on December 6, 2022, between Black Democratic incumbent Senator Raphael Warnock and the GOP Trump endorsed Black challenger Herschel Walker. In turn, Trump did not spend one penny on Walker's campaign, while GOP leader Mitch McConnell's Senate Leadership Fund delivered $15.4 million in campaign assistance.

Out of the $100 million left available in Trump's super PAC, only $15 million went toward electing Republicans in five Senate races, winning only one of those by J.D. Vance. The rest I suspect will be used by Trump in 2024. Back in November Trump transferred $40 million from his Save America PAC, which could not be used to fund his 2024 presidential candidacy, into a newly created PAC expressly for such purposes.[57] On December 15, 2022, Trump released a digital trading card collection at $99 a card. Backed by cryptocurrency technology, the proceeds from the NFTs or nonfungible tokens – images of the 2024 announced candidate for president – go directly to Trump.[58] These cards depict the former president as superhero cartoon characters, swinging a golf club, and a Top Gun-style fighter pilot. Incentives to purchase a card are entries into a series of sweepstakes to meet the Superhero in person or to golf at one of his properties.[59]

The slowly growing antipathy toward Trump was further aggravated when the former president admitted to late-night dining with antisemite Ye (formerly Kanye West) and white nationalist, Holocaust denying, and Neofascist Nick Fuentes at Mar-a-Lago on November 22.[60] Having his "cake and eating it too," you might say. After all, there is Trump with his daughter Ivanka having converted to Judaism, her husband Jared Kushner's Israeli-Palestinian Peace Plan (otherwise known as Trump's Peace to Prosperity plan) that heavily supported the Israeli policies of the right-wing, anti-democratic constituency of Benjamin Netanyahu. And President Trump's moving of the American embassy from Tel Aviv to Jerusalem in recognition of the latter as the capitol.[61] Finally, there is the desperate vote-seeking 2024 candidate Trump once again playing to his white nationalist, antisemitic, and QAnon conspiracy MAGA base.

As one of Trump's former national security advisers John Bolton in an interview with the Guardian less than two weeks before the run-off Senatorial election in Georgia maintained, word was getting out after the poor midterm elections that folks wanted Trump to be put out to pasture and that people were switching off Trump in their brain. As Bolton elaborated:

> Even if they loved his style, loved his approach, loved his policies, loved everything about him, they don't want to lose and fear is, given the results in November, that if he got the nomination, not only would he lose the general election, but he would take an awful lot of Republican candidates down with him.[62]

At his first 2024 campaign outings in New Hampshire and South Carolina during the last weekend of January 2023, GOP leaders almost exclusively on background or off the record were wishing that Trump would disappear. Though none of them were willing to say so publicly or to confront the former president to make it happen. They were hoping for a miracle or, consumed by magical thinking, were waiting for the criminal "prosecutors, an unsurvivable scandal, or even the Grim Reaper to sideline Trump."[63] Nevertheless, according to the national polling averages for the 2024 Republican presidential primary conducted by the FiveThirtyEight group in mid-April 2023, the former president was receiving 49.3%, Florida Governor Ron DeSantis 26.2%, former Vice President Mike Pence 5.8%, and former UN Ambassador Nikki Haley 4.3%.[64]

However, after Trump was finally criminally indicted in New York for the first time and found liable for sexual abuse and defamation of E. Jean Carroll, Trump was polling at 60% and DeSantis had dropped to 19% followed by those polling in single digits. Many Republican voters, especially the MAGA crowd, loved Trump's deposition tape revealing his sulkiness, entitlement, and misogyny. For example, when questioned about his comments from the Access Hollywood tape where Trump had stated that when you are a star "they let you grad them by the pussy," the predator-in-chief who has been credibility accused of sexual misbehavior by 26 women had this to say in his defense: "Historically, that's true with stars...If you look over the last million years, I guess that's been largely true. Not always, but largely true. Unfortunately or fortunately."[65]

Early in the 2024 campaign, the news media was engaging

> in endless false equivalency and "bothsidesism" where Biden's failures have been amplified while Trump and the Republican fascists' lawbreaking, criminality, and existential danger to American democracy and society have in many ways been downplayed. In essence, the news media as an institution has reasoned that 'they were not hard enough on Trump so, for reasons of "fairness" they must be equally, if not harder on Biden – even if it means

manufacturing "scandals." The mainstream news media must also for reasons of "balance" and "fairness" allow former Trump regime members a platform (and employment) to launder their befouled reputations.[66]

Meanwhile, after Biden's excellent state of the union address on February 7, 2023, polling revealed that the people thought Biden and Trump were both too old. Folks had turned out in huge record-breaking numbers for both in 2020, but now there was little enthusiasm for a rematch. More importantly, folks were craving something new, something different as everyone, left, right, and center knows that the system is broken. As surveys have repeatedly shown, the American people have increasingly regarded the two-party system, the courts, Congress, and other political and social institutions with skepticism if not cynicism, and with a lack of trust and respect, if not outright disgust and disdain.

Immediately after the GOP had regained control of the House not by a red tsunami of winners but with only a handful of bodies beyond the 218 seats required, they were as usual offering no affirmative policies to deal with any of the issues they may have raised during the campaign, such as inflation or crime. Immediately after taking over the House, the Republicans had as follows:

- Disbanded the Subcommittee on Civil Rights and Civil Liberties.
- Disbanded the Oversight Committee's environmental panel.
- Replaced the House Financial Services Committee's Diversity and Inclusion Subcommittee with one focused on digital assets and cryptocurrency.
- Renamed the Judiciary Committee's Immigration and Citizenship Subcommittee the Immigration, Integrity, Security and Enforcement Subcommittee

All along their primary agenda was one of revenge or payback in the forms of Congressional oversight, investigation, subpoena power, and pie-in-the sky wishful thinking that they will be able to impeach President Biden, Attorney General Merrick Garland,[67] and Homeland Security Secretary Alejandro Mayorkas for anything other than not being Donald Trump.[68] Their agenda also included investigations into Hunter Biden's business dealings, COVID-19 origins and policies, and the practices of the FBI. In the meanwhile, giving the former president a complete pass on all his lawlessness, obstructions of justice, and seditious behavior. Also, ignoring the conspicuous toadyness and impeachable behavior of Trump's third Attorney General Bill Barr, the new House Speaker Kevin McCarthy (R-CA) had this to say: "The Department of Justice has reached an intolerable state of weaponized politicalization. Attorney General Garland, preserve your documents and clear your calendar."[69] Never mind that Garland's calendar has been the fullest by far of any attorney general in the history of this Republic, not to mention the fact that Garland has moved the wheels of justice with extreme caution and political trepidation. And never mind that McCarthy and the rest of his "hole in the wall gang" have no ideas of what they would indict either President Biden or AG Garland for. But that had not stopped them from going after President Biden and his imaginary crime family while they were busy at work trying to protect the Racketeer-in-Chief.

By the end of its first year the 118th U.S. Congress under the chaotic "leadership" of the House GOP majority had become the least productive in modern history while Speaker McCarthy had been replaced by an ultra-right wing and white Christian nationalist Rep. Mike Johnson from Louisiana who previously had written an amicus brief challenging the "rigged" 2020 election which was signed by more than 100 Republican legislators.

## The Post Trump White House-in-Waiting

Should the GOP win the presidency in 2024 with or without Trump, it would prefer to do so without any violence or force. The Republicans would prefer to dress up their autocratic take-over with as much legality as they can muscle to further whitewash the January 6th failed insurrection, their own culpability, and threat to democracy. Should the Republicans gain control of the White House sooner rather than later, they will enjoy a key asset that was absent from the Trump transition back in 2017: "a sprawling infrastructure already preparing to staff a new administration and immediately enact major policies."[70] Back then, before Trumpism, there was factionalism between the new Trump loyalists, the Republicans in Name Only(RINOS), and the never Trumpers who together fueled the internal conflict that plagued the first two years of the Trump administration. By 2020 Trumpism and the GOP leadership had become one and the same especially because Trump had weeded out from his administration as best he could all but the die-hard Trump loyalists willing to defend lawlessness at any cost. Even after the lackluster performance in the 2022 midterm elections, Trumpism without Trump had become the preferred political modus operandi of the new GOP.

Although the Republicans had no affirmative platforms that they were willing to run publicly on in 2020 or 2022, they were very busy behind the scenes working on their anti-democratic agenda to take control of the state administrative infrastructure. In other words, should another America First and anti-woke candidate for president prevail in either 2024 or 2028, a constellation of conservative groups – many created since Trump left office – hope to cement the ideological brand of Trumpism throughout the administration, as well as in the formation and implementation of their anti-democratic agenda. As Trump's former Domestic Policy Council chief and the president of the America First Policy Institute (AFPI), Brooke Rollins, told Axios in an interview: "The next time around…there will be a whole new game in town that will be prepared for that presidency." Not unlike the Federalist Society and the GOP when Trump was elected President in 2016 and they were preparing to stack the Supreme Court with right-wing ideologues who would do the bidding for a whiter, Christian, and heterosexual America. As Rollins continued:

> A big part of that is having the personnel ready, the policy ready and the process understood so that on Day 1 of a new administration no matter who the president is, we will have 2,500 people ready to report to work to begin to implement that agenda.[71]

By the end of 2022 the annual tax filings by AFPI and other groups in the Trumpian network revealed that together these groups were pouring tens of millions of dollars into what effectively amounts to an administration-in-waiting. Their America first agenda to remake the federal civil service was to pick up where Trump left off by purging thousands of bureaucrats and replacing them with party loyalists for the purposes of deconstructing the administrative state and establishing an authoritarian apparatus of political control. In June of 2022, the nonprofit arm of America First Works and previously America First Policies, staffed by dozens of former Cabinet secretaries and senior aides, and employing about 160 people with an operating budget of $27 million in 2021, unveiled its American Leadership Initiative to develop strategies for future GOP presidential transitions, ideally without any future Democratic presidential transitions.

By mid-summer 2023, Trump and his allies assured that he would once again win the GOP nomination were promising that should the former president be returned to the POTUS in 2025, that their broadest goal was to "alter the balance of power by increasing the president's authority over every part of the federal government that" up to now has "operated, by either law or tradition, with any measure of independence from pollical interference by the White House."[72] Relying on the "unitary executive theory" or a theory of US constitutional law that holds that the President of the United States possesses the power to control the entire executive branch and that Congress can do nothing to limit the president's control. This type of imperial presidency would be similar to Benito Mussolini's fascist dictatorship of yesteryear or not unlike Viktor Orban's former democratic Hungary that has become a contemporary kleptocratic state curtailing the free press, eroding judicial independence, and undermining the nation's former multiparty democracy, and weighing in on the workings of the "free" market for the benefit of the oligarchs.

Among other details not discussed here. Trump intends to bring independent agencies like the Federal Communications Commission that makes and enforces rules for television and internet companies, and the Federal Trade Commission that enforces various anti-trust and other consumer protection rules against businesses, under direct presidential control. In an effort to "clean house" of the deep state and those governmental employees suspected of being disloyal to his administration, Trump "intends to strip employment protections from tens of thousands of career civil servants, making it easier to replace them if they are deemed obstacles to his agenda."[73] "The president's plan" would "fundamentally reorient the federal government in a way that hasn't been done since F.D.R.'s New Deal," said John McEntee, a former White House personnel chief who began Mr. Trump's systematic attempt to sweep out those viewed as disloyal "in 2020 and who is now involved in mapping out the new approach."[74] In tandem with Russell T. Vought, who ran the Office of Management and Budget in the Trump While House and runs a policy organization today, the Center for Renewing America, McEntee and Vought were now involved in Project 2025. This $22 million presidential transition operation led by the Heritage Foundation is busy preparing policies, personnel lists, and transition plans for any Republican who may win the 2024 presidential election.

These efforts were already being reinforced by other organizations with broader ideological ties to Trumpworld. These organizations, such as the Conservative Partnership Institute (CPI), led by former Sen. Jim DeMint (R, SC) and ex-Trump chief of staff Mark Meadows were aligning themselves with organizations founded by former Trump budget chief Russ Vought, top policy aide Stephen Miller, and former Housing and Urban Development secretary Ben Carson. According to tax filings, CPI's budget grew substantially from $7.1 million in 2020 to more than $45 million in 2021, including a $1 million contribution from Trump's leadership PAC. During 2021, American Moment, a CPI-backed nonprofit was born to cultivate America First talent for a variety of purposes, including the staffing of future GOP administrations.

These newer efforts in America First infrastructure development were also being buttressed by the more traditional conservative think tanks and organizations such as the Heritage Foundation, which had heavily influenced the early Trump administration. In conjunction with dozens of conservative groups, such as the Alliance Defending Freedom, the Claremont Institute, Hillsdale College, and the Center for Family and Human Rights,[75] Heritage was leading the 2025 Presidential Transition Project. An effort to help ensure a successful GOP administration in 2025 or 2029 with "the right conservative policy recommendations and properly vetted and trained personnel to implement them."[76] As Miles Taylor, a former chief of staff at the US Department of Homeland Security during the Trump administration, details in *Blowback: A Warning to Save Democracy from the Next Trump* (2023), Trumpism without Trump picks up where the Trump White House left off and is every bit as dangerous to democracy, the rule of law, and the deconstruction of the state as Trump was, if not more so.

In other words, despite the narrow 2022 electoral midterm defeats of the GOP and the survival of American democracy at least through 2024, the enemies of democracy or the movement for American autocracy are still as strong as ever. Even post-Trump and despite the turning of American public sentiment against the Big Lie and the insurrection of January 6, 2021 – thanks to the House Select Committee hearings and final report – Trumpism and the twin threats of political violence and anti-democratic schemes were infiltrating local and state politics. For example, far-right extremists, neo-Nazis, white supremacists, and paramilitary groups like the Oath Keepers and the Proud Boys that constituted the bulk of the violent insurrectionists were showing up at school board meetings, drag shows, and voting booths. They had provided Trump with violent force on January 6 and Trump had provided these folks with cover and legitimacy to seek their own alt-right pathways to power.

After the failed coup, paramilitaries and other extremists had adopted a decentralized strategy, "showing up, armed and intimidating, at events supporting white supremacy, school board meetings debating COVID policies or more inclusive curricula, LGBTQ-friendly events, and demonstrations in opposition to the Supreme Court's overruling of *Roe v. Wade*."[77] These same people were running for local and state offices, signing up as poll workers and precinct chairs, orchestrating recall elections "to replace moderate Republicans with election deniers and anti-government extremists," and ingratiating themselves with elected state and federal officials. Long after Trump's term in office had ended, these private paramilitaries and other extremists espousing political violence and illiberalism had "established themselves as a sinister force in American life."[78] Many of these extremophiles had been welcomed by pro-Trump operatives, Republican organizers, and others engaged in efforts to "Stop the Steal" or overturn the "rigged election." For example, the Select Committee Final Report "obtained texts between the anti-government Oath Keepers leader Steward Rhodes and Robert Weaver, a failed Trump political appointee who co-led the Christian Nationalist 'Jericho March' on Dec. 12, 2020," revealed that "in the weeks before January 6, Trump-aligned activists treated the Oath Keepers not as a pariah, but as a full-fledged coalition partner."[79] The Report also notes that Rhodes had been working with a January 6 rally organizer, Marsha Lessard, to ship tactical equipment to DC.

Another inextricable case related to election denial and insurrectionary enabling had to do with the selection of the 2023 Speaker of the House. After the 118th House of Representatives had failed to elect its new Speaker Kevin McCarthy for its 14th round of voting stretching from January 3 to January 6 – something that had not occurred since before the Civil War. Most viewers who had tuned into the televised voting had not been alerted to what had been fueling the inner party conflict or stalemate between 90% and 10% of the 222 members of the GOP conference. This lack of understanding had to do with what the mass media was not focusing on as well. Rather the media had been mislabeling the political dysfunctionality of the former party of Lincoln back in the day and before the emergence of the Southern Strategies after Reconstruction, after WWI and again after WW II.

The 20- or 21-persons opposing McCarthy on the first 11 votes were mislabeled as "rebels," "radicals," "extremists," and so on. Respectively, the *New York Times* and the *Washington Post* had referred to these politicians as "ultraconservatives" and as "election deniers" rather than as "state deconstructionists" or purveyors of "anarchistic chaos." At the same time, these labels falsely implied that there were ideological disagreements between the pro and con McCarthy factions. In fact, there were not any ideological differences between them, only differences in how to use the means of political power for their shared anti-democratic and non-legislative agendas except for hyper deregulation, reducing expenditures for the well-being of humans and other species, the environment, as well as exempting the wealthy multinational corporations from paying any taxes let alone their fair share. In terms of authoritarian and anti-democratic politics, McCarthy like the faction opposed to his becoming Speaker, as well as 126 out of 215 of those Republicans favoring McCarthy, all voted to overturn the 2020 election only hours after Trump's failed coup attempt, bringing the election lying deniers to more than 67% of the 117th Congress, including the latest GOP House Speaker Johnson.

As Amanda Marcotte wrote in real time:

There's no real daylight between the foaming-at-the-mouth fascists and McCarthy, much less other GOP leaders like Rep. Elise Stefanik of New York, a shameless coup booster and reborn Trump loyalist, and Rep. Steve Scalise of Louisiana, who once described himself as "David Duke without the baggage."[80]

Other political media distractors from "power" struggles were getting caught up in the "personal" conflicts or "personality" differences. McCarthy's opponents simply did not trust and/or like him. Marcotte also explained away why that explanation was not plausible. The "common factor uniting the 20 or 21 holdouts is not personality type but the fact that they come from safe seats in deep-red districts" where they cannot possibly lose an election. "These folks are far more worried about losing a primary to someone who runs on a more-fascist-than-thou platform than about losing to a Democrat."[81]

And from the lenses of the rise of A.I. engineers, and capitalists juxtaposed with the decline in the value of humans or the obsolescence of the humanities and humanity, the opinion columnist Maureen Dowd has argued that we cannot "deal with artificial intelligence unless we cultivate and educate the non-artificial intelligence that we already possess."[82] As she contends:

> It is not only the humanities and humanity that are endangered species. Our humaneness has shriveled. The dueling Republican clinchpoops, Trump and Ron DeSantis, are nasty and pitiless, the "unspeakable in full pursuit of the uneatable," as Oscar Wilde described fox hunting.
>
> Republicans have consecrated themselves to a war against qualities once cherished by many Americans. Higher principles – dignity, civility, patience, respect, tolerance, goodness, sympathy and empathy – are eclipsed.

The real lessons to learn from the 15 rounds of vote counting over McCarthy acquiring the speakership were never really about the leadership qualities of the representative from Bakersfield, California. Nor did the votes casted yea or nay or present have anything to do with either principles or ethics because both were absent from the majority and minority factions of the GOP. Another takeaway was that for the next two years, one-half of the federal legislating body would be mostly nonfunctional. Thus, the fight over the speaker's gavel had simply been a preview of what most every important vote in the House was going to look indistinguishably alike: "The speaker's fight is the debt ceiling fight is the budget fight is the Ukraine aid fight."[83] Finally, after the 15th vote was taken in the early hours of January 7, 2023, McCarthy became an exceptionally weak House Speaker, aided by the likes of Marjorie Taylor Green from Georgia. And the alt-right MAGA Freedom caucus with all kinds of rule changes and committee assignment concessions from Kevin became the driving force behind his ousting after only nine months and the of the nonfunctional 118th Congress.

By the end of its first full day of new business, January 10, 2023, a divided House had passed three resolutions to establish wide-ranging investigations, one of which received a bipartisan vote of 365 to 65 to form a special committee to investigate the Chinese government's economic, technological, and security progress, as well its competition with the United States. The other two votes were straight partisan votes 221 to 211. The first of these Republican resolutions was passed the day before approving an investigation into the coronavirus pandemic. Including "the origins of the virus, so-called gain-of-function research, the production of vaccines and the conduct of Dr. Anthony S. Fauci, President Biden's former chief medical adviser, whom Republicans have pledged to call before them for questioning."[84] The most controversial investigation was the approval of the formation of the Select Subcommittee on the Weaponization of the Federal Government. An Orwellian case where Trumpian insurrectionists and legislators alike are leading an investigation to interfere with the DOJ's investigation into a former president who had weaponized the Justice Department the likes of which the United States had not seen since the corrupt old days of J. Edgar Hoover, circa 1924–1972.

The Weaponization Subcommittee would be chaired by Representative Jim Jordan (R-OH), the incoming chairman of the Judiciary Committee, a staunch ally of Trump who blew off his subpoena to testify before the January 6 House Select Committee on the Capitol assault: "Mr. Jordan, who was deeply involved in Mr. Trump's efforts to overturn the 2020 presidential election, had for months been investigating what he says is a bias in federal law enforcement against conservatives." It had been his intent "to use his gavel and subpoena power to escalate and expand that inquiry, including searching for evidence that federal workers have become politicized and demanding documents about ongoing criminal investigations," including those involving January 6th, Mar-a-Lago, the discovery of classified documents in two locations of Joe Biden's, one in a security facility in Philadelphia discovered in November 4, 2022, and another in a locked garage on one of his two Delaware homes from his days as Vice President, as well as the laptop of his son Hunter Biden regarding his business dealings in Ukraine.[85] They were also planning to investigate claims that the federal government had encouraged discriminatory treatment of conservative or right-wingers on Twitter and at school board meetings and abortion clinics.

Moreover, the subcommittee was to have

> open-ended jurisdiction to scrutinize any issue related to civil liberties or to examine how any agency of the federal government has collected, analyzed, and used information about Americans. It also has authority to obtain some of the most sensitive secrets in the government, including information about covert actions that is usually the exclusive territory of the congressional intelligence committees.[86]

The Republicans with straight faces were trying to say that their Weaponizing Subcommittee was modeled after the well-respected Church Committee. They were referring to the 1970s investigation sparked by the dirty trickster Richard Nixon and led by Senator Frank Church (D-ID) that uncovered decades of intelligence and civil liberties abuses by J. Edgar Hoover and the Federal Bureau of Investigation (FBI), including the surveilling of civil rights groups.

Democratic representatives saw it much differently. Jim McGovern (MA) stated that the panel would have more in common with the infamous House Un-American Activities Committee, which had demonized Americans suspected of being sympathetic to communism. "I call it the McCarthy committee, and I'm not talking about Kevin; I'm talking about Joe," adding the subcommittee "is nothing more than a deranged ploy by the MAGA extremists who have hijacked the Republican Party and now want to use taxpayer money to push their far-right conspiracy nonsense."[87] Jerrold Nadler (NY) shared McGovern's sentiment. He argued that the goal of the panel was to "enable the House Republicans to interfere with the free operation of businesses they do not like, to inhibit the fight against domestic terrorism and to settle political scores on behalf of Donald Trump."[88] Oversight ranking Democratic member Jamie Raskin (MD) had quipped to colleagues that the panel was "insurrection protection" and told Axios: "It's an anti-law enforcement committee. It's meant to be obstructing law enforcement."[89]

After Jordan's committee began misfiring from its opening shots in February,[90] and after his first three "whistleblowers" had no incriminating evidence of any kind and turned out to be former disgruntled FBI agents in March,[91] the House Administration subcommittee on oversight led by Rep. Barry Loudermilk (R-GA), who like Jordan also failed to respond to a subpoena to the House Select Committee on January 6, decided to launch an investigation into the January 6 investigation. Fortunately, this only wasted the time of four Republicans and two Democrats examining roughly 2 million documents and records that were already made fully available to the public back in December 2022. The subcommittee hopes to investigate the securities failures leading up to and during the January 6th assault on the Capitol. Although there were indeed securities failures involved with the insurrection, rest assured that Loudermilk and company will not come up with anything of value as they uselessly spin their weaponizing wheels of administrative oversight.[92]

Lastly, in the midst of the 2024 GOP primary race for the presidency and the general election between its winner by a mile Trump and Joe Biden, there are going to be several criminal prosecutions, if not trials, of the former president where his former aids, advisors, and attorneys, and even his former Vice President Mike Pence also a candidate for the nomination as well as his "point man" on all things coup, Mark Meadows, will be testifying against Trump not to mention literally hundreds of other Republican witnesses who were involved in the fake elector slates from seven states across the country. This will have the effect of taking much of the steam out of Trump's third bid for the White House. Perhaps, giving Biden a landslide not unlike former California Gov. Ronald Reagan's trouncing of President Jimmie Carter in 1980 or incumbent President Lyndon Johnson's victory over Senator Barry Goldwater of Arizona in 1964.

### An American Democracy Still in the Making

The enemies of democracy who stormed the Capitol Building on January 6, 2021, aiming to overturn a presidential election were in effect privileging their votes over the majority of voters. After their side had lost the election, as well as the various recounts and court challenges, these rioters followed the lead of the losing incumbent president and attempted to prevent the certification of President-elect Joe Biden. After a ten-hour delay those members of Congress who voted later that night not to certify the election of Joe Biden shared an evident belief that all people are not in fact equally entitled to representation, and that some are more deserving of rights than others. In defiance of the law and the Constitution, these Trumpist loyalists were in effect weaponizing citizenship by "claiming a determinative right as 'real Americans,' the embodiment of the 'true America,' to place themselves in a category of citizenship enjoying certain" inalienable rights that are denied to others.[93]

Democracy, from its Greek roots *kratia*, means to rule by *demos* or the people. More precisely, democracy refers to a body polity ruled by free, as contrasted with unfree (or enslaved) people. This concept of democracy, which always embodies concepts of privilege and inequality, has its roots in the historical distinction between citizens with the franchise to vote and subjects without it. From its inception, our nation has always been something other than a democracy, as most members of American society were initially subjects of the law without representation.

Moreover, the United States has always been a federal republic of states and ruled today by 51 constitutions. In its earliest years the nation was ruled by elected US Representatives and appointed US Senators dependent on the voting power of white male property owners. Over the course of history, the nation has struggled over the expansion of the franchise as well as the contraction of privilege or inequality to become a more perfect union. The actions of the January 6th insurrectionists were rooted in a traditional division established by the Naturalization Act of 1790 that viewed citizenship as limited by ethnicity, religion, and gender. More than a half-century later, Chief Justice Roger Taney declared in the 1857 Dred Scott decision that Black people could never be citizens, since the Constitution was written by and for white men. After the Civil War, the 14th Amendment created a uniform standard of citizenship that temporarily included all males born or naturalized under the full and equal protection of law. Subsequently, legislators, congressmen, and judges "used the lesser citizenship status of women as an obvious justification for creating different legal castes" as in the imposition of segregation after the end of Reconstruction. Similarly, the Supreme Court stepped in to undermine the 14th amendment as well, "allowing full citizenship to be used as a weapon by elites against those who failed to be born white men," most notably in Plessy v. Ferguson, 1896.

Even after the passage of the 19th Amendment granting women the right to vote, which was ratified in 1920, numerous efforts to deny women full citizenship remained in place, often preventing them from owning property, engaging in "men's work," or barring married women from holding credit cards in their own name. Moreover, the denial of basic rights to Native

Americans, convict laborers, interned Japanese Americans – and most recently voter suppression laws or gerrymandering targeting Blacks and Latino voters in particular – can be viewed as constituting a citizenship caste system. These examples of the "weaponization of citizenship" operate daily to deprive those lacking full citizenship status the full protection of the law.

Until such time as the laws of this nation recognize that all American citizens are entitled to the same rights of citizenship, then the United States will continue to fall short not only of a "direct" but also of a "representative" democracy. As escaped slave Frederick Douglass and leading abolitionist guided by the natural rights tradition argued about the birth of this nation. There were two contradictory constitutions written as a compromise of sorts in the Philadelphia summer of 1787, one pro-slavery and the other antislavery. Otherwise, there may never have been a United States of America, certainly not at the turn of the 19th century. As Douglass wrote in 1850: "Liberty and Slavery—opposite as Heaven and Hell are both in the Constitution."[94]

Writing in his 1859 book, *On Liberty*, John Stuart Mill argued the tyranny of the majority or the tyranny of the masses was allegedly an inherent weakness to majority rule. This is due to the "self-interest" of the majority of people to pursue their own objectives at the expense of those minority factions. Mills went on to claim that rule by the majority would result in the oppression of minority groups comparable to that of a tyrant or despot. However, this view of the power of government, its defense of minority rule, and tyranny of or by an autocrat or despot ignores the political reality that a representative democratic rule by a minority or by an oligarchy of a few are all still tyrannies by any other name.

History has taught us that the weaknesses of democratic majority rule and the harm and oppression that it might cause would certainly be less than the harm caused by the rule of a democratic minority, and far less harmful than rule by oligarchy or autocracy have proven themselves to be – precisely because of the in-built propensities of self-interest. Hence, and as importantly, what has divided our nation from its origins to the Civil War and from the post-reconstruction South – despite the mid-20th-century Civil Rights era – to the present is a Constitution that is still "at war with itself" as Douglass once maintained. And as the US Supreme Court reaffirmed with its dialectically reasoned interpretations of the 14th Amendment on June 29, 2023, by its consolidated 6-3 and 6-2 rulings to end race-conscious affirmative action in college admissions after 45 years. Within hours of the announced decision, Uma Mazyck Jayakumar, as associate professor in the School of Education at the University of California, Riverside, and Ibram X. Kendi, a contributing writer for *The Atlantic* had dubbed the overturning of affirmative action as, "Race Neutral" Is the New "Separate but Equal."[95]

Of course not only are the legacies of race and racism still in place but so too is racism in contemporary America.

With American democracy in crisis and threatened by the rise of Republican authoritarianism, anti-woke neofascism, White Christian Supremacy, QAnon, the Proud Boys, the Oath Keepers, the Three Percenters, Moms for Liberty, and the rewriting of educational curricula across red America to deemphasize history and science, and to specifically "whitewash" racial, gender, and sexual identities make the time more than ripe to amend our US Constitution so that its legacies of privilege and inequality, bondage and domination, oppression and repression in all their ugly forms and dangerous arrangements are eliminated as best as possible. They certainly should not be reinforced by what Justice Ketanji Brown Jackson wrote in her dissent in the University of North Carolina case:

> With let-them-eat cake obliviousness, today, the majority pulls the ripcord and announces "colorblindness for all" by legal fiat. Today's ruling makes things worse, not better. The best that can be said of the majority's perspective is that it proceeds (ostrich-like) from the hope that preventing consideration of race will end racism. But if that is its motivation, the majority proceeds in vain.[96]

Of course, nobody seriously believes that this "majority" of six persons in the United States were interested in ending racism. On the contrary, their primary interest was in denying that racism still existed in America, and that it is time to move on. Well, perhaps someday the clock will run out on the need for affirmative action. However, that time has certainly not arrived early in the 21st century.

Other decisions of the supermajority conservative SCOTUS who have also become a superminority legislating body included a backlash to both the principles of "precedent" and "standing" and to a violation of the norms of liberty and freedom in terms of the protected classes or groups of people, as in women's reproductive rights and the overturning of Roe v. Wade, sexual rights of the LGBTQ+ communities and potentially more groups, and the rights of student loan forgiveness. All of these basic and fundamental changes in established law and practices are the outcome of alt-right politicalization of the Supreme Court rather than correcting unconstitutional behavior. Moreover, while SCOTUS had superseded its authority, it has also violated the Constitutional separation of powers of the three branches of government. Finally, the outcomes of all of these backlash decisions will have negative impacts on at least 100 million families in the United States, and the greatest negative impact will be on the poorest as well as the best-educated African-American women.

Historically, this is not the first time that an ultra-conservative SCOTUS has overreached and provoked intense backlash. After all, the Dred Scott decision helped to cause the Civil War. During the Progressive Era and again during the New Deal, a reactionary Court blocked federal programs and reforms. The Warren Court's liberal rulings especially around the rights of accused offenders provoked a backlash in the forms of the Burger Court that has not only continued more or less unabated for close to 50 years, and who's extreme Trumpian-appointed supermajority of judges corrupt personal behavior of two and judicial lawless behavior of six have brought the Court's popular ratings to its lowest point in American history. Not unlike the scandals surrounding the leaked *Dobbs* opinion of the 2021–2022 that had a huge impact on the 2022 midterms, the 2022–2023 decisions should be even more impactful in 2024. The time to reform a SCOTUS that is "out of control" and views itself falsely not only as an imperial lawmaker and not a judicial evaluator of the law is well past due for change. Two obvious reforms of the highest court in the land are the establishment and operation of an ethical code that no member of the Court can opt out of, along with, term limits that force justices of the highest court to automatically opt out.[97] Ultimately, Trump's three appointees and the decision-making of their supermajority (6-3) over the past three years have not been ultra-conservative. Rather they have been "reactionary" decisions and critics can make the case that these justices by violating both the spirit and letter of the Fourteenth Amendment are engaging in crimes against equal protection under the law. And, as we learned in the "fraud 'justice,'" and anti-LGBTQ decision, "far-right lawyers created a phony 'victim' in made-up case – and the justice with the stolen seat wrote the opinion"[98] for the now corrupted SCOTUS supermajority.[99]

Ideally, a democracy should be one person one vote, at least on those things that have an impact on the commonwealth and affect all of us. To this very day, the ongoing struggle to fulfill the ideals, if not truths, held by the authors of the Declaration of Independence (1776) that all people are equal and entitled to the same unalienable rights is still a work in progress. Likewise, the ongoing struggles to establish local, state, and national governments whose democratic powers are derived from the consent of all the governed are also a work in progress. The United States will remain an imperfect union until such time as all these political struggles are realized in full measure.

Rule by equals is the keystone of democracies because of its "fundamental moral commitment" to the democratic idea that "I have no greater or lesser right to decide how we will live together than you have."[100] When decisions are made that are binding on all women and men, the people must decide. Democratic majorities rather than representative minorities are the best stand-in for the people. Anchoring legitimate power to the people is not an end but only the means, or a prerequisite, for making democratic equality real in everyday life. As James Madison is credited for writing in *Federalist* Nos. 51 and 53, "You must first enable the government to control the governed, and in the next place oblige it to control itself."[101]

In the contemporary world democracy should mean that everyone within the political order has direct rather than indirect power or representation, as well as input into a system of nothing short of majoritarian rule. At its core, majoritarian democracy is the shared disposition of power by all the people constituting the body politic. For the purposes of collective decision-making on the fundamental questions whose resolution set the terms by which we must all live. These include but are not limited to taxes, education, health care, climate change, social security, law enforcement, and technology. By contrast, personal or individual sexual preferences, tastes about dietary consumption, art, literature, or religious faith, and so on, should be excluded from collective decision-making as these do not set the terms in which we must all live. Those expressions of life, liberty, and the pursuit of happiness should be of no interest to the state so long as these are not infringing upon or harming the rights of others to do the same.

Broader connotations of democracy involve ethical, constitutional, and cultural concerns. These are mostly about individual and common rights that a democracy needs to respect such as the equal protection of all people, including the losers and winners of elections, as well as the peaceful transference of power between those elected officials, or that no persons are above the law. Drilling down further, democracies should neither be about markets nor civil rights in and of themselves, or about "managing society toward a proper outcome" that has already been "set, let alone a synonym for eternal conversation." And "most certainly," they are not "ethnic 'real people's' control of a country." Democracies are to be ruled by equals. The ordinary shared power of the people should not be usurped by either the special interests of those hoarding power or the power of economists, judges, and other experts "thought to know what the future expects of us, or what the past requires."[102]

Jedediah Purdy in *Two Cheers for Politics* (2022), citing Alexis de Tocqueville's argument from *Democracy in America* (1835) that Americans never really believed in the "supremacy of the people" and from a 1930 essay by Walter Lippmann on the "dogma of democracy," both shared the cynicism of Americans toward politics and democracy that still seems to be a part of our national legacy in the 21st century. Purdy as well as others such as Russ Feingold and Peter Prendiville (2022)[103] has also written about what the United States can do to change the legitimate sources of democratic distrust. Their objective is the realization of a US majoritarian form of democratic government. In the final chapter, I turn to a vision of a new and amended democracy and to the nascent struggle for a majoritarian form of governing America.

## Notes

1 CQ Researcher. ND. *Anti-Radical Agitation.* https://library.cqpress.com/cqres earcher/document.php?id=cqresrre1935032800&type=query&num=criminal+ syndicalism&

2 Insha Rahman of the Vera Institute of Justice, quoted in James Van Bramer. 2022. Crime and the midterms. *The Crime Report.* November 10. https://thecrimerep ort.org/2022/11/10/crime-and-the-midterms/

3 John Hagan. 2012. *Who Are the Criminals? The Politics of Crime Policy from the Age of Roosevelt to the Age of Reagan.* New Jersey: Princeton University Press.

4 For the record, during the bill process of the CCCA of 1984, there were provisions initially for stiff punishment for white-collar and other financial crimes; however, these were all watered down until they became "slaps on the wrist." No matter because without enforcement of these crimes, there is really very little deterrent value, and besides these crimes are rarely prosecuted.

5 Parker Asmann and Steven Dudley. 2023. How US immigration policy foments organized crime on the US-Mexico Border: Executive summary and major findings. *Insight Crime.* June 28. https://insightcrime.org/investigations/executive-summary-major-findings-2

6 Gregg Barak, Paul Leighton, and Allison Cotton. 2018. *Class, Race, Gender, and Crime: The Social Realities of Justice in America.* 5th edition. Lanham, MD: Rowman & Littlefield.

7 Lila Kazemian. 2022. American exceptionalism in the 21st century: Can the United States get on par with peer countries? *The Criminologist*, 48(6) November/ December. https://asc41.com/publications/the-criminologist/

8 www.gunviolencearchive.org/

9 https://morelle.house.gov/issues/enacting-common-sense-gun-reform

10 For an examination of trends in financial lawlessness, see Gregg Barak. 2012. *Theft of a Nation: Wall Street Looting and Federal Regulatory Colluding.* Lanham, MD: Rowman & Littlefield. For an examination of multinational corporate lawlessness, see Gregg Barak. 2017. *Unchecked Corporate Power: Why the Crimes of Multinational Corporations are Routinized Away and What We Can Do About It.* New York and London: Routledge. For examinations of state and governmental crimes, see Gregg Barak, ed. 1991. *Crimes by the Capitalist State: An Introduction to State Criminality.* Albany, NY: SUNY Press; and Gregg Barak, ed. 2007. *Violence, Conflict, and World Order: Critical Conversations on State-Sanctioned Justice.* Lanham, MD: Rowman & Littlefield.

11 Mark Kennedy. 1970. Beyond incrimination: Some neglected facts of the theory of punishment. *Catalyst*, 5 (Summer): 1–37.

12 Barak, 2012. Ibid.

13 Although Bush and his gang of seven were found guilty of war crime in Malaysia by the Kuala Lumpur War Crimes Commission. See, Yvonne Ridley. 2012. Bush convicted of war crimes in Absentia. *Foreign Policy Journal.* May 12. www.forei gnpolicyjournal.com/2012/05/12/bush-convicted-of-war-crimes-in-absentia/

14 Jake Johnson and Common Dreams. 2023. Corporate prosecutions his record low in 2022 under Biden: Analysis. *AlterNet.* January 20. www.alternet.org/merr ick-garland-2659286649/

15 David Byler. 2023. How megadonors circumvent laws to give huge checks to politicians. *The Washington Post*. April 17. www.washingtonpost.com/opinions/2023/04/17/campaign-spending-megadonors-joint-fundraising-committees

16 Michael Waldman. 2022. Billionaires provided 15 percent of funding for the midterms. *Brennan Center for Justice*. November 22. www.brennancenter.org/our-work/analysis-opinion/billionaires-provided-15-percent-funding-midterms

17 Brian Schwartz. 2022. Federal and state spending on 2022 elections set to top $16.7 billion, making them the most expensive midterms ever. *CNBC*. November 3. www.cnbc.com/2022/11/03/2022-midterm-election-spending-set-to-break-record.html?utm_source=substack&utm_medium=email

18 Bill Allison. 2022. In battle for senate, super PACS tap big donors and dark money. *Bloomberg*. October 28. www.bloomberg.com/news/articles/2022-10-28/super-pacs-seeking-senate-control-tap-big-donors-dark-money-for-midterms

19 Johanna Chisholm. 2022. Herschel Walker tells bizarre story about vampires and werewolves to make point about "faith" in politics. *Independent*. November 17. www.independent.co.uk/news/world/americas/us-politics/herschel-walker-vampire-werewolves-speech-b2227315.html

20 Nick Reynolds. 2022. Herschel Walker's story about bull ditching pregnant cows raises eyebrows. *Newsweek*. October 11. www.newsweek.com/herschel-walkers-story-about-bull-ditching-pregnant-cows-raises-eyebrows-1750944

21 Domenico Montanaro. 2022. Almost $80 million is spent on TV ads for Georgia's 4-week Senate runoff. *NPR*. December 1. www.npr.org/2022/12/01/1139995258/georgia-senate-tv-spending-walker-warnock

22 Paul Waldman. 2014. How our campaign finance system compares to other countries. *The American Prospect*. April 4. https://prospect.org/power/campaign-finance-system-compares-countries/

23 Taylor Giorno. 2022. 2022 federal midterm election spending on track to top $9.3 billion. *OpenSecrets*. September 26. www.opensecrets.org/news/2022/09/2022-midterm-election-spending-on-track-to-top-9-3-billion/

24 Pete Quist. 2022. State-level midterm election fundraising on track to exceed $7 billion. *OpenSecrets*. October 19. www.opensecrets.org/news/2022/10/state-level-midterm-election-fundraising-on-track-to-exceed-7-billion/

25 Bill Allison and Mark Niquette. 2022. Out-of-state money is flooding midterm races – And drowning out local issues. *Bloomberg*. November 2. www.bloomberg.com/graphics/2022-midterm-election-campaign-finance/?leadSource=uverify%20wall

26 Brennan Center for Justice. 2022.

27 Waldman. 2022.

28 Brennan Center for Justice. 2022.

29 Ed Pilkington. 2022. Unregulated, unrestrained: era of the online political ad comes to midterms. *The Guardian*. November 4. www.theguardian.com/us-news/2022/nov/04/online-political-ads-us-midterms-2022

30 Ibid.

31 Ibid.

32 Daniel Dale. 2022. Fact check: The GOP's dishonesty-filled barrage of 'defund the police' attack ads. *CNN*. October 23. www.cnn.com/2022/10/23/politics/fact-check-defund-the-police-ads-2022-midterms

33 Daniel Dale. 2022. Fact check: How Democratic ads mislead on four candidates' abortion stances. *CNN*. October 17. www.cnn.com/2022/10/17/politics/fact-check-democratic-ads-abortion-esther-king-george-logan-april-becker-marc-molinaro

34 Quoted in Dale, 2022: October 23.

35 Quotes in Dale, 2022: October 17.

36 Marino Pino. 2023. George Santos, Sam Bankman-Fried, and Citizens United. *Brennan Center*. January 24. www.brennancenter.org/our-work/analysis-opinion/george-santos-sam-bankman-fried-and-citizens-united

37 Matt K. Lewis. 2023. *Filthy Rich Politicians: The Swamp Creatures, Latte Liberals, and Ruling-Class Elites Cashing in on America*. New York: Center Street.

38 David Feldman. 2022. It's the voter, stupid! *The David Feldman Show*. November 4. https://open.substack.com/pub/davidfeldman

39 Anthony Salvanto, Kabir Khanna, Jennifer De Pinto, Fred Backus. 2022. Republicans head into final week with lead in seats, voters feel things are 'out of control' – CBS News Battleground Tracker poll. *CBS News*. www.cbsnews.com/news/poll-republicans-lead-house-2022-10-30/

40 Chauncey DeVega. 2022. Former Obama lawyer Ian Bassin: The coming indictment of Donald Trump will break his power. *Salon*. November 28. www.salon.com/2022/11/28/former-obama-lawyer-ian-bassin-the-coming-indictment-of-donald-will-break-his-power

41 Garen Wintemute. 2022. Survey finds alarming trend toward political violence. *Violence Prevention Research Program*. July 20. https://health.ucdavis.edu/vprp/news/headlines/survey-finds-alarming-trend-toward-political-violence/2022/07

42 Ibid.

43 Chauncey DeVega. 2022. A big win for democracy? Not so fast: This was a welcome reprieve – but that's all. *Salon*. November 13. www.salon.com/2022/11/13/a-big-win-for-democracy-not-so-fast-this-was-a-welcome-reprieve--but-thats-all/

44 John Stoehr. 2022. We should drop the idea of the United States of America being one country. *Raw Story*. December 5. www.rawstory.com/raw-investigates/we-should-drop-the-idea-of-the-united-states-of-america-being-one-country/?rsplus

45 Ibid.

46 Ibid.

47 Ibid.

48 Jonathan Freedland. 2022. The winner of the midterms is not yet clear – but the loser is Donald Trump. *The Guardian*. November 9. www.theguardian.com/us-news/2022/nov/09/the-winner-of-the-midterms-is-not-yet-clear-but-the-loser-is-donald-trump

49 David Corn. 2022. J.D. Vance's flip-flop on the Nazi march in Charlottesville. *Mother Jones*. September 28. www.motherjones.com/politics/2022/09/j-d-vances-flip-flop-on-the-nazi-march-in-charlottesville-trump/

50 David Corn. 2022. J.D. Vance appeared with podcaster who once said: "Feminists Need Rape". August 25. www.motherjones.com/politics/2022/08/jd-vance-appeared-with-podcaster-jack-murphy-who-said-feminists-need-rape/

51 Reality Check. 2022. U.S. crime: Is America seeing a surge in violence? *BBC News*. October 24. www.bbc.com/news/57581270

52 Chris Cillizza. 2022. Why republican attacks on crime have been so devasting for Democrats. *THEPOINT*. October. 29. www.cnn.com/2022/10/29/politics/repu blicans-midterms-crime-ads/index.html

53 James Kai Chen, Chris Alcantara, and Emily Guskin. 2022. How different groups are voting according to exit pools and AP VoteCast. *The Washington Post*. November 9. www.washingtonpost.com/politics/2022/11/08/exit-polls-2022-elections/

54 Quoted in James Van Bramer. 2022. Crime and the midterms. *The Crime Report*. November 10. https://thecrimereport.org/2022/11/10/crime-and-the-midterms/

55 Allan Sloan and Cezary Podkul. 2021. Donald Trump built a national debt so big (even before the pandemic) that "it'll weigh down the economy for years. *ProPublica*. January 14. www.propublica.org/article/national-debt-trump

56 John Podhoretz. 2022. Here's how Donald Trump sabotaged the Republican midterms. *New York Post*. November 9. https://nypost.com/2022/11/09/heres-how-donald-trump-sabotaged-the-republican-midterms/

57 Kelly McClure. 2022. Trump is holding on to the bulk of his super PAC money for his favorite candidate, himself. *Salon*. December 14. www.salon.com/2022/12/14/is-holding-on-to-the-bulk-of-his-super-pac-money-for-his-favorite-candid ate-himself/

58 Neither a part of Trump's campaign nor the Trump Organization, it is an entity known as CIC Ventures with a lot of Trump overlap. The company that licensed Trump's terribly photoshopped images and likeness was "founded in 2021 by former Trump advisor Nick Luna and current Trump lawyer John Marion." The mailing address for this latest Trump scam is the same as the Trump International Golf Club in West Palm Beach. Quoted from Mathew Chapman. 2022. Mysterious company behind Trump's $99 trading card has same address as his West Palm Beach golf club. *Raw Story*. December 15. www.rawstory.com/trump-nfts-265 8971249/

59 Michael C. Bender and Maggie Haberman. 2022. Trump sells a new image as the Hero of $99 trading cards. *The New York Times*. December. 15. www.nytimes.com/2022/12/15/us/politics/trump-nft-trading-cards-superhero.html

60 David Mack. 2022. Trump admitted to dining with an antisemite (Kanye) and a white nationalist at Mar-A-Lago. *BuzzFeed News*. November 26. www.buzzf eednews.com/article/davidmack/trump-kanye-west-ye-dinner-fuentes-mar-a-lago. See also, Matt Lewis. 2022. Nick Fuentes and the illiberal right are America's homegrown Jihadists. *Daily Beast*. November 29. www.thedailybeast.com/nick-fuentes-and-the-illiberal-right-are-americas-homegrown-jihadists

61 Aaron David Miller. 2020. *What I Told Jared Kushner about His Middle East Peace Plan*. Carnegie Endowment for International Peace. February 7. https://carnegieendowment.org/2020/02/07/what-i-told-jared-kushner-about-his-mid dle-east-peace-plan-pub-81010

62 David Smith. 2022. Trump's act is 'old and tired', says his own former national security adviser. *The Guardian*. November 26. www.theguardian.com/us-news/2022/nov/26/donald-trump-old-and-tired-john-bolton

63 Ed Kilgore. 2023. Trump won't go away unless a Republican actually beats him. *Intelligencer*. January 30. https://nymag.com/intelligencer/2023/01/trump-wont-go-away-unless-a-republican-actually-beats-him.html

64 Nathaniel Rakich. 2023. Trump leads DeSantis in our new 2024 Republican Primary polling average. *FiveThirtyEight*. April 12. https://fivethirtyeight.com/features/trump-desantis-national-polls/

65 Amanda Marcotte. 2023. Trump's rape deposition tape shows exactly why MAGA loves him. *Salon*. May 9. www.salon.com/2023/05/09/rape-deposition-tape-shows-exactly-what-maga-loves-him

66 Chauncey DeVega. 2023. State of the Union: Americans are exhausted – and more vulnerable to a fascist takeover than ever. *Salon*. February 8. www.salon.com/2023/02/08/state-of-the-union-americans-are-exhausted--and-more-vulnerable-to-a-fascist-takeover-than-ever/

67 Chris Walker. 2022. Trump loyalists plan to impeach Biden if the GOP wins control of house in midterms. *Truthout*, August 30. https://truthout.org/articles/trump-loyalists-plan-to-impeach-biden-if-gop-wins-control-of-house-in-midterms/. While in the minority during the first two years of the Biden Administration, Republicans in the House introduced 14 impeachment resolutions, more than three times the number that Democrats introduced during the first two years of the Trump Administration.

68 Ryan Chatelain. 2022. Now in charge of House, Republicans expected to investigate Hunter Biden, Afghanistan withdrawal, more. *Spectrum News*. November 16/22. www.ny1.com/nyc/all-boroughs/politics/2022/11/15/house-republicans-expected-to-investigate-hunter-biden--afghanistan-withdrawal--more

69 Ibid.

70 Lachian Markay. 2022. D.C.'s emerging MAGA machine. *AXIOS*. December 21. www.axios.com/2022/12/21/trump-second-term-conservative-policy?utm_source=newsletter&utm_medium=email&utm_campaign=newsletter_axiossneakpeek&stream=top

71 Quoted in Ibid.

72 Jonathan Swan, Charlie Savage and Maggie Haberman. 2023. Trump and allies forge plant to increase Presidential power in 2025. *The New York Times*. July 17. www.nytimes.com/2023/07/17/us/politics/trump-plans-2025.html

73 Ibid.

74 Quoted in Ibid.

75 Project 2025: Presidential Transition Project. https://silver-squid-dlly.squarespace.com/advisory-board.

76 Markay. 2022.

77 Mary B. McCord and Jacob Glick. 2023. January 6th report exposes ongoing, converging threat of anti-democracy schemes and paramilitary violence. *Just Security*. January 6. www.justsecurity.org/84669/the-january-6th-report-exposes-the-ongoing-converging-threat-of-anti-democracy-schemes-and-paramilitary-violence/

78 Ibid.

79 Ibid.

80 Amanda Marcotte. 2023. McCarthy debacle comes with a lesson: There' a downside to being a party of fascist trolls. *Salon*. January 5. www.salon.com/2023/01/05/mccarthy-debacle-comes-with-a-lesson-theres-a-downside-to-being-a-party-of-fascist/

81 Ibid.

82 Maureen Dowd. 2023. Don't kill 'Frankenstein' with real Frankensteins at large. *The New York Times*. May 28. Sunday Opinion, p. 3.

83 Jonathan V. Last. 2023. The McCarthy speakership fight is only a preview. *Bulwark+*. January 6. https://thetriad.thebulwark.com/p/the-mccarthy-speakers hip-fight-is

84 Luke Broadwater and Catie Edmondson. 2023. Divided house approves G.O.P. Inquiry into 'Weaponization' of Government. *The New York Times*. January 10. www.nytimes.com/2023/01/10/us/politics/house-republican-committee-weapon ization-government.html

85 Ibid. See also MJ Lee, Phil Mattingly, Kaitlan, and Jeff Zeleny. 2023. Biden says he was surprised to learn government records, including classified documents, were taken to his private office. *CNN Politics*. January 10. www.cnn.com/2023/01/ 10/politics/classified-documents-joe-biden/index.html; Glenn Thrush. Classified documents found in second location associated with Biden. *The New York Times*. January 11. www.nytimes.com/2023/01/11/us/politics/biden-classified-docume nts.html; Eric Tucker. 2022. House GOP pushes forward with Hunter Biden probe despite thin majority. *PBS News Hour*. November 19. www.pbs.org/newsh our/politics/house-gop-pushes-forward-with-hunter-biden-probe-despite-thin-majority

86 Ibid.

87 Quoted in Ibid.

88 Ibid.

89 Hans Nichols and Zachery Basu. 2023. 1 big thing: GOP's escalating war with the feds. *Axios Sneak Peek*. January 10. www.axios.com/newsletters/axios-sneak-peek

90 Joshua Zeitz. 2023. Jim Jordan's 'Weaponization Committee' is misfiring. *Politico*. February 24. www.politico.com/news/magazine/2023/02/24/gop-church-commit tee-00083835

91 Annie Grayer and Alayna Treene. 2023. Jim Jordan's first FBI whistleblowers fact scrutiny from skeptical Democrats. *CNN*. March 2. www.cnn.com/2023/03/02/ politics/jim-jordan-whistleblowers-fbi-weaponization/index.html

92 Rebecca Shabad et al. 2023. Republicans launch an investigation into the Jan. 6 committee that examined the riot. *Yahoo News*. March 8. https://news.yahoo. com/republicans-launch-investigation-jan-6-215003642.html

93 Michael Bellesiles. 2021. Weaponizing citizenship. *Academic Letters*, Article 591: p. 1. https://doi.org/10.20935/AL591

94 Quoted in James Oakes. 2022. *The Crooked Path to Abolition: Abraham Lincoln and the Antislavery Constitution*. New York: W. W. Norton & Company.

95 See www.theatlantic.com/ideas/archive/2023/06/supreme-court-affirmative-action-race-neutral-admissions/674565

96 Nadra Nittle. 2023. The Supreme Court ends affirmative action in college admissions. *The19th*. June 29. https://19thnews.org/2023/06/supreme-court-overturns-affirmative-action-college-admissions

97 Michael Waldman. 2023. Supermajority: How the Supreme Court Divided America. New York: Simon & Schuster.

98 Amanda Marcotte. 2023. Fraud "justice": Anti-LGBTQ decision based on a fake case showcases the Supreme Court's illegitimacy. Salon. July 3. www.salon.com/ 2023/07/03/fraud-justice-anti-lgbtq-decision-based-on-a-fake-case-showcases-the-illegitimacy

99 Kim Messick. 2023. The Supreme Court's term of clear corruption and the innocence of influence. *Salon*. June 20. www.salon.com/2023/06/30/the-courts-term-of-clear-corruption-and-the-innocence-of-influence

100 Jedediah Purdy. 2022. *Two Cheers for Politics: Why Democracy Is Flawed, Frightening – And Our Best Hope*. New York: Basic Books, p. 16.

101 Ibid.

102 Ibid., p. 16.

103 Russ Feingold and Peter Prindiville. 2022. *The Constitution in Jeopardy: An Unprecedented Effort to Rewrite out Fundamental Law and What We Can Do About It*. New York: Public Affairs.

# 3

# OLIGARCHY, KLEPTOCRACY, AND THE MAESTRO OF LOOTING

Donald Trump and Jared Kushner besides being father and son-in-law share other things in common besides Ivanka Trump. These include biographies of migrating to Manhattan in their early professional careers, one from Queens, New York, and the other from Livingston, New Jersey. Their fathers Frederick Trump and Charles Kushner were both wealthy real estate entrepreneurs. Each had long histories of giving money to Democratic party machines and to governmental bureaucracies in New York and New Jersey to facilitate their economic ventures. Though separated by 35 years of age both men were raised in family businesses that were deeply connected to local and state politics. For the Trumps and the Kushners, these connections were always important for the accumulation of money. At the time of the 2016 presidential campaign, Donald and Jared had primarily separate financial and political relationships with access to different types of oligarchies and kleptocracies.[1] The former in international locales like Russia and Ukraine, the latter in Israel and the Middle East.

By the end of the Trump administration, both father and son-in-law had established financial and political relationships with the Saudis especially as they had each provided cover for Saudi Arabian Crown Prince Mohammed bin Salman (MBS) for the killing of *Washington Post* journalist Jamal Khashoggi. In the case of Jared, six months after leaving the White House, he secured a $2 billion investment from a fund led by the Saudi Crown Prince for his new private equity firm of which he had no experience whatsoever which is probably the reason that the fund's board had voted against the investment. Also, investing in Kushner's "startup" equity firm were Qatar, the UAE and other non-US Investors from the United States came to 1% (see Figure 3.1). As Steve Ratner commented about the Middle East shakedown

DOI: 10.4324/9781003390664-5

Kushner's Middle East Shakedown

**FIGURE 3.1** Kushner's middle east shakedown.

*Note:* Country totals are estimate based on outside reporting.

*Source:* Adapted from SEC, New York Times.

on MSNBC's Morning Joe, August 14, 2023: "I've been in this business 40 years, I've never seen somebody get two-thirds of their money from a single investor. Usually a single investor might be a few percent of the fund, might be 5 percent, maybe 10 percent." In the spring of 2022, the Trump Organization teamed up with Dar Al Arkan, one of Saudi Arabia's largest real estate companies to license its name for a planned golf course in Oman.[2] Chump change by comparison.

In short, both men on behalf of their family businesses were very agile and transactional when it came to changing their past practices of investing in political giving to the preferable practices of political receiving (bribery). Although the two men have very different personalities and do not necessarily see politics in the same tactical ways, they have been content to use one another for their mutual benefit. Unlike the larger "family" members of Boss Trump's inner business and/or political circles that were always expendable and subject to not being loyal enough, Donald and Jared were bonded by marriage. Finally, it is not known whether Kushner and Trump for the acquisition of several billion dollars "sold out their country and damaged prospects for peace in the world by helping MBS rise to power and then pushing Saudi Arabia toward Russia."[3] On the other hand, regarding the two emolument clauses of the US Constitution that forbid officials from taking gifts from foreign governments as a means of trying to prevent governmental corruption or limit foreign influence in this nation, there is little doubt that the two men violated the law.

### Oligarchs, Plutocrats, Kleptocrats

In an interview with *The Guardian* newspaper about his latest book, *It's OK to Be Angry about Capitalism* (2023), Senator Bernie Sanders informs us that "oligarchs run Russia. But guess what? Oligarchs run the United States as well." He also claims that oligarchs run Europe, the United Kingdom, and the rest of the world where "we're seeing a small number of incredibility wealthy people running things in their favour. A global oligarchy."[4] Under "uber" capitalism, governmental rule by the rich (plutocrats) or rule by the few (oligarchs) has become one and the same. Those richest few that are ruling – the governments whether democratic or autocratic – are simply referred to here as the oligarchy of the rich. These capitalist oligarchs are those individuals and entities that shape the global economies.

Uber-capitalism, laissez-faire markets, unfettered and unregulated capitalists, and regressive tax systems are epitomized by oligarchs like Jeff Bezos and Amazon.com, Inc. in the United States. Though there are plenty of other examples from the Kochs to Walmart to Starbucks to Elon Musk. The issues are always the same: unlimited greed, opposing the rights of workers to organize, and abusing power that hurts people and injures nations. In 2017 and 2018 Amazon paid no taxes. In 2021, Amazon had revenues of almost $470 billion and made a record-breaking $36 billion – a 453% increase from where it was before the pandemic. While some Amazon essential workers were literally catching COVID and dying during the first year of the pandemic, Bezos became $65 billion richer or a 57% increase in his fortune. Bringing his net worth to $170 billion, making him the second wealthiest human being on the planet behind Musk who had a net worth of $186.9 billion as of March 2023. As Saunders pointed out on the floor of the US Senate on April 26, 2022:

> Mr. Bezos has enough money to own a $500 million, 417-foot mega-yacht. He has enough money to afford a $175 million estate in Beverly Hills that includes a 13,600-square-foot mansion. He has enough money to afford a $78 million, fourteen-acre estate in Maui. He has enough money to own a $23 million mansion in Washington, D.C. with twenty-five bathrooms. He has enough money to buy a rocket ship to blast William Shatner to the edge of outer space. And yet, even though Mr. Bezos can afford all of those mansions, yachts and all those rocket ships, Mr. Bezos refuses to pay his [million] workers decent wages, deliver decent benefits, or to provide decent working conditions. This is what excessive greed looks like. And

this is why Amazon workers have been struggling to organize unions in warehouses across the country.[5]

Known on Wall Street as the Big Three – BlackRock, Vanguard, and State Street controlled more than $20 trillion or the equivalent Gross Domestic Product (GDP) of the United States at the beginning of 2023. Their portfolio consists of banks, transportation, health care, media, and real estate. Taken together these investment firms are the largest shareholders in the biggest banks in America, such as JPMorgan Chase, Wells Fargo, and Citibank. They are among the top owners of the four major airlines in the United States – American, Southwest, Delta, and United. They are also among the largest stockholders in Comcast, Disney, and Warner Brothers. On average they own 20% of the major US drug companies, and about one-third of the homes purchased in the nation in 2022. Finally, these oligarchs control the US democracy as they "spend tens of billions of dollars on campaign contributions to both major political parties" for the purposes of buying "politicians who will do their bidding. They spend billions more on lobbying firms to influence governmental decisions at the federal, state, and local levels."[6]

Modern-day oligarchies are associated with the dissolution of the Union of Soviet Socialist Republics (USSR) in the early 1990s. With the destruction of the Communist Party and the (Committee for State Security (KGB) networks as well as the rise of competitive politics and post-Soviet market economies came the formation of the national states of Eastern Europe and northern Eurasia under the strong influence of oligarchic groups. At the beginning of the 21st century, governments of post-soviet nations tried to end oligarchies in one of two ways – democratically or by systems of pyramid-like power. In the former, oligarchical corruption was fought in the public sector by strengthening the rule of law and calling for a clear division between the public and private sectors. In the latter, pyramid-like power systems were of two kinds: single-pyramid autocracies or multi-pyramid hybrid regimes with both democratic and nondemocratic political elements. For example, the success of the single-pyramid model in Azerbaijan, Belarus, and Russia gave birth to the current autocratic regimes in those countries. Multiple attempts, on the other hand, to "fight corruption have kept Georgia and Ukraine as hybrid regimes interpolated by many oligarchic groups and repeatedly oscillating between more and fewer political and economic freedoms."[7]

After Russia's invasion of Ukraine's Crimea region in 2014, sanctions from the United States, Switzerland, and the United Kingdom were imposed on "businessmen and officials believed to be in Mr. Putin's inner circle." The United States expanded its "sanctions in 2018 to Russians indicted by special counsel Robert Mueller for alleged interference in the 2016 U.S. election, and several other oligarchs and officials the U.S. government allegedly had been involved in various forms of 'worldwide malign activity'."[8] When Russia invaded Ukraine again in early 2022, the United States, the United Kingdom, and the European Union ratcheted up their sanctions on several of Russia's richest and most politically connected elites: "Western governments are chasing down the yachts, jets, and bank accounts of an expanding list of Russian billionaires and Kremlin elites, hoping to use them to pressure Russian Vladimir Putin to pull back from his country's invasion of Ukraine."[9] As it turned out, those sanctions were not enough to make Putin rethink his course of warfare with his much smaller neighbor. Similarly, federal prosecutors had been quietly issuing a series of subpoenas to seize US assets held by Russian oligarchs pretty much to no avail. So the Justice Department in late November "asked Congress for a new law that would streamline the process after delaying tactics by defense attorneys" were stymying their efforts.[10]

As Mykhailo Minakov writing for the Wilson Center has described:

After about thirty years of developing without hindrance in those states where they were not reined in by autocrats, the oligarchic groups have matured and evolved into stable and sophisticated informal structures. These structures typically consist of a core (comprising several oligarchic figures), public politicians (ministers, officials, MPs, mayors, etc.), and parties serving the interests of one or more of the following: their clan, individual judges or entire courts, parts of the law enforcement agencies, private companies, public companies informally controlled by the clan's management, media holdings, NGOs, philanthropic organizations, criminal and paramilitary groups, and foreign partners in the West and Russia. By controlling parts of the executive, legislative, and judicial branches of government, some governors, mayors, and local councils, the media, and civil society, each clan has a tendency to form a single pyramid. And as the clans compete for influence and control, they open a space for relatively free politics based on a zero-sum game.[11]

Oligarchies are not necessarily good or bad; however, where "rule is by the few," they tend to rule in favor of themselves. The term oligarchy varies or is amorphous and somewhat subjective. Globally, people argue about which countries should be listed as oligarchic and which should not. The World Population Review has recently identified China, Iran, Saudi Arabia, North Korea, Russia, Turkey, Ukraine, United States, Venezuela, and Zimbabwe.[12] The United States would constitute a multi-pyramid hybrid regime as Americans traditionally enjoy many features of a democratic government. However, over the past two decades powerful corporations and affluent individuals have had a significantly larger influence on policymaking than ordinary citizens due to changes in the campaign finance laws. Oligarchs as well as kleptocrats who use their power and money to buy or bribe politicians or to corrupt and/or steal from governments come from many other countries besides the ones listed. For example, these may include African despots as well as someone like Jean-Claude Duvalier, better known as Baby Doc, from the Caribbean nation of Haiti. In 1983 Baby Doc became Trump's first landed kleptocrat but not his last by any means.

Twelve years earlier, Baby Doc at just 20 years of age had ascended to the presidency of Haiti, following the death of his autocratic father. After smothering talk of reform and democratization, he spiraled into crimes against humanity. For example, he housed "political prisoners in jails dubbed the 'triangle of death' where many suffered unspeakably painful deaths." At the same time, his "regime supporters made sure any critical journalists were tortured or exiled for their reporting."[13] After looting state coffers, pillaging local populations, and pocketing Haiti's national wealth to the tune of upward of $800 million, Baby Doc with the help of a few friends opened an American bank account. Soon becoming on a smaller scale like the great kleptocratic American client of that era, the Philippines' Ferdinand Marcos whose looted wealth had been estimated to be worth between $5–10 billion. Back in those days, folks in Washington, DC, happily embraced dictators like Duvalier and Marcos because of their strong stances against communism. Back then, banks did not have to concern themselves over matters of servicing dictators' monies dripping in blood like they allegedly do today.

Baby Doc did not wish to make his investments transparent if he could help it. To obscure his finances, he found a shell company to use. "His American bank account kept growing, with millions in Haitians' missing money congealing for Baby Doc's use" where he spent more than $6 million on a schooner he liked from South Florida and another $6 million to secure a place to live in the middle of Manhattan on the 54th floor of the newly opened Trump Tower. According to

> the most comprehensive analysis available. Trump's American properties sold over 1,300 units – over one-fifth of Trump's total available condos – to buyers matching money laundering profiles: anonymously, to shell companies and cash buyers, often purchased in bulk and without ever revealing the identities of the ultimate beneficiaries.[14]

Kleptocracies or "rule by thieves" refer to those governments whose corrupt leaders use political power to expropriate the wealth of the people and the land. Like its sister institutions of oligarchy or oligarchic corruption, kleptocracies describe a specific type of corruption that occurs when state actors routinely loot not only hundreds of millions but also billions of dollars from national treasuries. In contrast to plutocracies (rule by the richest) or to oligarchies (rule by a small group of elites), kleptocracies refer to those corrupt politicians and their economic associates who clandestinely enrich themselves outside the rule of law by exchanging special favors, kickbacks, pay to play schemes, extortion, and so on. Also importantly, through the legal creation of "shell companies" that provide tax advantages and facilitate control over conglomerate companies, money laundering, and other illegal activities.

For nearly three decades, one country has acted as "the greatest offshore haven in the world, attracting hundreds of billions in illicit finance tied directly to corrupt regimes, extreme networks, and the worst the world has to offer." That center of global offshoring resides not in some Caribbean Island, Switzerland, or Panama City, but in the United States where states like Nevada, North Dakota, and Delaware have "perfected the art of the anonymous shell company."[15]

Wall Street and other global banking entities such as Deutsch Bank in the West have had a long history of legitimizing the inflow of questionable capital into the global pool of money. For example, in October 2020, Goldman Sachs Group revealed that "it was clawing back $174 million in executive compensation and had agreed to pay $2.9 billion over its role in Malaysia's Multibillion Dollar (MDB) corruption scandal," involving a government-run strategic development company where the then-Prime Minister Najib Razak had channeled approximately US$700 million.[16] This settlement between the Justice Department and Goldman Sachs over its misconduct with Malaysia's sovereign wealth fund "highlighted one of the most egregious, but entirely commonplace, examples of U.S. banks facilitating this process."[17]

As Sarah Chayes details in her 2015 book, *Thieves of State: Why Corruption Threatens Global Security*, this type of corruption underlies the spread of violent extremism involving terrorism, revolutions, and their aftermaths, as well as environmental degradation, not unrelated for example to bloody implosions in Iraq and Syria, East-West standoffs in Ukraine, Israel-Gaza or abducted schoolgirls in northern Nigeria.[18] Her investigative reporting has illuminated the connections between systemic corruption and violent upheavals around the world, from the Afghan insurgency to the revolutions of the Arab Spring. As Chayes underscores: "In some countries, the government is not a government that may be failing. It's a criminal organization that's succeeding."[19]

### Influence Market Corruption

Michael Johnston has identified "influence market corruption" to distinguish it from Elite Cartel, Oligarch and Clan, or Official Mogul styles of corruption that typically engage in deals and connections circumventing established institutions. Influence Market Corruption (IMC), by contrast, revolves around access to and operates from within established institutions. As Johnston explains, "Strong institutions reduce the opportunities, and some of the incentives, to pursue extra-system strategies, while increasing the risks." At the same time, "the very power of those institutions to deliver major benefits and costs raises the value of influence within them."[20] Sudhir Chella Rajan writes about "grand corruption" or what he has referred to as the unacknowledged "illegitimacy of elite networks exercising power over diverse social groups and ecosystems" and the "collective incapacity" of people to see their "complicity in maintaining elite collusion of economic and political power, which is manifested in our own daily habits and routines."[21]

Another way of getting at influence market or grand corruption is to say that like high-level white-collar and corporate crime, the key to these forms of doing political-economic business is to blend their deviant conduct with what people accept as "just the way things are." By normalizing these transactional forms of corrupt behavior, most people do not realize the actual extent of corruption or that people collectively are daily victims of politically organized crime.[22] For example, SCOTUS on November 28, 2022, heard oral arguments for two cases, *Percoco v. United States* and *Ciminelli v. United States*. Those cases are to decide when the federal government can prosecute private citizens for fraud and bribery who are influencing government decision-making. The issues revolve around a decades-long trajectory in the Court's decisions that "restricts the tools prosecutors can deploy to address public corruption." SCOTUS in the latter invalidated the Second Circuit's long-standing right-to-control fraud theory; in the latter it invalidated the test used by the same court for determining whether a private person may be convicted of honest-services fraud.

It has been the position of SCOTUS that prosecutors have been overreaching "in situations where vague laws mean public officials and those doing business with them were not on notice that their conduct violated the law." The court has "objected to what it views as overly expansive readings of criminal statutes by prosecutors." For example, in 2016 the Supreme Court ruled in *McDonnell v. United States* unanimously, 8-0 (during the period after Justice Scalia's death and while the Republican-controlled Senate refused to vote on the Obama nominee, Merrick Garland) to reverse on appeal, the then-Virginia's governor's bribery conviction prosecuted by Jack Smith.

As Joyce Vance elucidates, the Court held that "'merely' setting up a meeting, talking to another official, or organizing an event for a 'gift-giver' didn't qualify as the type of 'official act' in return for payment." In this case, the lavish gifts from a friend that included paying for part of McDonnell's daughter's wedding did not constitute a bride.[23] Moreover, recently there were the disclosures of the lavish "hospitality" and not "business" annual summer trips for decades worth millions on the dime of billionaire Harlan Crow.[24] There were other undeclared and falsely declared real estate subsidized by Justice Clarence Thomas' long-time billionaire friend.[25] Not to mention Crow's $500,000 donation to Liberty Central, a conservative political advocacy group founded in 2009 by Ginni Thomas.[26]

With respect to bribes and corruption, Paul Waldman has opined that before Trump became President "we had a relatively simple understanding of government corruption...officials using their positions of public trust to benefit themselves and their associates."[27] However, Trump has taught us that there is a lot more to corruption than meets the eye. In different words, the Donald "has offered us a corruption master class, presenting for our edification a kind of full-spectrum corruption" and in doing so "he has revealed that opportunities for corruption are far more numerous than we knew."[28] And from the project, Mapping Corruption: Donald Trump's Executive Branch:

> Trump has sowed corruption of a breath and brazenness unseen in the far-from-innocent annals of our nation's history. In three years as president, he has transformed the executive branch into a giant favor factory, populated with the agents or willing partners of virtually every special interest. Add up all the routine, daily outrages – the quasi-bribery and quasi-extortion, the private raids on public funds, the handouts to the undeserving, the massive flow of cash, jobs, and freebies back in return – and Trump's attempt to squeeze a little re-election help from the fragile government of a desperate Eastern European country does not loom particularly large in the reckoning.[29]

Much of this corruption may not necessarily be about acquiring capital or power, but the ability to use that power for political ends. For example, in the indictments of Rudy Giuliana's Ukrainian associates Lev Parnas and Igor Fruman pertaining not only to their work to discredit former Vice President Joe Biden and to investigate alleged Ukrainian interference in the 2016 election, but also to subsequently assist in the removal of US ambassador to Ukraine, Marie Yovanovitch. In addition, Parnas and Fruman were indicted for making contributions to US Political Action Committees (PACs) by unnamed politicians on the behest of an unnamed Ukrainian government official seeking energy independence for Ukraine. Finally, the indictments allege that Parnas, Fruman, and two other US citizens were using "political donations as part of an effort to get licenses for a planned marihuana venture."[30]

Trump has spent his dishonest life in search of money. His business history is filled with overseas financial deals and missed deals. Some of these have involved the Chinese state. The Donald "spent a decade unsuccessfully pursuing projects in China, operating an office there during his first run for president and forging a partnership with a major government-controlled company."[31] China along with Britain and Ireland are three nations where Trump maintains bank accounts. These foreign accounts do not show up on Mr. Trump's public financial disclosures where he must list his personal assets because these accounts are not in his name. In the case of China, the bank account is controlled by Trump International Hotels Management (TIHM), LLC, whose tax records reveal that TIHM paid $188,561 in pursuing licensing deals there from 2013 to 2015 that did not pan out.[32] Until 2019 China's biggest state-controlled bank rented three floors in Trump Tower stateside, a very lucrative lease that had generated accusations of a conflict of interest for the former president. Citizens for Responsibility and Ethics in Washington (CREW) in its January 15, 2021, report on corruption identified more than 3,700 conflicts of interest while Trump was President because of his decision while in office not to divest from his business interests.[33]

As far as offshore banking laws and accounts go, the releasing of Trump's taxes from 2015 to 2020 revealed that for at least 2016 he had an offshore bank account in the Caribbean nation of St. Martin, a popular place to avoid paying taxes. Nevertheless, recall when he was asked during the 2016 campaign whether US citizens should be allowed to save or invest in offshore bank accounts, Trump responded: "No, too many wealthy citizens are abusing loopholes in offshore banking laws to evade taxes."[34] Key planks in Trump's tax reform plan would allegedly also end the practices of US multinationals stockpiling offshore hundreds of billions of dollars and millions of jobs. For the record, the sheltered tax dollars did not come home nor did outsourced jobs ever come back to America. Those were merely from "talking points" that were never going to materialize in a Trump administration.

When it comes to "talking the talk" and not "walking the walk," nobody does it better than Trump like at the Republican National Convention in July 2016 when the GOP presidential nominee had this to say:

> Nobody knows the system better than me. Which is why I alone can fix it. I have seen first-hand how the system is rigged against our citizens just as it was rigged against Bernie Sanders, he never had a chance. But his supporters will join our movement because we will fix his single biggest issue trade deals that strip our country of its jobs and strip us of our wealth as a country. Millions of Democrats will join our movement because we are going to fix the system, so it works fairly and justly for every American.[35]

I doubt that more than a few of Bernie's supporters joined the Make America Great Again (MAGA) movement but the conventional wisdom and exit polling data did suggest that swing voters for Trump made the difference in his electoral college victory. Those included many who had previously voted for Barack Obama. They then learned that besides being a terrible President Trump was an out-and-out criminal and casted their votes for Biden in 2020.

Previously, many Democrats preferred to stay at home rather than to vote for Hillary Clinton – "crooked" or not thanks to FBI Director James Comey's public announcement that he found no criminal wrongdoing – in 2016. One of the reasons that Trump only loss the popular vote by 3 million in 2016 as contrasted with nearly 8 million votes in 2020.

Regardless of how people voted, the argument has been that Trump took presidential corruption to a whole new level. In the process, he transformed governmental corruption into a for-profit family business enterprise whose hidden and malicious intents were often but not always criminal in nature. Over the past three decades, numerous examples from investments to securities to control frauds (e.g., Savings and Loan, 1986 and 1995; BCCI, 1991; Waste Management, 1998; Enron, 2001; HealthSouth, 2003; Lehman Brothers, 2007; Wall Street; 2008; Bernie Madoff, 2009; Libor, 2011; Fannie Mae and Freddie Mac, 2011; FIFA, 2015; Wells Fargo, 2016; Volkswagen emissions, 2017) have repeatedly shown that when financial interests consist of profit, power, and/or pressure, these priorities tend to override and/or displace the interests of people, principle, policy, process, and practice. In turn, these untrustworthy activities increase the risks of disasters, crises, and scandals.[36]

Many powerful advisers whose financial backgrounds and inclinations both at home and abroad were at odds with regulations, the public interest, and reversing the trends in the social and economic growth of inequality tended to support Trump's routinization of governmental corruption. Most importantly, Donald's corporate and state-organized corruption was also steeped in a social milieu where nations, lobbyists, legislators, the Republican Party, businesses, the nonprofits, and so on all knew that to play in Trumpworld, they had to pay stipends directly or indirectly to the Trump Organization. And they usually had to pay not once but over and over. The more they paid Trump, the more they received from US domestic and foreign policy. Keep in mind that Trump always keeps tabulated records on the persons, corporations, and nations making deposits into his various properties and ventures.[37]

In effect, the Racketeer-in-Chief as President of the United States (POTUS) had established from the top down an administrative apparatus marked by placing self-interest, profiteering, and corruption above the public welfare. These networks of raising money and flowing cash loads of electronic money as well even helped to contribute to the "deadly insurrection that was rooted in the same self-serving ethos."[38]

### Stocking the Swamp with Free Marketers

Although Trump's political appointments included more than its share of high-rolling donors with no expertise in anything let alone with an appropriate area of specialty. As for those appointments where expertise was required, these were in business, finance, and law. The economic orientation or philosophy of these appointments generally reinforced a laissez-faire approach to regulation and taxation. These free marketers were not about recouping billions let alone trillions from the tax-avoiding and tax-evading dollars of the superrich or mega multinational corporations. Quite the contrary. Four of Trump's key economic appointments had been beneficiaries of shell companies and offshore banking accounts including Gary Cohn, Rex Tillerson, Steven Mnuchin, and Randal Quarles.

Chief economic adviser Gary Cohn was the driver behind the White House tax reform act. Leaked documents reveal that between 2002 and 2006 Cohn was either President or Vice President of 22 separate offshore entities in Bermuda for Goldman Sachs. That was before Cohn eventually became the President and (Chief Operating Officer (COO) of GS, one of the foremost banking, securities, and investment management firms in the world. As for Secretary of State Rex Tillerson, leaked documents reveal that before he ascended to chairman and CEO of ExxonMobil in 2006 and while still presiding as president of ExxonMobil Yemen division, Tillerson was also a director of Marib Upstream Services Company that was incorporated in Bermuda in 1997. And Treasury Secretary Steven Mnuchin before joining the Trump administration was an offshore specialist and deputy chairman of CIT Bank. Mnuchin provided "financing structures for personal aircraft priced at tens of millions of dollars, which customers used to legally avoid sales taxes and other charges."[39] Randal Quarles, Trump's most senior banking "watchdog," was also outed in connection with offshore banks and tax evasion as he appeared prominently in the infamous Paradise Papers.[40]

I could go on and discuss the three wealthiest cabinet members of the Trump cabinet, Secretary of Education Betsy DeVos, Secretary of Commerce Wilbur Ross, and Secretary of Transportation Elaine Cao the spouse of Republican Senator Mitch McConnell. As we all know the only shining accomplishment of President Trump was a $1.9 trillion tax gift or cut enjoyed primarily by super wealthy individuals, mega corporations, and multinational businesses who already had enjoyed the lowest tax rates in the corporate world to the ongoing financial detriment of the general population. According to a Joint Committee on Taxation, the 2017 Tax Cut and Jobs Act between 2021 and 2031 will have increased the governmental deficit by $1 trillion. The Tax Foundation analysis stated over the same period that the tax cuts would cost $1.47 trillion in decreased revenue while adding only $600 billion in growth and savings.[41] These economic projections are consistent with the negative consequences that occurred after the same types of not trickling down tax cuts by the Reagan and Bush II administrations for the corporate wealthy in the United States had also failed to increase production. These neoliberal taxing policies also yielded the same failures in such countries as Argentina, Brazil, Russia, and every other nation where they have been employed. In a nutshell, reducing the top income tax rates for the rich has to date had no appreciable effect on economic growth anywhere in the world.[42]

Why does this matter? Because these kinds of fiscal policies reinforce and escalate both inequality and criminal behavior. From preliterate to contemporary societies expanding inequality and relative rather than absolute, poverty has always been linked to rising rates of crime both in the suites and in the streets. Conversely, contracting the distribution of inequality in goods and services usually decreases crime at the top and the bottom of society because relative deprivation has always undermined the basic sense of fairness and collective trust shared by humans, primates, and even lower animals like the canines. These are the core fabrics that hold most families, tribes, packs, and nation-states together. When these basic qualities are violated the cynicism of "every man for himself" or it is a "dog-eat-dog" world out there unleashes, rationalizes, and normalizes hoarding, cheating, dishonesty, theft, exploitation, oppression, violence, and so on. In short, without cultural interaction and social cooperation based on fairness and trust, then shared values, emotional empathies, and group solidarities wither away as societies decline.

For example, think about the relationship between extreme tax cuts for the super wealthy, multinational corporations, and tax-free offshore accounts, on the one hand, and an underfunded Internal Revenue Service and underenforced business and tax laws, on the other hand. Because of inefficiencies, technicalities, or loopholes financial frauds continue unabated year in and year out, robbing the US coffers and taxpayer of several trillion dollars annually. These appropriations or stolen monies not only assault social solidarity and escalate class warfare, but according to Wealth-X so does the expected transfer of an inherited combined wealth of US$18.2 trillion between 2022 and 2030 by high-net-worth individuals and their families defined by US$5 million in net worth or more.[43] From an instrumental point of view, capturing the sheltered and stolen trillions annually, for example, could pay several times over for Biden's original Build Back Better agenda for $7.5 trillion over ten years to address climate change, infrastructural and human development as well as the amelioration of a myriad of social problems caused by our growing inequality and overall immiseration rates across society.

What most folks, criminologists, as well as non-criminologists fail to appreciate is the breadth and scope of the super wealthy normalization of the interconnected and overlapping relationships of the trillions of dollars annually looted by various forms of fraudulent capital formation and accumulation. These include money laundering, lobbying, and other expressions of organizational and white-collar crime. The magnitude or proportion of these thefts of capital from governmental coffers in relation to global wealth and its asymmetrical distribution is enormous and dwarfs both the human and financial costs of street crime dozens of times over. For example, criminal activities from drug trafficking to extortion to illegal mining to avocado cartels are all central to the worldwide global economy. According to the United Nations, these illicit activities generate an estimated $2.1 trillion in global annual proceeds or about 3.6% of the world's GDP. For perspective, according to Barron's, Forbes, and Lovemoney, total global wealth rose 7.9% in 2020 to US$431 trillion.

Making matters worse, people do not realize, nor do they focus their attention on the financial reality that the money derived by organized and syndicated criminals flows through the same global banking institutions that oligarchs and other tax cheats like Donald Trump and company use for their criminal and noncriminal enterprises. Politically, as Thom Hartmann wrote in *Salon* on July 22, 2021, the Republican Party "is so committed to making morbidly rich people even richer (and keeping them that way)" that Republican Sen. Rob Portman announced that he "wouldn't go along with funding a bipartisan infrastructure bill by letting the Internal Revenue System (IRS) hire more auditors to catch rich tax cheats." Other captured Republican senators including John Barrasso told *Axios* news that "spending $40 billion to super-size the IRS is very concerning" because law-abiding Americans "deserve better from their government than an army of bureaucrats snooping through their bank statements." And there was also Republican Senator Ted Cruz, the sleazeball from Texas that chimed in "Throwing billions more of taxpayer dollars at the IRS will only hurt Americans struggling to recover after the waves of devastating lockdowns." Ted's solution, "we should abolish the damn place."[44] This dribble coming from a Harvard law graduate, a former clerk for Chief Justice William H. Rehnquist, and a lawyer who has argued nine times before the United States Supreme Court. That was before he became a US senator and SCOTUS turned anti-constitutional with Trump's appointments of Neil Gorsuch, Bret Kavanaugh, and Amy Coney Barrett. Each was selected for the former president by the reactionary Federalist Society rather than the more neutral or politically balanced American Bar Association, which had once upon a time been charged with vetting potential supreme court justices.

## Paying to Play

Though Trump campaigned in 2016 to end the Washington insider culture of lobbying and favor seeking, he actually "reinvented it, turning his own hotels and resorts into the Beltway's new back rooms, where public and private business mix and special interests reign."[45] The line between the Trump Organization and the Trump administration was so thin that it is still unclear where the former president's public responsibilities ended, and his private financial interests began.

> Unlike any other modern president, Trump has forced the American people to ask if the decisions and policies his administration is implementing are because they're the best policies for the nation, or because they personally benefit him – either by helping his businesses directly or the special interests spending money there.[46]

Trump has never been about doing anything for the American people. More significantly the Corrupter-in-Chief in terms of personal benefits was able to monetize or convert the office of the presidency into a cash cow for both the Trump Organization and its family members.

Following his election to the White House, Trump pledged to recuse himself from running the operation of the Trump Organization that he did not do. A New York Times' investigation found that over 200 companies and special-interest groups and foreign governments reaped benefits from patronizing and spending monies at his various properties. Among Trump's fringe benefits was the granting of 67 foreign trademarks to his businesses, including 46 from China. With political interests at stake, 60 of those business customers found them advanced by bringing nearly $12 million into the Trump family businesses during the first two years of his presidency. The diversity of the patrons showing up at the Trump bazaar spanned the political spectrum and competing special interests were busy trumping one another there. Either way Trump and the family holdings made out like bandits as they doled out funding, laws, and land. Some of those winners and losers included: "foreign politicians and Florida sugar barons, a Chinese billionaire and a Serbian prince, clean-energy enthusiasts and their adversaries in the petroleum industry, avowed small-government activists and contractors seeking billions from ever-fattening federal budgets."[47]

By September 2020, the missing firewall between his businesses and the presidency had revealed 3,403 conflicts of interest or about 2 conflicts per day. These conflicts included foreign government officials conducting business or staying at Trump properties as well as other taxpayer and campaign spending at Trump businesses. They also involved Trump and family members or other politicos promoting an array of monetizing scams or rackets to raise capital. After 1,341 days in office: 88 political events had been held at Trump properties, including 13 foreign government events; 130 special interest groups events; 145 foreign officials; and 141 members of Congress had visited a Trump business for a total of 344 times. Most of these visits (284) were to the Trump Hotel in DC. Topping the list of pay to play was Senate Judiciary Committee Chairman Lindsey Graham with 27 visits, followed by Sen. Rand Paul (18) and Reps. Matt Gaetz (17), Kevin McCarthy (17), Jim

Jordan (13), and Mark Meadows (13). Not insignificant were the top ten political committees spending money at Trump properties[48]:

1  Trump Victory, $2,282,630
2  Republican National Committee, $2,425,472
3  Donald J. Trump for President, $2,307,127
4  America First Action, $600,322
5  Republican Governors Association, $412,721
6  Great America Committee, $237,967
7  Protect the House, $232,837
8  Senate Leadership Fund, $94,626
9  Republican Attorneys General Association, $85,205
10  National Republican Congressional Committee, $81,367

These tabulated and mutually reinforcing Trumpian interests may only be the tip of the pay-to-play iceberg.

During this period Trump paid 503 visits to Trump businesses mostly to his golf courses (303), costing the American taxpayers at least 1 million dollars spent at the properties as well as more than $100 million to shuttle him to his properties. In addition to Trump, some 334 administration officials visited his properties for a total of 885 times. First family members and senior advisors Jared Kushner and Ivanka Trump visited Trump properties "more than any other executive branch officials with 39 and 36 visits, respectively."[49] Following them were runner ups Vice President Pence with 33 visits, former Counselor to the President Kellyanne Conway with 27 visits, and Secretary of Treasury Steven Mnuchin with 23. Other visitors worthy of "dishonorable" mention were Wilbur Ross (19), Dan Scavino (19), Mick Mulvaney (18), Richard Grenell (17), and Sarah Huckabee Sanders (17).

Finally, 145 foreign officials from 75 governments had visited Trump properties with officials from Turkey leading the pack. At Trump's vaunted "Winter White House," Mar-a-Lago, the former president had hosted Chinese President Xi Jinping, the then-Japanese Prime Minister Shinzo Abe, and lastly the former President of Brazil, Jair Bolsonaro, and a slew of his Brazilian officials.[50] The Xi visit was the most successful promotional event in the history of Mar-a-Lago and an unparalleled moneymaker for Trump.[51]

## Anti-Democracy Corruption for Profit

As far as Donald Trump's lifelong schemes of conning goes probably none have been as financially rewarding to Trump as when he has run for the presidency of the United States. In this regard, I am more than speculating that Trump has both legitimately and illegitimately pocketed hundreds of millions of US dollars, Russian rubles, Saudi riyals, Emirati dirhams, Chinese renminbi, and even a few Euros tossed in for good measure. In between in his failed 2020 re-election campaign and the announcement of his 2024 bid for the presidency, on the afternoon of July 21, 2021, I received an email invitation from the Republican National Committee HQ informing me: "Gregg, Thanks to your loyal support of YOUR Party, you already PRE-QUALIFY to become an **Official 2021 Trump Life Member,** no application necessary." The body of the email read: "Once you join, you'll be a part of the most critical group of conservatives helping to push back against the constant LIES coming from Joe Biden and his allies in the Liberal News Media." The email finished, "We plan to finalize the membership roster soon, don't miss your chance to be included." All I had to do was make a modest contribution by 11:59 p.m. Even when I missed the deadline and after I had unsuccessfully unsubscribed daily for seven weeks, I was still receiving my "last chances" to become an official 2021 Trump member for life.

One of Trump's best grifts was the Big Steal that yielded Trump $75 million in the first six months of 2021. The fraudulent operation, Save America, was a leadership PAC that Trump created in the aftermath of the 2020 not "stolen election." In less than seven weeks, it amassed $31.2 million. And in less than eight months, the PAC raised more than $100 million. But wait folks that's not all. There was also an affiliated joint fundraising committee contributing more money to the Save America scam. This ongoing scam involved the Make America Great Again Committee that was splitting its donations with 75% of the money raised going to Trump's leadership PAC and the remaining 25% going to the Republican National Coalition for Life. So, add another $50 million to the $31 million by the end of 2020.[52] Additionally, during the first six months of 2021, Save America paid for lodging nine times at properties owned by Trump for a scant $68,000. Meanwhile, Make America Great Again spent about $200,000 on office and restaurant space in Trump Tower. Another Trump-backed PAC overseen by Corey Lewandowski one of his three campaign managers during the 2016 race paid $21,810 to rent space at the Trump National Golf Club in Bedminster, NJ.[53] According to ProPublica, these Republican campaign groups had paid about $348,000 to Trump properties in the first six months of 2021.[54]

Although Trump cannot legally spend the PAC cash directly on his 2024 campaign, he did use some of it to back election-denying candidates in the 2022-midterm elections. He also used this money to pay for some of his political co-conspirator's legal bills, to travel the country on his Boeing 757 Trump Force One, and to cover some of his own fees for multiple lawsuits. Trump's "slush fund" was also used as a revenue stream to cover his daily expenses that were spent at his own properties. As for his spending political money on other candidates or on his efforts to steal the elections in Arizona, Pennsylvania, Michigan, and Georgia, these expenditures were mostly for feeding the election lies and casting doubt on the integrity of the not rigged

2020 election.[55] At the same time, whatever Trump did not spend of other people's money on attorneys or other political candidates simply found its way into his baggy trousers.

The Capitol assault on January 6 was certainly one of his biggest moneymaking scams and helped Trump solidify his control over the Republican Party. At the other end of the financial ledger, the income from Trump's seditious activities and other political business dealings were being offset by his accumulating deficits from his more traditional businesses that started heading south during the early days of the 2016 campaign along with the loss increasingly of merchandising deals. Throughout the presidency the loss of his branding and management agreements continued and reached a low ebb when a wave of partners vowed to no longer do business with him after the Capitol attack.

To paraphrase Abraham Lincoln: "You can con all the people some of the time and some of the people all the time, but you cannot con all the people all the time." As for conning some of the people all the time I would not have believed it until Trump and his sycophantic cult followers proved otherwise. In a similar vein, while the Houdini of White-Collar and Organized Crime is the virtuoso of the con, he is also the connoisseur of corruption – a dynamic duo to say the least. Speaking of or exposing grand corruption on a Trumpian scale especially the sustainable and long-lasting kind becomes an exercise in identifying the small and overlapping elite networks of wealth, power, and privilege.

As Rajan explains these

> networks drive all criminal activity – from terrorist financing to manipulation of huge tax write-offs through shell companies and offshore accounts to protect ill-gotten wealth. Over time, laws may be changed to normalize these activities and to legalize the laundered financing of political campaigns, which entrenches white-collar criminal control of democracy.[56]

This political economy of social control and grand corruption is not importantly limited to those individual bureaucrats and politicians who episodically distort public goods for private gain. Rather, this is a global network of social relations in which inner circles of "prominent and wealthy individuals, political machines, and corporations may be involved in deceiving the public over a much longer time than a mere election cycle."[57] As many readers are probably aware, *Citizens United vs. Federal Election Commission* (2010) ruled to remove any limits on financial contributions from corporations to political campaigns. This terrible ruling by SCOTUS predictably amplified the scope of parties both left and right colluding with big business and resulting in the obscene kinds of spending on elections.

## Trump's Linked Elite Networks of Global Wealth and Power

What do the people listed below and the US nationals have in common? First, they are all part of the overlapping global networks of wealth and power linked to Donald Trump. Second, with the exceptions of Rudy Giuliani and Jared Kushner who have also been under investigation by various law enforcement agencies for similarly related activities, the rest either plead guilty or were convicted for crimes investigated by Robert Mueller except for Parnas and Fruman who plead guilty to other criminal matters and served short sentences in prison. Barrack was prosecuted and acquitted of other criminal matters discussed below. Before leaving high office Boss Trump pardoned several of his most loyal soldiers including Manafort, Flynn, Bannon, and Stone. One person who received a pardon from Trump on his last full day as President was Elliott Broidy.[58]

Broidy who had been a former top Republican fundraiser on March 30, 2023, was described as the "fixer" by Assistant US Attorney Nicole R. Lockhart in court, during one of many legally related cases arising from the looting of roughly $4.5 billion from Malaysia's state-owned investment and development fund. Lockhart explained further that Broidy had sought to use "his access to President Donald Trump in 2018 to advance one of several conspiracies tied to thievery [and money laundering] in Malaysia."[59] It was after Broidy pleaded guilty to illegally lobbying for foreign nationals in one of those corruption cases that Trump pardoned him. That was also after the Los Angeles-based investor and Trump fundraiser "in the wake of a report that he had paid a former Playboy model $1.6 million in exchange for her silence about a sexual affair" – arranged for by none other than Trump's personal attorney, Michael Cohen – "had resigned his position as deputy chairman for the Republican National Committee."[60]

However, political crimes and criminals like himself were not the only persons that Trump pardoned as political pay offs or for economic gain.[61] For example, back on February 18, 2020, President Trump "pardoned seven people and commuted the sentences of four others." By pardoning these white-collar criminals like Illinois governor Rod Blagojevich or former owner of the San Francisco 49ers Edward DeBartolo Jr., Trump was normalizing white-collar criminals while messaging "to the public that white-collar crime is just the 'price of doing business'."[62]

Team USA and Their Foreign Connections
George Papadopoulos, USA (Russia)
Paul Manafort, USA (Ukraine, Russia)
Michael Flynn, USA (Turkey)
Michael Cohen, USA (Russia)
Rick Gates, USA (Ukraine, Russia)

Steve Bannon, USA (Europe, Middle East)
Rudolph Giuliani, USA (Ukraine)
Jared Kushner, USA (Israel, Saudi Arabia)
Lev Parnas, USA (Ukraine)
Igor Fruman, USA (Ukraine)
Richard Pinedo, USA (Russia)
Roger Stone, USA (Europe)
Tom Barrack, USA (United Arab Emirates, Qatar)
Elliott Broidy, USA (Malaysia)
Indicted Foreign Nationals
13 Russian nationals, 12 GRU officers of the Russian military, and three
    Russian companies were all indicted, however, their lawsuits will never
    materialize.
Konstantin Kilimnik, a Ukrainian national (now living in Russia) was
    indicted along with Manafort and Gates, but the former will never find
    his way to trial.
Heads of Foreign States
Recep Tayyip Erdoğan, President of Turkey (Flynn)
Mohammed bin Salman, Crown Prince of Saudi Arabia (Kushner and DJT)
Vladimir Putin, President of Russia (Donald Trump)
Khalifa bin Zayed bin Sultan Al Nahyan, President of United Arab
    Emirates (Barrack)

One of those US citizens in the overlapping networks not convicted of a crime on behalf of Trump was Tom Barrack. Barrack was a senior adviser to the 2016 presidential campaign and chair of the 2017 inaugural committee. Barrack was not indicted for a series of related crimes until six months after Trump left office.[63] He was arrested July 20, 2021, on charges that he secretly acted in the United States as an agent for the United Arab Emirates. On November 4, 2022, a jury found Barrack not guilty of foreign lobbying and lying to the FBI.[64] The "sealed" federal indictment from US District Court of New York accused the 74-year-old Barrack of failing to register as a foreign agent, conspiracy, obstruction of justice, and four counts of making false statements to the FBI. He was no doubt acting secretly and not registering as an agent of a foreign government. But he was not acting without the knowledge of Trump. Quite the contrary. The two were in cahoots and have been bosom buddies for about three decades. Donald's long-time dirty trickster and collaborator Roger Stone has described Barrack as Trump's best friend. In the summer of 2016 Paul Manafort became Trump's second campaign manager on the recommendation of Barrack.

What is less known about Thomas Joseph Barrack, Jr., is that he made his fortune as an American private equity real estate investor in the Middle East and elsewhere. More specifically, in June 2018 *The NY Times* reported that Barrack's company "raised more than $7 billion in investments since Mr. Trump won the nomination" and that "about a quarter came from the Emirates and Saudi Arabia."[65] Hence, the $250 million bond secured by $5 million in cash to get out of jail was chump change for Barrack. For what it is worth, the "judge also ordered Barrack to wear a GPS location monitoring bracelet, barred him from transferring any funds overseas and restricted his travel to parts of Southern California and New York."[66]

In 1991 Barrack founded and became the executive chairman of the publicly traded Colony Capital, Inc. and subsequently Colony NorthStar. He divested all interests in 2019 and stepped down from his executive role in March 2021.[67] In 2016, Colony managed more than $58 billion in assets making it the fifth largest real estate company in the world. In 2017, Colony agreed to invest in The Weinstein Company to keep it afloat after the scandal broke about Harvey Weinstein's sexual misconduct. Barrack also helped rescue Trump's real estate empire back in the 1990s. In 2010, Barrack bought $70 million of Jared Kushner's debt on 666 Fifth Avenue. Most recently at the request of Trump, he agreed to reduce Jared's obligations to avoid bankruptcy.[68] Barrack was also Trump's top fundraiser for the 2016 campaign and gave more than $750,000 of his own money. Always preferring to remain his own person and behind the scenes, Barrack allegedly turned down a Cabinet position and he could also have been the White House chief of staff.[69]

To give the reader a sense of the indictment I quote from page 4, section IV. The Defendants' Actions in the United States as Agent of the United Arab Emirates, paragraph 13 reads:

> Government officials in the United Arab Emirates, including Emirati Official 1, Emirati Official 2, Emirati Official 3 and Emirati Official 4 tasked the defendants RASHID SULTAN RASHID AL MALIK ALSHAHHL, THOMAS JOSEPH BARRACK and MATTHREW GRIMES with, variously and among other things, (a) influencing public opinion, the foreign policy positions of the Campaign and the foreign policy positions of the United States government; (b) obtaining information about foreign policy positions and related decision-making within the Campaign and, at times, the United States government; (c) developing a back channel line of communication with the Campaign and, at times, officials of the United States government; and (d) developing plans to increase the United Arab Emirates' political influence and to promote its foreign policy preferences.

It is worth noting that Barrack and his two co-defendants were not charged with the more customary foreign-agent statute, the Foreign Agents Registration Act (FARA), but with "a lesser-known statue typically used to charge individuals accused of working at the direction of senior officials of a foreign government."[70] Unlike FARA the foreign-agent statue used for Barrack and company does not require proof that the defendants knew that their conduct was illegal. The prosecutor Mack Jenkins handling the bail hearings in Los Angeles where the three defendants had been living stated that the infrequently used foreign-agent statute reflected the elite circles involved: "We're talking about the highest levels at the UAE and the highest levels of the United States."[71] To repeat Barrack and his two co-defendants were not found guilty of being foreign agents.

Going forward with Barrack's prosecution apparently never raised questions involving another meeting at Trump Tower that occurred in August 2016 with Trump campaign officials. This meeting was not with Russians as the one that had occurred two months earlier in June. This meeting was between Donald Trump, Jr., George Nader at the time an advisor to Crown Prince Mohammed bin Zayed, the Emirates' de factoruler, and Joel Zamel, owner of an Israeli private intelligence company, Psy-Group, which had been discussed in a bipartisan US Senate Select Committee on Intelligence report about Russian election interference.[72] If the allegations in Barrack's indictment were true that Zamel was paid more than 1 million dollars for social media work done on behalf of Nader, "it means that while an adviser to the Emirates was offering Trump campaign election help, an Emirati agent was also shaping Trump's foreign policy, even inserting the country's preferred language into one of the candidate's speeches."[73] As Michelle Goldberg has written:

> Trump could scarcely have been a more accommodating ally to the Emirates and to Saudi Arabia, whose crown prince Mohammed bin Salman, was a protégé of Prince Mohammed bin Zayed. Trump's first foreign trip as president was to Saudi Arabia. He tore up the Iran deal, hated by Gulf leaders. Of Trump's 10 vetoes five dealt with concerns of the Emirates and Saudi Arabia. More significantly, he overrode Congress's attempt to end American military involvement in Yemen, where Saudi Arabia and the Emirates were fighting on one side of a brutal civil war.[74]

Aside from his overlapping networks of grand corruption, the routinization of corruption by Trump as a moneymaking enterprise is second to no other administration. Trump is in a league of his own; no other president is remotely close. Recall, for example, that Trump boasted in his recorded interviews with Bob Woodward for *Rage* that he had saved the Saudi crown prince after his agents murdered the *Washington Post* reporter and Saudi dissident Jamal Khashoggi.[75] I cannot imagine any future president coming along, no matter how full of conflicts of interest, ever giving the King-of-Corruption a run for anyone else's money. At the website Republic Report, a rank ordering of the 50 most disgraceful people in the Trump administration has the Donald finishing in first place with the following description:

> a shameless liar and con man, ugly racist and misogynist, vile coronavirus spreader, despicable attacker of the press and whistleblowers, amoral admirer of autocrats, erratic, ignorant, incompetent, pathetic narcissist, enabler of global climate disaster, corrupt, and kleptocratic abuser of the Constitution.[76]

Similarly, in an investigation of how money corrupts democracy, David Halperin posted at Republic Report, the Ten Reasons Trump is the Most Corrupt President in US History[77]:

1 Trump broke his promise to drain the swamp as he made it dirtier by giving top administration jobs to blatant grifters, such as Scott Pruitt, Ryan Zinke, Tom Price, Diane Auer Jones, and Mike Pompeo.
2 Trump while in office had personally pocked millions in taxpayer, lobbyist, donor, and foreign dollars; at least $2.5 million to rent high-priced rooms at his company's hotels, for example.
3 Trump corrupted the tax system with his tax cut for the wealthiest people and corporations while bragging about it but paid virtually no taxes of his own at the same time.
4 Trump gutted health care because of his hatred of Obama and did his best to eviscerate the Affordable Care Act, even as the COVID-19 pandemic raged, lying all the while that he had a new and better health plan, which never existed.
5 Trump sacrificed hundreds of thousands of lives to the pandemic because of his re-election strategy that necessitated the covering up and lying about the disease's contagiousness as he and his ilk became the super spreaders of virus and scientific denial.
6 Trump falsely claimed widespread voter fraud and that he won the 2020 election that has undermined the integrity of the US electoral system and has resulted in voter suppression laws passing throughout the nation thanks to Republican-controlled state legislatures.
7 Trump has been an ally of Russian dictator and murderer Vladimir Putin, praising him, endorsing his denials of election interference, and even delaying for months, beyond its legal deadline, the implementation of a bipartisan veto-proof margined bill to impose new sanctions on Russia.
8 Trump repeatedly engaged in the obstruction of justice and Congress with respect to Russia, Ukraine, and other matters, including the firing of several whistleblowers that testified before Congress and he also dismissed five inspector generals who were each investigating administration misconduct.

9  Trump and his hatched man Attorney General William Barr turned the US Department of Justice into an apparatus for doing the former president's corrupt bidding on behalf of his political allies and against his political enemies all the way up to the lost election and after only parting ways with the Donald in late December 2020.

10  Trump has driven racism and racist violence with far too many examples to enumerate here, including remarks to disparage Muslims, Mexicans, Black Lives Matter, members of Congress, the media, as well as defending the violent slogans and actions of white supremacists.

Two of the higher-ranking public enemies of Trump who found themselves caught in the cross-hairs of the former president's corruption and weaponization were former FBI Director Jim Comey and acting Director Andrew McCabe and their wives who came under scrutiny by the IRS for 2017 when they refused to do Trump's bidding. As Joyce Vance has asked, "What are the odds" that both of these families would have found themselves audited when only about 5,000 out of 153 million taxpayers a year undergo such auditing?[78] Other forms of abuse of power and corruption included Trump's firing of whistleblowers or folks like his second attorney general Sessions who would not do his bidding, or his removing of security clearances from people like former CIA Director John Brennan who had become an outspoken critic of President Trump.

The bottom line is that Donald Trump has been an "all-purpose" facilitator of corruption because of his acute dishonesty, unwavering fraudulent conduct, habitual abuse of power, and exceptional abilities to debase and transform any "good" or "bad" things to the "worst" of things from individuals to norms and institutions. Tucker Carlson had summed Trump up nicely or best when he stated well before January 6 that the man was "a demonic force."

### The Tax Audits that Never Were and the Tax Fraud that Got Away?

Trump's tax returns for six years including four while he was President were finally made public when the House Ways and Means Committee voted to release them along partisan lines on December 20, 2022. Trump had claimed since the 2016 presidential campaign and throughout his presidency that he was being audited and could not release his tax returns. Turns out that was one of the half-truths that Trump had spoken about to the American people. The Liar-in-Chief was in fact "still embroiled in an audit from 2009, with the IRS questioning the validity of a $72.9 million tax refund he received after declaring huge losses," and according to the New York Times, Trump "could end up owing more than $100 million," more cash than he probably has on hand.[79] In any case, an audit of any kind would not have prevented Trump from releasing his tax returns if he chose to. Of course, an interesting question remains as to why a dispute over $100 million between Trump and the IRS was still unresolved after 12 years?

Trump has never wanted to share his less-than-truthful tax returns with anyone let alone the American people as these are not apt to reflect favorably on the fraudster of a businessperson that he has always been. During the Trump administration, the IRS had no interest apparently in examining the president's tax filings until such time as the Ways and Means Committee Chairman Richard E. Neal (D, MA) sent a written request in April 2019 to obtain those records from the IRS. Ways and Means had suspected that Trump was not being audited even though tax audits of sitting presidents and vice presidents had been mandated since 1977, though yet to be codified in law.[80] With the court-ordered release of his tax returns, the world had learned that this committee had been correct in their suspicions.

Only in his third year of office on the very same day as the IRS received Neal's request did the IRS begin an audit which it never finished of Trump's tax returns. The IRS did not even bother to begin an audit of Trump's fourth year in office. Thus, Trump became the first and only POTUS since Jimmy Carter became the first President subject to annual mandatory audit reviews of his tax returns not to be audited once, let alone, four times for one term in office. This was the case even though, for example, the returns that the IRS possessed "showed there were 'tens of millions of dollars' in deductions 'claimed without any adequate substantiation.'"[81] Not to mention the fact that Trump and the Trump Organization had previously been punished for financial fraud on at least two occasions before becoming President and were also undergoing several pending criminal investigations for tax fraud. Call this another case of the lawlessness of the powerful residing beyond incrimination.

From the moment the IRS had received the letter from Ways and Means, Trump was doing everything in his power not to release or at least to delay his tax returns from being released to the House oversight committee as required by protocol, including appealing the request all the way up to the Supreme Court. Three and one-half years later after Trump announced his 2024 presidential run, SCOTUS finally ruled in November 2022 without giving any reason that Trump had to comply with the law and release his tax records to the Democrats who still controlled the House for only a few more weeks. Once the Republicans took back control of the House in January 2023, Ways and Means ignored the non-audits of Trump's suspicious tax returns just as the GOP has ignored the former president's failed insurrection, which several of them were a party to, including some of his inner circle who ignored their Congressional subpoenas to testify before the January 6th Committee.

Trump's tax returns for 2015–2020 raised the same types of concerns that his tax returns raised decades earlier when he paid zero dollars in federal taxes in 1978 and again in 1979 by way of real estate depreciation on those two occasions. Recall during the 2016 presidential debates when Hillary Clinton called Trump out for not paying federal income taxes for those two years, Trump responded "That makes me smart." It could make one smart, but in Trump's case it also makes him a crook. As his former attorney Michael Cohen testified before the House Oversight Committee in February 2019, Trump had once shown Cohen a big refund from the IRS stating that he "could not believe how stupid the government was for giving someone like him that much money back."[82] And when Clinton next "speculated that Trump might not have paid 'any federal income tax for a lot of years'" – which turned out to be the case – Trump said the government would have "squandered" the money anyway.[83] Another area in which Trump has expertise as he ran up the US deficit to an all-time high.

Trump's business model has always included a wide array of questionable credits and deductions, including those for charitable contributions, debts, business expenses, and conservation easements on his golf courses and other properties. Concerning recent examples, the IRS

> had begun to examine a number of these items, such as tax credits the Trumps claimed related to his development of the Trump International Hotel in D.C. and a $21 million payment the Trumps made to settle fraud claims against his online school, Trump University.[84]

Meanwhile, the released tax returns show that Donald and Melania Trump had lost more than $75 million and reported positive total income to the IRS in two out of six years.

Only in his second and third year of the presidency were the Trumps in the black. In 2018 and 2019, they reported income of $24.4 million and $4.4 million. Interestingly, it turns out the income from 2018 was the result of Trump selling off the last properties of his father's real estate empire. Revealing once again that Trump's businesses have always lost a ton of money, and that his wealth has always been his father's money. In 2015, 2016, 2017, and 2020, they reported losing $31.7 million, $32.2 million, $12.8 million, and $4.7 million. By claiming millions in deductions without any documentation, the Trumps reduced the net federal income taxes they paid to $750 in 2016 and 2017 and $0 in 2020. This snapshot into Trump's complicated taxes once again reveals that Trump's businesses have always lost a ton of money – hundreds of millions – and that his wealth has always one way or the other been a product of gifts, unpaid loans, or inherited money from his father who passed in 1999.[85]

The unaudited tax returns without any of the backup information customarily provided to prove the legitimacy of one's claims should have raised many red flags. Including those identified by the House's nonpartisan Joint Committee on Taxation, such as questionable "charitable" contributions, "loans" to his children that might have been taxable gifts, or "business" expenses that look like personal hobbies.[86] After the tax returns were finally returned to Ways and Means by the IRS revealing its own gross failures to perform its due diligence with the clock running out of time to investigate the matter further turns out we may never learn the truth behind Trump's tax returns. Many unanswered questions remain about the sources of Trump's revenues, the validity of the numbers submitted, and his egregious patterns of tax evasion.

Some light was cast upon Trump's post-presidency business dealings on April 14, 2023, when he was compelled to release a personal financial discloser after having requested multiple extensions. Warned that he would be fined if he failed to file within 30 days, he did so 28 days later. As required by the Federal Election Commission, the financial disclosure reveals the cumulative income from January 2021 to December 15, 2022, and the value of assets on the latter date. Among several takeaways from the 101-page filing according to *The NY Times* was that it was "light on specifics," and notably that the parent company of Truth Social had taken a big valuation hit, valued at between $5 million and $25 million considerably less than when Trump Media & Technology Group announced its merger with Digital World Acquisition Company, and estimated potential valuation of $9 billion back in October 2021.[87]

Other takeaways included that Trump's online trading cards showed that early sales were underwhelming. Trump paid off several outstanding loans valued at more than $50 million on the Trump Tower and Trump Doral, a golf club outside of Miami, the single-biggest revenue-generating property owned by the Trump family. He also took out similar loans on these properties for some $50 million dollars that seemed to be a wash. Trump also listed more than $200 million in debts. Trump was starting to make money listed as more than $5 million as first payments for a new deal backed by a Saudi Arabia-based real estate investment firm to build a new golf and hotel complex in Oman. Finally, with little specifics Melania Trump reported a fresh revenue stream of collectibles on the conservative social media site Parler, monetizing her ties to Trump and the White House.[88]

## Weaponizing the US Department of Justice

To grasp the corruption and criminality of Trumpworld at home and abroad, it helps to provide a portfolio of persons who have taken a criminal fall since the former president announced his candidacy in 2015. By the 2020 presidential election, at least 18 shady figures in the president's orbit had either been arrested or gone to jail on charges from fraud to battery to child pornography. Of course, those numbers pale in comparison to the more than 950 people who were arrested after the January 6 Capitol assault or to the 192 who had been sentenced to incarceration for an average of 16 months by January 2023.[89] Nor do these figures include those members of the Oath Keepers and the Proud Boys who were convicted of the serious crimes of "seditious conspiracy."

Prior to the January 6 assaults on the capitol, many of those criminal charges stemmed from former Special Counsel Robert Mueller's investigation into Russian election interference in 2016. When it comes to the investigation into the Russian investigation in particular[90] or to attorney general corruption in general,[91] Trump's third and last attorney general stands in a league of his own as a political "fixer" on behalf of a POTUS. Attorney General Bill Barr should have been impeached and disbarred for all his unethical, if not criminal, intervention at the Justice Department and elsewhere on behalf of conspiracy theories and the Trumpian narrative. Egged on by a regular litany of grievances from the former president about "witch hunts" beginning with the Mueller investigation, Barr "set out in 2019 to dig into their shared theory that the Russian investigation likely stemmed from a conspiracy by intelligence or law enforcement agencies" to go after Trump.[92]

Leading Barr's inquiry was the "hard-nosed" prosecutor John H. Durham who was subsequently granted Special Counsel status. After three years of investigation, he had failed to develop a single case that resulted in any convictions. In October 2022, the only indicted and tried analyst, Igor Danchenko, who had provided much of the research in the dossier involved in the Russian investigation was acquitted on four counts of lying to the FBI about one of his sources.[93] After almost four years – far longer than the Russia investigation itself – Mr. Durham's work was "coming to an end without uncovering anything like the deep state plot alleged by Mr. Trump and suspected by Mr. Barr."[94] Durham's final report of 303 pages released in May 2023 was critical of some FBI behavior and yet made no recommendations for reform. No matter the Department of Justice (DOJ) was already aware of some of those criticisms and had already made changes. What is most interesting about Durham's failed inquiry to find any wrongdoing in the origins of the Russia investigation came from a trip to Italy taken together by Durham and Barr. While searching for evidence against the legitimacy of the Russian probe they stumbled into evidence of another kind when they were tipped off by Italian officials about international crimes allegedly involving Donald Trump.

One year into the Durham inquiry, Barr declared that the attempt "to get to the bottom of what happened" in 2016 "cannot be, and it will not be, a tit-for-tat exercise. We are not going to lower the standards just to achieve a result."[95] More than two years later, investigative reporting by *The NY Times* revealed that the Durham inquiry had fractured and was "roiled by internal dissent and ethical disputes as it went unsuccessfully down one path after another even as Mr. Trump and Mr. Barr promoted a misleading narrative of its progress."[96] The former attorney general and the former president even contemplated issuing a misleading interim report two months before the 2020 presidential election but were persuaded otherwise.

When the curtains are drawn back on Durham's investigation into Mueller's investigation, there is no real irony here that what Trump and Barr were doing was precisely what Trump is always guilty of doing. Namely, "calling the kettle black" and projecting his weaponizing and criminality onto others. Here are three incriminating illustrations from the Durham inquiry:

- Mr. Barr and Mr. Durham never disclosed that their inquiry expanded in the fall of 2019, based on a tip from Italian officials, to include a criminal investigation into suspicious financial dealings related to Mr. Trump. The specifics of the tip and how they handled the investigation remain unclear, but Mr. Durham brought no charges over it.
- Mr. Durham used Russian intelligence memos – suspected by other US officials of containing disinformation – to gain access to emails of an aide to George Soros, the financier and philanthropist, who is a favorite target of the American right and the Russian state media. Mr. Durham used grand jury powers to keep pursuing the emails even after a judge twice rejected this request for access to them. The emails yielded no evidence that Mr. Durham cited in any case he pursued.
- There were deeper internal fractures on the Durham team than previously known. The publicly unexplained resignation in 2020 of his No. 2 and longtime aide, Nora R. Dannehy, was the culmination of a series of disputes between them over prosecutorial ethics. A year later, two more prosecutors strongly objected to plans to indict a lawyer with ties to Hillary Clinton's 2016 campaign based on evidence they warned was too flimsy, and one left the team in protest of Mr. Durham's decision to proceed anyway. A jury swiftly acquitted the lawyer.[97]

### A Postscript on "Anti-Corruption" as an Instrument of Political Exploitation

While this chapter has drilled down on numerous examples of concrete corruption, anthropological theories maintain that corruption should not be restricted by its provincial or puritanical connotations alone. This is because traditional models of legal, political, and economic corruption, despite explaining certain material facets of corruption, do not explain the roots of corruption as part of the larger culture of belief in corruption. Nor why corruption is so broadly accepted politically. Finally, they do not explain the "growing influence of corruption in today's public arena, with, most of the times, a detrimental effect on democracy by populistic politicians/governments."[98]

Anthropologists also maintain that corruption is something more subtle and complex. Like a conversation, a ritual, or a form of cultural exchange in society: "a polysemic relationship and an important part of the way in which individuals connect with the state." They continue that corruption and its rejection expressed by the discourse of "anti-corruption" have become the "most utilized and instrumentalized in the political arena." Hence, those politicians, even the most lawless, corrupt, and unethical like Donald Trump who have captured the cultural belief in, or the narrative of, anti-corruption are in excellent positions to effectively exploit this anti-corruption political-economic discourse most as an instrument of subversive power over democracy and the rule of law.[99]

Whether in psychoanalytic or social-psychological terms, this type of association, belonging, or connection with the state or the public arena provides individuals with a sublimation, a compensation, and/or a release of sorts from their alienation from work, community, and themselves. In part three of this book, I will return to these ideas of social order and social change as these intersect with American mythology, partisan politics, bipartisan alienation, and the need for a new constitutional democracy.

## Notes

1  Andrea Bernstein. 2020. *American Oligarchs: The Kushners, the Trumps, and the Marriage of Money and Power*. New York: W.W. Norton & Company. See also Casey Michel. 2021. *American Kleptocracy: How the U.S. Created the World's Greatest Money Laundering Scheme in History*. New York: St. Martin's Press.
2  Rae Hodge. 2023. Court proceedings reveal MBS paid Trump "millions in the past two years": Human rights group. *Salon*. January 17. www.salon.com/2023/01/17/proceedings-reveal-mbs-paid-millions-in-the-past-two-years-human-rights-group/
3  Thom Hartmann. 2023. How Kushner and Trump sold out America for billions while the media looked the other way. *Raw Story*. March 10. www.rawstory.com/raw-investigates/kushner-trump/
4  Tim Adams. 2023. Bernie Sanders: 'Oligarch run Russia. But guess what? They run the US as well'. *The Guardian*. February 19. www.theguardian.com/us-news/2023/feb/19/bernie-sanders-oligarchs-ok-angry-about-capitalism-interview
5  Bernie Sanders. 2023. *It's OK to be Angry about Capitalism*. New York: Crown, p. 176.
6  Ibid., p. 4.
7  Mykhailo Minakov. 2021. Fighting oligarchy or the oligarchs? Focus Ukraine. *Wilson Center* Blog Post. June 30. www.wilsoncenter.org/blog-post/fighting-oligarchy-or-oligarchs

8 Betsy McKay and Danny Dougherty. 2022. The orbit of sanctions around Vladimir Putin. *The Wall Street Journal*. April 15. www.wsj.com/articles/the-orbit-of-sancti ons-around-vladimir-putin-11650015002?mod=article_inline

9 Ibid.

10 Andrew Cohen. 2022. Commentary. *The Marshall Project*. November 28. https:// mail.yahoo.com/d/folders/1/messages/AJ-jSFAvYvb4Y4SmUQMsgMXFfB8

11 Minakov. 2021.

12 World Population Review. 2023. Oligarchy Countries. https://worldpopulatio nreview.com/country-rankings/oligarchy-countries

13 Michel. 2021, pp. 219–220.

14 Ibid., p. 221.

15 Ibid.: book jacket.

16 Sarah N. Lynch and Noor Zainab Hussain. 2020. Goldman to pay $3 billion, claw back executive pay over role in 1MDB corruption scandal. *Reuters*. October 22. www.reuters.com/article/goldmansachs-1mdb-settlement

17 Igor Litvinenko and Casey Michel. 2020. Global kleptocracy as an American problem. *Just Security*. December 4. www.justsecurity.org/73599/global-kleptocr acy-as-an-american-problem

18 Sarah Chayes. 2015. *Thieves of State: Why Corruption Threatens Global Security*. New York: W.W. Norton & Company.

19 Daniela Petrova. 2015. Sarah Chayes: Global kleptocracy. *Guernica*. July 15. www.guernicamag.com/global-kleptocracy

20 Michael Johnston. 2005. *Syndromes of Corruption: Wealth, Power, and Democracy*. Cambridge: Cambridge University Press, p. 42.

21 Sudhir Chella Rajan, 2020. *A Social Theory of Corruption: Notes from the Indian Subcontinent*. Cambridge, MA and London: Harvard University Press, pp. x–xi.

22 Gregg Barak, 2017. *Unchecked Corporate Power: Why the Crimes of Multinational Corporations are Routinized Away and What We Can Do about It*. London and New York: Routledge.

23 Joyce Vance. 2022. The week ahead. *Civil Discourse with Joyce Vance*. November 27. https://joycevance.substack.com/p/the-week-ahead-bc3?utm_source=subst ack&utm

24 Associated Press. 2023. Report says Justice Thomas accepted undisclosed luxury trips from Republican donor. *PBS News Hour*. April. 6. www.pbs.org/newshour/ politics/report-says-justice-thomas-accepted-undisclosed-luxury-trips-from-rep ublican-donor

25 Ashley Capoot. 2023. Supreme Court Justice Clarence Thomas reportedly has been claiming thousands of dollars annually from a shuttered real estate firm. *CNBC*. April. 17. www.cnbc.com/2023/04/16/clarence-thomas-has-been-claim ing-thousands-of-dollars-annually-from-a-shuttered-real-estate-firm.html

26 Accountable. 2023. Timeline shows Clarence and Ginni Thomas benefitted from Crow over decades. *Accountable.US*. April 17. https://accountable.us/research/ timeline-shows-clarence-and-ginni-thomas-benefitted-from-crow-over-decades/

27 Paul Waldman, 2020. How Trump's epic corruption reveals hidden weaknesses in the system. *The Washington Post*. October 29. www.washingtonpost.com/ opinions/2020/10/29/how-trumps-epic-corruption-reveals-hidden-weaknesses- system/

28 Ibid.

29 Jim Lardner. 2020. Mapping Corruption: Donald Trump's Executive Branch: An inquiry into how the Trump administration transformed Washington. *The American Prospect.* April 9. https://prospect.org/power/mapping-corruption-donald-trump-executive-branch/

30 Ben Schreckinger, Darren Samuelsohn, Ben Lefebvre, and Caitlin Oprysko. 2019. 2 Giuliani Ukraine associates indicted on campaign finance charges. *Politico.* October 10. www.politico.com/news/2019/10/10/rudy-giuliani-ukraine-associates-indicted-043873

31 Mike McIntire, Russ Buettner and Susanne Craig. 2020. Trump records shed new light on Chinese business pursuits. *The New York Times.* October 20. www.nytimes.com/2020/10/20/us/trump-taxes-china.html

32 During the same period and after, Donald was paying the IRS less than $1000 annually.

33 CREW, 2021. President Trump's legacy of corruption, four years and 3,700 conflicts of interest later. January 15. www.citizensforethics.org/reports-investigations/crew-reports/president-trump-legacy-corruption-3700-conflicts-interest/

34 ISideWith…, ND. Donald Trump's policy on offshore banking. www.isidewith.com/candidates/donald-trump/policies/economic/offshore-banking

35 PBS News Hour. 2016. Trump: The system is rigged against our citizens. July 21. www.youtube.com/watch?v=TExdmFEETPQ

36 Thang Nguyen, 2021. On human decisions with hidden and malicious intent in business and management. *American Letters.* Article 1014. https://dos.org/1020935/AL1014

37 Bernstein. 2020.

38 CREW. 2021.

39 Jon Swaine and Ed Pilkington. 2017. The wealthy men in Trump's inner circle with links to tax havens. *The Guardian.* November 5. www.theguardian.com/news/2017/nov/05/wealthy-men-donald-trump-inner-circle-links-tax-havens

40 Nick Hopkins and Helena Bengtsson. 2017. What are the Paradise Papers and what do they tell us? *The Guardian.* November 5. www.theguardian.com/news/2017/nov/05/what-are-the-paradise-papers-and-what-do-they-tell-us

41 Eric Estevez. 2021. *A review of How Much Trump's Tax Cuts Cost the Government* by *Kimberly Amadeo. The balance.* May 30. www.thebalance.com/cost-of-trump-tax-cuts-4586645

42 Tyler Fisher. 2017. How past income tax rate cuts on the wealthy affected the economy. *Politico.* September 27. www.politico.com/interactives/2017/gop-tax-rate-cut-wealthy/

43 Ibid.

44 Quoted in Thom Hartmann, 2021. How Republicans unleashed a new crime wave in America – through worsening inequality. *Salon.* July 22. www.salon.com/2021/07/22/how-republicans-unleashed-a-new-crime-wave-in-america--through-worsening-inequality_partner/

45 Nicholas Confessors, et al., 2020. The swamp that Trump built. *The New York Times.* October 10. www.nytimes.com/interactive/2020/10/10/us/trump-properties-swamp.html

46 CREW. 2021.

47 Ibid.

48 Ibid.

49 Ibid.

50 Ibid.

51 Sarah Blaskey, Nicholas Nehamas, Caitlin Ostroff, and Jay Weaver. 2020. *The Grifter's Club: Trump, Mar-A-Lago, and the Selling of the Presidency.* New York: Hachette Book Group.

52 Zach Montellaro and Elena Schneider, 2021. Trump stocks new PAC with tens of millions as he bids to retain control of GOP. *Politico.* January 31. www.politico.com/news/2021/01/31/donald-trump-pac-millions-gop-464250

53 Isaac Stanley-Becker and David A. Fahrenthold. 2021. His campaign is over. But Trump's political groups are still spending donor money at his properties. *The Washington Post.* August 1. www.washingtonpost.com/politics/2021/08/01/trump-pacs-hotels-spending/?utm_campaign=wp_post_most&utm_medium=email&utm_source=newsl

54 Derek Willis. 2021. Campaign spending at Trump properties down, but not out. *ProPublica.* July. 20. www.propublica.org/article/campaign-spending-at-trump-properties-down-but-not-out

55 Josh Dawsey and Rosalind S. Helderman, 2021. Trump's PAC collected $75 million this year, but so far the group has not put money into pushing for the 2020 ballot reviews he touts. *Washington Post.* July 22. www.washingtonpost.com/politics/

56 Sudhir Chella Rajan, 2020. *A Social Theory of Corruption: Notes from the Indian Subcontinent.* Cambridge, MA and London: Harvard University Press, p. ix.

57 Ibid.

58 Nicole Lewis, Justin George and Eli Hager. 2021. Trump's pardons show the process had always been broken. *The Marshall Project.* January 19. www.themarshallproject.org/2021/01/19/trump-s-pardons-show-the-process-has-always-been-broken

59 Paul Duggan. 2023. From rap royalty to federal court, Fugees star on trial in financial scheme. *The Washington Post.* March 31. www.washingtonpost.com/dc-md-va/2023/03/31/fugees-pras-michel-trial/

60 Matt Zapotosky. 2018. Ex-Justice Dept. employee admits to aiding lobbying effort meant to shut down Malaysian corruption probe. *The Washington Post.* November 30. www.washingtonpost.com/world/national-security/ex-justice-dept-employee-admits-to-helping-aid-lobbying-effort-meant-to-shut-down-malaysian-corruption-probe

61 Gregg Barak. 2022. *Criminology on Trump*, chapter three. New York and London: Routledge.

62 Stephanie Sarkis. 2020. Trump's pardons are meant to normalize white-collar crime. *Forbes.* February 18. www.forbes.com/sites/stephaniesarkis/2020/02/18/trumps-pardons-are-meant-to-normalize-white-collar-crime

63 On January 22, 2020, the District of Columbia Attorney General Karl Racine sued Trump's Inaugural Committee. The suit alleges that the Committee improperly used nonprofit funds to pay highly inflated prices to the Trump hotel in DC as well as to Ivanka Trump for renting the space and so on.

64 Dareh Gregorian. 2022. Jury finds Trump friend Tom Barrack not guilty of foreign lobbying and lying to FBI. *CNBC.* November 4. www.cnbc.com/2022/11/04/jury-finds-trump-friend-tom-barrack-not-guilty-of-foreign-lobbying-and-lying-to-fbi.html

65 Quoted in Michelle Goldberg. 2021. A foreign agent in Trump's inner circle? *The New York Times*. July 25: SR7.

66 Eric Orden, 2021. Trump ally Tom Barrack strikes a $250 million bail deal to get out of jail. *CNN*. July 23. www.cnn.com/2021/07/23/politics/tom-barrack-bail-hearing/index.html

67 Divorced in 2016 and the father of six, Barrack has been based in Los Angeles. He owns a 1,200-acre mountain ranch near Santa Barbara as well Happy Canyon Vineyards in Happy Canyon and a wine-tasting room in downtown Santa Barbara, California. Notably, Barrack bought a house in 2014 in Santa Monica and "flipped" it for $35 million, the highest price for a residence in the area at the time. In 2017, he purchased a home in Aspen, Colorado, for a modest $15.5 million. Back in 2010 Barrack partnered with Qatar investment authority to purchase Weinstein film production company Miramax for $660 million. Six years later he sold Miramax to the Qatari beIN Media Group at a fourfold profit.

68 David D. Kirkpatrick. 2018. Who is behind Trump's links to Arab Princes? A billionaire friend. *The New York Times*. June 13. www.nytimes.com/2018/06/13/world/middleeast/trump-tom-barrack-saudi.html

69 Michael Kranish. 2017. 'He's better than this,' says Thomas Barrack, Trump's loyal whisperer. *The Washington Post*. October 11. www.washingtonpost.com/politics/hes-better-than-this-says-thomas-barrack-trumps-loyal-whisperer/2017/10/10/067fc776-a215-11e7-8cfe-d5b912fabc99_story.html

70 Josh Gerstein. 2021. Trump adviser Tom Barrack arrested on foreign-agent charges. *Politico*. July 20. www.politico.com/news/2021/07/20/tom-barrack-arrested-foreign-agent-charges-500333?cid=apn

71 Quoted in Ibid.

72 Mark Mazzetti, Ronen Bergman, and David D. Kirkpatrick. 2018. Trump Jr. and other aides met with Gulf emissary offering help to win election. *The New York Times*. May 19. www.nytimes.com/2018/05/19/us/politics/trump-jr-saudi-uae-nader-prince-zamel.html

73 Goldberg. 2021.

74 Ibid.

75 Bob Woodward. 2020. *Rage*. New York: Simon and Schuster.

76 David Halperin. 2020. Final Reckoning: The 50 Most Disgraceful People of the Trump Administration ranked seventh through second as follows: Mike Pence, Vice President of the United States; Lindsey Graham, chairman, Senate Judiciary Committee; Rudy Giuliani, outside counsel to President Trump; Mike Pompeo, Secretary of State; William Barr, Attorney General; and Mitch McConnell, Senate Majority Leader.
Republic Report. www.republicreport.org/2020/final-reckoning-the-50-most-disgraceful-people-of-the-trump-administration/

77 I have condensed the ten reasons' sections into single sentences from David Halperin's 2020 post. www.republicreport.org/2020/ten-reasons-trump-is-the-most-corrupt-president-in-u-s-history/

78 Joyce Vance. 2023. Rudy, Rudy, Rudy, Do You Love Me? *Civil Discourse*. July 8. https://joycevance.substack.com/p/rudy-rudy-rudy-do-you-love-me

79 Quoted in Heather Digby Parton. 2022. Trump and the IRS: A massive tax cheat and a hapless, corrupt agency. *Salon*. December 21. www.salon.com/2022/12/21/and-the-irs-a-massive-cheat-and-a-hapless-corrupt-agency/

80 Michael Kranish, Jonathan O'Connell, Amy B. Wang, Azi Paybarah, and Marianna Sotomayor. 2022 House committee votes to make public Trump's tax returns. *The Washington Post*. December 21. www.washingtonpost.com/politics/2022/12/20/trump-tax-returns-house-democrats/

81 Quoted in Ibid.

82 Quoted in Parton. 2022.

83 Ibid.

84 Kranish et al., 2022.

85 Gregg Barak. 2022. *Criminology on Trump*. New York & London: Rutledge.

86 Catherine Rampell. 2022. Why did the IRS drop the ball on Trump's tax audits? *The Washington Post*. December 22. www.washingtonpost.com/opinions/2022/12/22/irs-trump-tax-return-enforcement-timid/

87 Michael C. Bender, Eric Lipton, Matthew Goldstein, and Ken Bensinger. 2023. Six takeaways from Trump's new financial disclosure. *The New York Times*. April 14. www.nytimes.com/2023/04/14/us/politics/trump-personal-financial-disclosure.html

88 Ibid.

89 Dinah Voyles Pulver and Doug Caruso. 2023. More than 950 people have been charged in the Jan. 6 Capitol riot, but investigation 'far from over'. *USA Today*. January 6. www.usatoday.com/story/news/politics/2023/01/06/how-many-people-charged-jan-6-riot/10965483002/

90 Charlie Savage, Adam Goldman, and Katie Benner. 2023. How Barr's quest to find flaws in the Russia inquiry unraveled. *The New York Times*. January 26. www.nytimes.com/2023/01/26/us/politics/durham-trump-russia-barr.html

91 Jake Laperruque. 2020. Injustice: Tracking Bill Barr's misconduct as Attorney General. *Pogo*. September 25. www.pogo.org/analysis/2020/09/injustice-tracking-bill-barrs-misconduct-as-attorney-general

92 Savage et al., 2023.

93 Charlie Savage and Linda Qiu. 2022. Acquittal of Russia analyst deals final blow to Trump-Era prosecutor. *The New York Times*. October 18. www.nytimes.com/2022/10/18/us/politics/igor-danchenko-russia-acquittal-trump.html.

94 Ibid.

95 CBS News. 2020. Barr doesn't expect investigations of Obama, Biden stemming from Russia review. www.youtube.com/watch

96 Savage et al., 2023.

97 Ibid.

98 Fernando Forattini. 2021. For a broader understanding of corruption as a cultural fact, and its Influence in Society. *Academic Letters*, Article 2245. http://doi.org/10.20935/AL2245

99 Ibid.

# 4

# ON THE DIVIDED HOUSE SELECT COMMITTEE INVESTIGATION OF THE CAPITOL ASSAULT

BENNIE G. THOMPSON Mississippi, Chairman
LIZ CHENEY Wyoming, Vice Chair
ZOE LOFGREN California
ADAM B. SCHIFF California
PETE AGUILAR California
STEPHANIE N. MURPHY Florida
JAMIE RASKIN Maryland
ELAINE G. LURIA Virginia
ADAM KINZINGER Illinois

House Resolution 503 instructed the Select Committee to "investigate and report upon the facts, circumstances, and causes relating to the January 6, 2021, domestic terrorist attack upon the United States Capitol Complex" and to "Issue a final report, containing findings, conclusions, and recommendations for corrective measures."[1] The Final Report of the Select Committee became a comprehensive amalgamation of more than 800 pages inclusive of the preliminaries, executive summary, narrative, recommendations, and appendices. During the first nine public hearings, the Select Committee hereafter referred to as the Committee presented testimony from more than four dozen Republicans from Trumpworld. These included two of President Trump's former Attorney Generals, his former White House Counsel, numerous members of his White House staff, and the highest-ranking members of his 2020 election campaign, such as the campaign manager and campaign general counsel. All totaled the Committee staff, contractors, and consultants had examined more than a million documents, and the principal

DOI: 10.4324/9781003390664-6

investigators had interviewed more than 1,000 people who were directly or indirectly involved in the Capitol insurrection.

Many of the witnesses who were subpoenaed to testify invoked their Fifth Amendment rights not to answer some of or all the questions posed. For example, two days after the final hearing the Committee released the transcripts of 34 witnesses who had "asserted their Fifth Amendment rights during all or at least part of their testimony."[2] Among those invoking the Fifth were Trump-aligned attorneys Jenna Ellis and John Eastman, Department of Justice (DOJ) official Jeffrey Clark, adviser Roger Stone, former national security adviser Michael Flynn, and conspiracy theorist Alex Jones. Several other Republican Party officials invoked their right not to answer questions as well, including Nevada GOP chair Michael McDonald and Michigan Republican National Committeewoman Kathy Berden. One of the more provocative persons to invoke the Fifth was the American white supremacist, political commentator, and live streamer Nick Fuentes who in late November 2022 had also been a dinner companion of Donald Trump and Kanye West at Mar-a-Lago. Among the things that I suspect Fuentes did not wish to talk about were his revolutionary comments at various rallies that led up to the Capitol assault, including the speech he delivered before a crowd of Trump supporters at Freedom Plaza on January 6 just prior to the attack:

> It is us and our ancestors that created everything good that you see in this country. All these people that have taken over our country – we do not need them. It is the American people, and our leader, Donald Trump, against everybody else in this country and this world. Our Founding Fathers would get in the streets, and they would take the country back by force if necessary. And that is what we must be prepared to do.[3]

In structuring their investigation and hearings, the Committee "began with President Trump's contentions that the election was stolen," "focused on the rulings of more than 60 Federal and State courts rejecting President Trump and his supporters' efforts to reverse the electoral outcome," and took testimony from nearly all of the President's men and a handful of women.[4] We quickly learned that even "those key individuals who worked closely with President Trump to overturn the 2020 election on January 6th *admitted* that they lacked actual evidence sufficient to change the election result, and they *admitted* that what they were attempting was unlawful."[5] At the same time, the Committee does not begin its narrative about Trump and his allies interfering with or attempting to overturn the 2020 election until after Biden was officially declared the winner a few days after the election in November. Their story begins back in the spring of April 14, 2020, at 10:24 AM to be exact. When Trump @realDonald Trump tweeted out in all caps: GET RID OF BALLOT

HARVESTING, IT IS RAMPANT WITH FRAUD. THE USA MUST HAVE VOTER ID., THE ONLY WAY TO GET AN HONEST COUNT!

However, the roots of Trump's "state of mind" or attempts to secure power unlawfully can be traced back to the presidential campaign of 2016. As I argued in *Criminology on Trump* (2022) and in several opinion editorials as well, Trump is one needy and mentally ill person, narcissistic to a fault, and sociopathic too. Although Donald may be crazy or a not "very stable genius" as he has claimed, Trump is not by any stretch of the imagination legally insane. Possessed as he is with more than his share of demons, Trump does not believe for a second any of his or other people's fraudulent con jobs, such as any of his Big Lies or the QAnon conspiracies. Trump is all performance with a touch of defensive guilt thrown in. Trump is always deceiving others but never deceiving himself. He always knows the difference between fact and fiction, right and wrong, and fake or alternative electors, for example. What makes Trump a master con and performer artist is his uncanny ability to get most everyone around him to believe in and/or to go along with the unadulterated nonsense that he is forever propagating no matter how absurd.

For example, on the very same day that his tax returns were finally released to the public, and one day after the public release of the Introduction to the Final Report on December 19, 2022, Trump was still demanding his reinstatement as president, calling for another coup to overthrow the government, and doubling down on his myriad of lies. From his Truth Social platform, the former president posted on December 20, 2022, at 8:20 PM:

> The FBI and Twitter COLLUDED to elect Joe Biden. In other words, the 2020 Presidential Election was RIGGED & STOLEN. It all began a long time ago, they SPIED on my campaign, and tried to "RIGG" the 2016 Election but failed. Remember our government is doing this, not a person or party. What should be done about such a terrible thing, or should we let someone who was elected by cheating and fraud stay in office and continue to destroy our Country?

Trump, of course, was referring to the Mueller investigation of Russian interference into the 2016 presidential election to defeat Hillary Clinton on behalf of Trump and to one of his favorite refrains that there was "no collusion, no obstruction" between his campaign and Russia. Even with this type of election interference in mind, it was not until the 2018 midterm elections when Trump came to fully appreciate the "necessity" of not playing fair or by the rules because of what the GOP was up against. According to the statistical analysis of the Associated Press, the GOP even with its gerrymandering advantages had lost the 2018 popular vote to the Democrats by 9.7 million votes, or 8.6%, the largest midterm margin for any party and the largest margin on record for a minority party. Thus, Trump understood that without cheating it would be highly unlikely that he would be able to defeat a mainstream Democratic challenger like Joe Biden. Ergo, his first move to undermine the 2020 election was that "perfect" phone call to President Zelensky when Trump tried to extort the newly elected leader of Ukraine into launching an investigation of the alleged corruption of Joe Biden. It did not matter if there was any there, there, or any substance behind an investigation into Biden corruption because Boss Trump in his characteristic strongarm methodology only wanted there to be an appearance of corruption. Trump and his people would then be able exploit this bogus investigation. Not unlike the hour-long conference call where the then-president pressured the Georgia Secretary of State Brad Raffensperger to "recalculate" the votes and say that he had found 11,780 more votes for Trump one more than the number he had lost to Biden by. Or like when in another phone conversation on December, 27, 2020 Trump stated to acting Attorney General Jeffrey Rosen: "Just say that the election was corrupt and leave the rest to me and the Republican Congressmen." And like when Trump and Republican National Committee Chairwoman Ronna McDaniel on November 17, 2020 were recorded in a phone conversation to Monica Palmer and William Hartmann, the two GOP Wayne County canvassers as reported by The Detroit News, Trump was pressuring them not to approve the certification where Biden had won Michigan by 154,000 votes.

Similarly, the origins of Trump's two related coup plans – political and violent – to steal the election were not primarily about whether Trump as well as his allies believed in the absence of any widespread evidence of fraud that the election was rigged. Rather, the Big Lies were simply a ruse for building up GOP resentment, mobilizing the MAGA base, and creating six slates of "alternative" electors stirring up enough post-election chaos to prevent the normal certification process from occurring. Hopefully, their plan would enable the election deniers to finesse procedurally the substitution of each of the 50 states with 1 vote a piece to determine the outcome of the election where the Republicans would have 27 votes for Trump and the Democrats would only have 23 for Biden.

While the politically peaceful coup plan "A" was ongoing (e.g., the election recounts and court challenges) and busy priming the stolen election pump, the violent and forceful backup plan "B" was also taking shape. Preparing the way for a different kind of action plan should the peaceful coup plot fail to materialize. Therein lies the premeditation or the criminal intent – not to mention the razor like focus – of Trump to remain in power vis-à-vis his multi-pronged seditious conspiracy to overturn one way or the other the results of the 2020 election.[6] In the midst of this conspiracy lies a couple of back-and-forth incriminating phone calls. The first was placed by Donald Trump and John Eastman to Republican National Committee Chair Ronna McDaniel to set up the false slate of electors. The next day there was a return call from McDaniel to Trump accepting their request. We also learn from the testimony of other attorneys that Trump had put Giuliani in control of the false slate of electors and that he was executing what the former president wanted him to.

We learned further from previously unshared testimony by the star witness Cassidy Hutchinson that not only had she been pressured by her first Trump-provided attorney "not to recall" what she clearly recalled. Hutchinson was also not only being bribed with future job opportunities for not recalling but also that her boss Mark Meadows had made dozens of calls trying to operationalize the false slate of electors' scheme. The persons involved in these federal crimes of "conspiracy to defraud the United States" and "conspiracy to make a false statement" had all been subpoenaed to testify by Special Counsel Jack Smith almost immediately after he took over the DOJ investigation of January 6 in the fall of 2022.

### The Final Select Committee Hearing

At its tenth and final public hearing, the Committee accused Donald J. Trump of inciting an insurrection, conspiracy to defraud the United States, obstruction of an act of Congress, and conspiracy to make a false statement. This became the first time in American history that the United States Congress had referred a former president for criminal prosecution. The evidence had led the Committee to the overwhelming conclusion that the central cause of January 6th was Donald Trump. The events of that day would never have occurred without Trump, social media, Fox News, and 80.3 million followers on Twitter alone taking in the daily Trumpian lies about one thing or the other.[7]

While the Committee identified other co-conspirators who assisted Trump referring five of them for potential prosecution, once again it concluded that the Insurrectionist-in-Chief should be the primary person held accountable for causing the assault on the Capitol. Those political co-conspirators recommended for prosecution included his fourth chief of staff Mark Meadows and four Trump lawyers – Rudy Giuliani, John Eastman, Jeffrey Clark, and Kenneth Chesebro – who had all assisted #45 in his illegal efforts to hold on to power. The Committee also referred four House Republicans – former House minority leader Kevin McCarthy (R-CA), Rep. Jim Jordan (R-OH), Rep. Scott Perry (R-PA), and Rep. Andy Biggs (R-AZ) – for sanctions by the House Ethics Committee for refusing to comply with the panel's subpoenas to testify. All in all, the report offers hundreds of pages of evidence of a multi-pronged subversive conspiracy, involving the words and actions of Trump and his various circles of co-conspirators that go well beyond the lawyers and politicians to QAnon believers, white nationalists, neo-Nazis, paramilitarists, and other domestic thugs. Whether or not the Justice Department prosecutes Trump for his notorious behavior, the Select Committee has provided an extensively researched and well-documented historical record, as well as a devastating indictment of the 45th president that is assessable to and easily read by the public at large.

During the final televised hearing in his opening remarks, chairman Bernie Thompson emphasized that the Committee had effectively rolled out a roadmap for prosecuting and holding accountable those responsible for January 6. However, it is important to point out before I continue that the Department of Justice operates under constraints that were not applicable to the Committee. Referrals from the committee for indicting the former president and others are by no means automatic. There is still plenty of work to be conducted "between receiving all of the committee's evidence and reaching the point where" the DOJ can make its "decision about whether charges can and should be brought."[8]

Some of the constraints facing the prosecution or the hurdles that the DOJ must clear before either Donald Trump or his allies can be indicted have to do with the federal rules of evidence that determine the type of evidence or testimony that may be introduced during a trial and heard by a jury. Most commonly the DOJ must evaluate the evidence gathered – their own and/or the Committee's – for issues of hearsay, relevance, and undue prejudice. Notably, unlike the adversarial process of adjudication where there are two contentious sides examining the presentation of evidence, the Select Committee's presentation was one-sided. There were no defenses of either the former president or his allies or cross-examinations of the state's witnesses. Hence, the DOJ will have to assess possible defenses and, if they do exist, determine whether there is enough other counter evidence to move forward with the indictments and prosecutions. Ultimately, the DOJ will have to decide whether they have enough evidence for a unanimous jury to convict Trump and/or his allies beyond a reasonable doubt.[9]

Keep in mind that while the House committee's jurisdiction does not extend to indicting somebody in a court of law, it does give Congress a directive to pass new laws designed to protect the nation from future threats to our democracy or to similar plots to overturn a secure and fair election. For example, the omnibus budget bill that was signed into law by President Biden at the very end of 2022 contained a provision to clarify the Electoral College Count Act of 1887. Trump and company were trying to use and/or distort this law so that they could ideally steal the election from Biden. The new Electoral Count Reform and Presidential Transition Improvement Act of 2022 updates or replaces the ambiguous provisions of the 19th-century law with clear procedures that maintain appropriate state and federal roles in selecting the President and Vice President of the United States as set forth in the US Constitution. This reformed law also makes it more difficult for a state's slate of electors to be challenged during the certification process. Previously, it only took one state representative and one state senator to challenge a state's electoral outcome. That was the case even when those challenges were without any legitimate concerns or were fictious and baseless claims. This tactic was the one that Trump and his alternative or fake slate of electors were trying to exploit as a means of overturning the election results. The new law now requires that before there can be the lodging of an objection or an election challenge, there must be at least 20% of the members of the state houses and senates alike.

## A Viable Select Committee from a Rejected Bipartisan Commission

> At the outset of our investigation, we recognized that tens of millions of Americans had been persuaded by President Trump that the 2020 presidential election was stolen by overwhelming fraud. We also knew this was patently false, and that dozens of state and federal judges had addressed and resolved all manner of allegations about the election. Our legal system functioned as it should, but our President would not accept the outcome.
>
> *Excerpt from the Foreword to the Final Report*
> *by Liz Cheney, Vice Chair*

> I also think about why the rioters were there, besieging the legislative branch of our government. The rioters were inside the halls of Congress because the head of the executive branch of our government, the then-President of the United States, told them to attack. Donald Trump summoned the mob to Washington, DC. Afterward, he sent them to the Capitol to try to prevent my colleagues and me from doing our Constitutional duty to certify the election. They put our very democracy to the test.
>
> *Excerpt from the Foreword to the Final Report*
> *by Bernie G. Thompson, Chairman*

> The Select Committee to Investigate the January 6th Attack has succeeded in bringing clarity and demonstrating with painstaking detail the fragility of our Democracy. Above all the work of the Select Committee underscores that our democratic institutions are only as strong as the commitment of those who are entrusted with their care.
>
> *Excerpt from the Foreword to the Final Report*
> *by Nancy Pelosi, Speaker of the House*

What I had been thinking about – call it criminological irony – long before the January 6 assault on the Capitol occurred, and months before Trump lost the 2020 election to Joe Biden, was that Boss Trump and his consiglieres had been working on different ways that they might disregard the rules of democracy and steal the election from #46 should he not be re-elected. Something which both Trump and his pollsters knew was more likely than not especially because of #45's terrible handling of COVID and the unnecessary deaths of some 300,000 persons.[10]

In any case, following Trump's loss to Biden, the lame duck Racketeer-in-Chief armed with a corrupt bunch of attorneys, as well as many unethical GOP officials and a cadre of thousands of gullible supporters, joined knowingly or unknowingly in a complex plot to help Trump try to unlawfully overturn the election. Recall that on the same day as the Capitol assault a bipartisan leadership group had come together, if only momentarily, to draw up papers that would have immediately impeached and convicted the Insurrectionist-in-Chief.[11] In part, that never occurred because House Republican Leader Kevin McCarthy did a 180 degree about face. Nonetheless, one week later the minority leader was all in favor of the creation of a fact-finding bipartisan commission to investigate January 6, asserting that "the President bears responsibility" for the "attack on Congress by a mob of rioters." During a press conference on January 21, 2021, the day after President Biden had been sworn into office, McCarthy repeated his support for a bipartisan commission. In relatively short order Trump would change his mind. The House minority leader would do another flip flop because the Boss did not want an investigation of any kind into that infamous day. Like most of the GOP leadership their preference became to pretend that nothing unusual had occurred at the Capitol on January 6, and if something bad had occurred, then it was not the fault of the former Insurrectionist-in-Chief.

Less than a month later most of the GOP acquitted Trump of impeachment for the second time. One day later February 15th House Speaker Pelosi sent a letter to the Democratic Caucus of her intention to establish an independent commission to report on the facts and causes related to January 6th. A few days later, McCarthy provided Pelosi with a "wish list that mirrored 'suggestions from the Co-Chairs of the 9/11 Commission' that he and the House Republicans hoped would be included in the House's legislation to establish the Commission."[12] Specifically, McCarthy was requesting "an equal ratio of Democratic and Republican nominations, equal subpoena power for the Democratic Chair and Republican Vice Chair." Closing his letter, McCarthy quoted the 9/11 Co-Chairs: a "bipartisan independent investigation will earn credibility with the American public."[13] Pelosi agreed to the equal ratio of Democratic and Republican members and to equal say in subpoena power.

After the details for the commission had been worked out between the House Homeland Security Committee (HSC) Chairman Bennie G. Thompson and his Republican counterpart, Ranking Member John Katko, Thompson announced on May 14, 2021, that an agreement had been reached on legislation to form a bipartisan, independent Commission to investigate the January 6th domestic terrorism attack on the Capitol and to recommend changes to protect the citadel of our democracy. The day before the House was to take up the legislation on May 19, McCarthy released a statement in opposition to forming a bipartisan commission. Pelosi immediately released a statement sharing the February 22 letter that McCarthy had sent to her with three requests that the Democrats had agreed to and stated: "Leader McCarthy won't take yes for an answer." Republican leader Katko also defended the bipartisan nature of the bill to create the Commission:

> As I have called for since the days after the attack, an independent, 9/11-style review is critical for removing the politics around January 6 and focusing solely on the facts and circumstances of the security breach at the Capitol, as well as other instances of violence relevant to such a review. Make no mistake about it, Mr. Thompson and I know this is about facts. It's not partisan politics. We would have never gotten to this point if it was about partisan politics.[14]

Then the House voted and passed a bill to establish a bipartisan National Commission to investigate the January 6th attack on the Capitol Complex, with 35 Republicans joining 217 Democrats voting in favor and 175 Republicans voting against. A few days later, the bill was killed in the Senate when only six Republicans joined the Democrats failing to reach the supermajority of 60 votes out of 100 required to pass the legislation. Next, things became more interesting yet when Pelosi announced on June 24 that she intended to create a House Select Committee to investigate the attack. On June 30, the House voted on H. Res. 503 to establish a 13-member committee by a vote of 222 Yeas and 190 Nays. Just two Republicans, Liz Chaney and Adam Kinzinger, voted affirmatively along with the Democrats. The next day, Pelosi named eight initial members to the Select Committee, seven Democrats and Liz Chaney.

On July 17, McCarthy proposed his selection of five GOP members, including Ranking Member of the House Judiciary Committee Rep. Jim Jordan and Armed Services, Veterans' Affairs and Education and Labor Committees Rep. Jim Banks. For the record, Jordan had been personally involved in the act and circumstances of January 6th and would become a target of the investigation. Banks had already stated publicly that he had reached his own conclusions and had no intention of cooperating in any objective investigation, stating, for example, that the Select Committee was created to "malign conservatives and to justify the Left's authoritarian agenda."[15]

On July 21, exercising her power under H. Res. 503, Pelosi announced that she would not approve the appointments of Jordan and Banks. The House Speaker expressed "concern about statements made and actions taken by these Members" and "the impact that their appointments may have on the integrity of the investigation." Pelosi also stated that she had informed McCarthy that she "was prepared to appoint" his three other proposed

Representatives Rodney David, Kelly Armstrong, and Troy Nehis. The Speaker also requested that McCarthy "recommend two other Members."[16] In response, the Minority Leader elected to remove all five of his Republican appointments. Pelosi then appointed Republican Rep. Adam Kinzinger and the nine member House Select Committee was completed.

### The 17 Findings of the Select Committee[17]

1  Beginning election night and continuing through January 6th and thereafter, Donald Trump purposely disseminated false allegations of fraud related to the 2020 presidential election in order to aid his effort to overturn the election and for purposes of soliciting contributions. These false claims provoked his supporters to violence on January 6th.

2  Knowing that he and his supporters had lost dozens of election lawsuits, and despite his own senior advisors refuting his election fraud claims and urging him to concede his election loss, Donald Trump refused to accept the lawful result of the 2020 election. Rather than honor his constitutional obligation to "take Care that the Laws be faithfully executed," President Trump instead plotted to overturn the election outcome.

3  Despite knowing that such an action would be illegal, and that no State had or would submit an altered electoral slate, Donald Trump corruptly pressured Vice President Mike Pence to refuse to count electoral votes during Congress's joint session on January 6th.

4  Donald Trump sought to corrupt the US Department of Justice by attempting to enlist Department officials to make purposely false statements and thereby aid his effort to overturn the presidential election. After that effort failed, Donald Trump offered the position of Acting Attorney General to Jeff Clark knowing that Clark intended to disseminate false information aimed at overturning the election.

5  Without any evidentiary basis and contrary to State and Federal law, Donald Trump unlawfully pressured State officials and legislators to change the results of the election in their States.

6  Donald Trump oversaw an effort to obtain and transmit false electoral certificates to Congress and the National Archives.

7  Donald Trump pressured Members of Congress to object to valid slates of electors from several States.

8  Donald Trump purposely verified false information filed in Federal court.

9  Based on false allegations that the election was stolen, Donald Trump summoned tens of thousands of supporters to Washington for January 6th. Although these supporters were angry and some were armed, Donald Trump instructed them to march to the Capitol on January 6th to "take back" their country.

10 Knowing that a violent attack on the Capitol was underway and knowing that his words would incite further violence, Donald Trump purposely sent a social media message publicly condemning Vice President Pence at 2:24 p.m. on January 6th.

11 Knowing that violence was underway at the Capitol, and despite his duty to ensure that the laws are faithfully executed, Donald Trump refused repeated requests over a multiple-hour period that he instruct his violent supporters to disperse and leave the Capitol and instead watched the violent attack unfold on television. This failure to act perpetuated the violence at the Capitol and obstructed Congress's proceeding to count electoral votes.

12 Each of these actions by Donald Trump was taken in support of a multi-part conspiracy to overturn the lawful results of the 2020 presidential election.

13 The intelligence community and law enforcement agencies did successfully detect the planning for potential violence on January 6th, including planning specifically by the Proud Boys and Oath Keeper militia groups who ultimately led the attack on the Capitol. As January 6th approached, the intelligence specifically identified the potential for violence at the US Capitol. This intelligence was shared within the executive branch, including with the Secret Service and the President's National Security Council.

14 Intelligence gathered in advance of January 6th did not support a conclusion that Antifa or other left-wing groups would likely engage in a violent counterdemonstration, or attack Trump supporters on January 6th. Indeed, intelligence from January 5th indicated that some left-wing groups were instructing their members to "stay at home" and not attend on January 6th. Ultimately, none of these groups was involved to any material extent with the attack on the Capitol on January 6th.

15 Neither the intelligence community nor law enforcement obtained intelligence in advance of January 6th on the full extent of the ongoing planning by President Trump, John Eastman, Rudolph Giuliani, and their associates to overturn the certified election results. Such agencies apparently did not (and potentially could not) anticipate the provocation President Trump would offer the crowd in his Ellipse speech, that President Trump would "spontaneously" instruct the crowd to march to the Capitol, that President Trump would exacerbate the violent riot by sending his 2:24 p.m. tweet condemning Vice President Pence, or the full scale of the violence and lawlessness that would ensue. Nor did law enforcement anticipate that President Trump would refuse to direct his supporters to leave the Capitol once violence began. No intelligence community advance analysis predicted exactly how President Trump would behave; no such analysis recognized the full scale and extent of the threat to the Capitol on January 6th.

16  Hundreds of Capitol and DC Metropolitan police officers performed their duties bravely on January 6th, and America owes those individuals immense gratitude for their courage in the defense of Congress and our Constitution. Without their bravery, January 6th would have been far worse. Although certain members of the Capitol Police leadership regarded their approach to January 6th as "all hands-on deck," the Capitol Police leadership did not have sufficient assets in place to address the violent and lawless crowd. Capitol Police leadership did not anticipate the scale of the violence that would ensue after President Trump instructed tens of thousands of his supporters in the Ellipse crowd to march to the Capitol, and then tweeted at 2:24 p.m. Although Chief Steven Sund raised the idea of National Guard support, the Capitol Police Board did not request Guard assistance prior to January 6th. The Metropolitan Police took an even more proactive approach to January 6th, and deployed roughly 800 officers, including responding to the emergency calls for help at the Capitol. Rioters still managed to break their line in certain locations when the crowd surged forward in the immediate aftermath of Donald Trump's 2:24 p.m. tweet. The Department of Justice readied a group of Federal agents at Quantico and in the District of Columbia, anticipating that January 6th could become violent, and then deployed those agents once it became clear that police at the Capitol were overwhelmed. Agents from the Department of Homeland Security were also deployed to assist.

17  President Trump had authority and responsibility to direct deployment of the National Guard in the District of Columbia but never gave any order to deploy the National Guard on January 6th or on any other day. Nor did he instruct any Federal law enforcement agency to assist. Because the authority to deploy the National Guard had been delegated to the Department of Defense, the Secretary of Defense could, and ultimately did deploy the Guard. Although evidence identifies a likely miscommunication between members of the civilian leadership in the Department of Defense impacting the timing of deployment, the Committee has found no evidence that the Department of Defense intentionally delayed deployment of the National Guard. The Select Committee recognizes that some at the Department had genuine concerns, counseling caution, that President Trump might give an illegal order to use the military in support of his efforts to overturn the election.

## Narrative Summaries from the Final Report

The Committee divided up their findings and expanded on these in eight chapters as they elaborated upon one continuous thematic narrative. In each of the first seven chapters, the Committee reviews the core features of the developing efforts of Trump and his allies to hold on to presidential power not only after but before he lost the election to President Biden. The eighth chapter provides an analysis and detailed timelines for the day of January 6, 2021. In this section, I rely on the keen "take aways" from *Civil Discourse with Joyce Vance*.[18]

### Chapter 1. The Big Lie

Trump intended to lie all along if he lost. There was no honest, sudden outrage over an election he truly believed he'd won that surfaced as the election results were announced. He knew he lost and he knew it wasn't due to fraud.

When he spoke to the country in the early morning hours after Fox News correctly called Arizona for Biden, Trump said, "This is a fraud on the American public. This is an embarrassment to our country. We were getting ready to win this election. Frankly, we did win this election. We did win this election." Trump's claim was free of any evidence the election had been tainted by fraud. But his statement came as no surprise to allies like Steve Bannon and Judicial Watch's Thomas Fitton, both of whom were in on a plan devised months earlier for Trump to call the election in his favor, no matter, and most likely despite, how it was going.

Roger Stone put it like this,

> I really do suspect it will still be up in the air. When that happens, the key thing to do is to claim victory. Possession is 9/10s of the law. No, we won. F*** you, Sorry. Over. We won. You're wrong. F*** you.

Among Trump's campaign advisors and staff, it was a different story. Only a "definitely intoxicated" Rudy Giuliani backed Trump on that night. His campaign manager told him it was too early to know the outcome of the investigation, and as the week advanced, Trump was told he'd lost. His own people told him there was no evidence of fraud.

The committee's judgment on Trump is harsh but fair,

> Donald Trump was no passive consumer of these lies. He actively propagated them. Time and again President Trump was informed that his election fraud claims were not true. He chose to spread them anyway. He did so even after they were legally tested and rejected in dozens of lawsuits. Not even the electoral college's certification of former Vice President Biden's victory on December 14, 2020, stopped the President from lying.

This of course wasn't a surprise to anyone who'd been paying attention. Trump had refused to commit to abiding by the result of the election if he lost. It was all like watching a slow-motion train wreck in progress. With his campaign staff, who dubbed themselves "Team Normal" refusing to go along with the Big Lie, Trump replaced them with Giuliani's team, bringing Christina Bobb, Cleta Mitchell, Sidney Powell, John Eastman, and Boris Epshteyn into his orbit. His decision to surround himself with people who were willing to advance the fraud narrative was deliberate.

We all know what happened next,

> Instead of accepting his defeat, President Trump attempted to justify his Big Lie with a series of increasingly preposterous claims. The President was not simply led astray by those around him. The opposite was true. He actively promoted conspiracy theories and false election fraud claims even after being informed they were baseless. Millions of President Trump's supporters believed the election was stolen from him. Many of them still do, but President Trump knew the truth and chose to lie about it.

The committee offers two case studies that document how "President Trump and his surrogates lied in the face of overwhelming evidence." One involves Dominion Voting Systems, which Trump continued to falsely claim ran software that "switched votes" and "rigged" the election after he was definitively told by people running his own campaign as well as Justice Department officials that those claims were not true. The second one involves the video footage taken at the State Farm arena in Fulton County, Georgia, as votes were being tallied and the fake narrative concocted around it. Trump and his allies fabricated a story about suitcases of ballots mysteriously appearing and claims he would have won in the absence of fraud. Those claims were baseless, and he was repeatedly told that they were not true. Even Georgia's Secretary of State told him they were false. Trump victimized two decent women, Ruby Freeman and Shaye Moss, whose only crime was their commitment to work to support free and fair elections.

In other words, Trump was not a passive participant in any of this. He sought out the lies, pushed them, and ran with them, intentionally misleading his base so they would rally around his cause. On the Ellipse the morning of January 6, Trump told the crowd-that-would-become-a-mob that the election had been stolen from him and falsely claimed there was widespread voter fraud. He repeated falsehoods about the election and fraud more than 100 times, a shocking betrayal for an American president.

### Chapter 2. "I Just Want to Find 11,780 Votes"

Far and away my favorite thing about the report is how the committee illustrates the title of many chapters with a characteristic Trump quote. They hit the spot, as here, perfectly illustrating different parts of Trump's scheme.

There is more information in the report about the extent of the pressure brought to bear on states than what we learned during the hearings. It extends beyond Georgia. Of course, there's the audio recording. The one where Trump, like any good mob boss, ultimately threatens and cajoles Georgia Secretary of State Brad Raffensperger, Georgia's chief election officer, to "find" enough votes to declare him the winner of an election he lost.

But the process was repeating in states across the country, and in what seems to be new evidence, the committee paints a picture of Mark Meadows, Trump's chief of staff, as deeply involved. Trump is included as well:

The Select Committee estimates that in the two months between the November election and the January 6th insurrection, President Trump or his inner circle engaged in at least 200 apparent acts of public or private outreach, pressure, or condemnation, targeting either State legislators or State or local election administrators, to overturn State election results. This included at least:

- 68 meetings, attempted or connected phone calls, or text messages, each aimed at one or more State or local officials;
- 18 instances of prominent public remarks, with language targeting one or more such officials; and
- 125 social media posts by President Trump or senior aides targeting one or more such officials, either explicitly or implicitly, and mostly from his own account.

The scope is mind boggling. Everyone knows about the January 2 call to Brad Raffensperger, but there's a lot more to the story and the report includes lots of detail. This is the chapter of the report to start with if you've only got time for one right now. Kenneth Chesebro, a name you may not yet be familiar with, surfaces here as someone who is an early adopter of the Big Lie and willing to push out marginal legal theories and urge them to take on a life of their own.

This was also where Special Counsel Jack Smith started sending out subpoenas designed to elicit evidence and testimony about the campaign and individual lawyers' engagement with state officials. Apparently, the Special Counsel sees smoke here.

### Chapter 3. Fake Electors and the "The President of the Senate Strategy"

This is a familiar part of Trump's scheme:

President Trump and his allies prepared their own fake slates of electoral college electors in seven States that President Trump lost: Arizona, Georgia,

Michigan, Nevada, New Mexico, Pennsylvania, and Wisconsin. And on December 14, 2020 – the date when true, certified electors were meeting to cast their electoral votes for the candidate who had won the popular vote in each of those States – these fake electors also met, ostensibly casting electoral votes for President Trump, the candidate who had lost.

Nothing here is a close call. It's a rank attempt to circumvent democracy. Even Republican Senator Mike Lee could see that:

> On December 30th, Senator Lee texted Trump advisor Cleta Mitchell that January 6th was "a dangerous idea," including "for the republic itself." He explained that "I don't think we have any valid basis for objecting to the electors" because "it cannot be true that we can object to any state's presidential electors simply because we don't think they handled their election well or suspect illegal activity." Senator Lee even questioned her about the plan's dangerous long-term consequences: "[w]ill you please explain to me how this doesn't create a slippery slope problem for all future presidential elections?"

### Chapter 4. "Just Call It Corrupt and Leave the Rest to Me"

We heard most of the information here in the committee hearings, where there was extensive coverage of Trump's efforts to subjugate DOJ to his political needs. When acting officials at DOJ refused to legitimize Trump's fraud claims, he tried to replace them with Jeffrey Bossert Clark, the head of the Environment and Natural Resources Division ("We'll call you when there's an oil spill," the Deputy Attorney General Rich Donoghue told him). Trump backed down when DOJ officials threatened to resign if Clark was put in place.

Donoghue testified that Trump asked him and acting AG Rosen to "just say the election was corrupt and leave the rest to me and the Republican Congressmen." Donoghue explained this "is an exact quote from the President." It's easy to believe him. It's the same approach Trump used, leading to his first impeachment, when he asked Ukrainian President Zelensky to do him a favor and open an investigation into then-candidate Joe Biden.

Ultimately there's the Clark letter – what the White House Counsel called a murder-suicide pact for anyone who touched it. It's a letter that, if sent, could have sparked a Constitutional crisis by telling states DOJ believed the election was tainted by fraud, and they could set aside their legitimate slates of electors. Had acting officials not stood firm at this point, the Justice Department would have become another tool in Trump's effort to hold onto power and perhaps one that would have sealed the deal.

### Chapter 5. "A Coup in Search of a Legal Theory"

By the time it got close to January 6, everything else Trump tried to launch the Big Lie had failed. All that was left was persuading the Vice President to play a role in the scam. This led to the intense pressure campaign on Mike Pence. We all know much of the narrative and have seen the video from January 6, so we understand how important the role Pence played was on that day.

But this chapter still leaves unanswered questions about Trump's January 5 phone call with Pence. We don't learn the details, because Trump and Pence were the only two on the call, hearing both sides, and because aides who heard one side of the call declined to testify about what Trump said, citing executive privilege. If any one event could seal the deal on Trump's criminal mindset, it would be this call, but the committee doesn't have the goods. It seems likely DOJ has more or can get it, since some of those witnesses have now abandoned their claims of privilege and have spoken with federal prosecutors.

### Chapter 6. "Be There, Will Be Wild"

One of the question marks in the narrative is the absence of direct evidence linking the militias on the ground to Trump's inner circle. That would be essential for DOJ to consider filing seditious conspiracy charges against anyone higher up than the leaders of the Proud Boys and the Oath Keepers.

The committee begins to build a circumstantial case. It argues that when Trump summons the mob, it activates a network of right-wing extremists and unites them under a Trump banner. The committee offers an in-depth treatment of right-wing extremism, moving through the Stop the Steal coalition, and engagement with the Proud Boys, Oath Keepers, and others, as well as individuals like Alex Jones, Ali Alexander, Roger Stone, and their friends.

This chapter deserves a more critical read than I've given it tonight. But it does pop into focus a bit more in Chapter 8.

### Chapter 7. 187 Minutes of Dereliction

In its hearings, the committee did a compelling job of showing us what Trump was doing while the mob was attacking the Capitol, his nonchalance as the crowd chanted "Hang Mike Pence" and went looking for Speaker Pelosi. Trump could have called off the mob, but he refused to. That's strong circumstantial evidence that he intended for the mob to interfere with the certification of the election.

The real shocker here is the lack of official documentation from inside of the White House during this critical period. No entries in the presidential diary, no call records. Everything that should be there is missing, precisely at this most important time. Why? Of course, we're all capable of drawing that obvious conclusion. It's important that the committee has documented what's missing, both for DOJ's purposes and for the historical record.

### Chapter 8. Analysis of the Attack

Prosecutors like timelines. You can learn a lot by looking at events in the context of what is going on around them. Here, there are important inferences to be drawn from the timeline.

It's before 1:00 p.m. on January 6 when the Proud Boys launch their pre-planned attack. They're doing it for Trump, and they want to obstruct Congress and prevent it from certifying the electoral college vote. (The Proud Boys' leaders' trial on seditious conspiracy and other charges related to this began in January 2023 and was expected to last a couple of months.)[19]

There has been some criticism of the argument that Trump bears any responsibility for these events because the Proud Boys launched their attack on the Capitol before Trump finished his speech. This line of reasoning says that Trump isn't responsible because he didn't set off the attack by sending the mob to the Capitol.

The committee's narrative can be used to construe those facts in a different light, showing that the Proud Boys intended to harness the power of the mob that they knew would be coming their way. A key piece of evidence the committee details is that the Proud Boys took down security barriers between Peace Circle and the Capitol. That meant that when Trump told the mob to go to the Capitol, they had a clear path. At that point, fighting had stalled on the Western Mall between the Proud Boys and Metro PD. It was the influx of the mob that allowed the Proud Boys to overrun the Capitol, leading to MPD's first ever fighting retreat.

We have yet to see direct evidence linking Trump to any of this. But the Proud Boys, and to some extent the Oath Keepers, were buddy-buddy with Roger Stone, who took the Fifth Amendment rather than confirm for the committee that he was communicating with Trump on January 5th and 6th. Draw your own conclusions for now. DOJ may well be able to access evidence and testimony the committee couldn't.

One detail that jumps out – and this section of the report is so rich in detail I'm sure we'll be reading it over and over to extract all the nuances – is that the Proud Boys cleared the security barriers at Peace Circle. Why do that if you didn't expect someone to be coming in that direction? Did the Proud Boys expect the crowd from Trump's speech to join them at the Capitol? Did someone tell them to expect it?

Examining the facts helps investigators develop the leads they use to work with witnesses and get to the truth of matters. It's why cooperating witnesses can make such a difference. And it's why coming out of the Oath Keepers and Proud Boys trials with defendants who might newly wish to cooperate could have a real impact. Why were the rooms at the Willard Hotel called war rooms? It doesn't seem like a moniker that would be used unless there was some type of attack to manage. Given that the war rooms were staffed by folks like Stone, Giuliani, and Flynn, there is undoubtedly a lot that prosecutors would like to know about what was going on and what lines of communication and coordination were open.

## Recommendations

There are 11 recommendations in the Final Report on a variety of subject matters related to the January 6 attack on the Capitol and the future. Here are brief overviews of these:

1  **Electoral Count Act:** To deter future corrupt attempts to overturn presidential elections by violating the Electoral Count Act of 1887 as in the efforts of Trump, Eastman, and others before, during, and after the 2020 election, the Committee recommended the passage of the "The Presidential Election Reform Act" to clarify and improve the 1887 law, which Biden signed into law during the last week of December 2022.
2  **Accountability:** Besides the criminal referrals to the DOJ, the Committee also recommended additional criminal and civil steps be considered to ensure accountability for anyone, especially attorneys, engaging in misconduct described in the Report.
3  **Violent Extremism:** Quoted in total from pages 689–690.

> "Federal Agencies with intelligence and security missions, including the Secret Service, should (a) move forward on whole-of-government strategies to combat the threat of violent activity posed by all extremist groups, including white national groups and violent anti-government groups while respecting the civil rights and First Amendment civil liberties of all citizens; and (b) review their intelligence sharing protocols to ensure that threat intelligence is properly prioritized and shared with other responsible intelligence and security agencies on a timely basis in order to combat the threat of violent activity targeting legislative institutions, government operations, and minority groups."

4  **Fourteenth Amendment, Section 3:** Consistent with this constitutional amendment, the Committee recommended that those individuals who had previously taken an oath to support the Constitution, and then either "engaged in an insurrection" or gave "aid or comfort to the enemies of the Constitution," should appropriately be disqualified and barred from holding government office.

5 **National Special Security Event:** Given what occurred on January 6, the Committee recommended that the Congress and the Executive Branch work together to designate that the same types of security provided for both the inaugural and the State of the Union be applied to counting the electoral votes.

6 **To the extent needed, consider reforming certain criminal statutes, including to add more severe penalties:** quoted in total from page 691.

"As indicated in the Report, the Committee believes that 18 U.S.C. § 1512(c)2 and other existing provisions of law can be applied to efforts to obstruct, influence, or impede the joint session on January 6th, including to related planning efforts to overturn the lawful election results on that date. To the extent that any court or any other prosecutorial authorities ultimately reach any differing conclusion, Congress should amend those statutes to cover such conduct. Congress should also consider whether the severity of penalties under those statutes is sufficient to deter unlawful conduct threatening the peaceful transfer of power."

7 **House of Representatives Civil Subpoena Enforcement Authority:** Because of the unclarity of the current authority of the House of Representatives to enforce its subpoenas, Congressional committees of jurisdiction should develop legislation to create a cause of action for enforcing its subpoenas in federal court.

8 **Threats to Election Workers:** Quoted in total from page 691.

"Congressional committees of jurisdiction should consider enhancing federal penalties for certain types of threats against persons involved in the election process and expanding protections for personally identifiable information of election workers."

9 **Capitol Police Oversight:** Quoted in total from page 691.

"Congressional committees of jurisdiction should continue regular and rigorous oversight of the United States Capitol Police as it improves its planning, training, equipping, and intelligence process and practices [related to] its critical incident response protocols, both internally and with law enforcement partners. Joint hearings with testimony from the Capitol Police Board should take place. Full funding for critical security measures should be assured."

10 **Role of Media:** Because of the false information that was repeatedly reinforced by all forms of media, congressional committees of jurisdiction should continue to evaluate policies of media companies that have had the effect of "radicalizing their consumers, including by provoking people to attack their own country."

11 **Discussion of the Insurrection Act**: Because of the evidence that President Trump was considering the use of the Insurrection Act to pull off his coup, the Committee recommended that Congressional Committees of jurisdiction should continue to evaluate all such evidence weighing the risks posed to future elections.

## Commentaries on the Appendices and the Footnotes

The Committee included four appendices: (1) Government Agency Preparation for and Response to January 6th; (2) DC National Guard Preparation for and Response to January 6th; (3) The Big Rip-Off: Follow the Money; and (4) Malign Foreign Influence. All combined these four appendices represented 15% of the Final Report or 121 pages. These appendices were primarily enlarged discussions that drilled down into the complexity of issues involved on January 6. For example, here is the heading/subheading outline for appendix 1, the most ambitious and overarching of the four appendices that are drilled down further in the three related appendices that follow:

INTRODUCTION
DISCUSSION
Intelligence Received by Government Agencies
Discussion of the Potential for Violence
Operationalization of January 6-related Intelligence
DC Government Preparation
DC Fire and Emergency Medical Service Department Preparation
Metropolitan Police Department Preparation
U.S. Capitol Police Preparation
GOVERNMENT AGENCY PREPARATION
Interagency Coordination
January 3$^{rd}$ Coordination Call
Deliberation on Agency Roles
Agency Actions on Permitting
January 5$^{th}$ Congressional Briefing
FEDERAL AGENCY RESPONSE ON JANUARY 6$^{TH}$

As Joyce Vance has written, "it may well be these sections of the report that are the most illuminating." After her first reading, Vance states that the first appendix "provides compelling information about law enforcement failures."[20] Three excerpted passages from appendix 1 and she continues with her review of the Final Report:

"The Committee has reviewed hundreds of thousands of new Secret Service documents, including many demonstrating that the Secret Service had been informed of potential violence at the Capitol before the Ellipse rally on January 6th," its authors wrote. "These documents were critical to our understanding of what the Secret Service and White House knew about the threat to the Capitol on January 6th."

As January 6th approached, some of the intelligence about the potential for violence was shared within the executive branch, including the Secret Service and the President's National Security Council. That intelligence should have been sufficient for President Trump, or others at the White House, to cancel the Ellipse speech, and for President Trump to cancel plans to instruct his supporters to march to the Capitol. Few in law enforcement predicted the full extent of the violence at the Capitol, or that the President of the United States would incite a mob attack on the Capitol, that he would send them to stop the joint session knowing they were armed and dangerous, that he would further incite them against his own vice President while the attack was underway, or that he would do nothing to stop the assault for hours.

Other agencies were also surfacing indications and receiving tips. On December 26, 2020, the Secret Service received a tip about the Proud Boys detailing plans of having "a large enough group to march into DC armed and will outnumber the police so they can't be stopped." It stressed, "Their plan is to literally kill people …. Please take this tip seriously and investigate further." On December 24th, the Secret Service received a compilation of social media posts from "SITE," a private intelligence group. One of them urged those protesters to "march into the chambers." Another, referring to President Trump's December 19th "will be wild!" post, wrote that Trump "can't exactly openly tell you to revolt," so the December 19th post was "the closest he'll ever get." Another understood the President's tweet to be urging his supporters to come to Washington "armed." Others were to the same effect ("there is not enough cops in DC to stop what is coming," "make sure they know who to fear," and "waiting for Trump to say the word").

At 10:43 a.m. on January 6, despite all of this, Vance writes that

Acting Deputy Attorney General Donoghue received an email from Matt Blue, Acting Chief of the Counter- terrorism Section, stating "[t]here are no credible threats as of the 10:00 brief." Twelve minutes later, Rosen spoke to White House Counsel Pat Cipollone via phone. Acting Attorney General Rosen admits that "in hindsight" no one at the Department contemplated "how bad that afternoon turned out to be." Nobody in the DOJ leadership could have predicted President Trump's actions that day.

To which, Vance comments to her readers, "Funny, it feels like we could have all told them that at this point." She acknowledges here: "The committee [can't] give us any closure on whether there was simple misfeasance or gross malfeasance at the Secret Service. But the report concludes that they knew violence was possible at the January 6 rally." Vance then opines that "in some ways, the appendices provoke more questions than answers," which I believe is not necessarily a criticism as these things go.[21]

Finally, Vance underscores what all Americans should already know.

> It's clear that a crime was committed. We saw the Capitol overrun. DOJ is prosecuting a multitude of people for it and has either convicted, or is in the middle of trying, members of two key militias on seditious conspiracy charges.

And then the Distinguished Professor of the Practice of Law raises the rhetorical, if not Socratic question, about "how high up does culpability go?" She then answers:

> It's the whiff of obstruction of the investigation at the top that should drive DOJ forward. If it was just the mob, acting spontaneously, then there'd be no reason for a broad swath of Trump allies to take the 5th and for so many people to try to avoid testifying, or to suffer from a sudden outbreak of bad memory.[22]

In a guest essay for *The New York Times*, Brenda Wineapple, author of *The Impeachers: The Trial of Andrew Johnson and the Dream of a Just Nation* (2019), discusses the impeachment similarities and differences between Johnson and Trump. With respect to the former president and the January 6 investigation, she underscores the unprecedented referrals suggesting that Trump not only violated the Constitutional oath of his office but that he also committed a series of indictable offenses. With respect to the violation of 18 U.S.C. 2383, assisting an insurrection or offering aid and comfort to its participants, this is the most important because, if convicted, Trump "shall be incapable of holding any office under the United States," which was arguably the point of his two impeachment trials. Wineapple ends her essay this way:

> Now, whatever the Department of Justice decides to do and whatever the special counsel Jack Smith discovers or determines, the Jan. 6 committee has achieved what the impeachment of Mr. Trump could not: a series of referrals that caps an expansive and heart-rending investigation into the abuse of power, the obstruction of Congress and the aiding and abetting of

a rebellion…That president will be remembered as lawless, indicted or not, and will be disgraced in perpetuity, as Andrew Johnson should have been.[23]

Some "final words" from *Salon* writer Chauncey DeVega[24]:

Donald Trump's coup attempt on Jan. 6 and the terrorist attack on the U.S. Capitol by his followers was one of the most spectacular crimes in American history, and also one of the most documented and most thoroughly investigated. The world has learned that the Jan. 6 coup plot was vast in scale and scope, and involved or intended to involve Congress, the court system, the national security state, right-wing militias and paramilitaries, conservative think tanks, lobbyists and funders, and the right-wing "news" media.

The Republican coup plot was also reliant on state-level operatives who sought to sabotage American democracy, overturn the results of the 2020 election and return the Trump regime to the White House through a combination of false claims, threats of violence, voter nullification and a calculated attack on the weak spots in America's electoral mechanisms.

Donald Trump was personally at the center of this coup conspiracy. He was not a hapless bystander or useful idiot simply swept up in the catastrophic events of that day.

Violence was central to the coup plot and not peripheral or somehow accidental to it. There remain many unanswered questions about the Trump cabal's coup attempt. What was the role of the Secret Service, and how badly were its agents compromised or implicated? Who planted the bombs that apparently targeted the Democratic and Republican national headquarters, as well as Vice President-elect Kamal Harris? Was there a stand-down order that prevented Capitol Police and the National Guard from defending the Capitol? How much influence did conspiracy theorist and coup supporter Ginni Thomas have?

While we still do not know the answers to most of these questions, on January 27, 2023, the Democrats on the Senate HSC released the most comprehensive report on what intelligence and law Enforcement agencies knew about the events leading up to and even after the violent assault on the Capitol had begun, and what they did or did not do with the information they had. "Our intelligence agencies completely dropped the ball," said Senator Gary Peters, Democrat of Michigan and the chairmen of the HSC. He also added: "Despite a multitude of tips and other intelligence warnings of violence on Jan. 6, the report showed that these agencies repeatedly downplayed the threat level and failed to share the intelligence they had with law enforcement partners."[25]

Finally, from Benjamin Wittes, a co-founder of the legal and national security affairs website *Lawfare* and co-author of *Unmaking the Presidency: Donald Trump's War on the World's Most Powerful Office* (2020) who spent nearly a month studying the January 6th Report's 4,286 endnotes and the related documents they support. Wittes has referred to these items totaling hundreds of thousands of accessible pages as a "huge trove of underlying material" including depositions, interview transcripts, court filings, newspaper articles, public statements, and tweets.[26] He concludes that most of the report's footnotes were merely citations that provide the "connective tissue between the document and source materials." Other notes told

> stories the committee chose not to share in the public hearings. Or ones they could not make all the necessary connections between such as the two types of post-election misconduct – one involving Trump's legal advisor John Eastman, the fake electors, and the pressure on Vice President Pence not to certify the election, and the other involving mid-level Justice Department official Jeffrey Clark and a meeting that had occurred in Trump's office three days before January 6.[27]

Wittes continues, the "perpetrators of these streams are frequently in touch with each other during the relevant period." And they are making arguments that substantially overlap. Yet the Select committee could not "breach claims of privilege and show they are actually working together."[28] In the end, with all the notes and leads provided by the House Select Committee, it reveals that the committee ran out of both time and authority to carry the seditious conspiracy "ball into the endzone. The Justice Department will need to pick up the ball if the public is to get to the truth" of the matter.[29]

## Notes

1   All quotations for this chapter except where noted are taken from two places: Directly from the Select Committee to Investigate the January 6th Attack on the United States Capitol: Introductory Material to the Final Report of the Select Committee, published online December 19, 2022: p. 1. www.documentcl oud.org/documents/23466415-introductory-material-to-the-final-report-of-the-select-committee. Hereafter referred to as the Introduction. Or, directly from the Final Report of the Select Committee to Investigate the January 6th Attack on the United States Capitol, published online December 22. www.cnn.com/2022/12/22/politics/full-jan-6-report/index.html. Hereafter referred to as Final.
2   Kyle Cheney and Nicholas Wu. 2022. Jan. 5 report committee releases 34 transcripts of witnesses who pleaded the Fifth. *Politico*. December 21. www.polit ico.com/news/2022/12/21/jan-6-final-report-trump-election-lies-foreign-adversar ies-00074965
3   Luke Mogelson. 2021. Among the insurrectionists. *The New Yorker*. January 15. www.newyorker.com/magazine/2021/01/25/among-the-insurrectionists

4 Introduction, p. 1.

5 Ibid., p. 4.

6 Gregg Barak. 2022. The final 187 minutes of a 'Multi-Prong' criminal conspiracy. *The Crime Report*. July 22. https://thecrimereport.org/2022/07/22/the-final-187-minutes-of-a-multi-prong-criminal-conspiracy/

7 Rachel Lerman. 2020. Trump says Twitter is trying to 'silence' conservatives. His growing numbers of followers suggests otherwise. *Washington Post*. May 28. www.washingtonpost.com/technology/2020/05/28/trump-twitter-by-numbers/

8 Joyce Vance. 2022. "Unfit for Any Office." Civil Discourse with Joyce Vance. December 20. https://joycevance.substack.com/p/unfit-for-any-office?utm_source=substack&utm_medium=email

9 Personally, I thought that the DOJ has more than enough evidence to convict without even hearing directly from Trump's co-conspirators, but of course the January 6 Special Prosecutor Jack Smith is pursuing that testimony with the approval of the courts. At the same time, I was never convinced beyond a reasonable doubt that the DOJ would prosecute Trump for obstruction of justice, let alone seditious conspiracy, without the testimony of his corrupt allies for their full panoply of treasonous crimes.

10 Gregg Barak. 2022. *Criminology on Trump*. New York and London: Routledge. See chapter five.

11 Bade and Demirjian. 2022.

12 Introduction, p. 99.

13 Quoted in Ibid.

14 Ibid.

15 Ibid.

16 Ibid.

17 Quoted from Introduction, pp. 4–6.

18 Quoted with permission from Joyce Vance. 2022. The Report. *Civil Discourse with Joyce Vance*. December 23. https://joycevance.substack.com/p/the-report?utm_source=substack&utm_medium=email. Vance is a former US Attorney for the Northern District of Alabama from 2009 to 2017, a Distinguished Professor of the Practice of Law, University of Alabama, an MSNBC contributor, and since 2021, she has been a co-host of the #SistersInLaw podcast with Jill Wine-Banks, Barbara McQuade, and Kimberly Atkins Stohr.

19 Central to the defense of the leader of the Proud Boys, Enrique Tarrio, and four other members on trial had been to blame Trump, and their attorneys have sought to subpoena the former president as a witness. See Ella Lee. 2023. Proud Boys on trial for January 6 riot want to subpoena Donald Trump to testify. Can they? *USA Today*. February 17. www.usatoday.com/story/news/politics/2023/02/17/proud-boys-seek-trump-subpoena/11126135002/

20 Vance, 2022.

21 Ibid.

22 Ibid.

23 Brenda Wineapple. 2022. Donald Trump is now forever disgraced. *The New York Times*. December 23. www.nytimes.com/2022/12/23/opinion/donald-trump-criminal-referral-insurrection.html

24 Some "final words" is quoted from Chauncey DeVega. 2023. Crime and un-punishment: Now Republicans have a roadmap for a better coup. *Salon*. January

19. www.salon.com/2023/01/19/and-un-punishment-now-have-a-roadmap-for-a-better-coup/
25 Luke Broadwater. 2023. Senate report details Jan. 6 intelligence and law enforcement failures. *The New York Times*. June 27. www.nytimes.com/2023/06/27/us/politics/jan-6-report-senate.html
26 Benjamin Wittes. 2023. The Jan. 6 committee report contains a treasure trove in fine print. *The Washington Post*. January 25. www.washingtonpost.com/opinions/2023/01/25/jan-6-committee-report-footnotes-guide/
27 Nor have the conspiratorial connections been made so far between these two types of post-election misconduct activity and that prior to the insurrection, Trump was calling into the Willard InterContinental Washington, DC Hotel at 1401 Pennsylvania Ave NW – AKA the Willard "War" Room – to his lieutenants Rudy Giuliani, Steve Bannon, Roger Stone, and John Eastman as reported by Robert Costa and Bob Woodward on MSNBC Morning Joe Show, October 21, 2021. See also, www.washingtonpost.com/investigations/willard-trump-eastman-giuliani-bannon/2021/10/23/c45bd2d4-3281-11ec-9241-aad8e48f01ff_story.html
28 Wittes. 2023.
29 Ibid.

# PART II

# Indicting Donald Trump for Vandalizing the Federal Republic

# 5

# THE PEOPLE OF THE STATE OF NEW YORK V. DONALD J. TRUMP

How "lucky" for Teflon Don that he was able to surrender himself for booking and arraignment without the traditional perp walk that has been going out of fashion with white-collar criminals. Nor did Trump have to take the traditional booking mug shot photos with identification number. However, never missing a grift to raise money for his legal defense funds, the Trump campaign immediately started selling "NOT GUILTY" T-shirts with a picture of Trump, a placard with the date April 11, 2023, and his head barely breeching the 6'5" line on the height ruler behind him.

Trump flew from his home in Palm Beach, Florida, on Trump Force One, landed at LaGuardia Airport in NYC, and from the airport with Cable Networks shooting video from the air he O.J. Simpsoned his way to Trump Tower in the afternoon hours so he could stay the night before his court appearance where he and his family had resided for many years. Four years earlier at the beginning of the third year of his presidency, Melania and Donald with their son Barron William relocated to Trump's Mar-a-Lago Golf and Country Club where they have taken up residency pending the outcomes of his more serious indictments where prison should be anything but off the table. As far as the overnight stay at Trump Tower in the heart of Manhattan's Upper East Side, I think under the arresting circumstances the expression "You can't go home again" made popular by Thomas Wolfe's novel of the same name may have been quite apropos. However, one week after his first criminal indictment occurred, Trump returned to Manhattan to answer seven plus hours of deposition questions pertaining to another ongoing New York investigation by Attorney General Letitia James involving a civil fraud case that could put the Trump Organization out of business.

DOI: 10.4324/9781003390664-8

The week after that also in Manhattan, defendant Trump was a "no show" in the civil defamation trial for remarks he made after leaving the office of the POTUS about an alleged rape against plaintiff E. Jean Carroll some 25 years before. On May 9, 2023, a jury of six men and three women found Trump liable for sexual abuse and defamation and awarded Carroll $5 million in damages. The next evening on a CNN Town Hall, Trump was defaming Carroll again, and two weeks later he was being sued by Carroll for defamation and the protection of the rule of law.[1] With punitive damages another conviction could result in as much as a $15 million payout. Moreover, in July the Department of Justice (DOJ) reversed its earlier position that Trump had been shielded from liability as a federal employee under the Westfall Act for a 2019 defamation suit filed by Carroll.[2]

It was most fitting if not poetic justice that after so many decades of lawlessness that Trump's first criminal indictment would come from the Manhattan district attorney on what used to be the former president's home turf. It was also most appropriate that if criminally convicted for the first time in his life it will be for tax fraud one of Trump's specialties.[3] Immediately, Trump's attorneys were creatively "trying to knock down the Manhattan" District Attorney Alvin Bragg's 34 felony fraud counts "to misdemeanors by looking at a U.S. Supreme Court decision in a decades-old hate crime case."[4] They had tried to use the same arguments to remove the case from state to federal court as a delay tactic that had failed previously in the E. Jean Carroll rape and defamation lawsuit.

In the former motion, they were trying to use the decision in *Apprendi v. New Jersey* (2000) involving a 1994 incident where "a white man got drunk and fired gunshots at a Black family's home that resulted in hate crime charges." In that case a state judge had decided that Charles C. Apprendi Jr. had been "motivated by racial bias and tacked two additional years onto a 10-year maximum sentence from the charges listed at the time of the indictment." But the Supreme Court "ruled that the founders had never considered 'elements' of a felony or 'sentencing factors,' and said basically anything not listed in an indictment cannot be used to impose additional jail time."[5] Aside from the very different crimes involved, the legal analogies between the two lawsuits are off point. As prosecutor Becky Mangold in her ten-page response pointed out with respect to the office's decision to leave out some important details from the indictment:

> Where an intent to commit or conceal another crime is an element of an offense, the People need not prove intent to commit or conceal a particular crime. The indictment need not identify any particular crime that the defendant intended to commit or conceal.[6]

In the latter and related motion not on downgrading to a misdemeanor, but in removal to federal court, speculation about those unidentified crimes in Bragg's indictment comes from MSMBC legal analyst Lisa Rubin's deep dive into the sealed documents from the Manhattan office's "memo of law" that Bragg is using to argue for keeping the case in the state's jurisdiction so that case can begin on March 25, 2024.[7] One of the "sealed exhibits appear to be a $130k check from Cohen's shell company to Stormy Daniels." Other evidence included Cohen's sham invoices for his "services" rendered; the Trump Organization's electronic accounting records reflecting each payment to Cohen 9 out of 11 of those were from Trump's personal bank account and signed by Donald. "And perhaps most damaging, the sealed exhibits appear to include proof Trump paid 'other personal & other unofficial expenditures in 2017 from his same personal bank account.'"[8] Another bit of evidence that came to light as Memorial Day weekend began on May 26 was that the DA possesses an audio tape that Michael Cohen has been telling the world that he possessed from 2016, a recording according to ABC News that contains a discussion of hush money plans to buy silence of Playboy model Karen McDougal prior to the 2016 election as well.[9]

Trump also returned to the Manhattan courthouse by way of a compulsory video hearing on May 23, 2023, with Judge Juan Merchan where the terms of his protective order effectively established the rules around Trump's abilities to inappropriately share publicly or otherwise discovered evidence. In effect, the judge had agreed with the prosecutor's motion for a protective order because Trump was not likely to abide by the procedural rules. The judge did not agree with the response of Trump and his attorneys to deny such a motion because he was a candidate for the presidency. The judge also made it perfectly clear that Trump retained his First Amendment rights to free speech as well as to run for the presidency unencumbered by the protective order. So grave had the concern been that Trump would violate the expected norms based on his pattern of misbehavior that he was limited in access to some of the discovery items without court approval and could only see other evidence in the present of his attorneys.

One week later, Trump attorneys were filing a motion seeking to have the judge recuse himself from the Manhattan case for alleged "conflicts" and that getting an "impartial" judge was "vital to stop this travesty of justice."[10] Seven weeks earlier Trump had lashed out and attacked Judge Merchan as he often does with most judges presiding over his lawsuits. In this case, Trump wrote on Truth Social that Merchan had "railroaded" former Trump Organization CFO Allen Weisselberg who was serving time at Rikers Island after having pled guilty to tax fraud charges. He continued: "The Judge 'assigned to my Witch Hunt Case, a 'Case' that has NEVER BEEN CHARGED BEFORE, HATES ME. His name is Juan Manuel Merchan, was handpicked by Bragg & the Prosecutors."[11]

The hearing had made it clear and compelled Trump to acknowledge for the court record that he understood that among the consequences for violating the protective order were criminal contempt charges and the potential additional legal sanctions. In the event that Trump would be later charged with criminal contempt, obstruction of justice, and/or convicted on one or more of the 34 felony counts in his first criminal trial beginning midway through the Republican primary season for the 2024 GOP presidential nomination, Trump undoubtedly will appeal these decisions and/or verdicts all the way to the Supreme Court should he be granted a *writ of certiorari*.

Leading up to and after Trump's first criminal indictment, I wrote five commentaries between March 20 and April 13, 2023, three for *The Crime Report* and two for *Salon*. These essays written in real-time capture the impending indictments as they were happening. Not only in relation to decades of Trump having eluded law enforcement, but also in terms of the legal, media, and political strategies to be used by the Litigator-in-Chief in his numerous criminal charges to come which may ultimately exceed a low three-digit number.

Salon

**Time's up: Trump has dodged prosecution his whole life,
but Judgment Day is coming**

March 20, 2023[12]

**By Gregg Barak**

Over the course of five decades in his rise to political and economic power, Donald Trump has been accused of numerous crimes, including but not limited to sexual assault, tax evasion, money laundering, non-payment of employees, and the defrauding of tenants, customers, contractors, investors, bankers, attorneys, charities, and finally the American people.

Not unlike the capitalists, conmen, and fraudsters of the 19th century, Trump was in the right place at the right time, albeit more than a century later under very different economic conditions – that is, he was in New York real estate and Wall Street finance. He also took advantage of the era of heightened and deregulated monopoly-capitalist fraud where lawlessness and corruption were in close alignment with rampant scamming and financial entrepreneurship.

After his improbable election as president, Trump used his time in the White House to consolidate his economic and political power. He broadened his fraudulent schemes and expanded his criminal enterprise by monetizing the powers of the presidency for his own benefit, including the Trump Organization and members of his immediate family.

At the peak of his power, and even after orchestrating a failed coup, the "Houdini of organized crimes" has this far managed to escape his smorgasbord of transgressions with all but a few scratches. Now with the impending and unprecedented criminal indictment of both a former president and a candidate for president, apparently to be brought forth by Manhattan District Attorney Alvin Bragg, we will all become witnesses to the ways in which Trump's standard legal tactics as a civil defendant – deny, deflect, and delay – will be employed in his new role as a criminal defendant.

As Joyce Vance has explained, criminal courts work on a different clock than civil courts do. That's literally true, in that "the Speedy Trial Acts puts criminal cases on a shorter fuse" and while such proceedings "can be delayed by pending motions and appeals, the prospects aren't indefinite as they can be in civil cases."

Look for Trump and his legal team to mount a broad offensive against Bragg the person and Bragg the supposed "political operative" as they try to portray any charges against Trump as having nothing to do with his apparent payment of hush money to Stormy Daniels and everything to do, as *The New York Times* put it recently, with "a coordinated offensive by the Democratic Party against Mr. Trump, who is trying to become only the second former president to win a new term after leaving office."

Over this past weekend, Trump went on Truth Social to tell the world that he believed he would be arrested on Tuesday and urged his followers to protest and to "TAKE OUR NATION BACK!" Personally, I do not think any arrest or indictment will come until later this week (if even that soon), but time will tell.

With so many different civil and criminal lawsuits or investigations revolving around Trump, his teams of lawyers are using the various probes against him to "discover" what cross-over information or evidence is out there. For example, Trump's attorney Alina Habba, as the Daily Beast reports, has tried "to use the New York attorney general's case to subpoena information on other Trump investigations—including ones he may not know about."

Trump's attorneys were already caught earlier this month, as another Daily Beast report suggests, trying to manufacture trial delays by agreeing to schedules that would end up conflicting and leading to delays down the road. One such federal case involves investors who say they were misled by fraudulent promotions connected to "The Apprentice," Trump's former reality TV franchise, and the other is the New York state attorney general's civil suit over the Trump Organization's allegedly fraudulent financial practices.

During his term as president, Trump attempted to corrupt or deconstruct various parts of the federal administrative apparatus, including the Environmental Protection Agency, the Consumer Protection Bureau, and the Department of Justice. With the help of his third attorney general, Bill Barr, he also sought to weaponize the DOJ against his enemies and on behalf of such criminal allies as former White House adviser and Trump campaign chief Steve Bannon and former national security adviser Michael Flynn.

Even after Trump's statement on Saturday about his alleged imminent arrest, Speaker Kevin McCarthy proclaimed that he had directed House committees to investigate whether federal funds were being used for "politically motivated prosecutors," tweeting: "Here we go again – an outrageous abuse of power by a radical DA who lets violent criminals walk as he pursues political vengeance against President Trump."

While Trump may not be the world's most successful economic and political outlaw, he is certainly the leading US candidate for the title. Other contenders in American history would extend from industrialist Henry Clay Frick and Ponzi-scheme master Bernie Madoff to previous disgraced presidents such as James Buchanan, Warren G. Harding, and Richard Nixon. None of those candidates, however, can hold a candle to Trump, who – even with the likelihood of multiple indictments before him in the near future – is still the leading contender in the 2024 Republican presidential primary race for president.

Explaining how these remarkable social realities are materializing is complicated and beyond the scope of this commentary. Nevertheless, part of the explanation is in the very essence of American democracy's enemy-in-chief as captured by David Remnick:

> In his career as a New York real-estate shyster and tabloid denizen, then as the forty-fifth President of the United States, Trump has been the most transparent of public figures. He does little to conceal his most distinctive characteristics: his racism, misogyny, dishonesty, narcissism, incompetence, cruelty, instability, and corruption. And yet what has kept Trump afloat for so long, what has helped him evade ruin and prosecution, is perhaps his most salient quality: he is shameless. That is the never-apologize-never-explain core of him. Trump is hardly the first dishonest President, the first incurious President, the first liar. But he is the most shameless. His contrition is impossible to conceive. He is insensible to disgrace.

There's no question that Trump's shamelessness, as well as his sociopathic personality, are among the key attributes that have served him well over the course of his life. What has prevented Trump from evading prosecution and ruin all these years, however, can be encapsulated in the various struggles to impeach or criminalize him. I refer to Trump's abilities to corral and maximize legal and political power, on the one hand, and, on the other hand, to his mob-boss tendencies to resist, fix, or intimidate not only other politicians and ordinary citizens, but also officials from law enforcement agencies such as the Internal Revenue System, the Security & Exchange Commission, the Federal Bureau of Investigation, and the US Justice Department.

People with that much power especially corrupt political leaders, Wall Street financiers, and multinational corporate executives often remain habitually above the law and well beyond incrimination for extended periods of time, at least until the rare occasions when they are actually held accountable for their deeds.

We will encounter a test case very soon, and not just from Alvin Bragg. In fact, I believe we will learn a great deal more about Trump's ruthlessness, power, and racketeering skills when Fulton County, Georgia District Attorney Fani Willis finally indicts Trump, and quite likely numerous others, under her state's RICO statutes. Among the things I'm eager to learn are these:

- What a real as opposed to a fake conspiracy to commit crimes looks like?
- How the Trump-inspired conspiracy to overturn the results of the 2020 presidential election in Georgia came together?
- Why exactly Trump and his allies failed?

Should Willis' prosecution and the ensuing trial materialize as I envision it, that will surely become the most famous RICO case in American history.

**The Crime Report**
**Here come the indictments. When will the trials come?**
**Not before summer 2024**
March 31, 2023[13]

**By Gregg Barak**

The first of several forthcoming criminal indictments against Donald Trump was announced early on the evening of March 30, 2023, shortly after a Manhattan grand jury voted to indict the former president – crossing for the very first time the Rubicon that no person is above the rule of law in the United States.

We still do not know what the exact charges are and will not find out until Tuesday when Trump is scheduled to surrender at the courthouse accompanied by one or more of his Secret Service agents, and to appear for his open arraignment subject to the usual booking process of being fingerprinted, photographed, and so on.

We do know from reading *The New York Times* that the indictment contains 34 separate charges or "counts" including multiple felonies, which likely will involve some kind of tax violation or federal campaign crimes.

This indictment has been a long time coming. It was back in 2018 when Trump's personal attorney and fixer Michael Cohen pleaded guilty and went to federal prison for paying hush money to cover up at least one sexual affair of his former Boss just days before the 2016 presidential election.

What we are already witnessing even before the charges are publicly known is that the "cult of the personality" leadership of the GOP is continuing to circle the wagons around Trump, to cast aspersions on the prosecutors of the rule of law, and to politicize the slowly turning wheels of due process and the administration of criminal justice.

For example, in the world of the Trumpian "pot calling the kettle black," the unannounced and assumed 2024 Republican presidential contender who is already polling a distant second behind Trump for the nomination, Governor Ron DeSantis (FL), immediately following the announced indictment posted his antisemitic tropes defending the former president @GovRonDeSantis:

> The weaponization of the legal system to advance a political agenda turns the rule of law on its head. It is un-American. The Soros-backed Manhattan District Attorney has consistently bent the law to downgrade felonies and to excuse criminal misconduct. Yet now he is stretching the law to target a political opponent. Florida will not assist in an extradition request given the questionable circumstances at issue with this Soros-backed Manhattan prosecutor and his political agenda.

This is, of course, "all bark and no bite" since Governor DeSantis will not be asked by District Attorney Alvin Bragg to extradite Trump from Florida since his attorneys have already asserted that he will voluntarily show up at the Manhattan courthouse on Tuesday.

From Trump's point of view, his imagined indictments and criminality were always a matter of the political struggle for power and the "rule of law" versus the "rule of mob" as these play out together in the courts of law and the courts of public opinion.

For example, on the day before the indictment when Trump had perhaps a momentary belief that his forthcoming Manhattan indictment might not materialize at all, or as he had predicted two weeks earlier about his surrendering on March 21 rather than on April 4, the ex-president was playing to the grand jurors that he hoped would not vote to indict him.

From @realDonaldTrump, the ex-president posted in all caps: I HAVE GAINED SUCH RESPECT FOR THIS GRAND JURY, & PERHAPS EVEN THE GRAND JURY SYSTEM AS A WHOLE. THE EVIDENCE IS SO OVERWHELMING IN MY FAVOR, & SO RIDICULOUSLY BAD FOR THE HIGHLY PARTISAN & HATEFUL DISTRICT ATTORNEY, THAT THE GRAND JURY IS SAYING, HOLD ON, WE ARE NOT A RUBBER STAMP, WHICH MOST JURIES ARE BRANDED AS BEING, WE ARE NOT GOING TO VOTE AGAINST A PREPONDERANCE OF EVIDENCE OR AGAINST LARGE NUMBERS OF LEGAL SCHOLARS ALL SAYING THERE IS NO CASE HERE. DROP THIS SICK WITCH HUNT, NOW!

Having his "cake and eating it too," Trump was posting @realDonaldTrump less than 24 hours later, and only minutes after his indictment was announced: These Thugs and Radical Left Monsters have just INDICTED the 45th President of the United States, and the leading Republican candidate, by far, for the 2024 Nomination for President. THIS IS AN ATTACK ON OUR COUNTRY THE LIKES OF WHICH HAS NEVER BEEN SEEN BEFORE. IT IS LIKEWISE A CONTINUING ATTACK ON OUR ONCE

FREE AND FAIR ELECTIONS. THE USA IS NOW A THIRD WORLD NATION, A NATION IN SERIOUS DECLINE. SO SAD!

Donald Trump, Jr chimed in from his podcast shortly thereafter – "Apparently, Soros-backed Manhattan DA Alvin Bragg is indicting my father. Let's be clear folks: This is Communist-level shit. This is stuff that would make Mao, Stalin, Pol Pot blush." This is all part of his dad's narrative on the campaign trail, "They're not coming for ME, they're coming after YOU – and I am standing in their way."

The antisemitic references to George Soros by DeSantis, Trump, Jr., and others should be concerning to all of us as Joyce Vance has written: "This sort of casual hate baiting is in the former president's wheelhouse as well. Trump has always been cavalier about the impact of his words on his followers' propensity toward violence. But if Trump summons a mob," Vance believes they will come. I am not so sure that after January 6 that they still will. Time will tell.

More likely as Vance underscores, "individuals have answered his call too, as with the attack on Speaker Pelosi' husband. It's appalling that neither the Trumps, nor apparently DeSantis, understand that real people" can fall victims to their hateful speech.

This won't be over for a long time, folks. With all the defense motions and due process to play out, a trial on the merits of this indictment will not likely happen before the summer of 2024.[14] In the meanwhile, look for several more criminal indictments against Trump to materialize. One from Fulton County, Georgia for trying to overturn its statewide presidential election. And two from the Justice Department, one for inciting an insurrection, and the other for deliberately stealing classified documents and lying about it.

**The Crime Report**
**A criminal case fifty years in the making**
April 4, 2023[15]

**By Gregg Barak**

The master fraudster's first criminal indictment has been coming for 50 years. It finally arrived with the Manhattan booking and arraignment of the ex-president earlier today.

A very bold and impressive broad-gauged indictment that few, if any, legal pundits, saw coming. Yet at the press conference and Q & A following the arraignment District Attorney Alvin Bragg told the world that the 34 felony charges brought against defendant Trump were nothing more than the Manhattan office engaging in its everyday prosecution of "bread and butter" white-collar crimes.

Turns out the payments of hush money to at least two women – misdemeanor offenses – were not really what these indictments were all about. Ergo, there were no misdemeanor charges, only first-degree felonies.

The unsealed indictment of The People of the State of New York against Donald J. Trump accused the former president both before and while he was the 45th POTUS of conspiring to falsify business records, with the intent to defraud and intent to commit other crimes including the repeated violations of campaign election laws and tax laws, by way of aiding and concealing the commission of these offenses by way of the business records of the Trump Organization.

With additional criminal indictments coming to courts in Georgia, Washington, DC, and possibly elsewhere the Houdini of organized crimes as well as most legal commentators are of the opinions that Trump is or should be most concerned about the stolen documents stored in his country club and home at Mar-a-Lago, Florida.

For example, only hours before his Tuesday arraignment in New York City, Trump was ranting about Special Prosecutor Jack Smith – who is investigating both his attempts to overturn the 2020 election on January 6 and to steal classified documents – for "leaking" massive amounts of information about his alleged obstruction of justice to *The Washington Post*.

I believe that all these cases if prosecuted pose serious threats to the viability of Trump's presumed GOP candidacy for 2024. At the same time, I also believe the legal case that could bring Trump down in the minds of the American people is a civil one scheduled for trial on April 25, 2023, should it materialize. This lawsuit stems from two lawsuits filed by E. Jean Carroll who had also accused Trump of raping her in the mid-1990s.

The first of these was filed in 2019 when she sued Trump for defamation; the second lawsuit was filed last year because of a recent New York law that allows sexual assault victims to sue years later.

In the most recent case filed in 2022 as reported by *The Washington Post*, Carroll said Trump "forcibly raped and groped her" and that he "knew he was lying" when he responded to her allegations. Carroll and Trump sought to combine the two legal cases into one; however, District Judge Lewis A. Kaplan rejected the merger.

Instead, Kaplan postponed indefinitely Carroll's first lawsuit that had been scheduled for April 10, 2023. The second lawsuit scheduled for the end of the month accuses Trump of battery and defaming Carroll and is seeking monetary damages. However, there is a hitch and Trump may once more escape legal accountability for his harmful behavior.

It all depends on the decision of the DC Court of Appeals that heard arguments this past January on whether Trump was acting within his job as president when he denied Carrol's rape allegation:

> Lawyers for the New York-based writer E. Jean Carroll argued that Trump acted as a private citizen when he denied raping Carroll, and therefore can be sued like anyone else. Trump's lawyers and an attorney

for the Justice Department countered that his responses were made as part of his job as president – which would effectively end Carroll's case against him because of protection government employees have from defamation suits.

At this point in time, the lawsuit could be dismissed, allowed to proceed, or postponed until a decision is reached. The issue will turn on whether the former president was acting on behalf of his interests or the interests of the presidency of the United States.

Though Carroll was precluded from pressing criminal charges against Trump because of the statute of limitations, Trump set himself up for a second defamation lawsuit when he sounded off publicly after Carroll told her story about Trump allegedly raping her in a Bergdorf Goodman dressing room in Manhattan.

Not only did Trump respond, as Amanda Marcotte writes, "in his usual way, by accusing Carroll of lying and adding a bunch of insults about her looks," but he also made what appears to have been threatening statements, such as "people have to be careful, because they are playing with very dangerous territory."

While Trump makes bullying threats of intimidation and worse to his adversaries all the time, many folks dismiss these as all bluster and buffoonery. As most of us understand, Donald's bluster can come with very real violent consequences.

However, what most people are not aware of is that in his 1987 book, *The Art of the Deal*, Trump brags about how he used to be an aggressive person who in the second grade gave his music teacher a black eye because he didn't think the man knew anything about music. Whether true or not, Donny's parents Fred and Mary Anne sent him off as a young adolescent because of "behavioral issues" to a military academy to complete his primary education where he graduated in 1964.

Although Trump has told the public that he has "absolutely no idea who she is," there are pictures of Trump, Carroll, and his first wife Ivanka together. By the way Ivanka had also accused her ex-husband of having raped her. As he often does when Trump is accused of sexual assault, and there are more than two dozen women who have claimed that he has done so, he typically claims that these women were "not his type."

Most interestingly, during the October 2022 disposition for the Carroll case, Trump mistook a picture of Carroll for his second wife, Marla Maples: "That' is Marla, yeah That's my wife."

For the most part the press and many legal analysts had dismissed the hush money lawsuit case involving Stormy Daniels as small potatoes. However, after the indictment of 34 felonies today, I think that will largely change more than a little.

As for the upcoming Carroll (or not) lawsuit, I agree with Marcotte who argues that Trump's abuse of women and his misogyny are not minor matters.

These will resonate more with women (and perhaps "woke" men) than some of the other pending cases against Donald Trump. They also represent cases of poetic justice in the sense that these lawsuits are at the front of the line to hold the former president accountable:

> As the protesters in the Women's March understood, how men treat women tells you a great deal about their character. When Trump entered the White House, one sure thing we all knew about him was that he didn't believe a woman had a right to say "no" to him. Over the next four years, he proved that this entitled attitude was not limited to sex or women. Trump doesn't think *anyone* has a right to say "no" to him. Not the president of Ukraine. Not various public officials he leaned on to break the law. And, ultimately, not the American people.

### The Crime Report
### Trump v. Cohen is another lawsuit about the plaintiff-in-chief weaponizing civil litigation
### April 13, 2023[16]

**By Gregg Barak**

On Wednesday former president Donald Trump sued his former lawyer and fixer Michael Cohen for more than $500 million in a federal court in Miami. The civil lawsuit accuses Cohen of violating his attorney-client relationship by testifying as a key witness before a Manhattan grand jury, revealing "confidences" and "spreading falsehoods" which resulted in Trump being charged on 34 felony counts of falsifying business records.

Looking backward from 2023 to 1973, Trump has been involved in more than 4,000 legal battles. At least until the other day at the Manhattan Criminal Courthouse in New York, when the former president was criminally arraigned for the very first time and looking so dejected and forlorn as he sat between his attorneys two flanked on either side, Trump had always loved to litigate as much as he loves to golf, to down his cans of Diet Coke and to consume fast food.

Now that Trump is playing for such high stakes, between this first indictment and the ones to come where his liberty and freedom are in jeopardy, the joy of litigation may have finally lost some of its luster.

Despite Trump's bravado as the pressure from his depositions, indictments, and trials continue to build over the next 24 months, it would not surprise me to see the former president have a complete "meltdown."

Meanwhile, Trump's indefatigable ego and his inflated id are still very much in play. Thus, don't look for Trump to surrender to his adversaries without a "fight to the death" and certainly not without filing every frivolous motion in his attorneys' arsenal to delay or to postpone every legal proceeding dogging him.

As James D. Zinn in his examination of Trump's lengthy litigation history prior to his becoming the 45th POTUS, *Plaintiff in Chief: A Portrait of Donald Trump in 3,500 Lawsuits*, has revealed about the "character and morality" of Trump:

> If you partner with Donald Trump, you will probably wind-up litigating with him. If you enroll in his university or buy one of his apartments, chances are you will want your money back. If you are a woman and you get too close to him, you may need to watch your back. If you try to sue him, he's likely to defame you. If you make a deal with him, you had better get it in writing. If you are a lawyer, an architect, or even his dentist, you'd better get paid up front. If you venture an opinion that publicly criticizes him, you may be sued for libel.

Trump has learned that when it comes to litigation, it is better to be a plaintiff than to be a defendant. His ratio of being the plaintiff compared to being the defendant is about 60% to 40%. Many of these lawsuits on both sides have been dismissed by judges, and others seemed to be unresolved according to public records. All in all, Trump's win-loss record before becoming president was an impressive one. According to Zinn, he had won 451 times and lost 38 times.

One of the things that Trump has always loved most about litigation is his ability to use the courts and the rule of law as a cudgel against his enemies.

Zinn contends that Trump's

> political worldview was molded in the courtroom. He sees law not as a system of rules to be obeyed and ethical ideals to be respected, but as a weapon to be used against his adversaries or a hurdle to be sidestepped when it gets in the way.

In the case of weaponization, Trump's lawsuit against Cohen alleges that his "most egregious breaches of fiduciary duty and contract" happened in connection with his tell-all books, *Disloyal* (2020) and *Revenge* (2022), in addition to those claims that Cohen has made on his podcast, "Mea Culpa."

Lanny Davis, Cohen's attorney, labeled the lawsuit as "frivolous" and from a statement he released and reported on by Kevin Breuninger for CNBC: "Mr. Trump appears once again to be using and abusing the judicial system as a form of harassment and intimidation," suggesting that Trump is "terrified by his looming legal perils and is attempting to send a message to other potential witnesses who are cooperating with prosecutors against him."

When it comes to hurdling or sidestepping the law, Trump's favorite tactic besides countersuing has always been to raise frivolous motion after frivolous motion for no other purposes than to wear down his opponents, to deflect from the merits of the cases, and to delay for as long as possible the trials from materializing.

For example, Reuters reported that on April 12, 2023, in a letter to US District Judge Lewis Kaplan in Manhattan, Trump through his lawyers blamed the media for why they are seeking to delay the defamation trial scheduled to begin later this month on April 25 between magazine columnist E. Jean Carroll, plaintiff, and Donald J. Trump, defendant – who allegedly raped her in an upscale Manhattan dressing room more than two decades ago.

To guarantee the former president's right to a fair trial, his lawyers asked for a four-week "cooling off" period. Their letter claimed that absent a delay, "many, if not most, prospective jurors will have the criminal allegations top of mind when judging President Trump's defense against Ms. Carroll's allegation" because of "the breathless coverage" of his alleged "extra-marital affair with Stormy Daniels still ringing in their ears."

However, the only common denominator about alleged negative media coverage, whether it has to do with the two Manhattan lawsuits, the attempt to illegally overturn an election in Fulton County, Georgia, or the attempt to steal top-secret classified documents and the investigations into these, is that the leaking and media coverage surrounding these cases has rarely been created by Trump's adversaries.

On the contrary, it is Trump and his minions who deliberately create the hubbub so that they may manipulate false or fake narratives about these crimes in the courtrooms of public opinion.

Salon
### Jim Jordan fights on doggedly for his lord and master –
### but there's no winning this battle
April 13, 2023[17]

**By Gregg Barak**
Last week, one of Donald Trump's apparent January 6 co-conspirators, Rep. Jim Jordan, R-Ohio, who chairs both the House Judiciary Committee and its misbegotten Select Subcommittee on the Weaponization of the Federal Government – which has been misfiring as badly as Special Counsel John Durham's investigation of supposed wrongdoing in the origins of the Russia inquiry – announced that the Judiciary panel would visit New York next Monday to hold a field hearing on "Victims of Violent Crime in Manhattan."

Let's recall that Jordan was among the four GOP members of Congress referred to by the bipartisan House Ethics Committee last December for defying a subpoena for testimony and documents issued by the January 6 select committee.

Last Thursday, Jordan also issued his first subpoena aimed at undermining Trump's Manhattan indictment, directed at Mark Pomerantz, a former prosecutor on the staff of Manhattan District Attorney Alvin Bragg.

Pomerantz previously helped lead the investigation into Trump's finances and his alleged hush money payments to Stormy Daniels but resigned in early 2022 after Bragg initially declined to move forward with the case. Pomerantz is also the author of "People vs. Donald Trump: An Inside Account," which concerns an earlier investigation by the Manhattan office to prosecute the former president.

According to *The New York Times*, Pomerantz has said he will "not be providing documents or testimony" to Jordan's committee, citing instructions from Bragg.

As Joyce Vance has written, there's a crucial difference between Pomerantz and politicians who have written books or spoken extensively in public but then decline to comply with congressional subpoenas:

> Pomerantz was involved in a grand jury investigation. While he went further than some might have in his public conversations, he did not disclose grand jury proceedings – to do so violates the law. And, in any event, the charges Bragg has indicted on are different from the charges Pomerantz wrote about.

This week Bragg fired back, with an unprecedented lawsuit filed in federal court in Manhattan. In his official capacity as New York County District Attorney, he sued Jordan and the other members of the Judiciary Committee, along with Pomerantz.

In the introduction to Bragg v. Jordan, the DA writes that this suit comes "in response to an unprecedented brazen and unconstitutional attack by the members of Congress on an ongoing New York State criminal prosecution and investigation of former President Donald. J. Trump." Jordan and his fellow House Republicans, Bragg argues, have conducted "a transparent campaign to intimidate and attack District Attorney Bragg, making demands for confidential documents and testimony from the District Attorney himself as well as his current and former employees and officials." Bragg specifically cites the subpoena served to Pomerantz just two days after Trump was arraigned in a New York courtroom.

Whereas most civil suits seek money damages, Bragg is asking the court for a permanent injunction against the Pomerantz subpoena, which he describes as "invalid, unconstitutional, *ultra vires* [i.e., outside legal authority], and/or unenforceable."

Judge Mary Kay Vyskocil, a Trump appointee but a well-respected member of the bench, rejected Bragg's request to enter a temporary restraining order against Jordan and his committee, which is not unusual in itself. That would have immediately prevented any enforcement of the Pomerantz subpoena, even before Jordan's lawyers could argue on its behalf.

Instead, Vyskocil has set a rapid schedule for considering whether to enter a preliminary injunction. She ordered Bragg to serve the lawsuit on the defendants on Wednesday evening, and the defendants have been ordered to respond by 9 a.m. on Monday, April 17, with a hearing on the matter set for April 19.

Congress certainly has wide jurisdiction when it comes to judicial oversight, but the principle that ongoing criminal investigations in state or federal courts are off limits is well established. Nevertheless, it's entirely possible that this lawsuit could wind its way up to the US Supreme Court.

So goes another battle, with several more to come, between Donald J. Trump and his minions on one side, and the rule of law in the United States on the other.

With the next indictments coming even later than most people had thought, Trump had taken to YouTube to declare that Joe Biden is guilty of crimes without any examples or evidence whatsoever. No matter. It's not the facts; it's the story. He also referred to the "Trump-hating" Special Prosecutor Jack Smith who was questioning all of Trump's insiders who were being compelled to talk about the federal investigations into January 6 and the classified documents by a "lunatic" who "should go get Biden for what he did. He's very guilty. I'm not." Of course, Trump is perfectly aware that President Biden has not been the focus of any type of criminal investigation, let alone charged and indicted for anything. As to whether "the felony charges in New York and the possibility of more charges coming from Georgia and Washington D.C. are really weighing on the former president" as David Pakman ponders or that his YouTube video message is simply Trump spinning more lies about his 2024 presidential opponent remains an open question for some.[18]

To me, not only is it a question of both pressure and spin, but it is also what Trump does best publicly, if not, legally. Namely, inverting the political narrative about his criminality, shifting what he has done or is doing on to others especially those investigating, indicting, or prosecuting him like New York Attorney General Letitia James, Manhattan District Attorney Alvin Bragg, Fulton County, Georgia District Attorney Fani T. Willis, and Jack Smith who in the spring of 2023 was investigating the former president not only about stolen classified documents and his role on the January 6th assault and the fake electors scheme, but also his fundraising activities following the lost 2020 presidential election. In these cases Trump called these four prosecutors out, three for being Black "racists" and the one white prosecutor Smith for his allegedly Jewish connections.

Regarding Smith, on May 19, 2023 the former president was stepping up his other than racist attacks (although Trump had previously questioned his ethnicity and his having supposedly changed his name to Smith from what we do not know) in a late-night posting on his Truth Social platform where he absurdly claimed that Smith, his family, and friends were on a "treasonous quest" whatever that means: "TRUMP Hating Special Prosecutor Jack

Smith, whose family and friends are Big Time Haters also, will be working overtime on this treasonous quest. They are scoundrels and cheats. THIS IS ALL ABOUT ELECTION INTERFERENCE." Trump was referencing

> A Poll just came out where I am way up on Biden in the General Election. What that means is that the Radical Left Democrats will step up their Fake Investigations on me because they now see they can't win at the Ballot Box.[19]

Alvin Bragg and the other prosecutors were not sitting back idly. Instead they were trying to thread the needle between a two-time impeached former president and 2024 candidate and his First Amendment rights to free speech, on the one hand, and the 5th and 14th Amendment rights of due process and equal protection under the law, on the other hand. Bragg struck first and appears to have succeeded with this "gag order" which undoubtedly will be challenged by Trump and appealed all the way up to the Supreme Court should he be held in contempt of violating the protective order and/ or convicted on any or all of the 34 felony counts. On May 23, 2023, Judge Juan Merchan held a video hearing with Trump as part of the Manhattan DA's criminal prosecution regarding the sharing of evidence revealed by the government to Trump in discovery with third parties or the public especially vis-à-vis social media posts. Previously, Judge Merchan had waned "both sides" regarding restrictions on sharing this kind of information. Now, the judge was setting Trump up for contempt charges should he violate "the order, by reviewing it with him, and confirming in court, on the record, that Trump understands the obligations the court has imposed and has the opportunity to respond and clarify as appropriate."[20]

For the record, Merchan scheduled the hearing on May 10th the day after Trump appeared on CNN's town hall viewed by three million people where he lied, offered bogus excuses for his past behavior, insulted people, and called the Manhattan indictment a case of fake charges. The protective order stipulated that "any materials and information provided by the People to the Defense in accordance with their discovery obligations…shall be used solely for the purposes of preparing a defense in this matter."[21] Trump was specifically singled out in the order and was "limited to reviewing some material in the presence of his lawyers" and could not even "be shown others, like witnesses' cellphone records, without prior court approval."[22] These kinds of protective orders are used when a "defendant's conduct threatens the safety and well-being of witnesses, victims, or anyone else related to the case."[23] Bragg's prosecutors had argued that they needed "safeguards that will protect the integrity of the materials," saying the "risk" that Trump would use them "inappropriately is substantial." While Judge Merchan agreed that Trump had a history of making "harassing, embarrassing, and threatening statements," he also noted that "I'm bending over backwards and straining to make sure that he is given every opportunity possible to advance his candidacy and to be able to speak in furtherance of his candidacy."[24]

In the meanwhile, jury selection was to start July 17, 2023, for a lawsuit filed by Cohen against the Trump Organization back in 2019, "claiming he incurred $1.9 million in legal fees during multiple congressional hearings, Special Counsel Robert Mueller's investigation and the criminal case again against him brought in federal court in Manhattan."[25] One of the persons who received a subpoena to testify in the case is Donald Trump Jr. However, on Friday three days before jury selection was to begin Cohen and the Trump Organization settled the case to their mutual satisfaction without revealing the terms of the settlement.

It should be acknowledged that had not enough Republicans engaged in "jury nullification" in the second impeachment vote of the former president on February 13, 2021, and had they instead joined the Senate majority to convict Trump of High Crimes and Misdemeanors, there would never have been the federal and state prosecutions of Donald Trump in Washington DC and Georgia. There would also not be three cases before SCOTUS, one to decide the immunity question or whether a President was a king or above the law, one to decide the question of the 14th amendment and Trump's eligibility and whether Trump would have been disqualified from running for office, and a third that indirectly could relate, but should not apply to the former president, about whether a man convicted of obstructing an official governmental proceeding on Jan, 6 could have been charged in the first place.

Finally. the failure of Republican Senators to convict Trump did not occur based on principal or because these public servants believed Trump was innocent as charged, but rather as Liz Cheney and Senator Mitt Romney have explained, it was because they were scared for their own and the safety of their families knowing what Trump and his people were capable of. On the other hand, the two other criminal prosecutions have nothing to do with the POTUS, as the hush money-tax evasion indictment case in New York was committed before Trump became president, while his stolen classified documents caper in Mar-a-Lago, Florida was committed after he left office.

## Notes

1 Benjamin Weiser. 2023. E. Jean Carroll seeks new damages from Trump for comments on CNN. The New York Times. May 22. www.nytimes.com/2023/05/22/nyregion/carroll-trump-cnn-defamation.html

2 Graham Kates. 2023. Justice Department reverses position, won't support shielding Trump in original E. Jean Carroll lawsuit. CBS News. July 11. www.cbsnews.com/news/e-jean-carroll-lawsuit-justice-department-wont-support-shielding-trump

3 Paula Junghans, Norman L. Eisen, Siven Watt, Joshua Stanton and Fred Wertheimer. 2023. The untold strength of tax crimes in the Manhattan DA's Case against Former President Trump. Just Security. May 24. www.justsecurity.org/86686/the-untold-strength-of-tax-crimes-in-manhattan-das-case-against-former-president-trump

4 Travis Gettys. 2023. Inside Trump's new plot to wriggle out of felony charges. RawStory. May 19. www.rawstory.com/donald-trump-indictment-2660297794/

5 Ibid.

6 Quoted in Ibid.

7 Matthew Chapman. 2023. Legal analyst sifts through new Trump New York filing to uncover some of the sealed documents. RawStory. May 30. www.rawstory.com/donald-trump-alvin-bragg-2660728452/

8 Quoted in Ibid.

9 Aaron Katersky. 2023. Secret audio tape among evidence collected by DA in fraud case against Trump. ABC News. May 26. https://abcnews.go.com/US/secret-audio-tape-reportedly-evidence-collected-da-fraud/story

10 Asher Notheis. 2023. Trump attorneys file motion seeking to have judge recuse himself from Manhattan case. Washington Examiner. June 1. www.washingtonexaminer.com/news/trump-attorneys-file-motion-recuse-judge-manhattan-case

11 Ben Feuerherd and Elizabeth Rosner. 2023. Trump lashes out at judge expected to preside over hush-money criminal case. New York Post. March 31. https://nypost.com/2023/03/31/trump-lashes-out-at-judge-who-may-preside-over-hush-money-case

12 www.salon.com/2023/03/20/times-up-has-dodged-prosecution-his-whole-life-but-judgment-day-is-coming/

13 https://thecrimereport.org/2023/03/31/here-come-the-indictments-when-will-the-trials-come/

14 I got this one wrong. David DePape was trield and convicted in the attack on Paul Pelosi on November 16, and could face up to 50 years in prison. www.cbsnews.com/news/david-depape-trial-paul-pelosi-attack-what-to-know/

15 https://thecrimereport.org/2023/04/04/a-criminal-case-fifty-years-in-the-making/

16 https://thecrimereport.org/2023/04/13/trump-v-cohen-is-another-lawsuit-about-the-plaintiff-in-chief-weaponizing-civil-litigation/

17 www.salon.com/2023/04/13/jim-jordan-on-doggedly-for-his-lord-and-master--but-theres-no-winning-this-fight/

18 David Pakman. 2023. The David Pakman Show. April 20. https://davidpakman.substack.com/p/desantis-suddenly-in-trouble-the?utm_source=substack&utm_medium=email

19 Quoted in Tom Boggioni. 2023. Trump accuses Jack Smith of trying to commit treason. RawStory. May 20. www.rawstory.com/donald-trump-jack-smith-2660335522/

20 Joyce Vance. 2023 The Week Ahead. Civil Discourse with Joyce Vance. May 21. https://joycevance.substack.com/p/the-week-ahead-5be

21 Quoted in Ibid.

22 Vance. 2023.

23 Ibid.

24 Quoted in Vance. 2023.

25 Ben Feuerherd. 2023. Michael Cohen and the Trump organization set for showdown at trial over attorney fees. The Messenger News. July 7. https://themessenger.com/news/michael-cohen-and-the-trump-organization-set-for-showdown-at-trial-over-attorney-fees

# 6

# THE MAR-A-LAGO CLASSIFIED DOCUMENTS CAPER

In November 2022, a team of ten lawyers with decades of experience as federal prosecutors and/or defense attorneys including Andrew Weissmann, Ryan Goodman, and Joyce Vance wrote a Mar-a-Lago Model Prosecution Memo at least six months before Special Prosecutor Jack Smith completed his investigation of the stolen classified documents and with the available public evidence at the time. As they wrote at the time of its release: "Our memo provides a sense of how prosecutors will assemble and evaluate considerations that they must assess before making a prosecution decision."[1]

"Pros memos" are internal documents and are not shared with the public even in the case of an indictment. As Vance explains:

> Before prosecutors indict a case, they draft a memo that outlines the charges they intend to bring, the factual basis for those charges, and any legal issues that need to be assessed. The memo is used in the indictment review process, where prosecutors and their supervisors determine whether the case should be indicted, evaluating it against the standards in the Principles of Federal Prosecution.[2]

I have no doubt that Jack Smith and his team of prosecutors had digested this memo by that Thanksgiving holiday weekend.

As the memo is 175 pages long, allow me to highlight from their executive summary. The memo's objective was to assess the potential charges against the former president in the fall of 2022 "emanating from his handling of classified documents and other government records since leaving office on January 20, 2021."[3] The memo evaluated the case for prosecution like any other case with similar evidence without regard to the fact that case focused

DOI: 10.4324/9781003390664-9

on the conduct of a former President of the United States. Accordingly, the authors underscore that the memo included "a balanced assessment of this particular case, and a thorough review of past DOJ precedents for charging similar cases."

With two caveats, one with respect to "exculpatory evidence" and the other "admissibility issues," those past cases demonstrated that "to decline to bring charges against Trump would be treating him far more favorably than other defendants, including those who were charged for less egregious conduct than his."[4] Their memo analyzed six federal crimes related to the removal and retention of national security information and the obstruction of the investigation into his handling of the documents:

Mishandling of Government Documents

1  Retention of National Defense Information (18 U.S.C. § 793(e))
2  Concealing of Government Records (18 U.S.C. § 2071)
3  Conversion of Government Property (18 U.S.C. § 641)

Obstruction, False Information, Contempt

1  Obstruction of Justice (18 U.S.C. § 1519)
2  Criminal Contempt (18 U.S.C. § 402)
3  False Statements to Federal Investigation (18 U.S.C. § 1001)

Based on the publicly available information at the time, the memo concluded that "a powerful case exists for charging Trump under several of these federal criminal statutes",[5] and that was long before the special prosecutor finished his investigation making the case that more powerful.

Salon
**Crimes of the powerful: Why the Mar-a-Lago "special master"
decision is so dreadful**
Our justice system is already deeply unfair.
Insisting on a higher bar for Trump's prosecution only
makes it worse
September 7, 2022[6]

**By Gregg Barak**
When it comes to the crimes of the powerful, whether we are talking about Wall Street fraudsters, multinational corporate offenders, or ex-presidents of the United States under investigation for seditious conspiracy or espionage, the bar for prosecution should be of a lower rather than of a higher nature. Why? Because the social realities of justice in America are already stacked in favor of the powerful perpetrators of crime.

To hold such accused perpetrators to a *higher* bar for indictment or prosecution only serves to reinforce the existing biases of our justice system, favoring the powerful at the expense of almost everyone else in society.

In the case of US District Judge Aileen Cannon's decision to appoint a special master in the case of Donald Trump's purloined documents, recently seized by the FBI in its search of Mar-a-Lago, Duke law professor Sam Buell tweeted that

> Donald Trump is getting something no one else ever gets in federal court, he's getting it for no good reason, and it will not in the slightest reduce the ongoing howls that he is being persecuted, when he is being privileged.

Similarly, Andrew Weissmann, a New York University Law Professor with 20 years of experience as a federal prosecutor and 10 years as a defense attorney, tweeted: "In none of the rare Special Master appointment cases — of attorneys like [Michael] Cohen and [Rudy] Giuliani — did the court ENJOIN the criminal investigation. Less factual merit and far worse legal ruling."

Weissmann refers to the fact that Cannon's order prevents the Justice Department from using the documents in question as part of its criminal investigation into Trump, at least until the not-yet-appointed special master has gone through those thousands of pages.

On MSNBC's "Morning Joe" on Tuesday, Weissmann predicted that Cannon's decision could delay a possible indictment for several months, possibly killing any prosecution of Trump altogether.

When it comes to prosecutorial discretion, the crimes of the powerful are far too often viewed as "beyond incrimination," as contrasted with the crimes of the powerless. Ordinary offenders are often prosecuted and punished for non-serious or even insignificant offenses that have few consequences for society.

But if we speak of the legal logic of criminalization or the goal of deterring the crimes of the powerful, such indictments should be made easier – not harder than they already are. Punishments in such cases should be harsher too, rather than ceremonious or possessed of little or no punitive value. For example, most convicted white-collar offenders receive financial "slaps on the wrist," which in nearly all cases represents forfeiting a smaller sum of money than they illegally appropriated.

The only logical conclusion to draw from these practices of extreme punitive leniency or outright non-enforcement of the law when it comes to corporate and state offenders is that their criminal behavior is consistently rewarded, both economically and politically. No individual in US history personifies this kind of class-based and political injustice as much as Donald Trump does.

With respect to current or former presidents, the excuses used in demanding a higher rather than lower bar for criminal prosecution have nothing to do with the crimes perpetrated and are entirely a function of politics. The proximate questions seem to be whether the political party with executive power is the same or different from the rule-breaker's party, and whether one party holds congressional power while the other holds executive power.

In the case of Trump, the first functional argument for a higher bar reflects the current legal-political discourse that has been circulating since January 6, 2021: That is, with a Democrat in the White House, the government is reluctant to pursue the prosecution of a former president that will inevitably be perceived as political retribution. The second functional argument was in play, in different ways, during and after Trump's two impeachment trials: The first occurred while Trump was in office, when Democrats had a majority in the House but not the Senate; the second occurred after Trump had left office, with Democrats holding narrow majorities in both chambers.

I would argue that all possible justifications for a higher prosecutorial bar, when it comes to indicting a former president who has habitually broken the law, before, during, and after possessing executive power, are and should be totally irrelevant. If, that is, we are supposed to have a constitutional democratic republic.

To take these questions of political power into account – or, even worse, questions of unknown potential political outcomes – when deciding to prosecute or not to prosecute is to politicize justice. Regardless of the intention, to politicize lawlessness and turn the justice system into an instrument of politics (which is exactly what Trump wanted as president) is nothing less than a full-frontal attack on the core American principles of due process and equal justice for all.

Let us observe that these justifications would never even be raised under the Biden administration if Attorney General Merrick Garland and the Justice Department were, for example, contemplating whether to indict Barack Obama for some reason. Instead, the government would likely be praised for its integrity and there would be near-total silence about a "higher bar," even as the relevance of critical race theory would play out within the chambers of prosecutorial discretion.

Similarly, when Republicans began to contemplate prosecuting Richard Nixon if he refused to resign from office in 1974, there were never any concerns that doing so would contribute to democratic breakdown, to overzealous enforcement of the law, to a precedent of backlash in which each new administration would investigate its predecessor or to the abuse of prosecutorial authority to score political points.

With respect to both the Watergate scandal and the entirely hypothetical Obama case, the fundamental argument for holding the powerful parties accountable would be quite the opposite. Not to hold such violators accountable would be understood as undermining the basic constitutional principle that justice is blind and applies to all, and that it does not matter who is being investigated or accused.

Unfortunately, reality in the United States is that we do not live by that principle. We have two contradictory standards of justice – one for those who hold power and another for those without it – and persons in the former category, especially corporate "persons," are treated as though they exist outside the law and cannot be held accountable for their serious harms against society. Meanwhile, those in the latter category – in effect, ordinary citizens – are treated as fully accountable for far less serious offenses and are far too often subject to overzealous penal sanctions.

By the weekend before Memorial Day May 29, 2023, the public knowledge of additional evidence against Trump for the mishandling of government documents, obstruction of justice, and criminal contempt had all grown much more incriminating. For example, in response to a May 2022 grand jury subpoena and the day before the FBI agents came to retrieve the classified documents at Mar-a-Lago in early June, Trump's attorney Timothy Parlatore had instructed his employees to move boxes of documents from one storage area to another, all of which was video recorded on the country club's security system. Evidence had also been gathered that Trump "at times had kept classified documents in a place where they were visible and sometimes showed them to others." Apparently, Trump and his aides carried out a "dress rehearsal" for when the agents showed up at Mar-a-Lago. Taken together, the new details of the classified documents investigation suggest a greater breadth and specificity to the instances of possible obstruction found by the FBI and Justice Department than had been previously reported suggesting that violations of the Espionage Act may have occurred. "It also broadens the timeline of possible obstruction episodes that investigators are examining – a period stretching from events at Mar-a-Lago [one year] before the subpoena to the period after the FBI search there on August 8, 2022."[7]

Two days after Memorial Day a CNN "exclusive" revealed that US prosecutors had "obtained an audio recording of a summer 2021 meeting in which former president Donald Trump acknowledges he held onto a classified Pentagon document about a potential attack on Iran... undercutting his argument that he declassified everything."[8] It also reveals Trump's intent and understanding of what he could not do with classified documents whether he actually had ever had a classified Pentagon document referred to in the conversation that he wished he could share. Then on June 2, 2023, following his receiving a subpoena for the missing document, it was revealed that Trump attorneys had not found the document referred to in the conversation with a person about a book that Mark Meadows was writing.[9]

Even before those revelations, we knew that it took the National Archives and the Department of Justice at least 18 months to allegedly get all of the documents back. That's a long time to be jerked around by anyone with classified documents, especially a former president. During that period of time Trump and/or his attorneys lied not once, but twice, that all the mishandled classified documents had been removed one way or the other from Mar-a-Lago. We know further that at least one of Trump's attorney-client privileged relationship had been pierced by the DOJ resulting in 50 pages of notes. We also know that attorney Parlatore had left the Trump legal team because of internal turf wars and/or some kind of deal may have been in the works as well. Finally, it had been reported repeatedly that Smith had virtually interviewed everybody who worked at Mar-a-Lago.

Trump's motive is not necessary for a conviction on any potential charges. If Jack Smith and the prosecution knew of any motive/s by early June 2023, these had not been revealed to the public. Regarding the criminal contempt or obstruction of an investigation charges, while Trump's knowledge of the law and his intent to violate both of these had been known publicly since before Memorial Day, it was not known until June 5th that a Mar-a-Lago employee back in October 2022 had "flooded the room where security footage was stored while draining the resort pool." An "incident that raised suspicions" among Justice Department investigators at the time and the flood coupled with other factors raised the possibility of the charge of "conspiracy to commit obstruction of justice."[10] All things considered, former Trump attorney Ty Cobb and former DOJ prosecutor Vance were both arguing that Trump should have, could have, copped a plea of guilty to a misdemeanor avoiding felony charges and a potential prison sentence with a maximum of 20 years for one of the most serious offenses alone.[11] Three of Trump's attorneys – James Trusty, John Rowley, and Lindsey Halligan – had requested a meeting with Attorney General Garland to stop the prosecution. They had to settle for Jack Smith and others from the DOJ on June 5. Again, not to negotiate a deal but to plead their case one last time not to charge Trump with anything whatsoever, especially because of what they believed to be misconduct on the part of Smith's investigation. Thus, making it extremely difficult for the Special Prosecutor not to criminally indict and prosecute the former president before a jury of his peers.

Upwards of 50 million or more Americans were anticipating and looking forward to the federal indictment of the former president on multiple charges during the one-year anniversary of the week that Trump received his first subpoena at Mar-a-Lago. The public was also aware that the prosecution had "evidence of a type it almost never has access to—notes made by one of Trump's lawyers, former prosecutor Evan Corcoran, about a meeting with his client."[12] Joyce Vance explains:

> Usually, that kind of material would be clearly protected by the attorney client privilege. But District of Columbia District Judge Beryl Howell permitted prosecutors to use the crime-fraud exception to the attorney client privilege. What's utterly fascinating here is that a person familiar with the contents of the sealed memorandum Judge Howell wrote to record her decision-making process told the New York Times that this is not a case of an attorney conniving with a client. Rather, "prosecutors believe Mr. Trump knowingly misled Mr. Corcoran about the location of documents that would be responsive to the subpoena...."[13]

As indictments appeared imminent, legal experts were surmising that there might be split-indictments not unlike the Manafort case in Washington, DC and Virginia where the crimes occurred in different legal jurisdictions. As it turned out, because of venue issues as in where the bulk of the alleged crimes occurred and the bulk of the testifying witnesses resided, the Mar-a-Lago classified documents lawsuit would play out in the federal courthouse in Fort Pierce, Florida. It also turned out from a possibility of only three other judges being assigned to the case that Judge Aileen Collins was randomly assigned to the criminal trial. She had presided over the civil lawsuit brought in 2022 by Trump to contest the classified documents investigation and was twice robustly overruled by the 11th Circuit Court of Appeals for her decisions in the matter.

Besides waiting and wanting to know the actual criminal charges, such as retention and/or dissemination of classified documents, the obstruction and/or contempt of justice, or conspiracy and/or espionage charges involved, especially regarding the Espionage Act violations that automatically kick into motion the Classified Information Procedures ACT (CIPA) which "protects both national security and due process and maintains checks and balances between the Executive and Judicial branches of government,"[14] there was still the question of whether this criminal indictment would lay out the charges like in the Manhattan "hush money" case according to the "notice" principle of who, what, where, and when or would it become a full-scale "speaking indictment" that spells out in much greater detail the criminal charges. As straightforward as the legal documents case against the former president is compared to some of his other civil and criminal matters, the Mar-a-Lago case becomes procedurally more complex because the charges of espionage involve substantively classified documents as well as the activities of the US intelligence communities and governmental relationships that are cloaked in secrecy, in addition to "a need to know" information basis about the strengths and weaknesses of our allies and adversaries alike.

As it turned out, on June 8, 2023, for the first time in US history a former president was criminally indicted in a federal district court located in Miami for the mishandling of classified documents. Trump was charged with seven counts including conspiracy to willfully retain national defense secrets in violation of the Espionage Act, making false statements to the National Archives, the FBI, and the DOJ, and engaging in a conspiracy to obstruct the government's efforts to reclaim those documents. Trump broke the news of the indictment as he took to Truth Social early Thursday evening and posted back-to-back @realDonaldTrump posts. With the exceptions of the fact that he was about to be indicted and would be arraigned on the following Tuesday, Trump spoke on Truth Social with his powerful lies and nonsense as usual:

Page 1: The corrupt Biden Administration has informed my attorneys that I have been Indicted, seemingly over the Boxes Hoax, even though Joe Biden has 1850 Boxes at the University of Delaware, additional Boxes in Chinatown, D.C., with even more Boxes at the University of Pennsylvania, and documents strewn all over his garage floor where he parks his Corvette, and which is "secured" by only a garage door that is paper thin, and open much of the time.

Page 2: I have been summoned to appear at the Federal Courthouse in Miami on Tuesday, at 3 PM. I never thought it possible that such a thing could happen to a former President of the United States, who received far more votes than any sitting President in the History of our Country, and is currently leading, by far, all Candidates, both Democrat and Republican, in polls of the 2024 Presidential Election. I AM AN INNOCENT MAN!

Joyce Vance took to social media at 8:31 p.m. where she tweeted @ JoyceWhiteVance: "Chief Justice Roberts should immediately amend the rules to permit cameras in federal courts. The American public is entitled to watch the proceedings against Trump in their entirety. Anything less would be an injustice." Perhaps Roberts will bow to political pressure and "do the right thing" as the Chief Justice surprisingly did when he and Justice Brett Kavanaugh also on June 8th joined with the court's three liberals in a 5-4 opinion, ruling that Alabama Republicans had violated the rights of Black voters during redistricting following the 2020 census. I also understood that the Chief Judge in the US District Court of jurisdiction could open the court up to at least audio if not video coverage gavel to gavel. By late afternoon Friday, the unsealed federal indictment had been released by the Justice Department three days before Trump's Miami early afternoon booking and arraignment at 3:00 p.m. on Tuesday, June 13, 2023.

## Charges against Donald J. Trump

- 31 Counts of Willful Retention of National Defense Information (The Espionage Act) – 18 USC 739 (e)
- 1 Count False Statements and Representations – 18 USC 1001 (a) (2), 2
- 1 Count of Conspiracy to Obstruct Justice – 18 USC 1512 (k)
- 1 Count Withholding a Document or Record – 18 USC 1512 (b) (2) (A), 2
- 1 Count Corruptly Concealing a Document or Record – 18 USC 1512 (C) (1)
- 1 Count Concealing a Document in a Federal Investigation – 18 USC 1519, 2
- 1 Count Scheme to Conceal – 18 USC 1001 (a) (1), 2

My commentary in the Sunday edition of Crash Course, June 11, 2023, was about the revelations of Special Counsel Smith's indictment and the reactions of the GOP body politic.

Salon

**Jack Smith's indictment of Trump is devastating:
A reckless criminal has finally met his match**

Trump loyalists will circle the wagons, of course.
But Smith's "speaking indictment" hit Mar-a-Lago like a tsunami
June 10 2023[15]

**By Gregg Barak**

The unsealed federal indictment released by the DOJ on Friday revealed that the Grand Jury charges and counts in *United States of America* v. *Donald J. Trump and Waltine Nauta* revolve around "the most sensitive classified documents and national defense information gathered and owned by the United States government, including information from the agencies that comprise the United States Intelligence Community."

Specifically, after his presidency, Trump retained classified documents originated by or implicating the equities of multiple intelligence community members and other executive branch departments and agencies, including the CIA, the NSA, the Pentagon, the State Department, the Department of Energy, and various other more obscure entities.

Before the federal indictment was released, many legal commentators were wondering whether we would see a bare-bones indictment comprising the most basic or essential elements of the crimes involved or what is called a "speaking indictment" that would – in this dangerous and unprecedented legal case – lay out as much detail as possible about Trump's alleged felonies relating to the mishandling of national security documents, obstruction of justice, and false statements to law enforcement.

As it turned out, Special Counsel Jack Smith indeed gave us a speaking indictment – and one recounted, at least in part, through the actual words of Donald Trump both before and after the first subpoena was served at Mar-a-Lago just over a year ago.

In Trump's own words from when he was a candidate for president in 2016, here's what he had to say about classified information:

- On August 18, 2016, Trump stated, "In my administration I'm going to enforce all laws concerning the protection of classified information. No one will be above the law."
- On September 6, 2016, Trump stated, "We also need to fight this battle by collecting intelligence and then protecting our classified secrets…. We can't have someone in the Oval Office who doesn't understand the meaning of the word confidential or classified."
- On September 7, 2016, Trump stated, "One of the first things we must do is to enforce all classification rules and to enforce all laws in relation to the handling of classified information."
- On September 19, 2016, Trump stated, "We also need the best protection of classified information."
- On November 3, 2016, Trump stated, "Service members here in North Carolina have risked their lives to acquire classified intelligence to protect our country."

As president, on July 26, 2018, Trump issued the following statement while discussing the revocation of security clearances to some former officials who had criticized him:

As the head of the executive branch and Commander in Chief, I have a unique, Constitutional responsibility to protect the Nation's classified information, including by controlling access to it…. More broadly, the issue of [a former executive branch official's] security clearance raises larger questions about the practice of former officials maintaining access to our Nation's most sensitive secrets long after their time in Government has ended. Such access is particularly inappropriate when former officials have transitioned into highly partisan positions and seek to use real or perceived access to sensitive information to validate their political attacks. Any access granted to our Nation's secrets should be in furtherance of national, not personal, interests.

Lastly, Smith's indictment quotes from an exchange between Trump and a staffer heard laughing during a recorded interview at Trump's New Jersey golf resort on July 21, 2021. He was speaking to a writer and a publisher concerning a proposed book and mentioned a "senior military official" – widely assumed to be Gen. Mark Milley, chairman of the Joint Chiefs of Staff – who had advised Trump against launching a military attack on a foreign nation designated as "Country A" (widely assumed to be Iran).

Upon greeting the writer, publisher and his two staff members, Trump stated, "Look what I found, this was [the Senior Military Official's] plan of attack." Later in the interview Trump stated,

> Well with [the Senior Military Official] – uh, let me see that, I'll show you an example. He said that I wanted to attack {Country A]. Isn't it amazing? I have a big pile of papers; this thing just came up. Look. This was him. They presented me this. This was him. This was the Defense Department and him.

The indictment also demonstrates Trump's frivolous, cavalier, indifferent, and reckless approach not only to the rule of law and global stability, but also to anything remotely reflecting the presidential oath of office and its mandate to "preserve, protect, and defend the Constitution of the United States."

Trump is "boxed in," so to speak, by his own big mouth, which has provided numerous examples that demonstrate his keen knowledge of the law – his understanding of what he could and could not do – as well as his clear intent not just to defy requests to hand over national security documents he had kept for his own purposes, but also to make false statements to the FBI and to instruct his aides to help him conceal numerous boxes of documents.

Trump's false statements along with his historical pattern of getting attorneys, accountants, commissioners, legislators, fixers, and so on to do his bidding are also evident here. Two of his attorneys, evidently reluctant to commit crimes on Trump's behalf, resigned from his defense team some 14 hours after the indictment was announced. In an immensely damaging turn of events for Trump, Special Counsel Smith successfully pierced the attorney-client relationship between Trump and his former lawyer Evan Corcoran, also apparently unwilling to risk prison time for the boss.

Factually, here are the only two things you really need to know about this legal case. First, between January 2021 and August 2022, Trump stored at least 300 classified documents in boxes scattered about Mar-a-Lago, including in a ballroom, a bathroom and shower, an office space, his bedroom, and a storage room. During this period, the Club hosted events for tens of thousands of members and guests – and was not, by any stretch of the imagination, "an authorized location for the storage, possession, review, display, or discussion of classified documents."

How serious were those documents? Smith's indictment reports that they

included information regarding defense and weapons capabilities of both the United States and foreign countries; United States nuclear programs; potential vulnerabilities of the United States and its allies to military attack; and plans for possible retaliation in response to a foreign attack.

So we're talking not just about US national security but the security of the world. Trump wasn't trying to retain letters, notes, cards, photographs, or random memorability but rather classified documents that were as sensitive as they can possibly get. Over the course of his four years in office, Trump was evidently collecting and retaining such highly sensitive material on a regular basis.

We could speculate on his motives for doing so, although they are irrelevant to his alleged crimes and unnecessary to obtain a conviction. They might include, for example, degrees of narcissism, pathology, and revenge, along with the possibility of using the documents for political leverage or financial gain in the future.

In introducing the charges and counts, Smith begins his narrative. On March 30, 2022, the FBI opened a criminal investigation into the unlawful retention of classified documents at Mar-a-Lago, and a federal grand jury began its work the next month. When the grand jury issued a subpoena requiring Trump to turn over all documents with classification markings, he actively tried to obstruct both the FBI and the grand jury and conceal his continued retention of such documents. His actions included

1  suggesting that his attorney falsely represent to the FBI and grand jury that Trump did not have documents called for by the grand jury subpoena;
2  directing Waltine Nauta. His co-defendant, to move boxes of documents to conceal them from Trump's attorney, the FBI, and the grand jury;
3  suggesting that his attorney hide or destroy documents called for by the grand jury subpoena;
4  providing to the FBI and grand jury only some of the documents called for by the grand jury subpoena, while claiming that he was cooperating fully; and
5  falsely representing that all documents called for by the grand jury subpoena had been produced, while knowing perfectly well that was not true.

A public coterie of Trump-Republican apologists, including the House Speaker Kevin McCarthy, Governor Ron DeSantis of Florida, Sen. Josh Hawley of Missouri, and Sen. Roger Marshall of Kansas, have been busy circling the wagons around Trump and gaslighting the public.

Hawley told Fox News host Laura Ingraham, "This is about whether the constitution is still real in this country. This is about if any American can expect the due process of the law." Marshall wondered whether this was part of a concerted effort by the DOJ and the FBI to take down the former president. "Every American should be alarmed by [this] indictment," he posted on Twitter, adding, "Sadly, once again, Lady Justice has taken off her blindfold."

As David Frum asks, does anyone really believe that "DeSantis — so badly trailing in the polls behind former President Donald Trump — is genuinely upset by his rival's indictment?" Or that "McCarthy — so disgusted by Trump in private — does not inwardly rejoice to see Trump meet justice?" Frum observes that their expressions of concern are "as sincere as the grief at a Mafia funeral."

Meanwhile, Fox News presented an incomprehensibly distorted version of the case, complete with a graphic announcing "Banana Republic" and images of President Biden flanked by Attorney General Merrick Garland and FBI Director Christopher Wray.[16]

Sean Hannity claimed that "despite a mountain of evidence of public corruption, the FBI, the DOJ, they have been protecting and continue to protect the Biden family, just like Hillary Clinton was protected in 2016 and before that, the Clinton Foundation was protected," but that now the DOJ was "apparently moving at lightning speed to prosecute Donald Trump. Why? Over some documents stored in a secure room that the FBI has access to months earlier at Mar-a-Lago."

One could politely describe those half-based falsehoods as a weak attempt at deflection and misdirection. If they make anything clear, it's that Donald Trump has no defense.

During this period, various news stories and headlines caught the precarious nature facing the American citizenry and what was at stake: "U.S. Justice System Put on Trial As Trump Denounces the Rule of Law"; "Trump Case Poses Tests to Justice System, Public Trust and Democracy"; "On Trump Indictment, Biden Stays Silent"; "Unanswered in the Indictment: Why Did Trump Hoard Documents?"; "Global Reaction to Trump's Latest Legal Woes Ranges From Outrage to Eye Rolls"; and "Trump Backers Unleash Wave of Violent Threats, Worrying Some Analysts." From the latter article: "In social media posts and public remarks, close allies of Mr. Trump – including a member of Congress – have portrayed the indictment as an act of war; called for retribution and highlighted the fact that much of his base carries weapons." His allies have continued to falsely paint Mr. Trump as a "victim of a weaponized Justice Department controlled by President Biden, his potential opponent in the 2024 election."[17]

Like the other defenders of the former president that "generally do not address the substance of the 37 counts against him" and have preferred instead to "make a case of selective prosecution that resonates powerfully among many Republicans" – "What about Mr. Biden? What about Hunter Biden? What about Bill and Hillary Clinton?" Regarding the GOP false equivalencies, we know about the obvious differences and the resolutions of these matters as they pertain to Biden, Bill and Hillary Clinton, and Donald Trump. As for the five-year investigation of Hunter Biden, we know that he pleaded guilty on June 20, 2023, to two misdemeanor tax violations. We know that he had previously paid the government back the 1 million dollars that he owed the Internal Revenue System (IRS) for his filings in 2017 and 2018. For these misdemeanors he received a probationary sentence. Biden also entered into a pre-trial diversion program in connection with his possessing a firearm and being a user or addict of illegal drugs at the same time. Those suspended charges were to be dropped and removed from his criminal record if he remains sober.[18] Then Biden's plea deal collapsed and he found himself facing nine criminal charges in a federal tax case that never would have happen to anybody else with the same set of facts whose name was not Hunter Biden.

Two of Trump's primary competitors for the 2024 GOP presidential nomination had this to say about the stolen classified documents case:

> Former Vice President Mike Pence compared the indictment to leaders of "third-world nations" who "use a criminal justice system in their country against their predecessors." Gov. Ron DeSantis of Florida said "the weaponization of federal law enforcement represents a moral threat to a free society."[19]

In short, the Republican Party allegedly of law and order as well as national security was once again deflecting away from and excusing Trump's lawlessness. Instead, they were once again weaponizing the administration of justice this time by "investigating the investigators" while doubling down on deep state and/or Democratic conspiracies and engaging in outright lies and disinformation about the military, the FBI, the DOJ, and other law enforcement and intelligence agencies. Jennifer Rubin correctly observed here: "Some people are blithely claiming that the indictment of former president Donald Trump on charges of violating the Espionage Act, obstruction, conspiracy and other crimes puts the justice system on trial. *Balderdash*." She continues, this "cliché has no meaning" except primarily to "improperly shift the attention and blame from a treacherous defendant alleged to have endangered U.S. national security."[20]

Not only was this indictment of Trump or the forthcoming ones that were about to occur tests about the weaponization of our justice system by Trump, but they were also testimonials to the strengths of our criminal justice systems and to the backbone of our legal system that at least aspires to practice law like no person, not even a former president, is beyond the rule of due process and equal justice for all people. Rubin had also correctly opined that the real test at this political juncture was about the GOP leadership who had failed miserably because of their fears of the MAGA base and the dictates of the Boss to repeatedly do the wrong thing: "When Senate Republicans adopted the 'big lie' and acquitted Trump in the second impeachment, they took the side of lawlessness, authoritarianism and contempt for the Constitution."[21] Moreover, days after the classified documents case, a less than unified GOP-controlled House was busy attempting to unimpeach the former president for January 6 – something unprecedented and illegal I suspect – as they were also trying to impeach Joe Biden – if only they could figure out something to charge him with besides being the imaginary leader of the Biden "crime family" as opposed to Boss Trump's politically organized Republican crime family. In short, Trump's days or should I say decades of conning, grifting, faking, and racketeering had by now already peaked with about 75 million American voters, including his MAGA base. By now, many of these folks were wishing and hoping that they could politically move on. In other words, Donald Trump, the Dobbs v. Jackson decision overturning women's rights to reproductive health, and the US Supreme Court were all unpopular with the majorities of the American people.

Meanwhile, by the middle of June 2023, the 2024 GOP field of candidates for the presidential nomination had grown to at least 13 including Trump, suggesting that it was likely as in 2016 that the Insurrectionist-in-Chief even with two impeachments, multiple indictments, and who knows how many convictions to come would still win the Republican nomination. This would probably mean that in a two-person race without a viable third-party interloper between the president and the former president, Biden would win the popular vote by at least 10 million votes. On the other hand, most of those deluded and non-competitive GOP candidates for the nomination were betting against the odds, which were unknown under these unprecedented conditions. With one failed insurrection under his belt, civil liabilities for sexual assault, two indictments, and more imminent, the Trumpocene was about to burst open throwing the party into what has become a slow death nail.

Leaving the Republican Party with mostly ill-equipped candidates to engage in the 2024 general election battle between the Democrats and the democratic constitutional republic, on one side, and the Republicans and anti-democratic, anti-rule of law authoritarians, on the other side. Unfortunately, with the possible exception of women's health rights, no other issue, including Biden's unmatched legislative victories on infrastructure and climate change, his "rebirth" of a new kind of manufacturing presence in the United States, and a "kick-ass" economy not seen since the 1960s or perhaps the 1990s, will be what determines the outcome in 2024. After all, what were the two leading candidates for the GOP nomination, Trump and DeSantis, talking about? Abolishing the independent Justice Department, deconstructing the state, and pushing an authoritarian agenda of the tyranny of a hyperminority.

The classified documents case was "laden with political implications for Trump, who currently holds the dominant spot in the early days of the 2024 Republican presidential primary." It also poses "legal consequences given the prospect of a years-long prison sentence."[22] Despite the gravity of the charges, Trump was publicly displaying his characteristic bravado and outrage, insisting as usual that he had "done nothing wrong" and was once again being "persecuted for political purposes." The probelm is the GOP loves Trump's martyr complex as much as they do his big lies. As Trump stated the day before the arraignment in an interview with Americano Media: "They're using this because they can't win the election fairly and squarely."[23]

The political reality was very different from Trump's conspiracy narratives. The former prosecutor and Chief Judge of the US Court of Appeals for the District of Columbia Circuit and Biden-appointed Attorney General Merrick Garland had always been reluctant and not very enthusiastic about indicting the former president in either the January 6 failed coup or the classified documents caper for no other reasons than political appearances, not wanting to criminally prosecute a former president, or setting a precedent against not doing so in the future. Even though he would be accused of committing numerous political crimes against the welfare of the United States. It had been reported that an "off-ramp" from prosecution would hopefully be found to spare Garland from pursuing criminal charges. Apparently, Trump was on the verge of being let off the hook until the DOJ obtained incriminating recordings of him "boasting about the documents" and later that he had been "sharing them with aides" as he met with people working on an autobiography of his former chief of staff and right-hand man Mark Meadows. Those recordings became the smoking gun that took an otherwise simple settlement off the table.[24]

Additionally, conspiracies to obstruct justice would also be charged coming later with a superseding indictment filed on July 27, 2023. As Norman Eisen who had served as counsel to House Democrats in the first Trump impeachment as well as White House ethics czar and ambassador to the Czech Republic in the Obama administration described, the new charging document shows that the benefits to the Special Counsel and his case are well worth the costs, should it even come to bringing about a further delay in the trial. The updated or amended indictment as we will see below strengthens two of the three parts of the original indictment – violating the Espionage Act and obstructing justice – the first having to do with allegedly sharing classified documents based on an Iran attack and the second with trying to delete security camera footage. The latter allegations of a surveillance tap conspiracy almost read like an organized crime operation:

> It features Trump employee and co-defendant Walt Nauta's surprise clandestine trip to Florida. And it is followed by Nauta and the new co-defendant, De Oliveira, observing and pointing out the surveillance cameras, and then De Oliveira having a conversation about "the boss"

wanting the IT server deleted so there would not be the video recordings of the classified documents boxes being moved around.[25]

Trump spent the night at Trump National Doral, a hotel and resort located about 11 miles from the Wilkie D. Ferguson court in Miami. In the early afternoon Trump accompanied by Secret Service officers motorcaded to the court in time for his booking and 3:00 p.m. arraignment. Released "on his own recognizance," Trump flew back on Trump Force One to his golf club in Bedminster, New Jersey where shortly after landing he gave some of his usual inane remarks that had nothing to do with the law or the facts of the case but are believed by 70% of the GOP.

For example, attracted by the "unitary executive theory" which suggests that all power flows from the POTUS, Trump promised that should he be elected president again in 2024 his second administration would fully jettison the post-Watergate norms of Justice Department independence: "I will appoint a special prosecutor to go after the most corrupt president in the history of the United States of America, Joe Biden, and the entire Biden crime family. I will totally obliterate the Deep State."[26] As a part of Trump's playbook of politicking, the former president was projecting his usual criminal and corrupt behavior onto the legitimate behaviors of his political adversaries.

Nobody expected Trump to do anything at the arraignment other than to sit there subdued and stoic, with arms folded periodically across his chest. Though Trump remained silent throughout the arraignment even as his attorney Todd Blanche pleaded not guilty on his behalf to the 37 counts within the first 5 minutes of the proceedings that lasted 47 minutes, the former president did whisper occasionally with his co-defendant Walt Nauta. His legal team had waved the reading of the indictment charges as if that could make them disappear. Barring the dismissal of a very strong case against Trump, many thought that the former president should have let his attorneys "cut a deal" with Jack Smith before the arraignment in order to escape a certain prison sentence. In fact former federal prosecutor Andrew Weissmann said on *Morning Joe* the day after the arraignment: "So there's no question that the right legal move is to plead if you want to avoid jail time," and there is precedent like the deal that General David Petraeus worked out to avoid jail.

Similarly, attorney George Conway was framing a plea-bargaining agreement from the perspective of the case being a slam dunk that would be able to prove all 37 counts. After all, Trump had the documents and

> he knew he had the documents, check, and he was asked for the documents back by the government, check. He didn't give the documents back when he was asked for them, and they had to come seize them, check, and then he was moving them around to hide them, check, and he lied, he caused people to lie to the government, check.

Finally, Convey asked, "Which of these facts is he going to dispute, and the answer is he can't dispute any of them." The same is true of his other criminal prosecutions. Trump has no defense other than to try to derail the cases or delay them procedurally. He may also try to lie that his attorneys told him it was okay for him to break the law. However, rather than ever admitting his guilt under any circumstances, and in order to survive to fight another day, Trump was gambling this time with unfavorable odds that he could somehow delay the trial from starting and finishing before the November 2024 election, or better yet from starting until after election or ideally not before New Year's Eve 2025. As of New Year's Eve 2024, with the assistance of Judge Aileen Cannon, a recent Trump appointee to the federal bench, she has been doing her best to slow walk this case. Although scheduled for May 2024, it may very well not occur before the November presidential election.

While most non-revolutionary outlaws would have cut a deal to stay out of prison, Trump behind the scenes and on social media platforms had been trying to stoke his base and threatening harm and violence to prosecutors and judges and other law enforcement personnel. Like a mafioso boss and Mussolini's blackshirts or storm troopers, Trump had been fomenting hate, scapegoats, and violence toward the "enemies-others" since his campaign rallies began in late 2015. When others may have been cutting a deal with Garland, Trump was instead trying to intimidate the attorney general by telling him how angry people are out there over the prospects of his criminal indictments of any kind: "The country is on fire. What can I do to reduce the heat?"[27] Trump was wishing that the nation was on fire; however, Trump's threat of or real mob violence had climaxed back on January 6 and that by June 2023 with several calls put out by Trump for mass gatherings of protesters to no avail at his first two arraignments in Manhattan and Miami, that collective violence on behalf of the Trumpocene was a thing of the past. At least without some kind of delusionary victory involved in the personal risks at hand, the DOJ's response to the assault on the Capitol had deterred this type of organized as opposed to spontaneous violence.

In part, this has had to do with the government successfully prosecuting, convicting, and imprisoning more than 700 illegal protestors as a deterrent to these types of violent behaviors with negative consequences. In part, this has had to do with historical circumstances that led up to and culminated in a failed coup by these revolutionary insurrectionists who believed in their heart of hearts that they had some kind of realistic chance of reversing the "stolen election" and stopping the certification of Joe Biden and returning Trump to the White House. It was already beginning to seep in that by 2025 it was more likely that Trump would be residing in a federal prison for a multiplicity of crimes against the United States. In short, even the MAGA folks were rational and self-interested persons not prepared to throw themselves under the bus for the soon to be imprisoned Racketeer-in-Chief without some kind of purpose other than to scare or intimidate the authorities into some kind of submission on behalf of the former president.

Most folks who follow these types of federal cases were believing that the trial could possibly begin before the end of 2023 even with the expected series of pre-trial motions that would be raised by the defense to dismiss the case or at least squash some of the state's evidence. However, by the end of 2023, many legal experts were of the opinion that the classfied documents case may not occur before the 2024 presidential election. Aside from the defense motions to challenge the prosecution by way of the latter's acquiring the subpoena to search Mar-a-Lago; engaging in prosecutorial misconduct before the grand juries; piercing the client-attorney privilege by way of the crime-fraud exception because Trump was using the services of attorney Evan Corcoran to facilitate crime or fraud; and the admissibility of such evidence gathered from Corcoran's copious note-taking for the eyes and ears of a trial jury, there is also the mandatory private hearing or consideration of the ways in which the classified documents can and/or will be used during the trial in order to protect secret documents according to the CIPA (see Figure 6.1).

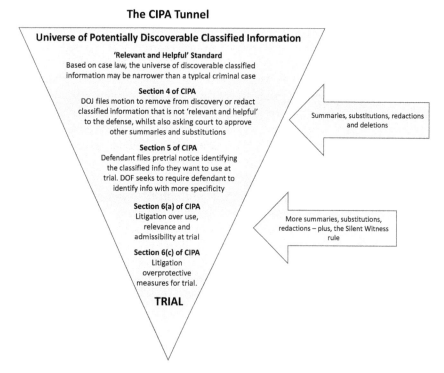

**FIGURE 6.1** The Quick Guide to Classified Information Procedures.

*Source:* Adapted from graphic by Brian Greer, The Quick Guide to CIPA (Classified Information Procedures Act), Just Security, July 17, 2023.

On June 23rd Special Counsel Smith filed a motion asking federal judge Aileen Cannon to move back the start of the trial to December 11, 2023, in order to provide time for Trump's defense lawyers to obtain their security clearances and to review the volumes of materials that the prosecutors had turned over to them. It would also allow for both sides to address the legal procedures surrounding the presentation of classified evidence. Smith's team argued that the case should nevertheless still be fast-tracked not only because of the political implications, but also because the case " 'involves straightforward theories of liability and does not present novel questions of fact or law,' nor is it particularly 'unusual or complex' from a legal perspective."[28] In turn, Trump's defense filed a motion to delay the start of the trial until after the 2024 presidential election. The two sides argued the motions before Judge Connor on July 18, 2023, and she ruled on July 21, 2023, that the trial would begin, at least for now, on May 20, 2024, more than a month before the Republican National Convention in early July.

Back in the fall of 2022 before the appointment of Special Counsel Smith to this case and to January 6, Cannon had made two different procedural decisions regarding the search of Mar-a-Lago and the ongoing investigation that were challenged by the Justice Department. These were both quickly overturned by an appellate court concerned about her equal protection and due process legal responses to the civil lawsuit filed by Trump to stop the DOJ's investigation into the alleged retention of classified documents.[29] It slowed up the investigation for nearly two months.

One year later Judge Cannon came out swinging at Special Counsel on August 7, 2023, "striking two sealed motions filed by Smith's team and directing him to address the legal propriety of an 'out-of-district grand jury' that is continuing to investigate the case."[30] Although Cannon had granted the prosecution a hearing over the conflict-of-interest issue over the co-defendants legal counsel in their motion, she had committed a faux pas with respect to the "legal propriety thing." Legal experts immediately raised concerns and wondered about the contents of Smith's appeal:

> "Looking like a good week to ask the 11th Circuit to replace the judge," tweeted former U.S. Attorney Joyce Vance. "If the DOJ filed under seal certain documents, and Judge Cannon just disclosed the existence of an otherwise confidential grand jury processing, we might be at the motion for recusal stage for the DOJ," added MSNBC legal analyst Katie Phang.
>
> "I'm betting that Judge Cannon's account of the out – of-district investigation is not the full story. But hard to see how she can justify not sealing her order referring to another Grand Jury." "Could this be a

possible vehicle for taking her up and seeking her recusal? Not clear yet," wrote former U.S. Attorney Harry Litman.[31]

Keep in mind that Smith's team had previously confirmed that they were continuing to use the DC and Florida grand juries after this indictment for the purposes of further investigating the obstructive activities of the former president. As former federal prosecutor Andrew Weissmann who served on Special Counsel Bob Mueller's Russian investigation explained: The "obstruction crimes that were investigated are charges that could have been brough in FLA or in DC and thus could be investigated in either district. And there was conduct that alleged to have occurred outside FLA." However, these rulings are resolved, Weissmann said that Cannon's ruling "clearly shows her ignorance (bias? Both?)"[32]

The prosecutorial tactics of this particular criminal indictment by Special Counsel Smith et al and the political-legal responses by Trump and his team of lawyers have perhaps taken their game of "cat and mouse" to the level where the state is making moves or not as a form of preventative defense from falling into any Trumpian traps of delay. Wanting to avoid as much as they possibly can from making "process fouls" that Trump might want to exploit for either political gain, legal delay, or raising matters of a fair trial. Even at the arraignment the prosecution was not making any requests for a posted bond, surrendering passports or limiting foreign travel. Moreover, the state had not filed a recusal motion to remove Judge Cannon based on her two previously overturned and lambasted rulings by the appellate court. And as Joyce Vance wrote at the time:

> It's not even clear they will challenge Judge Cannon's participation in the case if she makes another beyond the pale ruling that they have to appeal, although that would entail little if any delay if partnered with an appeal of a substantive ruling.[33]

This time around Magistrate Judge Bruce Reinhart had issued a protective order on June 19, 2023, to prohibit Trump and Walt Nauta, his co-defendant, from sharing any evidence federal investigators were scheduled to begin turning over to their lawyers as part of the discovery process:

> The Discovery Materials, along with any information derived therefrom, shall not be disclosed to the public or the news media, or disseminated on any news or social media platform, without prior notice to and consent of the United States or approval of the Court.[34]

That order had been raised by the government on the Friday before and Trump and his attorneys had agreed that the "Defendants shall only have access to Discovery Materials under the direct supervision of Defense Counsel or a member of Defense Counsel's staff."[35] Moreover, Trump and Nauta's access to materials were limited and prohibited them from retaining copies of Discovery. It barred Trump and company from "disclosing information about the government's case without explicit permission from a judge and warns they could face criminal contempt charges if they violate the order." While not a "gag order" it presented Trump with the difficulty of having to talk about the case and not look stupid or silly doing so. Which he was immediately doing on Fox News and elsewhere providing the prosecution with more usable evidence of guilt.[36]

Less than two days after the protective issue was ordered, Special Counsel Smith turned over his first batch of evidence in classified documents evidence to Trump's legal team. So confident were prosecutors of their case, which included unclassified evidence obtained through subpoena and search warrants; transcripts of grand jury testimony in both Washington, DC and Florida; witness interviews conducted through May 2023; and excerpts of closed-circuit television footage that they had provided the defense with a roadmap to their discovery. They had also invited the defense to contact DOJ to arrange for the inspection of any unclassified items that were sized at Trump's Mar-a-Lago resort on August 8, 2022. According to the prosecutors' filing, the first production of unclassified discovery included grand jury testimony of witnesses who would testify for the government. Meaning at long last, Trump would learn whether his former "point guard" Mark Meadows would be testifying on behalf of the government or as a hostile witness.[37]

When the prosecution filed its motion to delay the trial to the end of 2023, it also provided an estimate of the number of witnesses that might be called to testify as 84 whom the defense had already reserved the right to challenge. In any case, those names will be kept under seal. Naturally, Trump and his legal team did not share the prosecution's urgency, and the prosecution's filing also indicated that they would object to the Special Counsel's timeline. True to form, in their RESPONSE IN OPPOSITION TO THE GOVERNMENT'S MOTION FOR CONTINUENCE AND PROPOSED REVISED SCHEDULING ORDER filed to Judge Cannon on July 10, 2023, they asked that a trial be delayed at least until after the 2024 election.

In their 12-page response, they argued that

President Trump is running for President of the United States and is currently the likely Republican Party nominee. This undertaking requires a tremendous amount of time and energy, and that effort will continue until the election on November 5, 2024.

Regarding co-defendant Walt Nauta, his "job requires him to accompany President Trump during most campaign trips around the country. This schedule makes trial preparation with both of the Defendants challenging." His attorneys also noted that this will be more onerous on Trump and his attorneys as they will be involved in several criminal lawsuits that they will have to juggle with their busy schedules. All of these factors taken together will prohibit the former president and candidate for president as well as his co-defendant from receiving a "fair trial." The strategy of Trump's defense team in this case as well as in the forthcoming cases in Georgia and Washington, DC is to delay, delay, and delay and hope that they drag past the 2024 election and that somehow Trump can beat the odds as he did in 2016 and become the president-elect. Then, Trump could direct his first attorney general to drop the charges and wipe these cases off the books. In theory, Trump could try to pardon himself as he makes good on his promises to pardon many of the January 6 convicted insurrectionists.

On the remote possibility that the prosecution's case breaks down entirely as a result of exculpatory evidence, discovery, or one of several motions to limit the admissible evidence or to dismiss the case altogether, Ryan Goodman and Andrew Weissmann in either scenario construe that Jack Smith may still have even more serious charges up his sleeves to bring against Trump as in the *dissemination* of classified documents. They were referring to the fact that the Florida indictment states that Trump took classified records from Mar-a-Lago to his summer home in Bedminster, New Jersey where he not only showed them to others, but he also knowingly or unknowingly had been recorded on the phone talking about classified documents that he says he could have declassified before leaving the White House but that he did not do so. According to the speaking indictment Trump

> showed a map to a political ally and also showed a writer and a publisher a secret military plan to attack Iran. These two episodes were arguably the most egregious allegations of criminal wrongdoing mentioned in the indictment; they allege not just the improper retention of our nation's most highly classified information, but the intentional communication of such information.[38]

Goodman and Weissmann wrote further that

> Trump's Bedminster conduct, as described in the indictment, appears to fit the description of two federal offenses designed to keep America's national-security secrets safe. One makes it a crime to intentionally communicate national-defense information to people not authorized to receive it, and the other makes it a crime to intentionally disclose classified information to the same.[39]

What was perhaps the most fascinating and unexpected development on the day of arraignment was that Trump showed up to court without any experienced criminal defense attorneys by his side. Not that it matters who shows up for an indictment so long as they represent themselves as intending to remain counsel of record throughout the trial proceedings. In any case, back in May 2023 Timothy Parlatore had resigned over turf issues between Trump's various teams of lawyers and Trump's ringleader-attorney Boris Epshteyn. Next, after lawyers James Trusty and John Rowley resigned from the defense team following the criminal indictment, Trump found himself struggling to find any local criminal defense lawyers willing to join the classified documents team. Trump had been turned down by Howard Srebnick, David Markus, Benedict Kuehn, William Barzee, and Bruce Zimet. Hence, the ex-president showed up to court flanked only by former federal prosecutor Todd Blanche and former Florida solicitor general Chris Kise neither of whom had ever practiced any criminal defense work.[40]

The reluctance by attorneys to work for Trump stems from several things, including his tendency to stiff, to use, and/or blame his attorneys for his lawlessness. In terms of Trump's litigation style, it dates back to the 1970s under the mentorship of Roy Cohn his first fixer and attorney. Since Cohn's death in the early 1980s, Trump has had a long history of treating his lawyers as personal fixers and attack dogs. Now, after decades of fraud, corruption, and racketeering, Trump's litigious misbehavior had finally come back to bite Teflon Don and place him now in the most precarious legal jeopardy of his entire life. As they say, "what goes around comes around." Or, in the words of a former Assistant Attorney General and Acting Solicitor General of the United States, Neal Katyal, whose parents immigrated from India before he was born on American soil in 1970, the indictment was simply a matter of karma.

For example, in his first state criminal indictment in New York Trump's former fixer and personal attorney, Michael Cohen is expected to testify against Trump in the Manhattan state trial scheduled for March 2024. He will simply testify along with the corroborating evidence that he arranged illegal hush money payments during the 2016 campaign at Trump's direction. In the classified documents case, Corcoran's forced testimony "after a judge determined there was sufficient evidence that Trump used Corcoran to commit a crime" pierced the standard attorney-client relationship of privilege because Trump had "allegedly misled Corcoran by directing his personal aide, Walt Nauta, to move dozens of boxes containing classified records before Corcoran arrived at Mar-a-Lago to conduct the review."[41] Similarly, the unsealed indictment alleged that Trump's "legal team falsely certified to the Justice Department that all classified documents Trump had taken had been turned over in response to a subpoena."[42]

Recall back in 2017–2018 during the investigation into the Russian interference in the 2016 presidential election, the then-President Trump may have first attempted to obstruct justice "by ordering White House counsel Don McGahn to fire special counsel Robert Mueller."[43] However, McGahn pushed back and refused to do so. Then in 2019, Trump's lawyer Rudy Giuliani worked with President Trump to pressure the Ukrainian government to investigate Joe Biden, even trying to extort President Zelensky by holding up for several months congressionally approved financial aid to Ukraine. When Trump's so-called first "perfect phone call" was discovered that resulted in the first impeachment of President Trump. Then in 2020 in an attempt to overturn his election loss, Trump turned to a group of legal scholars led by former Trump attorney John Eastman and their false elector scheme that led to or contributed to the sentiment for the January 6 insurrection, a second impeachment of the now former president, the House Subcommittee hearings on January 6, and the subsequent criminal probes of Eastman's roles in the Capitol assault and in the attempt to overturn the presidential results in Georgia where Trump had a couple more of his perfect phone conversations recorded and listened to by the Fulton County grand jury before they made their unanimous recommendations to indict multiple persons for a RICO conspiracy to overturn the results of the presidential election in Georgia.

Robert Costa, who was in the courtroom during the Miami criminal indictment, reported @costareports that Special Counsel Smith was also present for the arraignment and that he never broke his stare from Trump during the proceedings. And as the former president slowly left the room gazing at some 20 reporters who were present in the courtroom though he never looked at or made eye contact with Smith. One of the conditions of Trump's bond was that he could not have contact with any witnesses involved in the case, including his co-defendant Walt Nauta who was still working full-time as Trump's personal valet and valued body assistant, making it rather impossible to police whether the two talk about the case or not. Interestingly, Nauta was arrested, booked, and digitally fingerprinted like Trump on June 13th. Unlike Trump, he took a mug shot that Trump did not have to take. Nauta was also sitting at the table with Donald and his two lawyers and the two co-defendants could be seen whispering to one another on a couple of occasions.

Because Nauta had yet to retain local counsel or someone who had been admitted in the Southern District of Florida to represent him, his arraignment did not occur that day. The 20-year Navy veteran was finally arraigned on July 6, 2023, represented by Sasha Dadan, a criminal defense attorney in South Florida with a history of having been a public defender but had no federal court experience. Nauta pleaded not guilty to six charges, including conspiracy to obstruct justice, withholding and corruptly concealing documents, and making false representations. As for his legal expenses, they were allegedly being picked up by one of Trump's political action committees.[44] The day before, Federal Magistrate Judge Bruce Reinhard had denied a request from several news organizations to release the entire affidavit DOJ had submitted in support of its request to search Mar-a-Lago. Because of the classified documents involved and grand jury secrecy rules designed to protect investigative sources and methods, a slightly less redacted version was released. Nevertheless, the newly released material from the affidavit confirmed that this was not a case about sloppiness or negligence on Trump's part. Rather, based on security camera video from Mar-a-Lago, Nauta was shown removing 64 boxes from the storage area, placing them in various locations within Trump's residence area before he returned 30 boxes back to storage where the FBI would not confine their search when they showed up almost two months later at Mar-a-Lago.

Before and during Trump's earlier arraignment, outside the courthouse there were cheers and jeers from small crowds of gathered people numbering a few hundred people far smaller than the anticipated crowd of some 50,000 estimated by law enforcement. After Trump left the courthouse and on his way to the airport, Trump paid a "surprised" trip to an iconic Cuban restaurant in Little Havana where he announced to a crowd of 200 supporters packed inside the Versailles: "Are you ready? Food for everyone." Moments later, the crowd began singing Happy Birthday to the former president who was turning 77 the next day. Trump's glad-handing and taking selfies with his minions lasted 10 minutes before he exited stage alt-right without providing anything, not even a Cuban coffee to go.

As we waited for the pre-trial motions to be resolved in anticipation of Trump's first 21st criminal trial of the century, and assuming that the government prevailed and can use attorney Evan Corcoran's lawyer-notes as evidence, I was looking forward to seeing whether Corcoran would remain a "hostile" witness or had become a witness for the prosecution. As Joyce Vance explains:

> If Corcoran isn't cooperative on the witness stand, the government can ask for permission to treat him as what's called a hostile witness, and under the rules of evidence, that entitles them to take his testimony using leading questions. Normally, when it's presenting the case, the government isn't permitted to lead a witness. It must ask open-ended questions starting with words like "where," "when," "who," and "how." But leading questions are permissible when eliciting testimony from a hostile witness. Leading questions let the questioner preview the expected testimony and solicit the witness's agreement: Isn't it true that Trump didn't tell you to search his office when you explained you needed to look every place where classified information might be located at Mar-a-Logo?

If the witness is combative or makes statements contrary to his notes, the government is entitled to read from it and confront the witness with his past statements. Ultimately, the government gets its desired testimony. It's possible Corcoran's posture vis-à-vis cooperation with the government could evolve in the months ahead of trial. Even if it doesn't, the government will be able to get the substance of the information in the indictment into evidence in a manner that is always compelling in front of a jury.[45]

What was disheartening to learn as we were waiting anxiously to see whether the next criminal indictments were forthcoming was the extent to which AG Garland and others at the Justice Department had been willing to go to let Trump off the hook for his extremely reckless, dangerous, and cavalier handling of top-secret classified documents. This was true even when nuclear data and information were among the stolen documents and there were (or still might be) risks to National Intelligence and the rest of the world. What kind of message would that have sent to our allies and enemies around the world had there been no criminal prosecution of the former president, especially when Trump's threat to national and international security had been well known since as early as 2016? Not to underscore that the Mar-a-Lago caper had followed right behind the January 6th failed coup and the nationwide fake electors' schemes. The stolen documents were simply more very concrete evidence of how unfit Trump was or is to become the US Commander-in-Chief once again.

The case also documents just how hazardous a narcissistic and sociopathic person like Trump can be to the well-being of society. Because even if the documents "weren't his," he still couldn't and wouldn't care less about the lethal risks to those that gather US intelligence, to anyone else, or in a twisted kind of way to himself even if it meant staying out of prison. As we already knew, Trump had passed that deal up back in spring 2023. So long as Trump believes that he can prevail to fight another day to retain and/or regain his former power, then the amoral and corrupt racketeer and wannabe dictator will unapologetically continue to transcend democratic norms and to resist the authority of the state even if it means destroying American society in the process. Something that he has been working on since he was sworn into office in 2017. Again, Trump does not care about any of these facts or any of these risks any more than he cared about or took responsibility for the 500,000 unnecessary deaths caused by COVID because of his denial and gaslighting of the American people regarding the "three alarm fire" as Bob Woodward described it. Donald also takes sadomasochistic pleasure in doing the wrong thing and getting over with his political conmanship. Very sad and that is the social truth of the matter and not fake news.

With all this and more, including the January 6 and Georgia imminent indictments coming, Jack Smith delivered a superseding indictment on July 27, 2023, incorporating the original charges and new ones as well a new defendant Carlos De Olivera. Like co-defendant Walt Nauta, De Oliveira is a Trump employee, once a valet who became a property manager in January of 2022. The superseding indictment added four new charges. The first was a willful retention of documents brought against Trump. There were two obstruction charges against three co-conspirators DJT, Walt Nauta, and De Oliveira for trying to destroy video footage from security cameras after DOJ had subpoenaed it. And the last count charged De Oliveira with lying to FBI agents during an interview.

> The old indictment contained 31 counts alleging Trump illegally retained national defense information after leaving the presidency. The new indictment adds new count 32, which concerns the document Trump infamously waived around at his Bedminster golf course in New Jersey concerning Mark Meadows' forthcoming book.

Turns out that this top-secret document contained battle plans for Iran, and that the DOJ had obtained the document well before the original indictment was filed. As Joyce Vance pointed out at the time of the superseding indictment, the

> document was important to charge because it wasn't "just" a document in a box in Trump's ballroom or bathroom, it was a document he pulled out, waived around, identified, and put in view of multiple people who lacked a security clearance.

Moreover,

> Trump's cavalier treatment of the Iran battle plan drives home how serious his crimes are, and it's an important inclusion among the retention counts. It's tough for a juror to look at this kind of evidence and refuse to vote to convict because it's not a serious crime.[46]

In sum, after the superseding indictments Trump and his co-conspirators now faced 40 charges, the newest ones for attempting to "alter, destroy, mutilate, or conceal evidence" as in conspiring to delete security footage – obstruction of justice – as well as making false statements to the FBI and the unlawful retention of at least one document containing national defense information that was also referred to in the original charges.[47] As is often stated, "it's not the crime, it's the cover up." In Trump's case, it is both the crime and the cover-up. What is perhaps the most compelling from Jack Smith's underlying and amended narrative is that the "tale is reminiscent of the hero's journey in mythology and literature" as well as in "countless Hollywood blockbusters, from *The Lord of the Rings to Harry Potter*. In this narrative, Employee 4 emerges as the hero who rejected Trump's villainous urges and then came forward with the truth, at his own peril."[48] Most significantly, as James Sample, a professor at Hofstra University's School of Law, told Salon: "Attempting to delete the surveillance footage has not only obstruction of justice ramifications but will also be useful to prosecutors in demonstrating consciousness of guilt… Innocent parties don't take steps to delete evidence of innocence." Finally, if Trump "is found guilty and does not strike some kind of sentencing deal, he may die in prison."[49] Of course, that's assuming that Trump loses the election, even if he does succeed in running out the clock before the 2024 election. True to form, back in December 2023 Trump's lawyers filed another delaying and frivolous motion for access to classified information that special counsel Smith was planning to redact before introducing it at the trial.

## Notes

1  Quoted in Joyce Vance. 2023. The week ends with chickens. *Civil Discourse with Joyce Vance*. May 24. https://joycevance.substack.com/p/the-week-ends-with-chickens?utm_source=substack&utm_medium=email

2  Vance. 2023.

3  www.justsecurity.org/84168/mar-a-lago-model-prosecution-memo/, p. 1.

4  Ibid., p. 2.

5  Ibid., p. 1.

6  www.salon.com/2022/09/07/of-the-powerful-why-the-mar-a-lago-special-master-decision-is-so

7  Devin Barrett, Josh Dawsey, Spencer S. Hsu and Perry Stein. 2023. Trump workers moved Mar-a-Lago boxes a day before FBI came for documents. *The Washington Post*. May 25. www.washingtonpost.com/national-security/2023/05/25/trump-classified-documents-mar-a-lago

8  Katelyn Polantz, Paula Reid and Kaitlan Collins. 2023. Trump captured on tape talking about classified document he kept after leaving the White House. *CNN Politics*. May 31. www.cnn.com/2023/05/31/politics/trump-tape-classified-document-iran-milley

9  Kaitlan Collins, Paula Reid and Katelyn Polantz. 2023. Trump attorneys haven't found classified document former president referred to on tape following subpoena. *CNN Politics*. June 2. www.cnn.com/2023/06/02/politics/donald-trump-iran-subpoena

10  Sara Dorn. 2023. Trump's swimming pool flooded surveillance video room at Mar-A-Lago. *Forbes*. June 5. www.forbes.com/sites/saradorn/2023/06/05/trumps-swimming-pool-flooded-surveillance-video-room-at-mar-a-lago-report-says

11  Joyce Vance. 2023. The smart move. *Civil Discourse with Joyce Vance*. June 4. https://joycevance.substack.com/p/the-smart-move

12  Joyce Vance. 2023. The week ahead: Civil discourse turns one!. *Civil Discourse with Joyce Vance*. June 4. https://joycevance.substack.com/p/the-week-ahead-civil-discourse-turns

13  Ibid.

14 David Aaron. 2023. Expert backgrounder: Secret evidence in public trials. *Just Security*. June 6. www.justsecurity.org/86812/secret-evidence-in-public-trials-pro tecting-defendants-and-national-security-under-the-classified-information-pro cedures-act

15 www.salon.com/2023/06/10/jack-smiths-indictment-of-is-devastating-a-reckless-criminal-has-finally-met-his-match/

16 As for the repetitive reference that many Republicans have made of the indictment as being "the stuff of a banana republic" as Trump's former acting attorney general Mat Whitaker put it. Many "liberal democracies" have also prosecuted current or formers heads of state and heads of government. Notable examples include such countries as France, South Korea, Israel, Italy, and Brazil.

17 Michael S. Schmidt, Alan Fewer, Maggie Haberman and Alan Goldman. 2023. Trump backers unleash wave of violent threats, worrying some analysts. *New York Times*. Sunday June 11, p. 19.

18 Turns out the Hunter Biden plea-deal fell apart and he is now facing criminal indictments on misdemeanor gun charges. www.pbs.org/newshour/politics/hun ter-biden-arrives-at-a-delaware-court-where-hes-expected-to-plead-guilty-to-tax-crimes

19 Peter Baker. 2023. U.S. justice system put on trial as Trump denounces the rule of law. *New York Times*. Sunday June 11, pp. 1 and 16.

20 Jennifer Rubin. 2023. The test isn't for the justice system. It's also for Republicans. *The Washington Post*. June 16. www.washingtonpost.com/opinions/2023/06/16/ newsletter-test-judicial-system

21 Ibid.

22 Eric Tucker and Alanna Durkin Richer. 2023. Trump to face judge Tuesday in historic court appearance. *The Associated Press*. June 13. www.mlive.com/news/ 2023/06/trump-to-face-judge-tuesday-in-historic-court-appearance.html

23 Quoted in Bernd Debusmann Jr. 2023. How Trump's arraignment in Miami federal courthouse will unfold. *BBC News*. June 13. www.bbc.com/news/world-us-canada-65881780

24 Aruna Viswanatha and Sadie Gurman. 2023. Trump prosecutors struggled over motives. Then they heard the tape. *The Wall Street Journal*. June 23. www.wsj. com/articles/trump-prosecutors-struggled-over-motives-then-they-heard-the-tape

25 Norman Eisen. 2023. The latest charges against Trump paint an even more damning picture. *CNN Opinion*. July 28. www.cnn.com/2023/07/28/opinions/ indictment-new-charges-donald-trump-damning-eisen

26 Jonathan Swan, Charlie Savage and Maggie Haberman. 2023. The radical strategy behind Trump's promise to 'Go After' Biden. *The New York Times*. June 15. www.nytimes.com/2023/06/15/us/politics/trump-indictment-justice-departm ent.html

27 Aila Shoaib. 2022. Trump sent cryptic message to Merrick Garland before warrant was unsealed: 'The country is on fire. What can I do to reduce the heat?' *Insider*. August 14. www.businessinsider.com/trump-asked-ag-garland-fbi-raid-warrant-2022-8

28 Glenn Thrush. 2023. Prosecutors seek to delay Trump documents trial to December. *The New York Times*. June 23. www.nytimes.com/2023/06/23/us/polit ics/trump-documents-trial-delay.html

29 Ann E. Marimow. 2023. Judge Aileen Cannon's pivotal role in Donald Trump's criminal trial. *The Washington Post*. June 12. www.washingtonpost.com/natio nal-security/2023/06/12/judge-aileen-cannon-trump-case

30 Gabriella Ferrigine. 2023. Experts: Cannon daring court to replace her after "coming out swinging" at Jack Smith in new order. *Salon*. August 7. www.salon.com/2023/08/07/experts-cannon-daring-to-replace-her-after-coming-out-swinging-at-jack-smith-in-new-order

31 Quoted in Ibid.

32 Ibid.

33 Joyce Vance. 2023. Hunter Biden & the rule of law. *Civil Discourse with Joyce Vance*. June. 21. https://joycevance.substack.com/p/hunter-biden-and-the-rule-of-law

34 Dareh Gregorian. 2023. Judge bars Trump from disclosing – or keeping – evidence in documents case. *NBC News*. June 19. www.nbcnews.com/politics/donald-trump/judge-bars-trump-disclosing-evidence-documents-case-rcna90016

35 Ibid.

36 Greg Sargent. 2023. Trump's confession on Fox News should prompt Democrats to step up. *The Washington Post*. June 21. www.washingtonpost.com/opinions/2023/06/21/trump-fox-news-baier-hunter-biden

37 Summer Concepcion and Daniel Barnes. 2023. Special counsel gives Trump's team first batch of evidence in classified documents case. *NBC News*. June 22. www.nbcnews.com/politics/donald-trump/trumps-team-gets-first-batch-evidence-classified-documents-case

38 Ryan Goodman and Andrew Weissmann. 2023. Jack Smith's backup option. *The Atlantic*. June 14. www.theatlantic.com/ideas/archive/2023/06/trump-indictment-florida-new-jersey-classified/674393

39 Ibid.

40 Hugo Lowell. 2023. Trump finds no new lawyers for court appearance in Mar-a-Lago case. *The Guardian*. June 13. www.theguardian.com/us-news/2023/jun/13/trump-finds-no-new-lawyers-mar-a-lago-documents-arraignment

41 Zachary Basu. 2023. Trump's attorney-client curse. *Axios*. June 12. www.axios.com/2023/06/12/trump-lawyers-indictment-classified-documents

42 Ibid.

43 Ibid.

44 Kevin Breuninger. 2023. Trump aide Walt Nauta pleads not guilty in classified documents case. *CNBC.com*. July 6. www.cnbc.com/2023/07/06/trump-aide-walt-nauta-arraignment.html

45 Joyce Vance. 2023. Chickens come home to roost. *Civil Discourse*. June 14. https://joycevance.substack.com/p/chickens-come-home-to-roost

46 Joyce Vance. 2023. A superseding indictment. *Civil Discourse*. July 28. https://joycevance.substack.com/p/a-superseding-indictment

47 Jacqueline Thomsen. 2023. Factbox: The charges in the Trump classified documents case. *Reuters*. July 28. www.reuters.com/world/us/new-charges-trump-classified-documents-case

48 Kimberly Wehle. 2023. Trump's legal turmoil just keeps getting worse. *The Atlantic*. July 28. www.theatlantic.com/ideas/archive/2023/07/donald-trump-indictment-jack-smith

49 Quoted in Areeba Shah. 2023. "Witnesses lie, recordings don't" ex-prosecutor pinpoints major problem for Trump in new indictment. *Salon*. July 29. www.salon.com/2023/07/29/witnesses-lie-recordings-dont-ex-prosecutor-pinpoints-major-problem-for-in-new-indictment

# 7

# THE PEOPLE OF FULTON COUNTY, GEORGIA V. DONALD J. TRUMP ET AL.

While the United States was waiting for the next two criminal indictments to befall Donald Trump, the former president had been busy fundraising off the first two indictments. For Trump, more indictments meant more money that he could legitimately raise for his legal expenses and more. This money was unlike the money that Trump fraudulently raised off the Big Lies which all totaled came to around $500 million. In the two weeks following his first indictment in New York, Trump raised $15.4 million compared to $18.8 million that he raised for the first quarter in 2023. Not only had the first indictment "turbocharged" his fundraising but it had also grown his fundraising base as "nearly a quarter of those who contributed to Trump during this period had never given to him before."[1] As previously noted in some detail, two weeks after his federal indictment for violating the Espionage Act among some 37 classified documents related charges and one week before the end of June 2023, Trump had strengthened his lead over the Grand Old Party (GOP )field of candidates, distancing his lead over the second highest polling candidate since the first indictment from 15% to 29%.

At this point in time, Trump's criminal defense expenditures were already "swallowing his campaign, just over half of the money he raised" during the second quarter of the year "went not to the campaign itself but to an affiliated PAC" that was "footing the legal bills." According to the Federal Election Commission of more than $35 million raised between March and June, the campaign received $17.7 million and the rest went to the Save America PAC, which had been "spending millions on lawyers representing Trump and allies in the multiple ongoing" legal cases.[2] It was then revealed that Trump's Save America PAC had spent $40.2 million by June 30, 2023, on legal fees related to his first two and forthcoming indictments.[3] Interestingly, as part of Fulton

DOI: 10.4324/9781003390664-10

County Superior Court Judge Robert McBurney's rejection of Trump's final bid to derail his potential prosecution – even before an alleged wrongful indictment had occurred – he made reference to the twice indicted and former president's ability to capitalize on his legal troubles: "And for some, being the subject of a criminal investigation can, a la Rumpelstiltskin, be turned into golden political capital, making it seem more providential than problematic."[4]

**The Crime Report**
**Reckoning with the Criminal Indictments of the 45th President**
June 28, 2023

**By Gregg Barak**
After the first two criminal indictments of the former president, the once-upon-a-time Teflon Don's *lead on the field of GOP candidates* had risen from 15% to 29% over the second-highest polling candidate and nobody besides Florida Governor Ron DeSantis at 22% was in double digits. Meanwhile, his "war chest" *to defend himself continues to grow* with *some 20%* of those giving having allegedly not done so before.

Last Sunday night Donald Trump made his first Michigan campaign speech in Novi months ahead of the 2024 election. Trump was as defiant as usual calling the indictments a "badge of honor." As Trump accepted the *Oakland County Republican Party's* Man of the Decade award, he also claimed that transitioning to electric vehicles would "decimate" the state of Michigan.

Trump's *other takeaways* included attacks on Joe Biden, transgender athletes, and Governor Gretchen Whitmer – not by name – for "giving away hundreds and hundreds and hundreds of billions of Michigan taxpayer money to Chinese companies."

Concerning the indictments and the other investigations, Trump stated:

> If these corrupt persecutions succeed, they will complete their takeover of this country and they will destroy your way of life in the United States of America forever. It will be forever destroyed; we'll never be able to come back from that.

The twice impeached, twice-indicted former president finished his rambling speech by saying, "In the end, they're not after me. They're after you, and I just happen to be standing in the way. We're not going to let anything happen to us."

Although many now expect Trump to receive the 2024 GOP nomination, and *odds makers* are giving the former president a 30% chance of defeating President Biden in a rematch, compared to his 8% chance of defeating Hillary

Clinton in 2016, I believe that Trump will lose the popular vote by more than 10 million votes should he still be the 2024 nominee of the Republican Party.

Accordingly, I contend that when the baneful saga of Donald Trump finally comes to a long overdue ending, his legacy, if the GOP can survive his political debacle will include a party that rejects American constitutionalism, is about deconstructing the state or emptying out as much as possible the executive branch, the Department of Justice, the Environmental Protection Agency, the Consumer Protection Agency, and so on by swapping in or substituting for those professional experts and public servants who have taken an oath to the US Constitution ideological true believers in Trump-like anti-democratic authoritarianism.

This preoccupation of Trump which has always been to clear out and not clean up the Department of Justice that has been investigating and now has indicted and will shortly be prosecuting the former president for his smorgasbord of political crimes and his strong desire to dissolve almost 50 years of an "independent" attorney general with a reconstituted and weaponized Attorney General as in the case of his last "fixer" AG Bill Barr who has also become a preoccupation of the former Republican Party.

In other words, it is not only whether Trump is elected President again in 2024, but also other Republicans such as DeSantis or former Vice President Mike Pence, or former South Carolina Governor and dark horse Nikki Haley. If not in 2024, or even in 2028, these Republicans would like nothing better than to perpetuate Trumpism without Trump but not without his MAGA base.

In a similar vein, as the so-called nationalist or populist conservatives grow increasingly "enthusiastic about using the state to enforce a particular social order" as in the decisions of the alt-right SCOTUS, the Republican Party has also "begun to take on the values and attitudes of the small-time capitalist and the family firm."

In many ways, this is simply Republican "business as usual" as "business owners have always been a critical part of state and local Republican politics."

After all, the nation's state legislatures and county boards of supervisors have always been full of family-owned businesses from car dealerships to food franchises and from construction companies to landscaping businesses.

Among those elements that distinguish these closely held models of ownership from multinational corporations are the degrees to which these businesses are understood to be extensions of the business owners who appear to exercise total authority over their places of production so long as their employees have not organized and established a union.

As New York Times political columnist Jamelle Bouie *concluded,*

If the nature of our work shapes our values – if the habits of mind we cultivate on the job extend to our lives beyond it – then someone in a position of total control over a closely held business like, say, the Trump empire might bring those attitudes, those habits and pathologies, to political office.

That was the case in spades with respect to Donald Trump where there was no separation between the POTUS and the Trump Organization. Moreover, as the Republican Party came to wrap itself around the lawless and fraudulent Trump, and as the GOP came to shape itself around the Trump persona, it also adopted his anomic and nihilistic worldview, and the ideology of a politically organized crime boss no less.

No longer content to run government for businesses' sake, the Republican Party as with Trump now wants to run the government as though it was their very own privately owned business. However, this "doesn't mean greater efficiency or responsiveness or whatever else most people (mistakenly) associate with private industry, it means instead, government as the fief of a small-business tyrant."

The current struggle between democratic and anti-democratic forces in the context of revolutions and civil wars – ours and other nations' – takes us to the heart of the matter in America as analyzed by biologist and climatologist turned political historian, Peter Turchin. In his recently published "End Times: Elites, Counter-Elites, and the Path of Political Disintegration" he addresses the iron laws of oligarchy and wealth pumps that always take from the poorest and the masses in order to giveth to the richest persons and corporations.

This is the historical situation in which the United States has found itself since President Ronald Reagan took office in 1980.

In a nutshell, the contemporary crisis in government is about intra-elite competition and conflict on the one hand, and about the weakened legitimacy of the state, its laws, and institutions, on the other hand, as both of these political conditions are exacerbated by the economic conditions of elite overproduction and popular immiseration.

Fortunately, the "reintegration" of these types of political-economic crises has been resolved in America's past. We can incorporate those successful remedies used previously.

However, going forward I am arguing in my forthcoming book, "Indicting the 45th President: Boss Trump, the GOP, and What We Can Do About the Threat to American Democracy," that in order to be most effective against the fight for authoritarianism and to preclude the next cycle of US institutional failure from happening again, we must also transform our present constitutional democracy from a "tyranny of the minority" to a "tyranny of the majority."

Indicting Donald Trump and others for their alleged conspiracy to overturn the 2020 presidential election on January 6 was also connected to seven states and teams of fake electors, as well as to other election and GOP officials. On July 18, 2023, 16 false Trump electors in Michigan found themselves facing felony charges for their involvement in a fake elector scheme. As Michigan Attorney General Dana Nessel stated during her announcement of the charges: "The false electors' actions undermined the public's faith in the integrity of our elections, and we believe, also plainly violated the laws by which we administer our elections in Michigan." She continued:

> My department has prosecuted numerous cases of election law violations throughout my tenure, and it would be malfeasance of the greatest magnitude if my department failed to act here in the face of overwhelming evidence of an organized effort to circumvent the lawfully cast ballots of millions of Michigan voters in a presidential election.[5]

This fake elector scheme in Michigan and six other states (PA, NV, WI, GA, AZ, and NM) revealed a pattern of organized efforts by Trump and Mark Meadows to engage in corruption, racketeering, and other crimes that were complicated by the multiple legal jurisdictions and geographical locations where the crimes were committed. In Fulton County (Atlanta), Georgia, after more than a two-year investigation by District Attorney Fanti T. Willis, a grand jury had voted unanimously to recommend multiple indictments. This criminal conspiracy not only overlaps with some of the criminal conspiracies of January 6 but is also reminiscent of both of Trump's two impeachment trials for different reasons. The investigation by Georgia prosecutors into Trump's second "perfect conversation" urging Georgia Secretary of State Brad Raffensperger to find enough votes to overturn the election by "recalculating" after three previous counts had found no fraud was not unlike another "perfect conversation" that revolved around extorting the Ukrainian President Zelensky.

Recall that Trump's first impeachment involved his withholding financial aid to Ukraine so that the newly elected president would announce publicly that his government was launching an investigation into the then former Vice President Joe Biden and 2020 Democratic contender for President. This resulted in Trump's first impeachment for High Crimes and Misdemeanors by the Democratic-controlled House and jury nullification by the Republican-controlled Senate. Thirteen months later the Senate Republicans would once again perform jury nullification for Trump's incited insurrectionary assault on the Capitol and the former president's failure to lift a finger to stop the violence for some 3 hours. By the time he made a statement for the rioters to go home, the failed coup had already been defeated by the Capitol Police. While glued to the television in the meanwhile, the Insurrectionist-in-Chief had tweeted out support to his armed comrades.

Thanks to the January 6th House Subcommittee and the DOJ, Trump and his organized co-conspirators would eventually be indicted for their efforts to deny the peaceful transfer of power and to remain the 45th President of the United States by force. This would play out at both the federal and state levels. At more or less the same time by way of Smith's Target Letter to Trump, it had also been confirmed by the middle of July that the Fulton County prosecutors were preparing racketeering charges against Trump and others as consistent with the RICO statute of Georgia. The requirements for prosecutors to invoke the state's RICO statute include showing the existence of an "enterprise" as well as a "pattern" of racketeering activity predicated on at least two qualifying crimes of a field that is more expansive than its federal counterpart. According to *The Guardian* those qualifying crimes were based on evidence of influencing witnesses and computer trespass.[6] In her court filings, Willis has described her investigation of the Fulton County probe as "multi-state, coordinated efforts to influence the results of the November 2020 elections in Georgia and elsewhere."[7]

Donald Trump and his attorneys have done their very best with less than little or no substance whatsoever to their motions to disrupt, stymie, and avert several criminal investigations and potential indictments against the former president. The Trumpian-controlled Republicans in the House of Representatives, armed with their rhetorical witch hunts, debunked conspiracies, and weaponized deep states, have spread their unadulterated propaganda and have done their worst to publicly attack, insult, and debase the Boss' prosecutorial adversaries from Manhattan District Attorney Alvin Bragg to US Special Counsel Jack Smith to New York Attorney General Letitia James. Arguably, Fulton County DA Willis has been the prosecutor most harassed by the GOP's offensive, threatening, and over-the-top MAGA behavior. The only judge to escape the wrath of Trump and his supporters' threats is U.S. District Court Judge Aileen Cannon of Florida, a newly appointed judge by Trump who by all judgments seems to be in Trump's hip pocket.

In June 2022, District Attorney Willis informed the public that she had taken extraordinary measures to protect herself and her family amid threats since the creation of a special grand jury to investigate efforts to overturn the 2020 election.[8] In April 2023, she had also asked for extra security when the time comes to announce the Georgia election probe results.[9] One month earlier the Georgia prosecutors announced that investigators had acquired a "large volume of substantial evidence related to a possible conspiracy from inside and outside the state," and that they were "considering bringing racketeering and conspiracy charges in connection with Donald Trump's effort to overturn the 2020 election in Georgia."[10]

In response to Trump's legal pushback and other nonlegal assaults, Willis had to fight back to remain as the prosecutor in charge of investigating and/

or indicting the former president and his allies for trying to interfere in the election. Trump's legal jeopardy stems from the phone calls he made

in the weeks after the 2020 election to pressure state officials to overturn the results there, and his direct involvement in efforts to assemble an alternative slate of electors, even after three vote counts affirmed President Biden's victory in the state.[11]

Back on March 20, 2023, Trump's lawyers filed three motions related to alleged prosecutorial bias. One to quash the final report of a special grand jury. A second motion sought to suppress any evidence or testimony derived from the investigation. And a third motion to disqualify and remove the office of Fanti T. Willis from the case. Trump and his lawyers were claiming that "the whole world has watched" grand jury proceedings that were "confusing, flawed and, at times, blatantly unconstitutional."[12] On July 17, 2023, Georgia's Supreme Court unanimously ruled that "Trump's lawyers had failed to make a persuasive case for shutting down the inquiry" led by District Attorney Willis. Their five-page decision denying the motions pending in the superior court stated that there was no showing that Trump has been prevented fair access to the ordinary channels, and that the sort of relief Trump was seeking was inappropriate given the circumstances.[13]

For the record, the Trump filing stated that Judge Robert C.I. McBurney of Fulton County Superior Court who will decide to hold a hearing or not on the matter of disqualification had made prejudicial statements against Trump. Even though McBurney had ruled in July 2022 that Willis' office could not pursue a criminal case against State Senator Burt Jones, then the Republican candidate for lieutenant governor in Georgia.[14] At the time of the Trump filing, the Fulton County special grand jury's report remained largely under seal. Finally, the jury had heard evidence for some seven months before they made their recommendations to indict more than a dozen people according to public statements and an interview given by the jury forewoman, Emily Kohrs, to *The NY Times* on February 2023.[15] Then on May 5th to the dismay of Trump and some of the other potential co-conspirators it was revealed that prosecutors for Fulton County had granted immunity to 12 out of 16 fake electors.[16]

On May 15, 2023, Willis asked Judge Robert C.I. McBurney to dismiss the motion: "The State now responds that the Motions should be dismissed or denied as inappropriate. The Movants advance constitutional arguments for which they have no standing and which fail to demonstrate the unconstitutionality of pertinent statues." Overall, the state had argued in its 24-page response that "the Motions are procedurally flawed and advance arguments that lack merit, and the state respectfully requests that this Court retain supervision of this matter and dismiss or deny the Motions as appropriate without a hearing."[17] By Memorial day weekend, it remained to be seen whether or not Judge McBurney would hold a hearing or settle the matter himself. It also remained unclear whether or not the "master of legal delay tactics" would be able to disrupt the timetable and the decision to prosecute. Ms. Willis had stated that criminal indictments were coming between July 11 and September 1, 2023.[18] McBurney did finally reject the latest motions primarily on the grounds that it was premature: While

> being the subject (or even target) of a highly publicized criminal investigation is likely an unwelcome and unpleasant experience, no court ever had held that that status alone provides a basis for the courts to interfere with or halt the investigation.[19]

During the first week of June 2023, it was also confirmed that like the January 6th probe that had expanded its investigation beyond Washington, DC, so too had Fulton County expanded its investigation beyond Georgia to include six other states. According to the *Washington Post*, Willis' office was exploring whether the efforts to overturn Trump's lost in Georgia were parts of a far-reaching multilevel and multistate criminal conspiracy scheme.[20] In this regard, it was disclosed that the two-year-long investigation was examining Trump's campaign "hiring two firms to find voter fraud across the United States and then burying their findings when they did not find any."[21] Specifically, information had been subpoenaed from Simpatico Software Systems and Berkeley Research Group who had been retained for a combined $1 million to find the nonexistent voter fraud.

My commentary in the Sunday edition of Crash Course, June 25 focused on John Eastman's central roles in the fake elector plots involved in both the January 6th insurrection and in the attempts to overturn the election results in Fulton County, Georgia, and several other swing states after the 2020 presidential election. My next commentary in Salon (shared below) focused on both Smith's second criminal indictment of Trump and the forthcoming Fulton County indictments and the role that Mark Meadows would play in these two trials

Salon
**Trump's "coup memo" lawyer may face disbarment – but that's the least of John Eastman's problems**
June 23–24, 2023[22]

**By Gregg Barak**
In January of this year, the State Bar of California announced the filing of a Notice of Disciplinary Charges against attorney John Eastman, precipitated by his central role in the scheme devised by Donald Trump and his allies in

several swing states to create and submit fraudulent election certificates and the now-infamous slates of "fake electors."

Eastman's plot to subvert the 2020 election and defraud millions of American voters will almost certainly be central to the next two indictments facing Trump, those being conspiracy charges likely to be filed this summer by prosecutor Fani Willis in Georgia and Special Counsel Jack Smith in Washington, DC.

Like so many other attorneys, advisers, and aides who have fallen under Trump's spell and done his bidding, Eastman must now face the consequences of his actions. Last week his trial before the California Bar Court began in Los Angeles, with prosecutor Duncan Carling arguing that Eastman should be disbarred as "the architect of a legal strategy aimed at keeping former President Trump in power, [who had] concocted a baseless theory and made false claims of fraud in an attempt to overturn the 2020 election."

All of Eastman's legal misconduct, Carlin continued, "was done with one singular purpose: To obstruct the electoral count on Jan. 6 and stop Vice President Pence from certifying Joe Biden as the winner of the election." Furthermore, the prosecutor argued, Eastman knew exactly what he was doing and was "fully aware in real time that his plan was damaging the nation."

Eastman, who cited the Fifth Amendment numerous times in declining to answer questions from the House committee investigating the January 6 insurrection, has offered the same defense all along: He was just asking questions or raising debating points. His defense attorney in the California bar trial, Randall Miller, told the judge that Eastman "was not there to steal the election or invent ways to make President Trump the winner" but was "merely engaging in what he said was a serious debate at the time about what authority the vice president had concerning the certification of the election." Eastman's goal, Miller contended, was not to reverse the election results but "to delay the counting of the electoral votes so that there could be reasonable investigation undertaken by those states."

Whether that claim will resonate with the court remains to be seen. The 11 charges against Eastman specifically allege that he assisted Trump "in executing a strategy, unsupported by facts or law, to overturn the legitimate results of the 2020 presidential election by obstructing the count of electoral votes of certain states."

As has been widely reported, Eastman drafted two "legal memos" that sought to create a rationale for "circumventing established procedures for the counting of electoral votes in front of the U.S. Congress," based on a radical reinterpretation of the vice president's ceremonial role in that process.

As the disciplinary charges in California make clear, "Eastman knew, or should have known, that the factual premise for his proposals — that massive fraud was at play — was false, and that Trump had lost his bid for re-election." By the time Eastman authored those memos for Trump, the Justice Department had reported that it had "not seen any election fraud on a scale that could have affected the election's outcome," and "multiple courts had rejected election fraud lawsuits."

Eastman also "ignored these truths," the disciplinary charges state, when he spoke at the White House rally on the morning of January 6, 2021, hours before a mob of Trump supporters stormed the US Capitol. In his speech, Eastman made unsupported allegations of widespread voter fraud, including claims that dead people had voted and that Dominion voting machines had manipulated the results. In the aftermath of the January 6 events, Eastman was forced to retire immediately from the law faculty at Chapman University, where he had taught since 1999.

If the California bar court finds Eastman culpable of the alleged violations, it can then recommend to the California Supreme Court that Eastman's law license be suspended or revoked. The outcome of this proceeding is surely of less importance to Eastman than his likely forthcoming indictments in Atlanta and Washington as a Trump co-conspirator.

Perhaps Eastman should have reflected on the career of Donald Trump, the most litigious person in US history, who is well known for his failure to pay attorneys, employees, and contractors of all kinds. Indeed, his history of stiffing his lawyers, especially after losing cases, has led to the humiliating circumstance that the former president must now pay attorneys up front for services not yet rendered.

Between November 2020 and this month, at least 13 attorneys have severed their working relationships with Trump, either resigning or being fired due to some version of "irreconcilable differences." There are also several attorneys who were never officially retained by Trump, and never paid by him, but who nonetheless acted in his interests, including Sidney Powell, Rudy Giuliani, and quite likely John Eastman. As of March 2023, 17 current or former Trump lawyers had been sanctioned by various courts, mostly because of their involvement in dubious litigation challenging the 2020 election.

Then there's the list of Trump lawyers who have had to hire lawyers of their own to fend off the consequences of their work for the former president. Most recently, Trump attorney Christina Bobb retained a defense attorney because of her entanglement in the Mar-a-Lago classified documents case. (In fairness, it seems likely that Bobb was misled by Trump into signing a false declaration that all relevant documents had been returned to the FBI.)

Disciplinary sanctions against Trump lawyers, up to and including disbarment, go all the way back to the notorious Roy Cohn, Trump's first personal attorney and mentor, in 1986, and of course include the disbarment and felony conviction of his longtime personal lawyer and "fixer," Michael Cohen, in 2019.

Is it any wonder that Trump is having a hard time finding a competent defense counsel to represent him in his upcoming criminal trial in Miami? It's a core principle of our legal system that every accused person is entitled to a defense attorney, but at this point not many lawyers are eager to defend the most heinous accused criminal in American political history.

As the anticipated indictments of multiple defendants implicated in the Fulton County investigation were soon to be revealed in the summer of 2023, many legal scholars including former US Ambassador and counsel in the first impeachment trial of Trump, Norman Eisen, were of the opinion (as was I) that the Fulton probe appeared "on tract to be treated like an organized crime ring given the allegations that Trump and others coordinated similar election coups across several states." Speaking on the June 14th podcast Talking Feds with Harry Litman, Eisen continued, "It's more likely than not to be a big sprawling RICO case because it was a big sprawling conspiracy to overturn the 2020 election."[23]

Salon
**One key figure is missing from the Trump indictment:
Will he be revealed as a MAGA "traitor"?**
August 8, 2023[24]

## By Gregg Barak

Let us consider the federal government's second criminal indictment and forthcoming trial of Donald J. Trump, as well as his likely impending criminal indictment and subsequent trial in Fulton County, Georgia. Both of these prosecutions are for conspiracies to subvert American democracy, disenfranchise voters, and defraud the government. There are also related charges and counts regarding the corrupt obstruction of a congressional proceeding on January 6, 2021, in the former case, and anticipated counts of obstructing justice according to Georgia's racketeering statutes in the latter case. Together, they make it perfectly clear why both of these trials must occur – and must be televised for the world to see.

As Jamelle Bouie of the New York Times writes in his latest commentary, even if Trump's Democratic opponents must ultimately "defeat him at the ballot box, it would have been untenable for the legal system to stay quiet in the face of an effort to put an end to the American experiment in republican self-government." It is also worth underscoring that Trump's attempt to overthrow our institutions, in Bouie's phrase, could never have occurred without the distinctively American and undemocratic Electoral College.

As almost everyone outside Trump's MAGA base knows, the ex-president is guilty of these crimes as charged whether he is convicted or not. What most people do not know and what Trump and his lawyers know all too well about these charges – despite their empty political rhetoric about "free speech" and "criminal intent," not to mention their "ace-in-the-hole" argument that #45 was simply relying on his attorneys – is that there is no legitimate legal defense to these criminal charges.

What passes for *substantive* legal defense is the argument that free speech has been weaponized by Trump opponents. That may work in the court of public opinion, but it will not in a court of criminal law. All Team Trump really has are *procedural* legal defenses. That is to say, Trump's attorneys will file a few serious motions – and as many frivolous motions as they can – aimed at indefinitely delaying the eventuality of a criminal trial. That's exactly what they did at 4:55 p.m. on Monday in their 29-page response to the prosecution's protective order motion regarding the rules of behavior during discovery.

In short, the Trump defense team's primary tactical goal is to run out the clock in hopes of preventing the trial from occurring before the 2024 election. If Trump regains the keys to the White House, he clearly intends to derail his own prosecution and continue what Times columnist Maureen Dowd has dubbed his "Coup-Coup-Ca-Choo, Trump-Style."

Dowd reminds us "we're mid-coup, not post-coup. The former president is still in the midst of his diabolical 'Who will rid me of this meddlesome democracy?' plot, hoping his dark knights will gallop off to get the job done." Dowd also notes, "While Trump goes for the long con, or the long coup – rap sheet be damned, it's said that he worries this will hurt his legacy."

I am not sure what "alternative" legacy Trump imagines for himself. As for the one he has cemented in American history, his real legacy is safe. Drawing a term from Gaelic folklore, Dowd calls him "the most democracy-destroying, soul-crushing, self-obsessed amadán ever to occupy the Oval."

As much as we know from Jack Smith's two criminal indictments of Trump and the forthcoming indictment in Georgia, we still know relatively little about the facts behind these indictments. That includes the vast amount of information and evidence gathered from the House select committee that investigated January 6 (but had no subpoena power) as well as that gathered by Smith and Atlanta District Attorney Fani Willis that almost certainly will not be shared with the American public until Trump faces a courtroom trial.

For example, to this point in time we do not know how many different groups of people were involved in the coordinated efforts across the seven states and the District of Columbia to steal the election from the American people. The number of knowing or unknowing participants in that conspiracy, at a minimum, will be over 100 and probably closer to 200.

As for the millions of dollars spent by pro-Trump PACs and supporters to fund the coup, or spent by federal and state governments to investigate it, we are all but clueless and still in the dark. Rest assured that Jack

Smith and company are following the money, as the hoary but useful saying holds.

Here's one more thing we do not know: what role Mark Meadows, Trump's last White House chief of staff and apparent point man for all things coup, will play in Smith's prosecution of the crimes leading up to the January 6 assault on the Capitol.

That's why the first thing I will look for in the Georgia indictment is whether Meadows is listed as an indicted or unindicted co-conspirator. Will he be left out of the document altogether, as he was in Smith's second Trump indictment?

If that happens again in the Georgia charges, it is safe to assume that Meadows will soon become Trump's No. 1 "traitor," ahead of even former Vice President Mike Pence (and Michael Cohen, Trump's longtime personal attorney). That would strongly suggest that Meadows will be a star witness for the prosecution, both in Washington and Atlanta.

This is of course a familiar scenario in classic racketeering cases regarding organized crime conspiracies. It is often the consigliere who brings down the boss – but never before has the crime boss in such a case been a former President of the United States.

Within 24 hours of the above post, we learned about an internal campaign "smoking memo" from one of the "unidentified co-conspirators" for January 6. lawyer Kenneth Chesebro dated December 6, 2020. Referred to as the "fraudulent elector memo" by the prosecution, it proposed "a bold, controversial strategy" that the Supreme Court would "likely" reject. However, Chesebro argued that the strategy (scheme) would focus attention on claims of voter fraud as well as "buy the Trump campaign more time to win litigation that would deprive Biden of electoral votes and/or add to Trump's column."[25] This all but turned out to be a pipe dream thanks to the "too honest" Vice President Mike Pence who refused to go along with the unconstitutional plan. We also learned on the same day that Special Counsel Jack Smith shortly after Elon Musk took over Twitter, now called X, had gotten permission by a federal judge to search Trump's dormant account without his knowledge because they believed he would interfere with the investigation by giving him "an opportunity to destroy evidence, change patterns of behavior" or "notify confederates."[26]

Trump and his attorneys had once again filed not one but two long-shot motions to throw out the special grand jury's investigative findings and to disqualify DA Willis from the proceedings. On Monday, July 17, 2023, the Georgia Supreme Court unanimously rejected Trump's attempt to quash the investigation before the indictments would occur. Then in response to a second amended motion and 650-page filing to disqualify Willis and quash the fillings of the special grand jury based, in part, on the district attorney's alleged "fundraising for her reelection campaign on the back" of the fake electors' scheme and investigation.[27] As investigative reporter for *The NY Times*, Danny Hakim, wrote at the time, "Mr. Trump's lawyers have assailed the Georgia case in their efforts to derail it ahead of any indictments."[28] Among their baseless arguments in their second amended filing, "It is one thing to indict a ham sandwich. To indict the mustard-stained napkin that it once sat on is quite another."[29]

On a more serious note Trump and some of his supporters in their racist communication and intimidation of prosecutors including Manhattan DA Alvin Bragg and New York AG Letitia James have especially exceeded any of their first amendment protections in the instance of Fani Willis. In a group email issued by Willis in the last weekend of July 2023, she warned a group of county leaders to "stay alert" and "make decisions that keep your staff safe." The email also forwarded an obscene message – calling Willis a "corrupt (the n-word)" and "You are going to fail, you Jim Crow Democrat (Whore)!" – that she had recently received as an example of the kind of verbal threats her office has gotten since opening an investigation into possible election interference by Trump and others in the 2020 Georgia presidential election. Willis explained that she was contacting them in case

> you are unclear on what I and my staff have come accustomed to over the last 2½ years. I guess I am sending this as a reminder that you should stay alert over the month of August and stay safe.[30]

She had previously instructed her staff to work from home during the first three weeks in August and had requested that judges clear their calendars for this period as well. In response to the group email, the Fulton County Solicitor Keith Gammage replied all: "The awful communication that you received is meant to threaten, harass and intimidate, not just you, but all of us. The sender and his or her ilk has and will continue to fail." Over the same weekend, heightened security related to the convening of the grand jury and the forthcoming indictment when orange barricades were placed outside the entrance to the Fulton County Courthouse.

As we were all on watch for the Georgia fourth shoe to fall, litigation was swirling all around Trump from E. Jean Carroll to the Mar-a-Lago classified documents case to the January 6 conspiracy charges. The court tossed out Trump's defamation case again Carroll on August 5. The same day in a response to the prosecution motion's about a conflict-of-interest claims involving the same attorney representing two of Trump's co-conspirators and another Trump employee who refused to erase the surveillance video, Judge Cannon put the issue off until she could get a response from the government as to why the prosecution was continuing to further investigate into the stolen classified documents in a jurisdiction outside of the Southern District of Florida. She invited the prosecution to respond and the defense as well if they chose to. According to Joyce Vance, by revealing this investigation to both the defense and the public, it may very well be appealed to 11th Circuit Court to remove her from trying the case. Meanwhile, on the very same day, the Magistrate and Trial Judge in Washington, DC, were expecting a filing in response to the prosecution's motion for a protective order so that discovery could begin and they could turn over their documents to the defense. But first, Trump would have to agree not to disclose any of that information to the public or otherwise.

Meanwhile, according to a three-decade former New York prosecutor Karen Friedman Agnifilo, the prosecutors were – I might say with good reason primarily to put off time-saving appeals – treating Trump with kid gloves. Not only was he being treated not as an ordinary defendant but he has been the recipient of privileges.[31] I quote extensively from Defendant Trump's Sweetheart Deal:

In the bizarre upside down world that has currently infected the right wing, there is a drumbeat narrative alleging that Hunter Biden has received a sweetheart deal from the Department of Justice, while Donald Trump is being "persecuted." However, it is the exact opposite and here is why: defendant Trump is treated differently than other similarly situated defendants and continues to be given pass after pass after pass by prosecutors and judges alike.

I have never seen a defendant treated as leniently as defendant Trump. He has a rap sheet with 3 open felony indictments, 78-charges, in 3 separate jurisdictions. He has repeatedly threatened prosecutors, judges, and potential witnesses and has his own 757 jumbo jet at the ready to fly anywhere in the world and can abscond at any time. And the nature of his charges is among the most serious there are – he is accused of stealing our nation's most sensitive secrets, trying to destroy evidence of his crimes, committing fraud in the oval office, and causing a violent insurrection in order to attempt to steal an election he lost, and our democracy.

The most recent example of Trump's flagrant potential middle finger in the face of justice is when, the day after he was arraigned in the blockbuster Democracy stealing indictment, he crossed a bright red line and fake treated: "IF YOU GO AFTER ME, I'M COMING AFTER YOU!"

This post on his personal social media platform Truth Social was a clear threat to the prosecutors when it was viewed in context with a photo of Biden, Willis, Bragg, James and Smith – where he labeled them all "the fraud squad." And let's not forget the post from several months ago where he posted two photos next to one another where he held a baseball bat next to a photo of Bragg's head and when called on it gave an excuse that not even a toddler would find credible.

In both of these instances, he has not only (allegedly) committed a crime, but he has also violated his terms of release from custody. Defendant Trump's release conditions are contextually quite lenient in all three of his open cases. I dare anyone to find any other defendant with a rap sheet like his with only these conditions.

Moreover, with respect to "obstruction of justice" and "jury tampering," Team Trump has taken these mediated crimes to a level never seen before in its minute-long ad titled "The Fraud Squad" that attacks President Biden's four prosecutors who were indicting him for more than 100 crimes. With respect to Fulton County DA Fani Willis' indictment that was announced on August 15/17, 2023, the ad ran on cable news channels in metro Atlanta between August 9 and 13. With respect to Willis, Trump has long accused her of being a "racist" and on a "witch hunt." In the video Willis is slandered, defamed, and lied about. Its most incendiary allegation is that Willis "got caught hiding a relationship with a gang member she was prosecuting" which was a total mischaracterization and was "flatly denied that she had a relationship with a former client and other rumors spread" on the first day that the campaign ad meant to prejudice a jury pool was aired. In an email to her colleagues, obtained by The Atlanta Journal-Constitution, Willis labeled the ad "derogatory and false."[32] The email begins Good Morning Fulton County District Attorney Family:

> It is my understanding that an ad was put in the Atlanta market to run between today 8/9 and 8/13 that will have derogatory and false information about me as the District Attorney of the Atlanta Judicial Circuit. Apparently a lot of money was spent to run this ad in the Atlanta market over the next 5 days. That means the ad will run quite frequently over the next 5 days. Each of you represents me. Especially, ADA's who all took an oath under my name. We often remind you if you are an ADA you are my personal staff and represent me. Many of you are quite kind to me, very protective, and will become very defensive if someone attempts to attack me, the office or your colleagues. You may not comment in any way on the ad or any of the negativity that may be expressed against me, your colleagues, this office in coming days, weeks or months. We have no personal feelings against those we investigate or prosecute and we should not express any. This is business, it will never be personal. We have a job to do. In this office, we prosecute based on the facts and the law. The law is non-partisan. You should feel no need to defend me. I shared with this office at last Friday's meeting 1/1000 of the negative or derogatory comments I receive. I invited you into an hour of my typical day. I am not concerned with the calls, emails, or ads and you should not concern yourself with them. This is a reminder that it is against office policy to comment on these matters on

social media or any public forum. No employee of this office may make any public comments related to the noise. Your instruction from me is to ignore all the noise and keep doing your job with excellence. Please make it an absolutely phenomenal day and stay safe.

To briefly summarize, the Fulton County investigation lasted some two and one-half years before the eventual indictment came on August 16, 2023. The inquiry had focused on five things that occurred primarily in Georgia in the weeks after the election. These include

> calls that Mr. Trump made to pressure local officials, including a January 2, 2021, call to Georgia's secretary of state, Brad Raffensperger, during which Mr. Trump said he wanted to "find" nearly 12, 000 votes, or enough to reverse his loss.

It included scrutinizing "a plan by Trump allies to create a slate of bogus electors for Mr. Trump in Georgia, even though Mt. Biden's victory had been certified several times by the state's Republican leadership." Ms. Willis' office also investigated harassment of local election workers by Trump supporters, as well as lies about ballot fraud that were advanced by Rudolph W. Giuliani as well as "other allies during legislative hearings after the election."[33] On the Sunday evening before the week of the fourth criminal indictment of Trump, Enythe Green wrote the poem, "Never Trump":

> If Trump is winning
> Americans are losing
> It's a simple equation
> That needs no explanation
> They hold him as hero
> When he is absolutely zero
> No ethics no morals no character
> or Grace
> We all know that he should not even be in the race
> A conman a grifter a bully -soon to be
> Indicted x 4
> And we wish that Republicans would show him the door
> But they are weak and spineless and
> clamor to kiss his ring
> He incites violence caused an insurrection
> That is his thing
> He said in his inauguration speech the carnage stops here stops now
> And in the White House we should never him
> Allow.

Fani Willis released the Fulton County indictments of Georgia v. Trump, et al to the public close to midnight on August 14, 2023. At the heart of these RICO indictments is *the usage of fake claims of election fraud to commit election fraud.* Ms. Willis named 19 defendants including Trump. She intends to prove they were part of a criminal organization that constituted an "enterprise" that engaged in a "pattern of racketeering activity" to "accomplish the illegal goal of allowing Donald J. Trump to seize the president's office." Willis gave the former president and 18 others charged with illegally conspiring to overturn the results of the 2020 presidential election until August 25 to turn themselves in. This fourth indictment of Trump in as many months had the effect of a homerun in the bottom of the ninth in the seventh game of the world series of criminal indictments because for the first time the principal organizers who conspired with the 45th POTUS to pull off an "inside" coup d'état were charged with crimes. Trump faces 13 counts, including violating the Georgia Racketeer Influenced and Corrupt Organizations Act, conspiring to commit forgery in the first degree and conspiring to file false documents.

The breadth and depth of this comprehensive 98-page speaking indictment also made 89 references to 30 unidentified co-conspirators as they are likely to be cooperating witnesses in what promises to become the longest and most significant RICO criminal trial in US history. As Palm Beach County Florida State Attorney Dave Aronberg explained why Willis' case was a tour de force on the Morning Joe show, August 15 – using the analogy that Jack Smith's prosecution was like a MAGA "tactical strike" to initially convict only Trump in a trial that was designed to last four to six weeks as contrasted with Fani Willis' "carpet bombing of MAGA forces to smithereens" whose trial could last as long as 12 months. I was pleased by the fact that there were 100 overt acts by Trump and his co-conspirators disclosed step by step in the indictment to further their attempt to steal the election. I was also pleased to learn that Georgia governors do not have pardoning power and that there was no rush to take these indictments to trial, and that should a trial materialize most likely not to many weeks before the November 2024 presidential election that it will be videoed live for the whole world to watch as when Trump was arraigned in Fulton County, Georgia Unlike his three previous criminal indictments that were all behind closed doors. Lastly, I was pleased to see that the serial criminal, lifelong fraudster and conman, and most recently, wannabe authoritarian and failed insurrectionist was finally being held accountable for his lawlessness, corruption, and criminal efforts to overturn democracy and the rule of law.

### The 41 Counts in the Georgia Indictment

22 counts related to forgery or false documents and statements
8 counts related to soliciting or impersonating public officers

3 counts related to influencing witnesses
3 counts related to election fraud or defrauding the state
3 counts related to computer tampering
1 count related to racketeering
1 count related to perjury

## The 19 People Named in the Indictment[34]

**DONALD TRUMP:** Then-President Donald Trump fixated on Georgia after the 2020 general election, refusing to accept his narrow loss in the state and making unfounded assertions of widespread election fraud there. He also called top state officials, including Gov. Brian Kemp, to urge them to find a way to reverse his loss in the state. In a January 2, 2021, phone call with Georgia Secretary of State Brad Raffensperger, Trump suggested the state's top elections official could help "find" the votes needed for him to win the state. Fulton County District Attorney Fani Willis opened an investigation into possible illegal attempts to influence the election shortly after a recording of that call was made public.

**RUDY GIULIANI:** During several legislative hearings at the Georgia Capitol in December 2020, the former New York mayor and Trump attorney promoted unsupported allegations of widespread election fraud in Georgia. Prosecutors have said Rudy Giuliani was also involved in a plan to have 16 Georgia Republicans serve as fake electors, falsely swearing that Trump had won the 2020 presidential election and declaring themselves the state's "duly elected and qualified" electors.

**JOHN EASTMAN:** A former dean of Chapman University law school in Southern California, John Eastman, one of Trump's lawyers, was deeply involved in some of his efforts to remain in power after the 2020 election. He wrote a memo arguing that Trump could remain in power if then-Vice President Mike Pence overturned the results of the election during a joint session of Congress where electoral votes would be counted. That plan included putting in place a slate of "alternate" electors in seven battleground states, including Georgia, who would falsely certify that Trump had won their states.

**MARK MEADOWS:** Trump's chief of staff visited Cobb County, in the Atlanta suburbs, while state investigators were conducting an audit of the signatures on absentee ballot envelopes in December 2020. Mark Meadows obtained the phone number of the chief investigator for the secretary of state's office, Frances Watson, and passed it along to Trump, who called her. He also participated in the January 2, 2021, phone call between Trump and Georgia Secretary of State Brad Raffensperger.

**SIDNEY POWELL:** A lawyer and staunch Trump ally, Sidney Powell, was part of a group who met at the South Carolina home of conservative attorney Lin Wood in November 2020 "for the purpose of exploring options to influence the results of the November 2020 elections in Georgia and elsewhere," prosecutors have said. Wood, who's licensed in Georgia, said Powell asked him to help find Georgia residents to serve as plaintiffs in lawsuits contesting the state's election results. Additionally, emails and documents obtained through subpoenas in an unrelated lawsuit have shown that Powell was involved in arranging for a computer forensics team to travel to rural Coffee County, about 200 miles southeast of Atlanta, to copy data and software from election equipment there in January 2021.

**KENNETH CHESEBRO:** Prosecutors have said Kenneth Chesebro, an attorney, worked with Georgia Republicans in the weeks after the November 2020 election at the direction of Trump's campaign. Chesebro worked on the coordination and execution of a plan to have 16 Georgia Republicans sign a certificate declaring falsely that Trump won and declaring themselves the state's "duly elected and qualified" electors.

**JEFFREY CLARK:** A US Justice Department official who championed Trump's false claims of election fraud, Jeffrey Clark presented colleagues with a draft letter pushing Georgia officials to convene a special legislative session on the election results, according to testimony before the US House committee that investigated the January 6, 2021, Capitol riot. Clark wanted the letter sent, but Justice Department superiors refused.

**JENNA ELLIS:** The lawyer appeared with Rudy Giuliani at a December 3, 2020, hearing hosted by state Republican lawmakers at the Georgia Capitol during which false allegations of election fraud were made. Jenna Ellis also wrote at least two legal memos to Trump and his attorneys advising that Pence should "disregard certified electoral college votes from Georgia and other purportedly 'contested' states" when Congress met to certify the election results on January 6, 2021, prosecutors have said.

**RAY SMITH:** A Georgia-based lawyer, Ray Smith, was involved in multiple lawsuits challenging the results of the 2020 election in Georgia. He also gathered witnesses to provide testimony before Georgia legislative subcommittee hearings held in December 2020 on alleged issues with the state's election.

**ROBERT CHEELEY:** A Georgia lawyer, Robert Cheeley, presented video clips to legislators of election workers at the State Farm Arena in Atlanta and alleged the workers were counting votes twice or sometimes three times. He spoke to the lawmakers after Giuliani.

**MICHAEL ROMAN:** A former White House aide who served as the director of Trump's election day operations, Michael Roman, was involved in efforts to put forth a set of fake electors after the 2020 election.

**DAVID SHAFER:** The chairman of the Georgia GOP, Shafer, was one of 16 state Republicans who met at the state Capitol on December 14, 2020, to sign a certificate declaring falsely that Trump had won and also declaring themselves the state's "duly elected and qualified" electors. He also joined Trump in a lawsuit challenging the certification of the 2020 election in Georgia.

**SHAWN STILL:** He was one of 16 Georgia Republicans who signed a certificate falsely stating that Trump had won the state and declaring themselves the state's "duly elected and qualified" electors. Shawn Still was the finance chairman for the state GOP in 2020 and served as a Georgia delegate to the Republican National Convention that year. He was elected to the Georgia state Senate in November 2022 and represents a district in Atlanta's suburbs.

**STEPHEN CLIFFGARD LEE:** Prosecutors say Stephen Cliffgard Lee, a pastor, worked with others to try to pressure Georgia election worker Ruby Freeman and her daughter after Trump and his allies falsely accused them of pulling fraudulent ballots from a suitcase during the vote count. Lee allegedly knocked on Freeman's door, frightening her and causing her to call 911 three times, prosecutors said in a court filing last year.

**HARRISON WILLIAM PRESCOTT FLOYD:** Also known as Willie Lewis Floyd III, he served as director of Black Voices for Trump and is accused of recruiting Lee to arrange a meeting with Freeman and Chicago-based publicist Trevian Kutti.

**TREVIAN C. KUTTI:** Prosecutors allege publicist Trevian C. Kutti claimed to have high-level law enforcement connections. They say Freeman met with Kutti at a police precinct, where she brought Floyd into the conversation on a speakerphone. Prosecutors say Kutti presented herself as someone who could help Freeman but then pressured her to falsely confess to election fraud.

**CATHY LATHAM:** One of 16 Georgia Republicans who signed a certificate falsely stating that Trump had won the state and declaring themselves the state's "duly elected and qualified" electors, Cathy Latham was also chair of the Coffee County Republican Party. She was at the county elections office for much of the day on January 7, 2021, and welcomed a computer forensics team that arrived to copy software and data from the county's election equipment in what the secretary of state's office has said was "unauthorized access" to the machines.

**SCOTT GRAHAM HALL:** An Atlanta-area bail bondsman, Scott Graham Hall, was allegedly involved in commandeering voting information that was the property of Dominion Voting Systems from Coffee County, a small south Georgia jurisdiction. Also charged in the scheme were Powell, Latham, and former county elections supervisor Misty Hampton.

**MISTY HAMPTON:** She was the elections director in Coffee County. Misty Hampton was present in the county elections office on January 7, 2021, when a computer forensics team copied software and data from the county's election equipment. She also allowed two other men who had been active in efforts to question the 2020 election results to access the elections office later that month and to spend hours inside with the equipment.

It is worth underscoring that the charges brought forth by Ms. Willis fall into several criminal baskets and that the indictments bundle together

> several efforts by Mr. Trump and his allies to reverse the election results in Georgia. None of the 19 defendants [were] accused of taking part in all of those different schemes, but under RICO law, prosecutors have to prove only that each one broke state laws as part of a continuing criminal enterprise with the same overarching goal.[35]

Several defendants tried unsuccessfully to move their cases to federal court including Eastman, Meadows, Latham, Shafer, and Still. Four of the 19 co-defendants had plead guilty to various charges in the fall 2023, including Scott Hall, Sidney Powell, Kenneth Chesebro, and Jenna Ellis. Only Ellis appeared remorseful and likely to be a strong cooperating witness for the prosecution.

Although this trial is scheduled to begin in August 2024, it is quite complicated and could take as long as one year to try. Several more co-defendants are likely to make a deal before the trial begins. However, District Attorney Willis has indicated that there would be no deals made with Trump, Meadows and Giuliani.

## Notes

1  Alex Isenstadt. 2023. Indictment turbocharges Trump's fundraising. *Politico*. April 15. www.politico.com/news/2023/04/15/trump-fundraising-indictment-data
2  Isaac Arnsdorf and Josh Dawsey. 2023. Trump prosecutions consume campaign funds and messaging as charges mount. *The Washington Post*. July 21. www.washingtonpost.com/politics/2023/07/21/trump-indictments-campaign-2024
3  Alayna Treene. 2023. Trump leadership PAC spends more than $40 million on legal fees amid indictments. *CNN Politics*. July 30. www.cnn.com/2023/07/30/politics/donald-trump-campaign-spending-legal-costs
4  Kyle Cheney. 2023. Georgia judge skewers Trump's bid to derail potential charges. *Politico*. July 31. www.politico.com/news/2023/07/31/georgia-judge-trump-charges-fulton-county
5  Craig Mauger and Beth LeBlanc. 2023. 16 false Trump electors face felony charges in Michigan. *The Detroit Free Press*. July 18. www.detroitnews.com/story/news/politics/michigan/2023/07/18/michigan-donald-trump-fake-electors-charged-felonies-attorney-general-dana-nessel
6  Hugo Lowell. 2023. Fulton County prosecutors prepare racketeering charges in Trump inquiry. *The Guardian*. July 21. www.theguardian.com/us-news/2023/jul/21/georgia-trump-charges-fraud-election

7 Holly Bailey. 2023 Atlanta braces for possible indictments in 2020 election investigation. *The Washington Post.* July 31. www.washingtonpost.com/national-security/2023/07/31/georgia-2020-election-investigation-trump

8 WSBTV.com News Staff. 2022. Fulton D. A.: Extreme security 'required for me to stay alive' after threats. *WSB-TV.* June 10. www.wsbtv.com/news/local/fulton-cou nty/fulton-da-extreme-security-required-me-stay-alive-after-threats

9 Dale Russell. 2023. Fulton County DA asks for extra security when she announces Georgia election probe results. *Fox 5 Atlanta.* April 26. www.fox5atlanta.com/news/fulton-county-election-probe-donald-trump-extra-security-investigation

10 Don Lemon and Jason Morris. 2023. Georgia prosecutors considering racketeering and conspiracy charges in probe of effort to overturn Trump's 2020 loss, source says. *CNN.* March 20. www.cnn.com/2023/03/20/politics/georgia-racketeering-conspiracy-trump-willis/index.html

11 Richard Fausset. 2023. Trump's Georgia lawyers seek to quash special grand jury report. *The New York Times.* March 20. www.nytimes.com/2023/03/20/us/tru mps-georgia-special-grand-jury.html

12 Quoted in Ibid.

13 Josh Gerstein. 2023. Georgia Supreme Court rejects Trump bid to head off potential indictment. *Politico.* July 17. www.politico.com/news/2023/07/17/geor gia-supreme-court-trump-indictment

14 Richard Fausset, Danny Hakim, and Sean Keenan. 2022. Prosecutor is barred from pursuing criminal case against Trump Ally. *The New York Times.* July 25. www.nytimes.com/2022/07/25/us/georgia-prosecutor-fani-willis-trump.html

15 Danny Hakim. 2023. Jury in Georgia Trump inquiry recommended multiple indictments, Forewoman Says. *The New York Times.* February 21. www.nytimes.com/2023/02/21/us/trump-georgia-grand-jury-indictments.html

16 Reuters. 2023. Georgia fake elector defendants accept immunity in Trump probe. *Reuters.* May 5. reuters.com/world/us/georgia-fake-elector-defendants-accept-immunity-trump-probe-lawyer-2023-05-06

17 In Re: Special Purpose Grand Jury. May 15, 2023. www.documentcloud.org/documents/23813446-fcda-response-5-15-23#document/p2/a2256252

18 William K. Rashbaum, Maggie Haberman, Charlie Savage and Jonah E. Bromwich. 2023. Donald Trump's time-tested legal strategy: Attack and delay. *The New York Times.* April 1. www.nytimes.com/2023/04/01/nyregion/trump-bragg-legal-defe nse-strategy.html

19 Quoted in Cheney. 2023.

20 Josh Dawsey and Amy Gardner. 2023. Trump-funded studies disputing election fraud are focus in two probes. *The Washington Post.* June 5. www.washingtonp ost.com/nation/2023/06/05/trump-funded-studies-disputing-election-fraud-are-focus-two   probes/?utm_campaign=wp_post_most&utm_medium=email&utm_ source=newsletter&wpisrc=nl_most

21 Reuters. 2023. Georgia probe of Trump expands to activities in other states, Washington Post reports. *Reuters.* June 2. www.reuters.com/legal/georgia-probe-trump-expands-activities-other-states-washington-post-2023-06-02

22 www.salon.com/2023/06/24/coup-memo-lawyer-may-face-disbarment--but-thats-the-least-of-john-eastmans-problems

23 Quoted in Stanley Dunlap. 2023. 'A big sprawling conspiracy': All eyes on Fulton investigation as Trump plots White House return. *Raw Story.* July 6. www.rawst ory.com/fulton-county-investigation

24 www.salon.com/2023/08/08/one-key-figure-is-missing-from-the-indictment-will-he-be-revealed-as-a-maga-traitor

25 Maggie Haberman, Charlie Savage and Luke Broadwater. 2023. Previously secret memo laid out strategy for Trump to overturn Biden's win. *The New York Times*. August 9. www.nytimes.com/2023/08/08/us/politics/trump-indictment-fake-elect ors-memo

26 Alan Feuer. 2023. Special counsel obtained search warrant for Trump's Twitter account. *The New York Times*. August 9. www.nytimes.com/2023/08/09/us/polit ics/trump-twitter-account-search-warrant

27 Holly Bailey. 2023. Trump attorneys again push to block Georgia 2020 election investigation. *The Washington Post*. July 21. www.washingtonpost.com/national-security/2023/07/21/trump-georgia-investigation

28 Danny Hakim. 2023. For Trump and Allies, outcome of Georgia election inquiry nears. *The New York Times*. July 23: National, p. 19.

29 Quoted in Ibid.

30 Patricia Murphy, Greg Bluestein and Tia Mitchell. 2023. The Jolt: Fani Willis warns Fulton leaders 'stay alert' ad decision looms. *The Atlanta Journal-Constitution*. July 31. www.ajc.com/politics/politics-blog/the-jolt-fani-willis-warns-fulton-lead ers-stay-alert-as-decision-looms

31 Karen Friedman Agnifilo. 2023. Defendant Trump's sweetheart deal. *MTN*. August 6. www.meidastouch.com/news/defendant-trumps-sweetheart-deal

32 Tamar Hallerman. 2023. 'Derogatory and false': Fulton DA denies rumors circulated by Trump. *The Atlanta Journal-Constitution*. August 9. www.ajc.com/ politics/derogatory-and-false-fulton-da-denies-rumors-circulated-by-trump

33 Danny Hakim and Richard Fausset. 2023. Georgia grand jury likely to hear Trump case next week. *The New York Times*. August 8. www.nytimes.com/2023/ 08/08/us/trump-georgia-election-grand-jury.html?campaign

34 Tim Darnell. 2023. Here are the 19 people named in the sweeping indictment against Donald Trump. *ANF*. August 14. www.atlantanewsfirst.com/2023/08/15/ here-are-19-people-named-sweeping-indictments-against-donald-trump

35 Richard Fausset and Danny Hakim. 2023. Trump Indicted in Georgia: Prosecutors accuse Trump of 'Criminal Enterprise' to overturn election. *The New York Times*. August 14/15. www.nytimes.com/live/2023/08/14/us/trump-indictment-georgia-election

# 8

# TRUMP'S CONSPIRACIES TO OVERTURN THE 2020 ELECTION THAT LED TO THE JANUARY 6TH ASSAULT ON THE CAPITOL

On Sunday, July 9, 2023, events were scheduled outside secretaries of state offices in California, Colorado, Georgia, and Oregon. These actions were led by the advocacy organizations Free Speech for People and Mi Familia Vota among other groups and legal scholars. They not only cited Section 3 of the 14th Amendment and provided examples of other elected officials who had taken an oath to support the US Constitution, "engaged in insurrection or rebellion," and were subsequently barred from holding office again even without having been indicted for these activities. Theses activists were making the case with a week of rallies that Trump's incitement of the January 6 attack on the US Capitol had disqualified him from holding office again. Meanwhile, secretaries of blue states were taking seriously the matter of disqualifying the frontrunning Republican presidential nomination in 2024 after having orchestrated a failed coup before leaving the White House as the 45th president in 2021.[1]

Although we did not know for sure at the time, it seemed that Special Counsel Jack Smith with respect to January 6 was most heavily invested in going after a conspiracy by Donald Trump and others to stop the peaceful transfer of presidential power after his 2020 loss to president-elect Biden. This was most evident by those witnesses subpoenaed for testimony revolving around the fake electors scheme spread over seven states. All totaled there were 84 fake electors who had signed documents falsely declaring Trump the winner of their state elections. Relatedly, another 50 or so individuals testified before the federal grand jury. They had either received subpoenas

DOI: 10.4324/9781003390664-11

or spoke voluntarily to investigators about the efforts to stop the peaceful rather than nonpeaceful transfer of power. These included such high-profile politicos as:

- Former White House lawyers Patrick Philbin and Pat Cipollone
- Former Trump White House officials Stephen Miller and Dan Scavino
- Former Department of Homeland Security official Ken Cuccinelli
- "Stop the Steal" leader Ali Alexander
- Former Republican Speaker of the House Newt Gingrich
- Trump's Political Tactician Steve Bannon
- Former Arizona House Speaker Rusty Bowers
- Georgia Secretary of State Brad Raffensperger
- Former deputy director of Election Day operations for Trump, Gary Michael Brown

Other political luminaries and Trump associates numbering another 40 or so persons included Rudi Giuliani and his attorney Robert Costello, former New York City Police Commissioner Bernard Kerik, Justin Clark, Sidney Powell, Jenna Ellis, John Eastman, MyPillow CEO Mike Lind, and Rep. Scott Perry.[2] By "hook or crook," most of these folks will have taken the fifth preferring to be indicted along with Trump, or they will have to cut a deal, if they have not already done so, to reduce the severity of their sentences or possibly in some instances to receive total immunity for "spilling the beans."

As the "model prosecution memorandum" and *Just Security* concluded on July 13, 2023,

> there likely is sufficient evidence to obtain and sustain a conviction of Trump for his three-step plan to overturn the election:

1. Trump knew he lost the election but did not want to give up power, so he worked with his lawyers and others on a wide variety of schemes to change the outcome. Those schemes included creating fraudulent electoral certificates that were submitted to Congress, implicating statutes such as 18 U.S.C. § 371, which prohibits conspiracies to defraud the United States in the administration of elections.
2. When all the other schemes failed, Trump and his lawyers ultimately concentrated on using the false electoral slates to obstruct the constitutionally mandated congressional certification of the election on January 6, implicating statutes such as 18 U.S.C. § 1512, which prohibits obstruction of an official proceeding. Their primary objective was to have Vice President Mike Pence in his presiding role on that day either block

Congress from recognizing Joe Biden's win at all or at least to delay the electoral count.

3  When Pence refused, Trump went to his last resort: triggering an insurrection in the hope that it would throw Congress off course, delaying the transfer of power for the first time in American history. This implicated statutes such as 18 U.S.C. § 2383, which prohibits inciting an insurrection and giving aid or comfort to insurrectionists. (Section 2383 is rarely charged, and as we discuss below, this is a charge DOJ will use only with extreme caution. We believe there is sufficient evidence to pursue it – as did the Select Committee in making a criminal referral of Trump under that statute – but prosecutors may make different choices. Much will depend on the evidence the Special Counsel develops.)[3]

One day earlier FBI Director Christopher Wray, a lifelong Republican and a Trump appointee, testified before the House Judiciary Committee hearing on "oversight of the Federal Bureau of Investigation" and the alleged politicalization of law enforcement against the former president. As Amanda Marcotte argued the next day, "Being a 'good' Republican means embracing the anti-government ideology that led to the 1995 Oklahoma City bombing." On its surface,

> these anti-FBI conspiracy theories are further evidence there is nothing too low for Republicans when it comes to running interference for Trump. It's never that Trump is such a massive criminal that he overcomes law enforcement's unwillingness to deal with him. No, it must be an ant-Trump conspiracy.

It goes without saying, the "notion that the FBI is a leftist organization out to destroy the American right is…among the dumbest ideas ever generated by human brains."[4]

Even after Trump announced on Truth Social on the morning of July 18, 2023 that he had received a "target letter" from the Special Counsel two days earlier and that another indictment was imminent, the "good" Republicans and nearly all of the dozen or so Republican primary candidates for the 2024 presidential nomination were as usual busy circling the wagons and echoing Trump's nonlegal defenses that he posted @ realDonald Trump about witch hunts, crooked Joe Biden and his injustice department, prosecutorial misconduct, election interference, and more fabrications. Later the same say on an Iowa radio show, the self-destructive Trump was warning everyone that it would be "very dangerous" should the "deranged" Special Prosecutor jail him, since his supporters allegedly now had "much more passion than they did in 2020." Something that had already been thrown into question by the missing crowds of supporters as well as their apathetic responses to the first two indictments – except to dole out money for his defenses. In any case, if anyone is to jail the "petulant child" Trump before the January 6 trial begins, it will be Judge Tanya Chutkan for continuing to violate the gag order imposed by her after several warnings.

Most succinctly and setting the record straight on *The Katie Phang Show* on Sunday, July 23, 2023, US Representative Jamie Raskin (D-MD) and member of the January 6 House Select Committee responded to the likes of former Vice President Mike Pence and Governor Ron DeSantis. Both of these 2024 candidates for the GOP presidential nomination were taking to the airwaves. Each was trying to maintain that the assault on the Capitol was spontaneous and simply got out of control. Raskin maintained to the contrary that "this was a very carefully orchestrated and choreographed plot to overthrow the election. There was nothing spontaneous or out of control about it."[5] While discussing the conspiratorial scheme behind January 6, Raskin further elaborated that the scheme included:

> Trying to get state legislatures to void out the Biden slates and replace them with Trump slates. It included direct overtures to state election officials like Secretary of state Brad Raffensperger in Georgia to get them to just find 11,780 votes. It involved an attempt to conceivably overthrow the Department of Justice leadership and install someone who would assert corruption. And finally, it involved a very concerted plan to try to get Vice President Pence to step outside of his constitutional role and to exercise lawless extra-constitutional powers simply to declare Trump president or to kick the whole election into the House of Representatives for a so-called contingent election where the states would be voting one state, one vote, rather than each of us members voting in that way.[6]

Nonetheless, at campaign rallies in Erie, Pennsylvania on Saturday, July 29, 2023, and from New York on Sunday the next day, Trump was not denying his guilt or claiming that he was an innocent man. Although he was still claiming victimhood and that he was being unfairly persecuted by the Deep State and its weaponization of the DOJ. Trump was also calling on Republicans to impeach President Biden and to go after the Biden "crime family" for doing "worst things" than Hillary Clinton. At the same time, his political discourse was about claiming that he was only being indicted because he was winning the 2024 GOP primary for president. The 4,000 people gathered at the Erie rally were loving each and every absurdity flowing from the mouth of the gaslighter-in-chief.

Salon
## Jan. 6 assault reflected a deep American division: Whose democracy is it?
Trump's rioters represented a deep, dark current in American history:
Restricting democracy to a chosen view
December 20, 2022[7]

**By Gregg Barak**
The enemies of democracy who stormed the US Capitol building on Jan. 6, 2021, aiming to overturn a presidential election were in effect privileging their votes over those of the majority of voters. After their side had lost the election, as well as the various recounts and court challenges, these rioters followed the lead of the losing incumbent president in his attempt to overturn the election results by force and violence. That president has now been referred to the Justice Department for possible prosecution on a number of criminal charges, an unprecedented step taken by the House select committee investigating the insurrection, which is sure to be dissolved with the new Congress next month.

The actions of the lame-duck president's supporters and those members of Congress who voted later that night not to certify the election of Joe Biden shared an evident belief that all people are not in fact equal, and that some are more deserving of rights than others. In defiance of the law and the Constitution, these Trumpist loyalists were in effect weaponizing citizenship, in the phrase of Michael Bellesiles, by "claiming a determinative right as 'real Americans,' the embodiment of the 'true America,' to place themselves in a category of citizenship enjoying certain" inalienable rights that are denied to others.

Democracy, from its Greek roots *kratia*, means to rule by *demos* or the people. More precisely, democracy refers to a polity ruled by free, as contrasted with unfree (or enslaved) people. This concept of democracy, which always embodies concepts of privilege and inequality, has its roots in the historical distinction between citizens with the franchise to vote and subjects without it. From its inception, our nation has always been something other than a democracy, as initially most members of American society were subjects of the law, not citizens or rulers of the law.

To this point, the United States has been a federal republic of states, ruled today by 51 constitutions. In its earliest years the nation was ruled by elected and appointed representatives dependent on the voting power of white male property owners. Over the course of its history, America has struggled over the expansion of the franchise as well as the contraction of privilege or inequality to become a more perfect union.

The actions of the January 6 insurrectionists were rooted in a traditional division established by the Naturalization Act of 1790 that viewed citizenship as limited by ethnicity, religion, and gender. More than a half-century later, Chief Justice Roger Taney declared in the 1857 Dred Scott decision that Black people could never be citizens, since the Constitution had been written by and for white men. After the Civil War, the 14th Amendment created a uniform standard of citizenship that temporarily included all males born or naturalized under the full and equal protection of law.

Subsequently, legislators, congressmen, and judges "used the lesser citizenship status of women as an obvious justification for creating different legal castes" as in the imposition of segregation after the end of Reconstruction. Similarly, the Supreme Court stepped in to undermine the 14th Amendment as well, "allowing full citizenship to be used as a weapon by elites against those who failed to be born white men," most notably in Plessy v. Ferguson.

Even after the passage of the 19th Amendment granting women the right to vote, which was ratified in 1920, numerous efforts to deny women full citizenship remained in place, often preventing them from owning property, engaging in "men's work" or barring married women from holding credit cards in their own names. Likewise, the denial of basic rights to Native Americans, convict laborers, and interned Japanese-Americans – and, most recently, voter suppression laws or gerrymandering targeting Black and Latino voters in particular – have constituted a citizenship caste system.

As 19th-century historian Michael Bellesiles, also quoted above, has written:

> The concept of equality shapes definitions of citizenship. If we think that some people deserve more rights than others, then citizenship takes different forms for different groups. The January 6 insurrectionists expressed a certainty that their opinions mattered more, reflecting a heritage that has denied the full citizenship of non-whites. In some ways, their perspective is accurate, since the inequality of citizenship rights is built into our political system. The Senate and Electoral College ensure that some people always matter more than others. For instance, Wyoming's 575,000 people have the same representation in the Senate as California's 40 million ... while the 700,000 residents of Washington, D.C., have no political citizenship in the Senate.

Ideally, a democracy should be one person, one vote, at least on those things that impact the commonwealth and affect all of us. To this very day, the ongoing struggle to fulfill the ideals, if not truths, held by the authors of the Declaration of Independence that all people are equal and entitled to the same unalienable rights, is still a work in progress. Likewise, the ongoing struggles to establish local, state and national governments whose democratic powers are derived from the consent of all the governed is also a work in progress. The United States will remain an imperfect union until such time as all these political inequalities are done away with.

Rule by equals is the keystone of democracies because of its "fundamental moral commitment" to the democratic idea that "I have no greater or lesser right to decide how we will live together than you have." When decisions are made that are binding on all women and men, then the people must decide. Democratic majorities rather than representative minorities are the best stand-in for the people. Anchoring legitimate power to the people is not an end but only the means, or a prerequisite, for making democratic equality real in everyday life. As James Madison is credited for writing in Federalist Nos. 51 and 53, "You must first enable the government to control the governed, and in the next place oblige it to control itself."

Three days after Trump announced his 2024 candidacy for the presidency on November 15, 2022, Attorney General Merritt Garland appointed Special Counsel Jack Smith to take over the investigations of both January 6 and the Mar-a-Lago classified documents cases. At the time he was nursing a broken leg in the Netherlands where he had been working at the International Criminal Court in the Hague investigating and prosecuting war crimes. The DOJ had stated that Smith had been conducting "sensitive investigations" of foreign government officials and military members related to war crimes, crimes against humanity, and genocide. He had also conducted similar work at the Hague from 2008 to 2010.

In between these two international tours of duty, from 2010 to 2015, Smith served as the head of the DOJ's public integrity unit that includes "tackling cases like bribing government officials and election crimes, investigating and prosecuting elected and appointed officials of all levels."[8] In this capacity, Smith and his team prosecuted Virginia's former governor, Robert McDonnell, on a series of corruption charges, as well as former CIA officer Jeffrey Sterling for leaking classified information and obstruction of justice. In announcing Smith's appointment Garland had stated that Smith was "the right choice to complete these matters in an even-handed and urgent manner."[9]

**The Crime Report**
**RICO case for Trump may be a little less unlikely**
**under New Special Counsel**
November 22, 2022[10]

**By Gregg Barak**
Last week Attorney General Merritt Garland appointed former career Justice Department prosecutor and former chief prosecutor for the special court in The Hague, Jack Smith, to serve as Special Council to oversee two ongoing criminal investigations, one involving the failed insurrection on January 6th and the other involving stolen classified documents and presidential records found at the former president's country club and part-time residence, Mar-a-Lago.

As described in court documents filed in the District of Columbia, the first investigation revolves around whether any person or entity unlawfully interfered with the transfer of power following the 2020 presidential election and/or during the certification of the Electoral College voting process on or about January 6, 2021.

As described in court filings pending before the Southern District of Florida, the second investigation revolves around misappropriated documents and whether former President Donald Trump obstructed justice during the Department of Justice investigation into the matter.

At the public pronouncement about the Special Counsel, AG Garland stated:

> Based on recent developments, including the former President's announcement that he is a candidate for President in the next election, and the sitting President's stated intention to be a candidate as well, I have concluded that it is in the public interest to appoint a special counsel. Such an appointment underscores the Department's commitment to both independence and accountability in particularly sensitive matters.

I initially had mixed feelings about the appointment of a Special Counsel as did many other commentators, some reluctantly in favor and others vehemently opposed.

Ultimately I sided with Joyce Vance, who also had reservations about the appointment, because of the failure of Special Counsel Bob Mueller to hold Trump accountable. Among other reasons, Vance makes the critical distinction between the two Special Counsel assignments.

"Mueller was bound by the Office of Legal Counsel memo that prohibited indicting a sitting president. With Trump out of office, there is no policy like that to prevent Smith from indicting Trump," Vance wrote.

"His consideration will be whether, based upon admissible evidence, he believes DOJ would likely be able to obtain and sustain a conviction."

Garland will adhere to the decision reached by Special Counsel Smith.

Moreover, as readers of *The Crime Report* and *Salon* know, for the better part of 2022 I have been making the argument for why Trump should be indicted under the Racketeer Influenced and Corrupt Organization Act (RICO), both for the crimes of racketeering and for operating a criminal enterprise.

While I have never believed that the DOJ will ultimately use RICO against Donald Trump, the Trump Organization, his campaign entities, attorneys, associates, and others who may have been involved in January 6, Mar-a-Lago, and the greater efforts to overturn the 2020 presidential election results, I do believe that Special Counsel Jack Smith's resignation as the chief prosecutor for the special court in The Hague in order to take on and oversee the two ongoing DOJ investigations makes the possibility of a RICO case a little less unlikely.

Smith hit the ground running shortly after the first of the year. The likelihood that Trump would be indicted for trying to obstruct the congressional count of the electoral college votes on January 6, 2021, were given two shots in the arm. One on February 17, 2022, and the other on March 20, 2022. In the first instance, US District Judge Amit P. Mehta refused to dismiss three lawsuits against Trump by Democratic House members and police officers seeking damages for physical and emotional injuries they incurred in the assault. In his 112-page opinion, the federal judge completely rejected the former president's claim of "absolute immunity" from lawsuits accusing him of inciting a riot at the Capitol on January 6. Mehta said that Trump's own words and conduct in falsely alleging a "stolen" election were not immune on separation-of-powers ground because they served only his personal aim of retaining office, falling beyond the "outer perimeter" of a president's official responsibilities. Mehta wrote:

> The President's actions here do not relate to his duties of faithfully executing the laws, conducting foreign affairs, commanding the armed forces, or managing the Executive Branch. They entirely concern his efforts to remain in office for a second term. These are unofficial acts.[11]

In the second instance, US District Judge David O. Carter determined in a ruling addressing the scores of sensitive emails that Trump ally and lawyer John Eastman had resisted turning over to the House Select Committee investigating the Capitol riot and related efforts to overturn the results of the 2020 presidential election based on a preponderance of the evidence. It is "more likely than not" that Trump committed federal crimes. The Court found that President Trump corruptly attempted to obstruct the Joint Session of Congress on January 6, 2021. Judge Carter who is based in California had jurisdiction because Eastman as a residence filed his case there claiming that his communications with the president were protected by attorney-client privilege. Carter's 44-page opinion concluded that the House select committee lawmakers were "entitled to have 101 of the 111 documents they sought."[12]

Additionally, the 11th District Court of Appeals in late December 2023 citing a previous U.S. Supreme Court ruling that presidential immunity did not extend further than the "outer perimeter" of a President's official responsibility, the three-judge panel rejected once again Trump's argument that his conduct should be considered part of his official duties as they "constituted speech on matters of public concern."

In both the Mar-a-Lago and the January 6 cases, the DOJ had begun around September 1, 2022, to interview Trump's legal counselors and other key persons in the Trump Administration, which would continue throughout the first five months of 2023. First up were Pat Cipollone, the former White

House counsel and the former White House Deputy Counsel Pat Philbin. Both of these attorneys were accompanied by their attorney Michael Purpura. Other people who were initially interviewed and/or had their phones confiscated (e.g., Jeffrey Clark, Trump's appointed Assistant Attorney General for the Environment and Natural Resources) before and after Smith came on board included Vice President Mike Pence's chief of staff, Marc Short, and Pence's top counsel Greg Jacob.[13] Eventually, White House Chief of Staff Mark Meadows, Pence, attorney Rudy Giuliana, and others were subjects of the January 6 grand jury probe.

On June 23, 2023, a CNN exclusive disclosed that Jack Smith in his sprawling criminal investigation into efforts to overturn the 2020 election had compelled at least two Republican fake electors to testify to a federal grand jury in Washington by giving them limited immunity. In signaling that Smith may be close to filing criminal indictments against Trump and others for January 6, it was also revealed that prosecutors had been playing hardball with those who had signed false certificates involving the fake electors' scheme by refusing to grant extensions to grand jury subpoenas to testify and by demanding that they testify or face charges of contempt. In short, the prosecution had now locked in incriminating witness statements by agreeing that these persons would be protected from potential prosecution.[14]

We also learned that weekend, according to an NBC news poll taken after his second criminal indictment, that Trump's polling over the other candidates had risen from 46% in April to 51% in June. Meanwhile, Florida Gov. Ron DeSantis in second place had declined from 31% in April to 22% with candidates Mike Pence and Nikki Haley in third and fourth place rising from 6% to 7% and from 3% to 4%, respectively. We already knew that nearly 70% of GOP voters were standing behind Trump after his first criminal indictment.[15] We also heard that weekend from Trump at the Faith & Freedom Coalition Conference in Washington, DC, where he was the keynote speaker in relation to the failed Wagner coup in Russia, how he could once again end the Russian-Ukraine "in one day."[16]

Then on Monday June 26th we learned that about a half dozen Secret Service agents complying with subpoenas had testified before the grand jury concerning the former president's role in the riot at the Capitol on January 6. No doubt their testimony would be about firsthand experiences with Trump regarding his intent to march with his insurrectionists to the Capitol corroborating the testimony before the House Select Committee on January 6 of Cassidy Hutchinson, a former top aide to Trump's White House chief of staff Mark Meadows. And those Secret Service agents were not related to the two dozen Secret Service agents that had been interviewed in Washington, DC, concerning the investigation into the classified documents case before it had been moved to Miami.[17]

We also learned on the same day that Smith and his team were "barreling forward on multiple tracks," focusing "on ads and fundraising pitches claiming election fraud as well as plans for 'fake electors' that would swing the election to the incumbent president."[18] The investigators were interviewing witnesses about the actions of lawyers Rudy Giuliani, Jenna Ellis, John Eastman, Kurt Olsen, and Kenneth Chesebro, as well as then-Justice Department official Jeffrey Clark, and whether they were following specific instructions from Trump or others, and what those instructions had been. These attorneys along with Mark Meadows were all likely a part of the conspiracy to overturn the election.

The next day on the 27th the Supreme Court issued its opinion in *Counterman v. Colorado*, an important First Amendment decision. There were complicated arguments involved in the 7-2 decision with Justices Clarence Thomas and Amy Coney Barrett in dissent. The decision wiped away a Colorado Court of Appeal's ruling that had convicted Billy Counterman and it established a higher bar for prosecuting threats under the first Amendment. Although the crime of inciting violent or lawless actions is not the same as a "true-threat" crime, the nine judges had agreed that the former does require establishing specific intent, and not just recklessness. In the words of Justice Elena Kagan, it was a way of ensuring that "efforts to prosecute incitement would not bleed over, either directly or through a chilling effect, to dissenting political speech at the First Amendment's core."[19] The implications of *Counterman* for indicting Donald Trump for the crime of inciting an insurrectionary assault on the Capitol are that it just became less likely, more difficult, but not an unsurmountable evidentiary burden.

According to *Lawfare*, before *Counterman*, it had been "unclear whether the government would have to establish that Trump specifically intended the violence that occurred or whether he was merely profoundly reckless as to the possibility of that violence." After *Counterman*,

> no responsible prosecutor – certainly not special counsel Jack Smith – will bring an indictment against Trump unless they feel confident that they could prove, beyond a reasonable doubt, that at least part of what motivated Trump to speak and act the way he did on Jan. 6 was a desire to see his supporters forcefully disrupt the certification of the electoral college vote.[20]

Back on the first of June, House Judiciary Committee chairman and Trump Lieutenant Jim Jordon (R-OH) had sent a letter to attorney general Merrick Garland seeking information about several things, including details about the FBI's involvement in Special Counsel Jack Smith's sprawling investigations of the former president. Part of the smokescreen for Jordan's queries had to do with his concerns about FBI election interference in the upcoming

2024 presidential contest, even after a five-year investigation failed to find any evidence of a "deep state" conspiracy or witch hunt against the former president. Jordan was conflating Durham's failure to convict anyone for a crime though he tried twice and with Durham's report which allegedly eviscerated the agency's effort to undermine voters in 2016.

Jordan as usual was either confusing or projecting the election interference by the Russians on behalf of Trump in 2016 and by Trump and his associates including himself to overturn the presidential election in 2020. As for those deficiencies identified with respect to FBI practices or protocol noted by Durham, the FBI claimed to have implemented dozens of corrective actions by early 2022. As for information pertaining to Smith and the involvement of the FBI in the three ongoing investigations of Trump, Jordan might as well have been banging his head against the wall.[21] Considering that Jordan graduated from Capital University Law School in 2001, he should have known better. Then again, Jordan is not a lawyer. Jordan claimed he never took the bar examination.[22] I cannot imagine that he did not want to be a lawyer in the worst kind of way, and had failed the exam? In any case, I should note that the strength of the January 6th insurrection case like that of the Mar-a-Lago classified documents case and the fraudulent electors' case in Georgia is that the testimonial evidence for each of these investigations was provided exclusively by former Trump employees, allies, or other Republican officials.[23] There were no Democrats to the best of my knowledge. Although I do imagine that there may have been some.

Shortly after the classified documents had been revealed and Trump and his first co-conspirator in the case had been arraigned, public sentiment not to be confused with public polling was beginning to change from "How can we indict without becoming a banana republic?" to "How can we fail to indict without becoming a banana republic?" While MAGA Republicans remained devoted to their cult anti-hero and most Democrats viewed Trump as a villain, polling during and after the January 6 hearings revealed that majorities thought Trump did something illegal and/or should be indicted.[24] At the time there were at least four reasons why the January 6 indictments were pending.

First, as we already knew the Justice Department had already obtained multiple convictions on the most serious charges including seditious conspiracy as well as long prison terms for multiple military group members whose violence Smith should be able to connect to Trump assuming that he indicts multiple co-conspirators whether he charges them with violations of RICO or not. Second, there was already available evidence from a state filing in Georgia about the phony or fake elector scheme and Trump's efforts to cajole Georgia officials to "find" 11,780 votes, just enough to flip the state to Trump, that Smith can use as the two cases are overlapping or inseparable. Third, as noted above, US District Judge Carter in Eastman's assertion of attorney-client privilege had ruled that Trump had "attempted to obstruct an official proceeding by launching a pressure campaign to convince Vice President Pence to disrupt the Joint Session on January 6."[25] Fourth, Smith had all the goods on Trump that he needed. He had the massive amounts of evidence gathered from the House select committee, he had testimonies from former Mike Pence, former chief of staff Mark Meadows and other former White House lawyers.

Without knowing the Special Prosecutor's full theory of the case, we knew from Smith's target letter sent to Trump on July 16, 2023, that the former president was probably facing a broad prosecution that would include not only the events of January 6th but also a monthslong conspiracy by numerous people to disrupt the peaceful transfer of power. The target letter informed Trump that he could be charged under at least three statutes. One involving the obstruction of an official proceeding as in Congress's certification of the 2020 election results at the Capitol. A second charge involving Trump's attempt to defraud the United States vis-a-vis his fake elector certificate scheme. The most intriguing charge would strike at the heart of a constitutional democracy. It involves Trump's violating Section 241 of Title 18 of the US Code that makes it a crime to "conspire to injure, oppress, threaten, or intimidate any person… in the free exercise or enjoyment of a right or privilege secured to him by the Constitution or laws of the United States." This provision was originally part of the Ku Klux Klan Acts of the Reconstruction era. They were designed to protect Black male voters from intimidation and physical violence. Section 241 remains a vital safeguard against all forms of election subversion. For example, it has been used to prosecute public officials who had attempted to omit valid ballots from a vote count as well as private actors who had sought to coerce or bribe voters as well as a Twitter user who gave false instructions about voting by text to divert votes away from Hillary Clinton in 2016.

There are other compelling reasons to indict the insurrectionist-in-chief in connection with lies about a stolen election and other lies to defraud the American people by fundraising emails and other communications related to defending Trump from his multiple litigations – civil and criminal. There had also been the conflating of Trump's "criminal interests and fascist demagoguery with those of 'the peoples'."[26] In this type of existential struggle, Chauncy DeVega has argued that violence is, therefore, necessary and reasonable – even unavoidable. In Trump's own incriminating words following the classified documents indictment:

> The price to save our country is high in Crooked Joe's America: vicious attacks, endless witch hunts, and politically charged indictments and arrest. But if this is the cost to see our mission through to the end, to restore our free Republic, and to revive the greatest country in the history of the world, then it's a price I'm willing to pay. You see, Biden, the radical

Democrats, and the Deep State all believed that after Soros' hand-picked state prosecutor failed to break us, that this federal indictment would finally bring our movement to its knees. The truth is, I could walk into the courthouse tomorrow, throw in the towel, denounce our mission to save America, and end our 2024 campaign, and magically, the charges would disappear. But rest assured, Friend, I will NEVER, EVER SURRENDER our country to the Left's tyranny![27]

The narrative of the democratic rule of law and his being held accountable for so many obvious crimes was also being framed as a matter of persecution or a type of warfare being waged against him personally, and by implication, his followers. For example, fundraising emails were repeatedly mentioning the Trump family and "God" and "country" and "patriotism" and how his persecution was a matter of his being a courageous defender of "real America." Code words for White right-wing Christians and red state America. Similarly, the campaign emails were depicting an America that was "on the verge of some type of Stalinist or Maoist totalitarian regime under President Biden." When in "truth is stranger than fiction" reality the GOP was in the process of becoming the Leninist-Bannonist party of the deconstruction of the state and its constitutional legal system. Moreover, Trump's emails were deploying "threatening language" that was "designed to trigger death anxieties and retaliatory eliminationist violence"[28]:

> The Left would gladly destroy every single American value of liberty, justice, and the rule of law in order to remain in power and stop YOU from having a say over your own government. That's why I continue to say that 2024 truly is the final battle. Either we win. Or we lose more than just an election…we lose our country.

The long-awaited Trump indictments related to the assault on the Capitol on January 6th came down as Criminal Case NO. 1.23-cr-00257-TSC in the United States District Court for the District of Columbia on August 1, 2023. Those violations or four counts charged in the UNITED STATES OF AMERICA v. DONALD J. TRUMP include:

*Count 1: 18 U.S.C. § 371*
*(Conspiracy to Defraud the United States)*
*Count 2: 18 U.S.C. § 1512(k)*
*(Conspiracy to Obstruct an Official Proceeding)*
*Count 3: 18 U.S.C. §§ 1512(c)(2), 2(Obstruction of and Attempt to*
*Obstruct an Official Proceeding)*
*Count 4: 18 U.S.C. § 241(Conspiracy Against Rights)*

In a fundraising email the very next day, one day before his third criminal arraignment on August 3rd, Trump told his supporters that he could potentially face hundreds of years in prison should he be convicted of the crimes: "With Crooked Joe's corrupt DOJ having unlawfully INDICTED yours truly yet again, reports indicate that I could now face a combined 561 YEARS in prison from the Left's witch hunts."[29] Since people have done the math, the actual number of years serving prison time for these three criminal indictments combined would come to 641 years. On the day of the arraignment like millions of other Americans I received the following email from Donald J. Trump with a banner heading in red, white, and blue with five stars on the top and 2024 on the bottom with TRUMP and MAKE AMERICA GREAT AGAIN! in between.

It read as follows:
Gregg,
I have a lot to say in this email – but it all comes from the HEART.

Since the moment I rode down the Golden Escalator at Trump Tower to announce my presidential campaign as a political outsider, the Deep State has put a bull's eye on my back.

My private communications were SPIED on, I was slandered by the Fake News, and a dossier was fabricated in an attempt to FRAME me as an asset of the Russian government.

*But then, a line was crossed on August 8, 2022 at 9:00 in the morning when my own home was RAIDED by the FBI and staged to look like a made-for-TV crime scene.*

*When the Deep State invades your own home, it's a sign that our nation has entered uncharted territory and things are about to get far worse.*

The raid on my home was a stern warning from the federal government not to run for president in 2024 – and a sign of what's to come if I chose to defy their demands.

I could've obeyed. I could've said, "I got to be one of only 45 Americans to ever be president. We did a tremendous job in those 4 years. Now, I can just spend the rest of my life by the beach with my beautiful family."

But that thought never even crossed my mind.

*I could never turn my back on the country that gave me everything I ever could've dreamed of. America will always be worth saving.*

Surrendering our country to tyrannical bureaucrats who've become drunk with power never was and never will be an option.

So, when I announced my re-election campaign in November of 2022, I knew the imminent storm I was walking straight into…

…I have since been INDICTED *THREE* TIMES as an innocent man. I've been ARRESTED for crimes that I did not commit. And the rabid left-wing prosecutors have signaled that this is only just the beginning.

They've made it clear that their end game is to **JAIL ME FOR** *LIFE* **as an innocent man.**

Many pundits have remarked that if I were to drop out of the presidential race, the phony charges against me would be dropped and I would be guaranteed to live as a free man.

*But here in America, our liberty is not a bargaining chip. Our freedom doesn't come from a deal brokered by the government, our freedom is a natural right from God.*

*The second we allow our liberty and justice to be used as weapons of extortion, our nation will have forever succumbed to the dark forces of tyranny.*

So, I will address those who are wondering if I would accept a deal with the Deep State and what this THIRD sham indictment means for the fate of our campaign...

...Let me make myself 100% clear: *OUR CAMPAIGN GOES ON AND IT WILL CONTINUE TO GO ON UNTIL WE THE PEOPLE WIN BACK THE WHITE HOUSE ON NOVEMBER 5, 2024.*

We've built the greatest political movement in the history of our country – and I will NEVER ABANDON it.

**We are on a mission to save our country from a corrupt, self-serving ruling class – and I know in my heart, that we will prevail just as we always have, and on November 5, 2024, We the People will be celebrating America's** *TRIUMPH OVER TYRANNY.*

Gregg, if you are doing poorly due to the very sinister people who are destroying our country, then you can stop reading here. I only wanted to share this note with you.

*But, if you can, never forget that even just $1 has the power to beat Crooked Joe and save America, because your $1 is never alone. It's backed by millions of other patriots who share your values and love for our country.*

**Please make a contribution of even just $1 to show that you will peacefully stand by my side and NEVER SURRENDER our mission to SAVE AMERICA – for 1,500% impact.**

Thank you and God bless you,
Donald J. Trump
45th President of the United States

First and foremost, this criminal indictment is about a President of the United States defrauding the American people and conspiracy to deprive US voters of their Constitutional right to participate in an election and to have their votes counted. It is also about the former president's organized schemes to overturn the 2020 presidential election results involving fake electors from seven battleline states as a means of illegally keeping the 45th POTUS in the White House. It is also about a "too honest" former Vice-POTUS Mike Pence who had refused to become another criminal co-conspirator and whose contemporary notes and subsequent testimony before the grand jury will make him a significant witness to Trump's state of mind by way of their person-to-person conversations leading up to the days before the assault and even after in those delayed hours before the certification occurred around 11:00 p.m. on the evening of rather than at 3:00 p.m. in the afternoon of January 6.

Like in the classified documents case, Special Prosecutor Smith brought forth another speaking indictment against the former president and his co-conspirators whether they were charged or not. In this instance he did not name or identify six co-conspirators but it was obvious that five were Trump attorneys, including Rudy Giuliani, John Eastman, Sidney Powell, Jeffrey Clark, and Kenneth Chesebro. The last co-conspirator was described as a "political consultant" who had allegedly helped to implement a plan to submit the fraudulent slates of presidential electors. He too was believed to be a nonpracticing attorney. Chances are sometime in the future these unindicted co-conspirators may be charged in a separate criminal conspiracy case. The fact that Mark Meadows who was central to all things fake electors and knee deep in more than just talk and who did not become another uncharged co-conspirator, suggests that he will be testifying as a "cooperating" witness. However, the type of cooperating witness Meadows will become was not yet known at the time of the indictment and would ultimately depend on whether he cut a deal with DOJ for full immunity or for lesser charges and/or reduced punishment.

Once again, Smith delivered a compelling and linear narrative in prose that any nonlawyer could easily understand. This time the narrative was about three related conspiracies using essentially the same set of facts as evidence of organized efforts to overturn the 2020 presidential election that Trump knew all along he had lost. Even if the former president had truly believed that the election was stolen from him that would not have legitimated his scheming plots to steal the election from president-elect Joe Biden. In the real world, since Trump first learned of the factual reality that he had lost the 2020 election, he has been free to exercise his First Amendment rights to lie about the election results to the American people which he still continues to do. Similarly, between his November 2020 election loss and his January 6, 2021, failed insurrection, Trump had already exhausted his lawful rights to challenge the election results as fraudulent in courts of law across the nation where he had lost 62 times and won 0 times.

Not including the imminent charges that were coming from Georgia at the time, the total number of Trump counts had stood at 78 from his first three 2023 criminal indictments with maximum prison sentences of 35 years each for both the conspiracies leading up to January 6 and for those conspiracies involved in the classified documents caper at Mar-a-Lago. For the record, the four counts brought forth in the US District Court of Columbia in Washington, DC, on August 1st had nothing to do with the First Amendment rights of citizen Trump that both he and his supporters have been spuriously yapping about and trying to use to defend the indefensible behavior of the former president and his sordid supporters. They had been doing so since the GOP Senate made up its mind to nullify the charges brought forth in the second impeachment trial of Trump in February 2021. After all, this criminal case is not about political speech, but about factual frauds and tasks agreed to for the purposes of stealing the election from the president-elect and denying the American people their right to vote. However, since Trump had (and has) no factual or legal basis for defending himself from his multitude of crimes before, during, and after his presidency he has had no other choice but to continue to politically lie about the history of his fraudulent and corrupt behavior in the courts of public opinion.

Much of the legal narrative with a bit more anecdotal evidence gathered from grand jury testimony was reflective of the same evidence gathered and conclusions reached by the House Select Committee on January 6 as well as by those introductory remarks by Republican Representative Lynne Cheney from Wyoming in her opening statement at the first publicly televised hearing of the Select Committee on June 22, 2022. Perhaps one of the most damaging bits of new information was learning that after Trump had told his insurrectionists to leave the Capitol and go home in peace around 4:00 p.m. that he and some of his Congressional allies were still conspiring and trying to persuade, well into the evening, Pence at a minimum to delay the certification for ten more days if he still was refusing not to certify Joe Biden as president.

Although Trump was not charged with "seditious conspiracy" or "inciting an insurrection," the indictment does accuse Trump of trying to "exploit the violence and chaos" during the January 6 insurrection. However, those charges not brought would have been more complicated and difficult to prove beyond a reasonable doubt than those charges brought. Similar to the assumed rationale for not prosecuting the other six co-conspirators as part of this criminal case, such additional charges and defendants would probably have resulted in the "big lie" criminal conspiracies trial to interrupt the peaceful transference of presidential power and to subvert the norms and institutions of American democracy occurring after, rather than before, the November 2024 presidential election. As Randall D. Eliason, a former chief of the fraud and public corruption section of the US Attorney's Office for the District of Columbia wrote: "The charging decisions in the indictment reflect smart lawyering...The beauty of this indictment is that it provides three legal frameworks that prosecutors can use to tell the same fulsome story." It allows not only for the "prosecutors to put on a compelling case that will hold Mr. Trump fully accountable for the multipronged effort to overturn the election," but at the same time, it also "avoids legal and political pitfalls that could have delayed or derailed the prosecution."[30]

Like the House Select Committee on January 6th, all of the critical evidence against Trump has come from Trumpers – those who liked, supported, and voted for him in 2020 – and not from a weaponized Deep State and/or some democratically controlled Justice Department. There were also Republican election officials from across the seven fake elector states who resisted Trump et al. and who had refused to go along with the conspiracies that make up much of the bulk of the evidence against Trump. Hopefully, this allegedly public trial will be televised not only because it is the most important criminal trial in American history, but also because it is precisely what the United States needs to help save our constitutional democracy from the abyss it is facing due to the existential threat posed by one Donald Trump et al. It may also help to restore faith in the norms and institutions of the rule of law. Equally important, this trial is not only about Donald Trump's criminality and accountability, but it is also a "trial" of those American people who defend and support Trump to see whether or not his criminality actually matters, whether convicted or not.

At the same time there were critics from the Black community who thought that the indictment was "whitewashed" as it did not seem to zero in on or speak to the centrality of trying to suppress the Black votes in cities like Detroit, Atlanta, and Philadelphia. The echoes from the racist rhetoric of the Big Lie that had relied heavily on claims that votes in cities with large Black populations were "fraudulent" was front and center once again when Trump lawyer John Lauro told CBS News that he is going to ask for a change of venue to West Virginia, claiming that it is "more diverse" than Washington, DC. In other words, Trump was arguing that he could not get a fair trial in the heavily Democratic nation's capitol with a predominantly Black population.[31]

As for the arraignment itself, it was pretty much boilerplate and lasted about 28 minutes. There was some back and forth between the government and Trump's attorneys Todd Blanche and John Lauro about when the first hearing would occur before District Judge Tanya Chutkan on August 28, 2023. Magistrate Judge Moxila Upadhyaya informed the prosecution that they had one week to make their arguments for when the trial could begin and that the defense would have a week after that to make its case. On the 28th of August Judge Chutkan set the trial date for March 4, 2024. What was perhaps the most interesting aspect of the arraignment was the admonition that Magistrate Upadhyaya gave defendant Trump before adjourning. It is pro forma at most arraignments for judges to say to those who are being released on money bail or on their own recognizance like Trump that they should not commit any further crimes. What came next is not typical and usually only comes when dealing with organizational criminals. Because of Trump's history of tampering with witnesses and his multiple charges of obstruction of justice pending, Upadhyaya spelled out a few more things that Trump should not engage in or be subject to confinement while awaiting the trial.

> I want to remind you that it is a crime to try to influence a juror, or to threaten or attempt to bribe a witness or any other person who have information about your case, or to retaliate again anyone for providing information about your case to the prosecution, or to otherwise obstruct the administration of justice.

### From Civil Discourse with Joyce Vance, August 5, 2023, "If you go after me..."[32]

Today, Donald Trump issued what can only be construed as a shot across the bow, after the Magistrate Judge Moxila Upadhyaya admonished him during arraignment yesterday that he must not commit any new crimes while on a pre-trial bond – the thing that's keeping him out of jail before trial – and that efforts to influence or intimidate witnesses, jurors or others involved in the case were illegal.

So, Trump posted this on Truth Social this afternoon.

"IF YOU GO AFTER ME, I'M COMING AFTER YOU!"

It couldn't be more clear that this is a threat to Jack Smith and the prosecutors and investigators involved in the case against him. It's readily construed as a threat against state court prosecutors like Alvin Bragg in New York and Fani Willis in Georgia and could even be seen as a threat to people like E. Jean Carroll who have the temerity to hold him accountable for civil misconduct.

That's a threat, made by a defendant in a criminal case, after being warned by a judge that there were consequences for violating conditions of release. Trump may think he can be cute and deny it if confronted. Maybe he'll use his usual line: it's just a joke. But we can all see it for what it is.

The Special Counsel's office alerted the Judge to the post tonight, as part of its motion seeking a protective order for the discovery materials it will be releasing to Trump in the case. The government wants assurances, in the form of a protective order, that Trump won't make the discovery materials public.

There is good reason for this. Some of the discovery contains personal identifying information for witnesses. If publicly disclosed, that could put them at risk of doxing, identity theft or other harm. There is also grand jury testimony from witnesses, who might be put at risk if they find themselves suddenly in the public spotlight. As the government explains in its motion,

If the defendant were to begin issuing public posts using details – or, for example, grand jury transcripts – obtained in discovery here, it could have a harmful chilling effect on witnesses or adversely affect the fair administration of justice in this case.

Prosecutors haven't asked the court, at least not yet, to revoke Trump's bond. That, of course, would be a step that would trigger prolonged litigation and possibly delay the trial. That seems to be the one thing Jack Smith is trying to avoid at all costs. He has made strategic decisions, for instance, only indicting Trump and leaving the co-conspirators unindicted, that streamline the process. He clearly wants his trial before the election.

A motion to rescind Trump's bond based on this one post might not be successful. But he has a history of threatening prosecutors, as well as of making nasty statements about judges and witnesses. It's more than just the one statement. It wouldn't be inappropriate to force him to explain why his bond shouldn't be revoked at this juncture. But Smith is taking the high road, not because he's showing any special deference to Trump, but because he wants to avoid distraction and keep his case moving toward trial. That's his clear north star.

The government has to establish that a defendant is a flight risk or a danger to the community in order to detain him in pre-trial custody. The statute that governs release or detention of a defendant pending trial, 18 USC § 3142, permits the court to craft conditions of release that prevent the defendant from endangering the community, if he would present a risk if released without them. At arraignment, the judge imposed the condition specifically authorized by the statute, that Trump's release was "subject to the condition that the person not commit a Federal, State, or local crime during the period of release." This is remarkable when you think about it. The former president of the United States presents such a danger to the community that he could not be released without imposing the condition designed to prevent him from harming people.

All in all, as The Guardian's David Smith observed the arraignment of Trump on August 3, 2023, at the Prettyman federal courthouse in Washington, DC, was a humbling experience for **Mr.** Trump as the Magistrate addressed the former president after making him sit and wait for 15 minutes before the arraignment was called to order. As he entered his plea of not guilty to the four charges Trump was "meek, shrunken, stripped of bravado and any sense of control."[33] Smith further argued that Trump's "smallness and demeanor" at the hearing was an excellent reason for broadcasting the trial gavel to gavel for all to see without any need for commentary. At the pre-trial hearing on August 11 called by Judge Tanya Chutkan to establish a standard (as contrasted with a classified) protective order about what Trump and his lawyers could publicly disclose about evidence – some 5 million pages of documents and transcribed witness interviews from a yearlong investigation – the government argued that Trump and his lawyers could undermine the process by making them public before trial. Chutkan did and did not side with defense's request to narrow the restrictions on what they could disclose as she ruled that they were free to discuss non-sensitive materials, on the one hand, and as she broadly defined sensitive information as inclusive of most everything the government had submitted and was prepared to turn over to defense as discovery.

While she added no other constraints on what Trump could say about the case, the effects of Chutkan's courtroom comments were to put Trump and his attorneys on notice. For example, if Trump "continues to flout judicial warnings, she could place a more formal gag order on him," and "if he ignores that directive, she will likely issue additional warnings considering a criminal-contempt citation" and ultimately send him to jail.[34] This was the case with lesser-known public figures, including Trump ally Roger Stone and Trump foe Michael Avenatti who once upon a time represented Stormy Daniels. At the end of the day, Noah Bookbinder, a former federal prosecutor who heads the anti-corruption advocacy group Citizens for Responsibility and Ethics in Washington, described the citation of Trump's post as "a brushback pitch" and that the government was closely watching the former president's public statements.

However, both Smith and Chutkan may still be reluctant to call for and implement these sanctions against Trump. Should "push comes to shove" (which it probably will), fighting with Trump "over a gag order could distract from where the government wants to focus the case—on Trump's alleged crimes—and it could indulge his desire to drag out the trial."[35] And, possibly strengthen his martyr complex narrative. As Bookbinder pointed out the Special Counsel had to weight those concerns against the possibility that an out-of-control defendant Trump could jeopardize the safety of prosecutors and/or witnesses alike. His "strong suspicion is that Jack Smith doesn't want to go there." He added, "I think at some point he may have little choice."[36]

### What the "Indictment Wars" Foreshadows for the Upcoming Presidential Showdown[37]

*I may be a crook, but I am your crook. Vote for me and we'll get revenge on them all* as Susan Glasser has written in her piece for The New Yorker: "2024 Preview: Bidenomics Versus the Trump Freak Show."[38] With Trump having won the messaging wars over his four indictments in New York, Florida, Washington, DC, and Georgia[39] and with his having normalized the Big Lie that presidential elections are fraudulent enterprises – all the while escalating his threats of aggression toward his opponents in general as well as prosecutors, judges, witnesses, and jurors in particular – the potential for political violence should continue to escalate as we get closer to Trump's second defeat in a row to Joe Biden. Since the failed coup attempt on January 6, the GOP has been all about defending the indefensible with the false equivalences of everybody else is corrupt and by trying to criminally justify his and the GOP leadership's feeble attempts to retain political power over country, democracy, and the rule of law.[40] Similarly, by most of the other GOP candidates running for the 2024 presidential nomination spilling Trump's same poppycock narrative and demonizing the democratic norms and institutions of our society, they are only further solidifying the authoritarian and anti-rule of law threat to American democracy posed by the Republican majority that transcends Boss Trump.

What all Americans especially Republicans should have learned at least from the 2022 midterm elections is that Trump's Big Lies are a losing campaign message for the Republican Party especially in any general election. In short, by the GOP adopting the former projectionist-in-chief's defense of his lawlessness and corruption – "I'm rubber, you are glue, whatever you say, bounces off me and sticks to you" – is that the Republican Party finds itself inextricably caught up in an absurd fictional reality of disinformation. Namely, the illogical conspiratorial notion that Trump is some kind of martyr being pursued by the Deep State and that he is some kind of heroic MAGA warrior standing between his "fellow crazies" and the onslaught from the elitist and corrupt Biden administration that as Trump bellows is "coming for you through me."

Such nonsense in the face of all the evidence to the contrary will simply not wash with the overwhelming majority of the American people. As a consequence, come November 5, 2024, even with the Electoral College's structural bias in favor of the Republican Party, there will still come the inevitable landslide popular victory for the rule of law, democracy and Joe Biden over the chaotic, corrupt, and neofascist world of the criminal Trump wannabe dictator.

Finally, what we have been witnessing since the indictments and with the 2024 primary season now underway and leading up to the formal GOP presidential nomination this July and the general election to follow in November, is the comingling and cojoining of Trump's four prosecutions and his legal teams' attempts through numerous motions to dismiss or delay the upcoming trials against the former president. Most, if not all of these motions, have had nothing to do with Trump's guiltiness or innocence of the 91-felony charges. For these actual crimes, Trump and his lawyers have no legal or factual defenses to make. In other words, their only "defenses" for preventing Trump from being convicted beyond a reasonable doubt by juries of his peers are jurisdictional or procedural in nature. They have nothing whatsoever to do with the substantive law or the charges against

Trump. These are exemplified by their two favorite objections or challenges to Trump's indictments, namely presidential immunity or that violations of the First Amendment are being committed against Trump. Neither of these unprecedented legal challenges by a former president will succeed with a court of law tossing out any of these criminal cases against Trump. But that is not really the purpose of these legal challenges by Trump and his attorneys. Their purpose is to try to prevent these trials from occurring before the 2024 election as their appeals wind their way upward to the Supreme Court of the United States.

After exhausting his procedural motions and without any substantive defenses for his crimes, Trump and his attorneys have only one strategy left: "jury nullification." To enter evidence into the trial, if they can, that is not relevant to the charges against him, and is designed to sway the jury to acquit him for impermissible reasons. As a "prevent offense," on December 27, 2023, Jack Smith filed the government's "motion in limine" according to Rule 401 (Test for Relevant Evidence) to bar Trump from launching political attacks and making irrelevant claims such as blaming others for the January 6 attack in this federal election subversion case.

## Notes

1 Rafael Bernal. 2023. Activists want to disqualify Trump from ballot in key states under 14th Amendment. *The Hill.* July 07. https://thehill.com/homenews/campa ign/4086124-activists-want-to-disqualify-trump-from-ballot-in-key-states-under-14th-amendment

2 Ryan J. Reilly and Michael Mitsanas. 2023 Dozens of witnesses have testified as the Jan. 6-focused grand jury probes Trump. *NBC News.* July 9. www.nbcnews. com/politics/justice-department/dozens-witnesses-testified-jan-6-focused-grand-jury-probes-trump

3 Norman L. Eisen, Noah Bookbinder, Donald Ayer, Joshua Stanton, E. Danya Perry, Debra Perlin and Kayvan Farchadi. 2023. Trump on trial: A model prosecution memo for federal election interference crimes. *Just Security.* July 13. www.justsecurity.org/87236/trump-on-trial-a-model-prosecution-memo-for-fede ral-election-interference-crimes

4 Amanda Marcotte. 2023. GOP war on the FBI: Republican attacks on Christ Wray echo ideology of Oklahoma bomber Timothy McVeigh. *Salon.* July 14. www.salon.com/2023/07/14/on-the-fbi-on-chris-way-echo-ideology-of-oklah oma-bomber-timothy-mcveigh

5 Brandon Gage. 2023. 'A very clear concerted plot': Jamie Raskin lays out details of Trump's election theft scheming. *Raw Story.* July 23. www.rawstory.com/ trump-election-theft

6 Ibid.

7 www.salon.com/2022/12/20/jan-6-reflected-a-deep-american-division-whose-democracy-is-it

8 Dustin Jones. 2022. Who is DOJ special counsel Jack Smith. *NPR.* November 18. www.npr.org/2022/11/18/1137847204/who-is-doj-special-counsel-jack-smith

9 Carrie Johnson and Ryan Lucas. 2022. DOJ names Jack Smith as special counsel to oversee Trump criminal investigations. *NPR*. November 18. www.npr.org/2022/11/18/1137736663/special-counsel-trump-justice-department-jan-6-mar-a-lago

10 https://thecrimereport.org/2022/11/22/rico-case-for-trump-may-be-a-little-less-unlikely-under-new-special-counsel

11 Crime and Law. 2022. Opinion denying Trump motion to dismiss Jan. 6 lawsuits by House lawmakers and police. *The Washington Post*. February 18. www.washingtonpost.com/context/opinion-denying-trump-motion-to-dismiss-jan-6-lawsuits-by-house-lawmakers-and-police

12 Matt Zapotosky and John Wagner. 2022. Judge: Trump 'more likely than not' committed crime in trying to block Biden win. *The Washington Post*. March 28. www.washingtonpost.com/politics/2022/03/28/judge-says-trump-more-than-likely-committed-crime

13 Sarah N. Lynch. 2022. Former Trump White House attorneys appear before grand jury probing Jan. 6. *Reuters*. September 2. www.reuters.com/world/us/former-trump-white-house-lawyer-appears-before-grand-jury-probing-jan-6-2022-09-02/

14 Katelyn Polantz, Sara Murray, Zachery Cohen and Casey Gannon. 2023. Special counsel trades immunity for fake elector testimony as Jan 6 probe heats up. *CNN Politics*. June 23. www.cnn.com/2023/06/23/politics/special-counsel-fake-electors-immunity-testimony-jan-6

15 Rachel Scully. 2023. Trump expands lead over GOP field after indictment: poll. *The Hill*. June 25. https://thehill.com/homenews/4066726-trump-expands-lead-over-gop-field-after-indictment-poll

16 Fred Kaplan. 2023. When Trump promises to end the Ukraine Ware, here's what he really means. *Slate*. June 23. https://slate.com/news-and-politics/2023/06/trump-ukraine-russia-war-diplomacy-deal.html

17 Julia Ainsley. 2023. Five or six Secret Service agents have testified before the Jann. 6 grand jury, sources say. *NBC News*. June 26. www.nbcnews.com/politics/donald-trump/secret-service-agents-jan-6-grand-jury-trump-rcna91182

18 Josh Dawsey and Devlin Barrett. 2023. Justice Dept. asking about 2020 fraud claims as well as fake electors. *The Washington Post*. June 26. www.washingtonpost.com/nation/2023/06/26/justice-dept-asks-about-election-fraud-claims-well-fake-electors

19 Alan Z. Rosenshtein. 2023. What counterman means for prosecuting Trump over Jan. 6. *Lawfare*. June 27. www.lawfareblog.com/what-counterman-means-prosecuting-trump-over-jan-6

20 Ibid.

21 Tristan Justice. 2023. Jim Jordan probes the FBI role in Trump special counsel investigation. *The Federalist*. June 2. https://thefederalist.com/2023/06/02/exclusive-jim-jordan-probes-fbi-role-in-trump-special-counsel-investigation

22 Does anyone else besides me believe that Jordan is telling the truth about not wanting to be a lawyer?

23 There were no Democrats to my knowledge. Though perhaps there were a few.

24 Meredith Deliso. 2023, 6 in 10 Americans say Trump should be charged for Jan. 6 riot: POLL. *ABC News*. June 19. https://abcnews.go.com/Politics/10-americans-trump-charged-jan-riot-poll/story

25 Katelyn Polantz. 2022. Judge: 'More likely than not' that Trump 'corruptly attempted' to block Congress from counting votes on January 6. *CNN Politics*. March 28. www.cnn.com/2022/03/28/politics/john-eastman-memo/index.html

26 Chauncey DeVega. 2023. Don't let your guard down: MAGA: Right-wing foot soldiers fall back as the generals in the GOP ramp up eliminationist rhetoric. *Salon*. June 16. www.salon.com/2023/06/16/dont-let-your-guard-down-maga-is-still-plotting

27 Trump quoted in Ibid.

28 DeVega. 2023.

29 Phillip Bump. 2023. How much prison time might Donald Trump actually face? *The Washington Post*. August 3. www.washingtonpost.com/politics/2023/08/03/how-much-prison-time-might-donald-trump-actually-face

30 Randall D. Eliason. 2023. What makes Jack Smith's new Trump indictment so smart. *The New York Times*. August 2. www.nytimes.com/2023/08/02/opinion/jack-smith-trump-indictment

31 Tatyana Tandanpolie. 2023. Legal experts mock Trump's demand to move trail from D.C. to "more diverse" West Virginia. *Salon*. August 3. www.salon.com/2023/08/03/legal-experts-mock-demand-to-move-trial-from-dc-to-more-diverse-west-virginia

32 Joyce Vance. https://joycevance.substack.com/p/if-you-go-after-me

33 David Smith. 2023. From 'Mr President' to 'Mr': Strongman Donald Trump cut down to size in court. *The Guardian*. August 4. www.theguardian.com/us-news/2023/aug/04/trump-court-arraignment-power-dynamics-january-6

34 Russell Berman. 2023. Is Trump daring a judge to jail him? *The Atlantic*. August 11. www.theatlantic.com/politics/archive/2023/08/trump-arraignment-charges-judge-first-amendment

35 Ibid.

36 Quoted in Ibid.

37 It is also worth keeping in mind that while, on the one hand, the four indictments may have been what helped to seal the deal on the 2024 GOP nomination, on the other hand, had Trump not been gaming the system by announcing his candidacy a full two years before the election, the earliest announcement in US history, thinking it would put off his first two federal indictments altogether, instead, it backed fired when Garland immediately appointed Special Counsel Smith. Had Trump announced his candidacy in the late spring as is usual, chances were good that if indicted, his trials would not be able to occur until after the election unlike those which now have a good chance of occurring before the general election.

38 Susan B. Glasser. 2023. 2024 View: Bidenomics versus the Trump freak show. *The New Yorker*. August 10. www.newyorker.com/news/letter-from-bidens-washington/2024-preview-bidenomics-versus-the-trump-freak-show

39 It is worth noting that while most people are focusing on the four most prominent criminal indictments, this only scrapes the surface of his legal cases when civil cases are added to the calendar mix unfolding in federal and state courts alike. Beginning in October 2023 with the New York civil fraud case against the Trump Organization which could potentially eliminate his doing further business in New York and elsewhere (like Enron),

40 These work in two ways. First, with respect to the false equivalencies of the Trump and Bidden crime families. Second, with respect to the weaponization

of the Justice Department and the House of Representations. As for the two impeachments of Trump, House controlled GOP in 2023 has pursued two courses of action: contemplating if they can undo Trump's two impeachment from history as though they never occurred, and trying to impeach Joe Biden, or at least having an inquiry about the impeachment of Biden. The latter because without evidence gathered themselves or by Trump's two attorney generals Sessions and Barr as well as the Special Prosecutor Durham appointed by the former AG Barr, there is zero evidence of wrongdoing of Biden. As for Hunter Biden the private citizen and his tax problems while allegedly an addict as contrasted with Trump's eldest daughter and her husband who were both higher-ups in daddy's administration and who each monetized the state's political interests with their personal economic interests to the tune of millions of dollars in licensing products in China for Ivanka Trump and a $2 billion investment in son-in-law Jared Kushner's various ventures, was a hands off approach by Biden-Garland over not one but two Trump appointed Special Prosecutors pursing crime wherever it existed or not. Conversely, in the case of the Trump crime family, both the GOP House and Justice Department took the approach of The Three Wise Monkeys who "see no evil, hear no evil, and speak no evil."

# PART III

# Liberty, Justice, and American Democracy

# 9

# AMERICAN MYTHOLOGY, BIPARTISAN ALIENATION, AND PARTISAN POLITICS

Back in 2019 federal prosecutors charged 50 people in a brazen scheme to secure slots in the freshman classes at Yale, Stanford, the University of Southern California, and other prestige institutions of higher education.[1] At least 33 affluent parents were involved in this nationwide bribery and fraud scheme. They were charged with various felonies. Twelve of the defendants were also indicted on racketeering conspiracy charges for operating a fraudulent criminal enterprise.

In American mythology and the narrative world of crime and crime control, the use of Racketeer Influenced and Corrupt Organization (RICO) statutes to bring wealthy felons to justice helps to demystify the notion that "crimes in the suites" are not serious crimes committed by real criminals. Those criminal indictments and convictions of powerful white-collar offending moms and dads reveal that there are other forms of organizational crime and lawless conspirators besides gangsters and mob bosses. In the case of the Trump Organization and Teflon Don or other powerful business-criminal enterprises that have routinely operated lawless rackets or schemes for money and power and who have successfully eluded criminal justice mechanisms for decades, RICO may be viewed as the ideal tool in the crime control tool box for bringing these perpetrators to culpability. In the words of Elie Honig who has prosecuted his share of mob bosses, "Trump and other leaders in finance, entertainment, and politics use tactics that mirror the actual strategies used by mob bosses... exploiting the insulation afforded by their positions atop the power hierarchy, deterring potential cooperation by paying for lawyers for lower-level players, using fear to intimidate witnesses and jurors, limiting contacts with co-conspirators, and using coded language to convey orders," all as means of escaping the scales of justice.[2]

DOI: 10.4324/9781003390664-13

Those persons and businesses indicted under RICO for participation in a racketeering conspiracy to gain fraudulent admissions to elite colleges included the head coach of men and women's tennis at Georgetown University; an associate athletic director, the head and assistant coaches of women's soccer, and the water polo coach all at USC; the head coach of men's soccer at UCLA; the women's volleyball coach at Wake Forest University; an assistant teacher at a public high school in Houston who was also a standardized test administrator for the College Board and American College Test (ACT); the president of a private tennis academy and camp in Houston; the director of a private elementary and high school as well as a compensated standardized test administer in Los Angeles; and a formerly employed accountant and financial officer as well as another employee at the Edge College & Career Network (a for-profit college counseling and preparation business) and at the Key Worldwide Foundation (a nonprofit charity) in Newport Beach, California. The latter two entities "constituted an 'enterprise' as defined by Title 18, United States Code, Section 1961(4) (the "Key Enterprise"), that is, an association engaged in, and the activities of which affected, interstate and the foreign commerce." The Key Enterprise was "an ongoing organization whose members functioned as a continuing unit for the common purpose of achieving the objectives of the enterprise."[3]

These "snowplow parents,"[4] who were subsequently convicted of conspiracy to commit mail fraud and/or money laundering, collectively paid out millions of dollars to Key Enterprise for falsifying their child's test scores and/or fabricating their athletic statuses. Thereby displacing or victimizing other students who had lost their admissions and/or scholarships to those students who had cheated them out of a rightful spot. William Singer, the ringleader of this criminal enterprise and his conspiring associates were convicted of the more serious crimes. Singer, a middle-aged consultant, "who worked in the college counseling business for the better part of three decades, was behind an elaborate effort to bribe coaches and test monitors, falsify exam scores, and fabricate student biographies."[5] Ultimately, Singer had accumulated more than $25 million from his parent clients and paid out more than $7 million in bribes. He received the harshest penalty of any of these convicted felons. He was sentenced to three and one-half years and ordered to pay $10 million in restitution to the federal government.[6] Meanwhile, some of those parents who had paid hundreds of thousands of dollars to open college doors for their children were now turning to paying more money to consultants, doctors, and community service projects to reduce their penalties and hopefully avoid doing jail time.[7]

Since the emergence of the federal or state RICO statutes in the 1970s, they have rarely been used to pursue white-collar and corporate criminals. Racketeering crimes are reserved for catching organized or syndicated criminals. Mafia types or drug cartels are typical. White-collar offenders and corporate offenders, even when they are subjects of criminal law which is rare, are almost never prosecuted using RICO statutes. Their offenses are mostly handled as civil or administrative violations, torts rather than felonies. Think of the fines that Trump paid for his misuse of Trump Foundation in relation to his imaginary charitable contributions or to the class-action settlements reached with Trump University students and finalized by a judge to pay them a total of $25 million as victims of a fraudulent educational scam. Trump's schemes were of a "worse" nature than those rackets of Singer and company who had at least delivered academic admissions and athletic scholarships (while depriving the unprivileged) unlike Trump who had in comparison delivered zippo educational instruction. Trump's lawlessness also appears to have reaped larger sums of money than Singer did. At least two questions remain: (1) Why weren't Trump and Trump University indicted and charged for the crime of racketeering conspiracy under the RICO statutes? (2) Why haven't Trump and the Trump Organization for all their other fraudulent economic and political activities been indicted under RICO for operating a fraudulent enterprise?

The crimes of the powerful when addressed are usually dealt with as civil matters well beyond the administrative processes of criminalization. As was pointed out in Chapter 2, according to TRAC, only 31 businesses or corporate entities in the United States were charged with a crime in 2022, the lowest number since the Reagan administration. Compared to the much harsher punishments for the less harmful behavior of the crimes of the powerless, the overly lenient sanctions for the crimes of the powerful typically consist of fines that are less than the illegal profits reaped from their violations. These noncriminal fines plus the expense of white-collar criminal defense attorneys on legal retainers who bill at the rate of $1000–$1500 per hour are simply the costs of doing business. Sometimes these costs are even tax deductible.

Even when these costs are not legitimate tax-deductible expenses, fraudsters like Trump will claim false deductions anyway as in the hush money payments to Stormy Daniels for not disclosing their extramarital sexual relationship before the 2016 presidential election. These types of inequities in the structural distribution and measurement of crime and punishment, or in the differential applications of law and the administration of justice, have to do with a network of complex factors. These begin first and foremost with the legal-state-political *definitions of crime* that are neither arbitrary, inherent, or free of impartiality. Rather, these are typically "legally" reasoned constructions of competing economic, social, and political interests. In different words, the historically uniform and/or discretionary administrations of the criminal law have been a supportive, protective, or guarded usage of *mala prohibita* on behalf of the crimes of the powerfully affluent. Moreover, the institutionalized treatment and routinization of the patterned crimes of the powerful as something other than criminality, such as a tort, an administrative offense, or a civil violation, have in effect prevented, reduced, or removed these harms and their offenders from the criminal lexicons of social injury. In the process, these mostly unsanctioned crimes of the powerful with rare criminal accountability reproduce twin myths. One, there is not very much corporate crime in the first place. Two, even when these crimes are seldom pursued, the message is that these crimes of the powerful are not very serious because the punishments do not as a rule include incarceration. Because accountability and liability has amounted to financial fines without loss of liberty.

Since the rise of "crime control" or the management of the crimes of the powerful as well as the crimes of the powerless during the development of 15th and 16th century capitalism, the substantive relations of property rights and bourgeois legality have structurally usurped the procedural due process rights of individual liberty and equal protection for all under the law. In other words, dual systems of bourgeois justice were established with the introduction of capitalist legality and post-feudal legality. One system of justice for those committing crimes of capital accumulation such as colonization and slavery. Or more commonly from labor exploitation, securities fraud, multinational chemical terracide, and so on. Another system of justice for mostly those resisting immiseration or committing assaults against various forms of property. Pragmatically, these two systems for administering justice find themselves competing for scarce resources. These are subject to "cost-benefit" and "system capacity" analyses that depend on such factors as the densities or geographies of the types of crimes committed and the availabilities of the criminal, white-collar, and corporate lawyer service providers. Ultimately, the systemic capacity of these forms of "bureaucratic justice" assumes that "legal sanctioning—the celerity, certainty, and severity of punishment—depends, to a considerable degree, on the organizational structure of the court and also on factors external to the criminal justice system."[8]

Many factors outside the formal law affect the unequal distributions of civil liabilities and penal accountabilities. These may include, for example, the privileges or inequalities playing out in individual life histories, their opportunities or obstacles, their nepotistic connections or earned merits, and so on. These external factors are also reflective of cultural identities as well as caste systems of gender, ethnicity, and class expressed as a function of both financial wealth and social capital. For example, in cases of contemporary tax fraud, tax avoidance, or tax evasion in the United States, opportunities for auditing the very rich are very rare indeed because the system capacity or financial resources provided to the Internal Revenue Service by the Congress have been systemically underfunded since the Wall Street implosion in 2008/2009. Consequently, the super wealthy and mega corporations alike with often complicated tax returns find themselves paying little to no taxes annually, knowing that their chances of being examined by the IRA are slim to none.

Even though the tax audits of US Presidents are annually mandatory, Trump managed to become the first and only POTUS not to be subject to one, let alone any completed audits during his four-year term in office. Meanwhile, those ordinary American taxpayers with relatively meager incomes and simple tax returns are far more likely to be audited by the IRS. In other words, the US tax system is systemically biased or skewed away from auditing wealthy tax compliers, avoiders, or fraudsters. Once again, so much for the constitutional-democratic myths of "equal protection under the law" and "no person is above the law."

Since the publication in 1984 of the pioneering work *Myths that Cause Crime* by Hal Pepinsky and Paul Jesilow, criminologists have been studying the legal misconceptions and political assumptions that serve as the foundation for American criminal justice.[9] Numerous books have been written on the various myths that surround the landscapes of crime and crime control in the United States. As Victor Kappeler and Gary Potter have written in *The Mythology of Crime and Criminal Justice*, the fifth edition of their nontraditional textbook: "media and advocacy groups shine a spotlight on some crimes and ignore others. Street crime is highlighted as putting everyone at risk of victimization, while the greater social harms from corporate malfeasance receive less attention." They continue, "interest groups promote their agendas by appealing to public fears. Justifications often have no basis in fact, but the public accepts the exaggerations and blames the targeted offenders."[10] Not to oversimplify, it is the social, political, and economic concerns rather than the amounts of actual harm and injury inflicted on society that shapes the social values or philosophical ethics that define crime, punishment, and justice.

Reflecting on the myth propelling America's violence police culture, Sue Rahr a former Sheriff of King County, Seattle asked herself rhetorically as she watched the videos of a 29-year-old African American father of a 4-year-old Tyre Nichols being beaten to death by five African American police officers all in their mid-20s, "Why does this keep happening?" But Rahr knew the answer: "It's police culture—rooted in a tribal mentality, built on a false myth of a war between good and evil, fed by political indifference to the real drivers of violence in our communities." Rahr was referring to the continued use of "police to maintain order as a substitute for equality and adequate social services. It will take a generation of courageous leaders to change this culture, to reject this myth, and to truly promote a mission of service" that will not "drive officers to lose their humanity."[11] Unfortunately, previous generations of courageous police leaders have not changed the violent culture of the "thin blue line" separating the criminals from the rest of us. Nor are leaders likely to alter this culture of violence without the passage of significant police-legal reform. For example, it is well pastime that federal legislation be passed to exempt law enforcement officers from *qualified immunity* that protects all government employees from legal liability in lawsuits over alleged violations of constitutional rights.

The demystification of the study of crime and criminal justice in the United States can be traced further back than the *Myths that Cause Crime* to the Berkeley School of Criminology. And specifically to more than a dozen revisionist-historical doctoral dissertations, circa early 19th to early 20th century. These dissertations were all written between 1967 and 1980.[12] Several of these were subsequently published as books beginning with Tony Platt's *The Child Savers: The Invention of Delinquency* in 1969.[13] My 1974 dissertation, In Defense of the Poor: On the Origins of the Public Defender System in the United States (1900–1920), was later published as *In Defense of Whom? A Critique of Criminal Justice Reform* in 1980.[14] Among other things, my analysis was a demystification of equal protection under the law, a rebuttal to or reinterpretation of Anthony Lewis' award-winning *Gideon's Trumpet*, a 1964 book based on the story behind the 1963 landmark Supreme Court case *Gideon v. Wainwright*. This decision ruled that criminal defendants facing felony charges even if they could not afford an attorney of their own were entitled to a state-supported attorney.

Unlike the Constitutional-judicial story told by Lewis that became the legal gospel and conventional wisdom, I told a very different legislative-interests story about the emergence of public defenders. My story of "public defenders" as contrasted with "private defenders" began in the 1880s within the criminal bar associations of Portland, Oregon, and Los Angeles County. I revealed how the idea and the establishment of a public defender system began as a radical idea and subsequent reform movement to reduce the number of costly criminal trial days, to extricate criminal attorneys from increasingly more *pro bono* criminal defense work, and to institutionalize plea-bargaining. Beginning in 1886, several times legislative bills failed for different reasons not the least of which was the fear that public defenders would "socialize" criminal defense work for poor and rich defendants alike. Eventually, 1914 saw laws passed to create systems of public defenders in both Oregon and California where members of the bar in each of those jurisdictions were freed as officers of the court from doing their share of *pro bono* work without compensation.

Long before the highest court in the land ruled on behalf of Clarence Earl Gideon's right to a state-appointed attorney free of cost, indigent defendants were being represented by full-time public defenders working in these two West Coast states. Ultimately, the establishment of public defenders throughout the United States had more to do with streamlining and regulating the system of adversarial justice for indigent defendants than it did in providing legal representation. During the 19th-century indigent defendants in many jurisdictions were being represented by court-appointed attorneys when plea-bargains were accounting for one out of every three persons criminally indicted. At the turn of the 20th century, public defenders were initially introduced in California and Oregon as a means for institutionalizing plea-bargaining for those who could not afford private counsel. This not only reduced the expenditures of criminal trials, but it also helped to modernize the laissez-faire system of criminal justice. This reform and others such as the creation of systems of juvenile justice helped to turn the adversarial system of justice into an assembly-line system of bureaucratic justice. By the turn of the 21st century, adversarial justice for criminal defendants without private criminal defense attorneys had all but been eliminated with less than 5% of all criminal defendants today ever having their day in court with a trial by a jury of their peers.

## Politics, Logos, and Mythos

Politics are often a blending of logos and mythos. Logos are forms of knowledge that have to do with how things work in the real world. Mythos are forms of knowledge that have to do with the meanings of things from the mundane to the exotic. Societal myths generally provide people with the contexts that help them make sense of their day-to-day lives. Myths may be secular, and these may or may not direct people's attention from the narrow to the universal meanings of life. Myths may be nonsecular, and they may or may not direct people's attention from the transient to the eternal meanings of the afterlife. While myths are primarily concerned with the meanings rather than the pragmatics of things, myths can and often do become parts of social reality. This occurs when myths are embodied in cults, rituals, and ceremonies that provide believers or followers with significance in their otherwise boring, empty, or meaningless lives, as in QAnon conspiracies about rigged elections.

In the post-modern world of contemporary myths, unlike the myths of ancient times, these are usually free from supernatural beings or events. Myths, old school or new, are about looking backward and forward at the same time. With respect to the future, myths may be viewed as aspirational and/or representative of idealism over realism. In any society, the key myths whether rational, functional, structural, or psychological are often constructed as stories about a state, a region, or a nation's origins and development. These varying types of constructed narratives are often used to alter, cover up, or whitewash the truth.[15] In the case of the United States, democratic freedom has always been a double-edged sword or a struggle between the individual freedoms in the Bill of Rights or liberties versus the freedom of property bearers and their rights to oppress other peoples. As Jeff Shesol has written in his review of *Freedom's Dominion*: "This book is essential reading for anyone who hopes to understand the unholy union between racism and the rabid loathing of government."[16] In different words, the contemporary alliances between racists and those who hate the US government like a significant proportion of today's GOP base are not a byproduct of Donald Trump or Trumpism. Quite the contrary, as Ralph Waldo Emerson remarked about Americans shortly after the Civil War: They are "fanatics in freedom" who "hate tolls, taxes, turnpikes, banks, hierarchies, governors," and "almost all laws."[17] Perhaps, a bunch of Bakuninian revolutionary farmers and collective anarchists?

While myths can serve to form peoples' worldviews, they may also be specifically about places and events, past or present, helping to explain their practices, beliefs, and ongoing social movements. Myths may be based on facts, fictions, or a combination of the two. Likewise, myths may be true, false, or partially true and false. Myths may be subject to uniform interpretations or subject to competing interpretations. The latter instances, for example, like the countering success myths associated with gaining admission to prestige universities based on "what you know" ("meritocracy") or on "who you know" ("nepotism"). Successfulness in legitimate or illegitimate pursuits alike are usually based on a combination of what and who you know. The same goes for the prosecution or not of white-collar or corporate criminals.

During historical periods of "cultural crisis," paradoxical myths of success or failure are often animated by misinformation. At the same time, these partisans or competing myths are not as important as bipartisan myths. These shared bipartisan myths tend to be more influential or powerful than partisan myths. Because over time, these myths are dispersed throughout society, and therefore, they are more hegemonic. Similarly, as they are less contentious, they are also more absorbable or believable, and they are less likely to rise or fall in popularity over time. Bipartisan myths are also more malleable and better retrofitted as rationales for implementing policies and programs. Over the course of time, bipartisan myths have more staying power than partisan myths especially when multiple mythic stories are strung together, as in those bipartisan myths surrounding the logos of the "Founding Fathers" of the United States.

Political myths are characterized as bipartisan when majorities of both major parties identify with them. This is the case whether the Republicans or Democrats are referring to similar or dissimilar connotations, such as the bipartisan myth of "American Exceptionalism" both with its negative and positive meanings.[18] At the same time, bipolar myths and their narrative stories may be dueling and in conflict with each other. Like the contradictory myths in the contemporary movements associated with "democracy" and "fascism" that may very well be "empty words on the edge of the abyss."[19] As Andrew O'Hehir has argued, these overloaded labels often "float above our flattened cultural landscape unmoored to anything real, are meant to be reassuring (at least to those of us who say we we're in favor of the former) but in fact are precisely the opposite...." This is because "we project our hopes, dreams, fears, and fantasies onto them," as well as "our anxieties."[20]

Culturally, "bipolar" myths, "anti-myths" myths, and materially grounded realities are all integral to the power of myth making and myth breaking, as are the likely successes or failures of American democracy versus American dystopia in an era where mass entertainment has already become a matter of "captivity rather than escape."[21] We may, indeed, all be living in some semblance of Gil Scott-Heron's "B" Movie.[22] Complicating the world of changing mythological developments are the social realities that mystification and demystification are in constant states of becoming and unbecoming. This is evident in the contemporary "cultural wars" that have been playing out in America. As the two political scientists who edited *Myth America* (2022) have underscored, the current war on facts versus fictions has unfolded across multiple fronts:

> The fields of science, medicine, law, and public policy, among others, have been the subject of sustained assaults. But history too has come under attack, and for obvious reasons. As George Orwell famously observed in his dystopian novel *1984*, "Who controls the past controls the future."[23]

Perhaps nobody has tried harder than the "cultural warrior" Governor Ron DeSantis (R-FL), aka the wannabe Censor in Chief, to control history past and present. So it was a bit rich when he was critiquing GOP rival candidate for second place Nikki Haley and suggesting she needed a history lesson on the reasons for the Civil War when she failed to mention slavery as one of those reasons when asked by an audience member at a rally in New Hampshire a few days before New Years Eve 2024. As DeSantis stated at a Pensacola rally one week before his decisive 2022 re-election victory, Florida is "where woke goes to die," and he warned that "wokeness" could destroy America.[24] Nevertheless, by April 2022, the governor's first two censorship bills signed into laws, the Transparency in Technology Act and the Individual Freedom Act otherwise known as DeSantis' "Stop WOKE Act," had been declared unconstitutional by appellate courts as they were both clearly in violation of "protected speech" guaranteed by the First Amendment. The latter law prohibited public schools and private businesses from referring to certain races or sexes as privileged or oppressed, and from teaching people to allegedly feel guilty for historical events committed by people of their race or gender. Like many other states, Florida had also banned "critical race theory" from K–12 school curricula where it had never been taught in the first place.

In late January 2023 under the leadership of DeSantis, the Florida Department of Education rejected an Advanced Placement course on African American Studies that high school seniors can usually take for college credit because the course allegedly indoctrinates students with "a political agenda," teaches about Black Lives Matter too and considers reparations for the ancestors of US slavery. Educators and critics have maintained that

DeSantis' Florida has obviously been attempting to whitewash history by rejecting African American Studies. Three Florida high school students with the aid of civil rights lawyer Ben Crump have challenged the state of Florida's decision in court where it too will most likely be found to be in violation of the First Amendment. This is how it flows for those who are all about censorship in the name of Orwellian freedom. Worse yet, should Florida teachers or librarians violate their school district's media evaluators of vetted and sanctioned banned books they could find themselves guilty of a felony offense.

The attempts by DeSantis and other Republican-minded leaders have been to take the organized and rising K–12 schoolbook banning movement aimed primarily at censoring racial and sexual content to the college level.[25] For example, on January 31, 2023 standing at a podium labeled Higher Education Reform, DeSantis announced his wide-ranging plan to alter and censor higher education in Florida with these contradictory remarks straight out of 1984: "We're centering higher education on integrity of the academics, excellence, pursuit of truth, teaching kids to think for themselves, not trying to impose an orthodoxy." His plan that was immediately denounced by college educators in Florida and across the nation would include an anti-multicultural, Western-civilization-based core curriculum; greater authority for trustees and college presidents to hire and fire even tenured faculty members; and "other proposals that would, if enacted, encroach on the autonomy of the state's public colleges."[26]

### Bipartisan Myths that Democracy Should Be Available for All the People

Before the rise of capitalism and the emergence of modern democracies following the demise of feudalism in the late 16th to early 19th centuries, popes, kings, queens, plutocrats, pharaohs, and emperors had not allowed democracies for two related reasons. First, democracies were a threat to their wealth and power. Second, those leaders believed that democracies would render their nations unstable, and therefore, uncontrollable. Like contemporary anti-democratic "strongman" versions of oligarchic monopolistic power that emerged in those former short-lived democracies in Hungary, Poland, Turkey, Egypt, the Philippines, and Russia, a movement to limit and restrict democracy in the United States has been active since the 2016 presidential election, including the nationwide voter suppression laws that have passed in Republican-controlled state capitols. The re-emergence of GOP anti-democratic policies of governing were set in motion as far back as the election of President Ronald Reagan in 1980 who also wanted to make America great again. Post the GOP resignation of President Nixon on August 8, 1974, Reagan was picking up the ball dropped by Republican

Senator Barry Goldwater from Arizona who despite his landslide loss in 1964 to Lyndon Johnson for the presidency has been credited for sparking the resurgence of the American conservative political movement.

In reaction to the 1960s and less so by the 1970s, the Republicans were pushing back against the loose coalition or federation of activists and protesters that revolved around four political movements for social change: (1) the Women's Liberation Movement kicked off by the legalization of the birth control pill in 1961 and its widespread use by 1964, which allowed women to control their reproductive bodies while demanding equality in the workplace; (2) the Free Speech sit-in demonstrations on college campuses in the early 1960s that by the middle of the decade had morphed into the much more powerful Peace and Antiwar Movements against the illegal war in Vietnam; (3) the nonviolent Civil Rights and Voting Rights Movements throughout the 1960s that combined with a series of urban rebellions in Black and brown ghettos across the nation demanding an end to police occupation and brutality; and (4) the labor movements of the 1960s and 1970s, from the farm workers in California to the auto workers in Michigan to the steelworkers in Pennsylvania, where in 1970 there were more than 3 million workers who had walked out from work for a total of 5,716 strikes, all of which were helping to propel workers into the still expanding middle class. Sooner or later, some kind of backlash was coming to deflate these all empowering and contagious social movements against discrimination and for social justice.

By the late 1960s the precursors to the neoconservative Republicans of the 1980s believed that the middle class and their Age of Aquarius college acquiring offspring, as well as their Black, Brown, Red, and Yellow comrades were feeling too entitled for their caste statuses and acting too big for their baby boomer britches. Together, these "anti-American" protesters were disobeying, rejecting, and threatening to tear up the idyllic white "Leave It to Beaver" America of the 1950s. In a few words, the under 30 dope smoking and acid dropping generation was "out of control" and fomenting "social revolution" in the streets. Something would have to be done to squash these struggles for civil, human, and environmental rights. The "push back" would not occur until after Watergate, the Arab oil embargo, stagflation, and 12% interest mortgage rates combined with Ronald Reagan's 1980 electoral defeat of President Jimmie Carter.

The Reagan Revolution was not simply a story about *helping* rich people and giant corporations get richer and more powerful, which it did successfully accomplish and continues to do so to this very day. Reaganomics or "Voodoo Economics" as George H.W. Bush referred to it or supply side "trickle-down" economics as it became known was also a story about *hurting* ordinary Americans especially the most marginalized members of society. Think about these numbers. In 1980 there were zero home-grown or domestic billionaires living in the United States and by 2020 there were more than 700. Meanwhile, the federal minimum wage in 1980 had been $3.10 per hour and by 2023 was $7.25, the exact amount as it had been back in 2009. Without a federal minimum income raise in 14 years, a dollar of consumer spending at the beginning of 2023 was buying 72.3% as it did in 2009. Most recently, extreme economic inequality was bolstered by Trump's $1.5 trillion tax cut for the wealthy which lowered their income tax rate by one-half, making it less than the rate paid by working-class Americans grossing $50,000 annually.

At the same time, Trumpism and cultural Reaganism on steroids both revolve around a similar group of reactionary, white supremacist, and Christian social values. Economically, both have also shared the same free market ideologies of deregulation and anti-unionism. Post new wave GOP branding, such as the former president's MAGA rhetoric and before President Barack Obama's rhetoric of HOPE, there was the rhetoric of "compassionate conservatism" of the Bush II presidency. Unfortunately, the rhetorical slogans and policies of the GOP since 1980 have never had anything to do with improving the general welfare of society, let alone, helping the marginalized and disadvantaged, or alleviating poverty, hunger, or oppression in America. For example, these Republican agendas have always been against universal health care for all, whether publicly or privately financed, and always in favor of reducing social security, medicare, and veteran benefits for ordinary taxpaying Americans. Likewise, the GOP opposes mandatory maternity and/or paternity leave for newborn babies as well as expenditures for childcare or homecare. Ask yourself, "why are all of these policies in place in every other developed and most developing nations in the world?"

The authentic values or ideologies underpinning their political agendas ascribe to beliefs that there is too much government spending on everyday Americans, and too much regulation on businesses, economics, guns, the environment, the commons, and pretty much everything else except conspicuously on the reproductive freedom of women and girls, as well as the first amendment right to the freedom of knowledge. Neoconservatism or neoliberalism as it later became known was always of the belief that there was too much democracy in America because the middle class had become too assessable to too many people, and the MC had become too powerful for the maintenance of the status quo ruled by the employer classes. Taken together these historical realities of an expanding middle class were viewed as destabilizing as they posed a threat to the prevailing political and economic arrangements because of the inevitability of the demand for more equity, fairness, and justice throughout society by a MC with the leisure time to organize and protest. The roots of these alleged societal problems of a middle class that was "too big" stemmed from the 1950s expanding the democratic power of the fastest growing middle class the world had ever seen, which was accompanied by their offspring's' activist movements of the 1960s. And the periodic falling or pushing back against, and the rising or pushing for, a more egalitarian, gender inclusive, and multicultural democratic society.

With conservative historical and philosophical insight, Reagan and his Republican policy makers were looking "back at the 'solutions' England used around the time of the American Revolution" and that were advocated by Edmund Burke and other like-minded thinkers. They saw a remedy to their crisis, and "it had the side effect of helping their biggest donors," and hence, "boosting their own political war-chests." They reasoned that if "working people, women, minorities, and students were a bit more desperate about their economic situations," then "they'd be less likely to organize, protest, strike, or even vote." Hit them in their pocketbooks and in their wallets, and then "the unevenness, the instability, the *turbulence* of democracy in the 1960s would be calmed."[27]

To accomplish these goals, the Reagan administration not only cut taxes massively on the rich, but it also raised taxes on working-class Americans 11 times in eight years. Some of Reagan's specific diabolical reforms included the following:

- Reducing the top tax bracket for millionaires and multimillionaires from 74% to 27%
- Introducing taxes on Social Security income, unemployment benefits, and restaurant tip incomes
- Ending the tax deductibility on credit cards, car-loans, student-debt interest, and declaring bankruptcy due to student debt
- Declaring war on labor unions and crushing the 1981 strike of the Professional Air Traffic Controllers Organization (PATCO) in less than one week, setting in motion the great decline in union membership from about 1/3 of the American non-government workforce when he came into office to around 10% in 2023
- Doubling down on the War on Drugs in the streets, ignoring them in the suites, and imposing a variety of federal and state forfeiture laws

These reforms were "successful" in meeting their goals of both shrinking the middle class and immiserating the working class in America. The War on Labor "cut average inflation-adjusted minimum and median wages by more over a couple of decades than anybody had seen since the Republican Great Depression of the 1930s."[28] The War on Students and the reductions in state-subsidized education by nearly 60% over several decades have significantly raised the cost of higher education and have presently saddled an entire generation with more than $1.7 trillion in student debt.[29] The War on Street Crime decimated Black communities and grew the prison population exponentially to the largest in the world in absolute numbers as well as a percentage of the US population.

The key to selling these terrible ideas and social policies to the American people was the notion that liberal democracies should not protect the rights of workers, subsidize education, or enforce Civil Rights laws because the government was incompetent, self-serving, and dangerous. In other words, the government was not the solution, it was the problem. As Reagan told the American people in his first inaugural address, the nine most frightening words in the English language were "I'm from the government and I'm here to help." Throughout the 1980s and into the present, Reagan Republicans have built an infrastructure of think tanks and media outlets to promote and amplify this narrative about the dangers of too much democracy. By the 1990s the Democratic President Bill Clinton was echoing the Republicans saying such things as, "The era of big government is over" and "This is the end of welfare as we know it." All "welfare queen" mothers and "dead beat" fathers were to take notice.

In effect there was a great deal of symmetry between Reagan, Bush I, and Clinton's "third way" Democrats who were all leaning into the global international trends in which "liberal, labor, and socialist parties" were abandoning public ownership of major industries, as well as tax and spending government programs that had been aggressively seeking to redistribute income. A bipartisan right of center political agenda was briefly forged in the United States.[30] For example, during Clinton's first term in office, he signed the bipartisan Violent Crime Control and Law Enforcement Act, responsible for bringing down street crime, ignoring white-collar crime, and establishing mass incarceration in America. He also picked up the moribund 1947 General Agreement on Tariffs and Trades that Reagan and Bush had been husbanding. This allowed Clinton to facilitate the creation of the World Trade Organization, and in opposition to both trade unions and environmentalists, ratify the North American Free Trade Agreement that "opened a floodgate for American companies to move manufacturing overseas, leaving American workers underemployed while cutting corporate donor's labor costs and union membership."[31]

During his second term in office Clinton signed the bipartisan welfare reform legislation establishing "workfare," cutting social benefits overall, and reducing the welfare rolls. He also signed into the law the Gramm-Leach-Bliley Act, also known as the Financial Services Modernization Act of 1999, which repealed parts of the Glass-Steagall Act of 1933 and part of the Bank Holding Company Act of 1956, opening markets among financial institutions, and allowing consolidation between commercial banks, investment banks, security firms, and insurance companies. Without adequate regulatory oversight, this would result in inflated credit ratings, high-risk mortgage lending, investment banking abuse, the development of all types of derivative instruments, and the Wall Street implosions of 2008 and 2009. The Financial Services and Markets (FSM) Act of 2023 helped to complete the deregulation of financial markets that had begun nearly two decades earlier with the 1982 Joint Current Resolution that placed the full faith and credit of the US government behind the Federal Savings and Loan Insurance Corporation, as well as the Congressional passage in the same year of the Garn-St Germain Act that allowed savings and loans to offer other types of accounts particularly money market funds, free from withdrawal penalties or interest rate regulation. These financial legal changes precipitated the Savings and Loan debacles that had occurred by the end of the 1980s.[32]

Next, enabled by the 9/11 attacks on the Twin Towers, the Iraq War, and George W. Bush's massive tax cuts for the rich in 2001 and again in 2003, the bipartisan coalition held together until Barrack Obama was elected president in 2008 when racist America raised its voices once again to fuel the partisanship that has only intensified into the full-blown cultural wars that divide contemporary Republicans and Democrats.

Peter Turchin's June 2, 2023, essay in *The Atlantic*, America Is Headed Toward Collapse, published in conjunction with the release of his *End Times: Elites, Counter-Elites, and the Path of Political Disintegration*, asked three questions: How has America slid into its current age of discord? Why has our trust in institutions collapsed? Why have our democratic norms unraveled?

Using a database built by his research team and based on hundreds of societies over a period of 10,000 years, Turchin answered: "We found that the precise mix of events that leads to crisis varies, but two drivers of instability loom large." The less significant of the two drivers was "popular immiseration" or "when the economic fortunes of broad swaths of a population decline." The more significant driver was "elite overproduction" or "when a society produced too many superrich and ultra-educated people, and not enough elite positions to satisfy their ambitions."[33]

Turchin reveals that what the United States has been undergoing over the past 50 years, it has experienced twice before. He is referring to those economic periods of time when the material conditions and the earnings from production and the accumulation of capital are grossly uneven across society. Between 1970, the year after the medium income peaked in the United States, and 2020, Turchin reiterates that "despite overall economic growth, the quality of life for most Americans has declined." During this current episode of political disintegration, the wealthy have once again become wealthier, while the incomes and wages of the medium American family have stagnated or declined. Over the same period, the United States was overproducing graduates with advanced degrees which resulted in our "social pyramid" becoming top heavy. Moreover, with the development of technology, robotics, and the emergence of artificial intelligence, more and more people have found themselves competing over a relatively fixed, or even declining, number of desirable positions. Turchin argues that such competition has "corroded the social norms and institutions that govern society."[34] During these anomic periods, cheating and dishonesty are enhanced and normalized as "everybody does it."

The first time this happened in US history, it culminated in the Civil War. The second time following the Wall Street Crash-Great Depression, it led to broad-based postwar prosperity derived from earlier Progressive Era reforms and buttressed some two decades later by New Deal legislation that established Social Security, introduced a minimum wage, and guaranteed unions' right to collective bargaining. American elites "entered into a 'fragile, unwritten compact' with the working classes, as the United Auto Workers president Douglas Fraser later described it."[35] Turchin continues that this contract included,

> the promise that the fruits of economic growth would be distributed more equitably among both workers and owners. In return, the fundamentals of the political-economic system would not be challenged. Avoiding revolution was one of the most important reasons for this compact (although not the only one). As Fraser wrote in his famous resignation letter from the Labor Management Group in 1978, when the compact was about to be abandoned, "The acceptance of the labor movement, such as it had been, came because business feared the alternatives."[36]

As Turchin concludes:

> We are still suffering the consequences of abandoning that compact. The long history of human society compiled in our database suggests that America's current economy is so lucrative for the ruling elites that achieving fundamental reform might require a violent revolution. But we have reason for hope. It is not unprecedented for a ruling class – with adequate pressure from below – to allow for the nonviolent reversal of elite overproduction. But such an outcome requires elites to sacrifice their near-term self-interest for our long-term collective interests. At the moment, they don't seem prepared to do that.[37]

### The Economic Reality Behind the Bipolar Myth of American Exceptionalism

The myth of "American Exceptionalism" is particularly salient because of its polarized double meaning. As Princeton University historian Daniel A. Bell has articulated:

> It first arose as an analytical term, referring to the proposition that the social and economic structures of the United States represent an exception

to normal laws of historical development. To the extent that the analysis came away with a value judgment attached, that judgment was negative. The United States was a historical aberration – a country that was failing to evolve in the proper, desired direction.

More recently, though, the analytical meaning has been overshadowed, in the political sphere, by a prescriptive, moralizing one that refers less to American difference than to American superiority. When politicians today invoke "American exceptionalism," they almost always mean that the United States has desirable qualities that other nations lack and has a special, chosen, superior role in human history.[38]

So how has the bipolarity of American exceptionalism played out in our developing economic-democratic republic? Not very well. According to the United Nations Human Development Index (HDI), American exceptionalism across the index is inferior to some thiry other developed nations in the world.

In the century following the Civil War with the rise of the US economy, empire, and the remarkable upswing of white American's standard of living, the "employer classes" were not only patting themselves on their backs, but they were claiming three other things of importance. First, that profits for them caused prosperity for all. Second and third, capitalism was the best economic system in the world and American capitalism was its best expression. Richard D. Wolff further maintains that "employers and their ideologues invented the notion of 'American exceptionalism,' based on a self-serving interpretation of Adam Smith's work." The logic of this interpretation "held that because the U.S. facilitated the highest profit maximization for each employer, the economy was able to achieve the greatest wealth and growth, as if led by an invisible hand to that happy outcome."[39]

When Milton Friedman was reiterating that interpretation nearly a century later and US capitalism was still peaking before the globalization of capital, his book *Capitalism and Freedom* (1962) was on route to becoming the bible of economic neoconservatism. At the beginning of the 1970s, Friedman was arguing that the time had come to do away with the policies of FDR's New Deal and LBJ's Great Society. As already suggested, the Reagan, Bush I, Clinton, and Bush II administrations were to varying degrees on board with the virtues of unregulated laissez-faire capitalism. Even though US capitalism since the 1970s has been delivering stagnant real wages to the "employee classes" because with productivity rising, stagnation meant that growing output accrued as rising profits chiefly to employers. Hence, with inequality between the employer and employee classes growing and welfare or social capitalism declining, the employer classes found themselves increasingly uncomfortable about their indefensible positions.

Had there not been an explosion in consumer credit during the same period, the chances are that US capitalism would have crashed. Instead, the "soaring profits enabled by the stagnant wages were partly lent back to the employees who borrowed to buy homes and cars, use credit cards, and afford costlier higher education."[40] Rising personal debt and raising the federal debt ceilings became means of sustaining capitalism as employees chasing the American Dream, and governments conducting business, were now not only producing profits for their immediate employers but also interest returns for their financial lenders or bond holders from whom they borrowed. The United States had entered a period of rapidly growing income inequality and wealth favoring the employer and financial classes over the employee or working classes from which it has still not extricated itself. During the last quarter of the 20th century, rising household debts became increasingly costly and anxiety-producing as stagnant real wages moved the middle and working classes alike nearer to unsustainability even when interest rates were low. Eventually, this led to the credit system collapsing, the Wall Street implosion of 2008/2009, and the Great Recession that followed, cushioned by low interest rates for the next 14 years.

Beyond the massive economic losses in wealth, the Great Recession in conjunction with the underlying wage stagnation and deepening inequality led to a fundamental questioning of US capitalism. The anti-capitalist spirit of the Occupy Wall Street movement in 2011, however, was short lived. Even Senator Bernie Sanders' very moderate socialism did not prevail within the corporate-controlled Democratic Party, and much of the Democratic international public discourse in response to Trump's isolationism and autocratic identification has returned to where it was during the days of the Cold War. Similarly, it was not until the impending post-pandemic recession was staring the Biden administration in the face and the Federal Reserve finally started to raise interest rates for the carrying charges for the massive old and new debts alike that had been rendered minimally unsustainable. After several interest rate increases in two years to bring down the high rates of inflation and to contain the size of the foreseeable recession, interest rates were back to where they were before the Wall Street implosion in 2008. As a result of these changing relations of capital sustainability, conceptions of both capitalism and socialism have changed. Capitalism became less about who owns the means of production and the distribution of goods, services, resources, and products, by way of free markets; socialism shifted from a macroeconomic focus on the state as owner and planner to a microeconomic focus on the democratic organization of enterprises inclusive not only of worker participation in democratic decision-making, but also in the development of worker collectives.[41]

These changes are reflective of a changing consciousness that aspires to hold employers and investors socially responsible for what they do as the controlling classes. For example, the climate change movement has targeted the fossil fuel industry and other manufacturers for the environmental decisions they make. In another vein, the #MeToo movement has been about establishing greater accountability against sexual misconduct and gender discrimination in the workplace and beyond. Increasingly, it is the employers or lenders who have become the targets of those seeking progressive social change. For capitalism's victims and critics, the buck no longer stops with governmental leaders who in the United States are viewed as puppets of corporate dollars but nowadays also includes the employer and lending classes that are viewed as the puppeteers.

## Attachment Styles and Bipartisan Alienation

Over the past several decades, Americans regardless of political party have been losing their trust or faith in one another as human beings. People of both parties are not feeling as "connected" as they once did. They are a bit colder, harder, meaner, and less empathetic. People are increasingly avoiding other people and are self-isolating. In fact, many people enjoyed the imposed isolation during COVID as it made avoiding other people so much easier especially when they could bubble with whom they wished. Bipartisan alienation reflects not only a decline in *secure* attachments as well as an increase in *dismissive* and *fearful* attachments, but also a growing dissatisfaction with the current political, economic, and cultural conditions. Overall, there have been rising anxiety and cynicism in the United States – warranted and unwarranted – about government, religion, media, corporations, and the capacity of "legal politics" to adjudicate environmental conflicts from gun violence to climate change to financial plundering to reproductive conduct, and from gun violence to the January 6th insurrection. The accumulating anxiety and cynicism are not indivisible from spiraling rates of "mental illness" or the bipartisan malaise regarding the potential loss and/or demise of American democracy as an existential crisis.

Demographically, the United States is not exceptional as human anxieties and political discontents are on the rise worldwide. Here in America the data is supportive of the idea that we are living in an "insecure-attachment" period.[42] Discomfort with intimacies of all kinds not only sexual are on the rise and are to be avoided not only among those with *avoidant* or *dismissive* attachment styles who are committed to their independence free of taxing partners or offspring. But also among those adults with *fearful* or *preoccupied* styles of attachment that both crave intimacy.[43] All of which suggests that mental health or well-being may very well be in slight decline. With respect to the four attachment styles and the three insecure styles combined – dismissing, preoccupied, and fearful – these increased from 51.02% in 1988 to 58.38% in 2011. And during the same period, the percentage of people with a commitment to independence and unattachment had increased from 11.93% to 18.62%. Notably, anecdotal evidence and recent research also suggest that Americans are growing wary of their own colleagues, neighbors, friends, partners, and parents. A growing number of people want to be left alone to self-isolate. While many more people are longing for personal attachments and social connections.

Individualized alienation – feelings of disconnect or of not belonging – is widespread throughout American culture. According to a nationally representative survey taken in 2022 using the Belonging Barometer, people are experiencing belonging ambiguity or exclusion. More people than not feel disconnected from three out of five life measure markings. Those people not belonging or feeling disconnected included the following: 64% with their work, 68% with their nation, and 74% with their local communities. Moreover, 20% of Americans do not feel a "fit" with their friends and families. This research also disclosed who those people were that were more likely than not to feel that they belonged or were connected.

> Americans are more likely to report belonging if they see themselves as better off or much better off economically than the average American; are older; identify as a woman or a man (vs. another gender); or identify as heterosexual (straight) or homosexual (gay) rather than bi/pansexual, asexual, or queer.[44]

Neither negative attachment styles nor social alienation are inevitably self-destructive. Both are subject to self-agency, or a conscious will to change. These "fixed" attachment styles or tendencies of social interaction may vary among different relationships and are continuously being shaped by those relations. When it comes to partisan politics and social policies affecting alienation on others or us, the Democrats have been about "we feel your pain" and the GOP has been about "we are your pain." Likewise, the Democrats have been pushing a multicultural, racial, and gender inclusive agenda-society with expansive individual rights for all, while the Republicans have been pushing a mono-national, white, and heterosexual exclusive agenda-society.

## Partisan Politics

Based on the medium income in 2021 and the margin of victory by political party in the 2022 midterm elections, the 118th Congressional districts captured the Great Partisan Realignment that has been reconstituting over the past several decades. Currently, nine of the ten wealthiest districts are represented by Democrats, while Republicans now represent most of the poorer half of the nation. The Republicans are now the party of rural America, whereas they used to be the party of suburban country clubs. Sixty-four percent of congressional districts with median incomes below the national median are now represented by Republicans, whereas these used to be Democratic. Similarly, the highest and lowest college degree-holding districts have inverted as well.

What is paradoxically the most interesting about these demographic changes and realigning politics is that the Republicans are still serving and deferring to the interests of the wealthy against the interests of their new base of voters. Conversely, the Democrats are still doing more for the interests of the poor and working classes, whether urban or rural. As importantly, trumping the policy disagreements between Democratic and Republican politicians over the economy, racial justice, climate change, law enforcement, criminal justice, and international conflict are the "cultural" differences. What drove the voters to the polls in 2020 and 2022 was mutual contempt and fear of the other political party. One month before the election, roughly eight in ten of the registered Democratic and Republican voters said their differences with the other side were about core American values, and roughly nine in ten – again in both camps – worried that a victory by the other would lead to lasting harm to the United States.[45]

Since 2016 the Pew Research Center (PRC) has been tracking and comparing cross-party attitudes in the context of political polling that they have been conducting for the past three decades. Negative partisan views of the opposition parties have been growing substantially. About six in ten Republicans (62%) and more than half of Democrats (54%) in 2022 had very unfavorable views of the other party. At the same time, both Republicans and Democrats have become more positive about the people in *their* own party. For example, the percentage of Republicans who thought that "members of their party are a lot more or somewhat more moral that other Americans" rose from 51% in 2016 and 2019 to 63% in 2022. For Democrats, those percentages rose from 38% in 2016 to 51% in 2022.[46]

PRC has demonstrated among other things that frustration with the two-party system has been growing as partisan hostility grows. Nearly half of the younger adults polled, "wish there were more parties to choose from."[47] More viable as opposed to marginalized political parties might become a remedy for reducing "negative partisanship" or hatred of the opposing party, especially as the survey conducted between June 27 and July 4, 2022 found "negative sentiment – the belief that the opposing party's policies are harmful to the country—remains a major factor in *why* Republicans and Democrats choose to affiliate with their party." However, to fix our broken hyperpartisan system as I have been arguing will require other structural changes as well. In any case, while partisan polarization has long been a fact of life in the United States' two-party political system, increasingly both Republicans and Democrats "view not just the opposing party but also the *people* in that party in a negative light. Growing shares in each party now describe those in the other party as more closed-minded, dishonest, immoral, and unintelligent."[48] Between 2016 and 2022 the proportion of both Democrats and Republicans sharing these negative beliefs about the other party have nearly doubled.

Dr. Abdul El-Sayed who was runner up to Gretchen Whitmer in the 2018 Democratic primary race for Michigan governor wrote in *The Incision* about his hate and love affairs, respectively, with The Ohio State University and the University of Michigan following the latter's crushing win over the former on November 26, 2022:

> While rooting against the other team rather than for your own may be harmless in sports. It is far more caustic for our politics. It degrades the entire system. Democracy is premised on the notion that we can persuade one another – that ideas can move us. Engaging in democracy with the goal of winning people to our side implies maintaining an ability to persuade them. That requires you to believe in their ability to change. Negative partisanship is antithetical to persuasion – antithetical to democracy.[49]

The recent 2022 midterm elections and the narrow presidential victories since 2000, and again in 2020, have revealed that "an era of radical reform that repairs our broken democracy" had not occurred as George Packer had wished for during the race between Trump and Biden.[50]

Back then Packer wrote, "We have one more chance—in Lincoln's words, a 'last best hope'—to bring our democracy back from the dead." I believe that hope to save democracy is still very much alive. Packer also maintained that the "new progressivism is in the streets, in the classrooms, on social media—everywhere but the places with the power to solve problems."[51] Well that was not exactly true either. Especially given that Biden's 2020 campaign was probably the most progressive one in American history thanks to the influence of Bernie Sanders' *Our Revolution*. Moreover, Biden's legislative accomplishments in his first two years of office, despite almost unanimous opposition from the GOP and resistance from the likes of Democratic Senators Joe Manchin from West Virginia and Kyrsten Sinema from Arizona, were certainly the most successful since President Lyndon Johnson's Great Society back in the 1960s. Equally important, Packer was ignoring the new authoritarianism of Trump in the streets, on social media, and in those places of power controlled by the GOP like SCOTUS. Since Biden's victory was a narrow one with slim majorities lasting in both the House and the Senate for only two years, the Republican agenda to strip away civil liberties like reproductive freedom and the right to vote or "just say no" to spending of any kind except for looting the US Treasury on behalf of the superrich and corporate America has not yet been repudiated.

The problem of democratic change, however, runs deeper than the polarization and the need for bipartisanism. As John Sides, Chris Tausanovitch, and Lynn Vavreck have argued, US politics have calcified over the past couple of decades: "American electoral politics doesn't feel malleable. It seems set in stone."[52] Calcification they argue is derived from more than long-term polarization. It is rooted in "divides between the parties on issues tied to racial, ethnic, national and religious identities."[53] Calcification is also fueled by those issues that "Americans consider most important," which "tend to exacerbate their differences, not mitigate them."[54] During the 2020 campaign, for example, the "most salient issues to Republicans included opposing Trump's impeachment, building a border wall, and fighting reparations for slavery. Democrats' priorities included impeaching Trump, opposing Trump's restrictions on immigrants from Muslim-majority countries, and abortion rights."[55] In a few words, the GOP has been primarily about anti-identity politics and discrimination and the Democrats primarily about social inclusion and economic justice. As for the few issues of bipartisan agreement in the 2022 midterm elections, such as taxing those making over $250,000 a year or even some issues on crime control, these have tended to take a back seat to issues of immigration, women's health care, and school children's right to be secure from gun violence.

At the same time, calcified politics co-exist with frequent changes in which party controls the government, something that did not exist throughout most of the 20th century. In different words, Democratic advantage in party identification is around four percentage points the smallest it has been for more than 70 years. As Sides et al have claimed: "Calcified politics and partisan parity combine to produce a self-reinforcing cycle. When control of government is always within reach, there is less need for the losing party to adapt and recalibrate."[56] Likewise, voters have less of an incentive to revise their politics or loyalties to one party or the other. At the same time, increasingly more voters than in the past are identifying as Independents. What we have also learned from the aftermath of the 2020 election and Trump's failed insurrection on January 6, these appear to have increased the incentive for Republican lawmakers and voters to support the Big Lies, Fox News, conspiracy theories, and undemocratic behavior to win at any costs.

As for the dominion of the mostly GOP partisan investigations of "revenge politics" that were initiated after regaining control of the House in January 2023, these kept the election deniers' promises to "investigate the investigators" of the House Select Committee investigation of Trump and the January 6th assault on the Capitol. The rest of their partisan investigations included the Biden administration, from the US "military's bloody withdrawal from Afghanistan to the alleged weaponization of the Justice Department and the FBI" to the alleged "open border" policies, Hunter Biden's stolen laptop, China, and the COVID-19 origins.[57]

Another way to understand the GOP committee changes and America's top ten most partisan topical divides is from a Pew survey conducted between January 18 and 24, 2023. Among these interesting and not surprising findings were the following: 20% of Republicans versus 67% of Democrats believe that protecting the environment should be a top presidential priority; 13% of Republicans versus 49% of Democrats think that racial issues should be a top priority.

Similarly, political surveys from Bright Line Watch conducted in 2021 found "deep partisan polarization in perceptions of what is right and wrong with American democracy and the steps that should be taken to fix it."[58] Whether the 2018 and 2022 midterms as well the 2020 presidential elections may have saved the federal republic for the time being, the seesawing effect or not of regaining majorities in the future precludes the realistic possibility that either party will do much, if any, self-searching, renegotiating, or compromising with the opposition, all necessary prerequisites for bipartisanism and for maintaining the US constitutional-democratic republic of the "tyranny of the minority."

Meanwhile, on President's Day February 20, 2023, Margorie Taylor Greene called for a "national divorce" between the liberal and conservative states as she tweeted out, "We need to separate by red states and blue states and shrink the federal government." As for the MAGA agenda, Wyoming GOP Chair Mike Brest @MikeBrestDC had also floated the idea of secession as far back as 2021 after the failed coup and following @Liz_Cheney's (R-WY) vote to impeach Trump: "Many of these Western states have the ability to be self-reliant, and we're keeping eyes on Texas too and their consideration of possible secession." The polling from Bright Line Watch also found that 66% of Southern Republicans supported leaving the United States and forming a new country, while 47% Democrats in the West supported separation.

One way of moving beyond the structural bipartisan paralyses of the existing representative tyranny of the democratic minority would be to re-establish the Constitutional Republic into a new representative tyranny of the democratic majority. However, neurologically at least that is easier said than done. This is because political partisanship or the polarization of Democrats and Republicans is typically based on semantic representations, for example, as in "abortion," "immigration," or "police" and have a neurobiological grounding. Accordingly, brain research has suggested that these representations can become embedded in the deep wiring of the brain where they become powerful shapers of political ideology through our neural processes. In other words, restoring civil discourse and cooperation around and between the partisan divides in America may be very difficult indeed.[59]

### Partisan Power, the Alt-Right Agenda, and the Threat to US Democracy

Because of the polarity of US politics, the margins of victory and defeat in national elections have been slim:

> The Republican majority that gave President George W. Bush a second term in the White House – and inspired, however, briefly, visions of a permanent Republican majority – came to 50.7 percent of the overall vote.

President Barrack Obama won his second term by around four percentage points, and President Biden won by a similar margin in 2020. Donald Trump, as we know, didn't win a majority of the voters in 2016.[60]

Despite gerrymandering advantages to the Republicans, control of Congress is evenly matched as well:

Majorities are made with narrow margins in a handful of contested races, where victory can rest more on the shape of the district map than on any kind of political persuasion. That's the House. In the Senate, control has lurched back and forth on the basis of a few competitive seats in a few competitive states. And the next presidential election thanks to the Electoral College, will be a game of inches in a small batch of closely matched states rather than a true national election.

With the absence of bipartisanism and the prevailing power of partisanship and the fact that neither party can any longer obtain a lasting advantage over the other party, the US democracy as a political system has become static, ossified, and destructive. As we prepare for another presidential election in 2024 it is déjà vu 2020 more or less all over again with another Biden-Trump showdown. Only this time the race for the White House has been simplified as the issues have been condensed to only one: democracy versus autocracy. And future presidential elections without changing the rules of the political game, should become Groundhog daylike.

By the spring of 2023, the former president and leading candidate for the 2024 GOP nomination had already begun outlining his vision for a second term in office. Faced with local, state, and federal criminal investigations, including for the alleged crimes of obstruction of justice, seditious conspiracy, and illegal campaign fundraising to name three that arose from his unsuccessful efforts to overturn the 2020 election, his campaign advisors were nonetheless still trying to play the "law and order" card emphasizing that public safety and law enforcement would be Trump's top priority. They were also stressing the former commander-in-chief's commitment to collaborate with state authorities and with a "straight face" or no "wink-wink" to work within the law. The fact of the matter was that post the 2022 midterm elections the old and busted GOP or the so-called party of "law and order" (always a mythical misnomer if there ever was one) had become the new Trumpian party of lawlessness. Remember back in the late summer of 2016 when Steve Bannon was the campaign chairman of Trump's first successful bid for the White House and Bannon declared that he was a Leninist out to deconstruct the state and destroy the conservative establishment.[61] Well, some six years later the Trumpian leadership of the Republican Party were all Bannonists and most of the GOP candidates running for their party's nomination were all out to destroy the state and its democratic institutions in deference to Donald Trump and authoritarianism.

On the campaign trail, as part of his unfinished business and the "new and improved" authoritarian agenda going forward, Trump was vowing that there would be mandatory stop-and-frisk orders by the police, the death penalty for drug dealers, and criminal charges against whistleblowers. He would deploy the military to fight street crime, break up gangs, and deport immigrants. Trump was also promising to purge the federal workforce by making it easier to fire them, and he was proposing a new civil service exam. At the same time, Trump was "proposing to apply governmental power, centralized under his authority, toward a vast range of issues that have long remained outside the scope of federal control."[62] At his Waco, Texas rally in March 2023 Trump told his adoring supporters:

> Together, we are going to finish what we started. With you at my side, we will totally obliterate the deep state, we will banish the warmongers from our government, we will drive out the globalists, and we will cast out the communists and Marxists, we will throw off the corrupt political class, we will beat the Democrats, we will rout the fake news media, we will stand up to the RINOs, and we will defeat Joe Biden and every single Democrat.[63]

Central to Trumpism these "talking points" on the campaign trail seem to blend seamlessly with the embrace of conspiracy theories, the distrust of scientific and academic knowledge, and the division of people into believers or non-believers in the manner of the gnostic tradition with its emphasis on illusion and enlightenment. Less conceptually the appeal of or the rise of anti-democratic extremism and what animates far-right circles has as much to do with what Jeff Sharlet also refers to as "the undertow of civil war" and the anticipation of the next civil war.[64]

In the real world, most of Trump's ideas are impractical, self-defeating, illegal, reckless, or dangerous. Some of those ideas are as absurd as they are outlandish as when Trump was doing an interview with the Nelk Boys in April 2023 and he commented that if he were the president of a South American country, then he would "dump the prison and mental institution populations into the United States."[65] At least in the short run, this is politically both good and bad news. The good news is that should Trump win the nomination and barring no viable "third party" candidate to carve up the 2024 presidential vote, then there is little chance that Trump could defeat the incumbent "old man" Biden.

The bad news, however, is that Trump's articulate vision of a more coercive and punitive agenda –MAGA on steroids – is not only resonating with and finding common ground with his leading rival for the 2024 Republican nomination Ron DeSantis and 64% of voting Republicans, but also with the community of right-wing political organizations and "think tanks." The Heritage Foundation's 2023 Presidential Transition Project and partner organizations like the Conservative Partnership Institute and the Center for Renewing America, as well as the American First Policy Institute, and America First Legal, are all on board. As Larry Diamond, a senior fellow at the Hoover Institution who studies democracy has stated about the alt-right movement in America, "We need to take it very seriously" because as "we've learned about Trump and authoritarian populists like him," their rhetoric is much more than "idle language and toothless roar."[66]

In fact, with all the chaos and legal matters engulfing the former president, the Republican elites are getting aboard the Trump train much more quickly in 2024 than they did in 2016. This makes sense even though the train may be headed off a cliff because it is well known that authoritarians cannot succeed on their own. And seldom do they pull off coup d'états while not in power or without the military on board. It is also well known that authoritarians do not just take power. They "are *given* it" and "the people who give it to them are their enemies."[67] In other words, successful authoritarians are those politicians who have co-opted enough of the prevailing political establishment by any means necessary. The Republican establishment in this instance was full of many leaders who disliked and strongly opposed Donald Trump before he won the 2016 GOP primary. Thereafter, sooner or later all but a few conformed themselves to the will of the Racketeer-in-Chief. Think about the pre-Trump establishment conservatives and the Never Trumpers like Senator Lindsey Graham who eventually became all in with Trump and a regular golfing buddy after that latter's take-over of the Republican party. By 2023 Graham had become one of Trump's staunchest defenders. As Jonathan Last reminds us about those who become corrupted and captured by authoritarians like Trump: "First they oppose him. Then they accept him. Then they believe they can manage him. Then they defend him. Finally, they become his supplicants."[68]

Meanwhile, on the ground across red America Republican leaders have been "adopting increasingly autocratic measures, using the police powers of government to impose moralized regulations, turning private citizens into enforcement officers," expelling and limiting the power of "defiant elected Democrats" in Florida, Mississippi, Georgia, and Montana "just as county Republican parties [were] electing militia members, Christian nationalists and QAnon believers to key posts."[69] Even more importantly, the GOP has been very busy tweaking the rules. Passing legislation to suppress the votes of those who would not likely vote for them on the bogus grounds of election fraud.[70] Establishing supermajorities to replace simple majorities to pass statewide referendums. Blocking efforts to get initiatives on the ballot. And doing pretty much all they can to suffocate democracy and the will of the people both legislatively and judicially.

In the contemporary "cultural wars" between the Republican vision and practice of less democracy for all, less political inclusion, less equity and fairness, and fewer individual rights versus the Democratic vision and practice of more democracy, more political inclusion, more equity and fairness, and more individual rights for all, perhaps nothing is as insidious and yet obvious as the anti-democratic usage by Republicans of what are known as "state pre-emption" laws to usurp local, or city and county rule. Once upon a time these state laws were used exclusively to curb discrimination and anti-democratic practices of local communities. Now, they are being used in red states across the country to either pass legislation invalidating the policymaking and practices of Democratically controlled, urban big cities, including anti-discriminatory and diversity policies, as well as the votes cast and election results there in national elections, or by Republican lawmakers making it more difficult or impossible for the people to enact laws or constitutional changes by either prohibiting ballot initiatives and referendums, or by requiring supermajorities for their passage.[71]

Finally, the polarity of the two democratic visions for America reveals what is truly at stake if democracy as we have known it is to survive, or better yet, if a new and improved constitutional democracy can emerge from the current existential threat to its demise. In the case of the Democrats, there are the four freedoms first famously articulated by Franklin Roosevelt in his 1941 State of the Union address that is best representative of the Democratic Party, especially the progressive members: "freedom of speech and expression," the "freedom of worship," the "freedom from want," and the "freedom from fear." In the case of today's Republican party, there are four very different kinds of freedoms: "freedom to control" or restrict the bodily autonomy of women and to repress the existence of anyone that does not conform to traditional gender roles; "freedom to exploit" by allowing owners of businesses and capital to weaken labor and take advantage of workers as they see fit; "freedom to censor" and suppress ideas that challenge and threaten the dogmas of the anti-democratic; and the "freedom to menace" or to carry weapons, to brandish them in public, and to turn the right of self-defense into a right to threaten other people.[72]

Of course, the Republican vision is not one of liberal democracy but is rather one of illiberal democracy, if not, autocracy. As Jamelle Bouie contends:

> Roosevelt's four freedoms were the building blocks of a humane society – a social democratic aspiration for egalitarians then and now. These Republican freedoms are also building blocks not of a humane society but of a rigid and hierarchical one, in which you can either dominate or be dominated.[73]

## Notes

1 Jennifer Medina, Katie Benner, and Kate Taylor. 2019. Actresses, business leaders and other wealthy parents charged in U.S. College entry fraud. *The New York Times*. March 12. www.nytimes.com/2019/03/12/us/college-admissions-cheating-scandal.html

2 Elie Honig. 2023. *Untouchable: How Powerful People Get Away with It*. New York: HarperCollins. Quoted from the inside book jacket.

3 Quoted from www.govinfo.gov/app/details/USCOURTS-mad-1_19-cr-10081

4 Claire Cain Miller and Joana E. Bromwich. 2019. How parents are robbing their children of adulthood. *The New York Times*. March 16. www.nytimes.com/2019/03/16/style/snowplow-parenting-scandal.html

5 By The New York Times. 2019. College admissions scandal: Your questions answered. *The New York Times*. March 14. www.nytimes.com/2019/03/14/us/college-admissions-scandal-questions.html

6 BBC. 2023. William Singer: US College admissions architect will go to jail. *BBC News*. January 5. www.bbc.com/news/world-us-canada-64165326

7 Kate Taylor. 2021. Parents paid to open college doors. Now they're spending to limit prison time. October 8. www.nytimes.com/2019/10/03/us/college-admissions-scandal-consultants.html

8 Henry Pontell. 1982. *A Capacity to Punish: The Ecology of Crime and Punishment*. Bloomington, IN: Indiana University, p. 36.

9 Harold E. Pepinsky and Paul Jesilow. 1984/1992. *Myths That Cause Crime*. Santa Ana, CA: Seven Locks Press.

10 Victor E. Kappeler and Gary W. Potter. 2018. *The Mythology of Crime and Criminal Justice*. 5th edition. Long Grove, IL: Waveland Press, Inc.

11 Sue Rahr. 2023. The myth propelling America's police culture. *The Atlantic*. January 31. www.theatlantic.com/ideas/archive/2023/01/police-brutality-shootings-derek-chauvin/

12 Gregg Barak. 2020. *Chronicles of Radical Criminologist: Working the Margins of Law, Power, and Justice*. New Brunswick, NJ: Rutgers University Press. See chapter 1, Coming of Age at the Berkeley School of Criminology for the other dissertations referenced here.

13 Anthony M. Platt. 1969/1977/2009. *The Child Savers: The Invention of Delinquency*. Chicago, IL: University of Chicago.

14 Gregg Barak. 1980. *In Defense of Whom? A Critique of Criminal Justice Reform*. Cincinnati, OH: Anderson Publishing Company.

15 Jefferson Cowie. 2022. *Freedom's Dominion: A Saga of White Resistance to Federal Power*. New York: Basic Books.

16 Jeff Shesol. 2023. Taking Liberties: When freedom meant the freedom to oppress other people. *The New York Times Book Review*. January 8: p. 11.

17 Quoted in Ibid.

18 American exceptionalism with the exception of cancer deaths, in virtually all other non-economic life and death categories, the United States when compared to all other developed or comparable nations in the world is literally dead last in every one of these categories that any rational nation would strive to be first in. See David Wallace-Wells. 2023. Why is America such a deadly place? *The New York Times*. August 9. www.nytimes.com/2023/08/09/opinion/mortality-rate-pandemic

19 Andrew O'Hehir. 2023. Democracy and fascism: Empty words on the edge of the abyss. *Salon.* January 29. www.salon.com/2023/01/29/democracy-and-fascism-empty-words-on-the-edge-of-the-abyss/
20 Ibid.
21 Megan Garber. 2023. We've lost the plot. *The Atlantic.* January 30. www.theatlantic.com/magazine/archive/2023/03/tv-politics-entertainment-metaverse/672773/
22 Gregg Barak. 2023. With support for gun control more popular than ever, where's the people's mandate. *The Crime Report.* January 26. https://thecrimereport.org/2023/01/26/with-support-for-gun-control-more-popular-than-ever-wheres-the-peoples-mandate/
23 Kevin M. Kruse and Julian E. Zelizer. 2022. *Myth America: Historian Take on the Biggest Legends and Lies about Our Past.* New York: Basic Books, p. 4.
24 Alec Schemmel. 2022. DeSantis says Florida is 'where woke goes to die,' warns 'wokeness' could 'destroy' U.S. *Wear News.* November 1. https://weartv.com/news/local/desantis-says-florida-is-where-woke-goes-to-die-warns-wokeness-could-destroy-us
25 Johnathan Friedman and Nadine Farid Johnson. 2022. Banned in the USA: The growing movement to censor books in schools. *Pen America.* September 19. https://pen.org/report/banned-usa-growing-movement-to-censor-books-in-schools/
26 Francie Diep and Emma Petit. 2023. DeSantis's higher-ed push just got bigger. Fresh resistance is starting to bubble up. *The Chronicle of Higher Education.* January 31. www.chronicle.com/article/desantiss-higher-ed-push-just-got-bigger-fresh-resistance-is-starting-to-bubble-up
27 Thom Hartmann. 2023. New report details why wealthy people really oppose democracy. January 31. www.rawstory.com/raw-investigates/documentednet/
28 Ibid.
29 Gregg Barak. 2022. Debt relief reforms are not enough to alter the relations of inequality and harm reproduction: The case of educational debt and the need for structural reconstruction. *Critical Criminology.* 30(3): 575–587.
30 Thomas B. Edsall. 1998, Clinton and Blair envision a 'Third Way' international movement. *The Washington Post.* June 28. www.washingtonpost.com/archive/politics/1998/06/28/clinton-and-blair-envision-a-third-way-international-movement/0bc00486-bd6d-4da4-a970-5255d7aa25d8/
31 Hartmann. 2023.
32 Gregg Barak. 2012. *Theft of a Nation: Wall Street Looting and Federal Regulatory Colluding.* Lanham, MD. Rowman & Littlefield.
33 Peter Turchin. 2023. America is headed toward collapse: History shows how to stave it off. *The Atlantic.* June 2. www.theatlantic.com/ideas/archive/2023/06/us-societal-trends-institutional-trust-economy/674260
34 Ibid.
35 Ibid.
36 Ibid.
37 Ibid.
38 Quoted in Kruse and Zelizer. 2022, p. 13.
39 Richard D. Wolff. 2023. The social changes we need, the class obstacle we face. *Brave New Europe.* February 2. https://braveneweurope.com/richard-d-wolff-the-social-changes-we-need-the-class-obstacle-we-face
40 Ibid.

41 Gregg Barak. 2017. *Unchecked Corporate Power: Why the Crimes of Multinational Corporations are Routinized Away and What We Can Do About It*. London and New York: Routledge.
42 Faith Hill. 2023. America is in is insecure-attachment era. *The Atlantic*. April 27. www.theatlantic.com/family/archive/2023/04/insecure-attachment-style-intimacy-decline-isolation
43 Sarah H. Konrath, William J. Chopik, Courtney K. Hsing and Ed O'Brien. 2014. Changes in adult attachment styles in American college students over time: a meta-analysis. *Personality and Social Psychology Review*. April 12. https://journals.sagepub.com/doi/10.1177/1088868314530516
44 Nichole Argo and Hammad Sheikh. 2023. The Belonging Barometer: The State of Belonging in America. Over Zero: American Immigration Council, p. 50. http://belonging@projectoverzero.org
45 Michael Dimock and Richard Wike. 2020. America is exceptional in the nature of its political divide. *Pew Research Center*. November 13. www.pewresearch.org/fact-tank/2020/11/13/america-is-exceptional-in-the-nature-of-its-political-divide/
46 Pew Research Center. 2022. As partisan hostility grows, signs of frustration with the two-party system. *Pew Research Center*. August 9. www.pewresearch.org/politics/2022/08/09/as-partisan-hostility-grows-signs-of-frustration-with-the-two-party-system/
47 Ibid.
48 Ibid.
49 Abdul El-Sayed. 2022. Michigan Ohio state, and negative partisanship. *The Incision*. November 29. https://abdulelsayed.substack.com/p/michigan-ohio-state-and-negative
50 George Packer. 2020. America's plastic hour is upon us. *The Atlantic*. October print edition. www.theatlantic.com/magazine/archive/2020/10/make-america-again/615478/
51 Ibid.
52 John Sides, Chris Tausanovitch and Lynn Vavreck. 2022 A hard 2020 lesson for the midterms: Our politics are calcified. *The Washington Post*. September 16. www.washingtonpost.com/outlook/2022/09/16/midterms-2020-election-polarization/. See their book, *The Bitter End: The 2020 Presidential Campaign and the Challenge to American Democracy*. Princeton, NJ: Princeton University Press.
53 Ibid.
54 Ibid.
55 Ibid.
56 Ibid.
57 Masood Farivar. 2023. Five key house republican investigations. *VOA News*. January 09. www.voanews.com/a/five-key-house-republican-investigations-/6911266.html
58 Bright Line Watch. 2021. Still miles apart: American and the state of U.S. democracy half a year into the Biden presidency. *Bright Line Watch*. http://brightlinewatch.org/still-miles-apart-americans-and-the-state-of-u-s-democracy-half-a-year-into-the-biden-presidency/
59 Eric Laursen. 2023. Is politics all in the mind? *Rosenberg Quarterly*. April 29. https://rozenbergquarterly.com/is-politics-all-in-the-mind/

60 Jamelle Bouie. 2023. Something's got to give. *The New York Times*. May 7. Sunday Opinion, p. 3.

61 Ronald Radosh. 2017/2018. Steve Bannon, Trump's top guy, told me he was 'a Leninist'. April 13/August 22. www.thedailybeast.com/steve-bannon-trumps-top-guy-told-me-he-was-a-leninist

62 Isaac Arnsdorf and Jeff Stein. 2023. Trump touts authoritarian vision for second term: 'I am your justice'. *The Washington Post*. April 21. www.washingtonpost.com/elections/2023/04/21/trump-agenda-policies-2024/

63 Quoted in Ibid.

64 Jeff Sharlet. 2023. *The Undertow: Scenes from a Slow Civil War*. New York: W. W. Norton & Company.

65 www.youtube.com/watch?v=NI6zob8rufM

66 Quoted in Arnsdorf and Stein. 2023.

67 Jonathan V. Last. 2023. Don't look now: But republican elites are already getting aboard the Trump train. *The Triad*. May 9. https://thetriad.thebulwark.com/p/dont-look-now-but-republican-elites

68 Ibid.

69 Thomas B. Edsall. 2023. The republican strategists who have carefully planned all of this. *The New York Times*. April 12. www.nytimes.com/2023/04/12/opinion/republican-party-intrusive-government.html

70 Voting Laws Roundup: February 2023 revealed that state legislators had introduced 150 restrictive voting bills and 27 election interference in red states. *Brennan Center for Justice*. February 27. www.brennancenter.org/our-work/research-reports/voting-laws-roundup. According to Morning Joe on May 22, 23, the number of restrictive bills had increased to 188.

71 The Editorial Board. 2023. States are stifling the voices of cities and their voters. *The New York Times*. Sunday Opinion, p. 11, June 4.

72 Jamelle Bouie. 2023. The four freedoms, according to republicans. *The New York Times*. May 21. Sunday Opinion, p. 3.

73 Ibid.

# 10

# TYRANNY OF A MINORITY OR TYRANNY OF A MAJORITY

For more than a half century, this nation has been frozen in a kind of constitutional stasis of democracy. "Despite deep changes in our society, we have made no formal changes to our national charter, nor have we added states or rearranged the federal system or altered the rules of political competition."[1] As historian and director of the Amendments Project, Jill Lepore has argued the best way to save American democracy and stave off constitutional extinction is to amend the original document.[2] Reform and change of that charter and related matters are well past due. As Steven Levitsky and Daniel Ziblatt have argued in their latest book *Tyranny of the Minority: Why American Democracy Reached the Breaking Point* (2023), the United States will either "become a multiracial democracy" or it will "cease to be a democracy at all."

One way to facilitate a multiracial democracy would be to establish a multiparty democracy. These two developments in tandem would go a long way toward fixing polarization and escaping from the current zero-sum game of US politics or winners take-all partisanships. By contrast a system of proportional representation with larger districts in the lower chambers of Congress that would elect multiple representatives each with seats parceled out according to the percentage of the vote that each party received would be less polarizing. These reforms would also help to transform the US political system from a two-party or bipartisan democracy to a multiparty less partisan democracy that naturally moves power away from minority rule and toward rule by the majority.

Let me be clear and underscore once again that the prevailing economic and political conditions of democracy are much more than a matter of *agency* or politicians doing the morally right thing for the benefit of the people. Within

DOI: 10.4324/9781003390664-14

the presently constructed federal constitutional republic of the United States, the increasingly divisive polarities and episodic paralyses of governing are also a function of the *structural* arrangements that reflect the reproduction of an economically and politically symbiotic or orchestrated system that favors the interests of a minority over the interests of the majority. In other words, both the bipartisan and hyperpartisan arrangements of American democracy have always supported a "tyranny of a minority" as the byproduct of the undemocratic rules of the political contests derived from the Electoral College, gerrymandering, the filibuster, *Citizens United v. Federal Election Commission*, and the Uber capital legalistic system from its regressive taxing policies to its lack of universal health care to its inadequate ecological protocols to its contradictory policies of debt relief.

Transitioning away from the old tyranny of the minority and toward the new and improved tyranny of the majority requires that we transform the rules of these political and economic arrangements. Dialectically, this involves pushing back against and resisting those Republican forces that have been doubling down on contracting the tyranny of the minority by using the "counter majoritarian features of the system to build redoubts of power, insulated from the voters themselves." For example, there is the Supreme Court that has been using "its iron grip on constitutional meaning to accumulate power in its chambers, to the detriment of other institutions of American governance." There is also an authoritarian movement "led and animated by Trump, that wants to renounce constitutional government in favor of an authoritarian patronage with Trump's family at its center." As New York columnist Jamelle Bouie has been arguing, each of "these forces are trying to game the current system. But there's nothing that says we have to play this anti-democratic game or that 'we can't write new rules'."[3]

For example, one democratic structural change would be to expand the number of House of Representatives. As Danielle Allen has argued, "growing the House of Representatives is the key to unlocking our present paralysis and leaning into some serious democracy renovation."[4] Originally, the House was supposed to grow with every decennial census. James Madison had even proposed in the Bill of Rights an amendment "laying out a formula forcing the House to grow from 65 to 200 members" and to expand after that as well.[5] Moreover, the one and only time that George Washington spoke at the Constitutional Convention was on its final day when he endorsed an amendment lowering the ratio of constituent members to 30,000. The rationale was that responsive representation required allowing representatives to meaningful know their constituents and vice-versa as a means of taking care of business. Presently, House members represent approximately 762,000 people each, a number that is projected to become 1 million by 2050:

The number has gotten so high because the 1929 Permanent Appointment Act has as a de facto matter capped the size of the House. The bill set the decennial reapportionment of the House on autopilot. It assigned the Census Bureau the job of reporting a new 435-seat apportionment plan for the House to the president following each decennial census. The president in turn simply reports the new apportionment to Congress. Congress can change this number if it wants to, but it has not wanted to for nearly a century.[6]

More representatives mean a bit less power per representative. Individual power aside, the Republicans would most likely all be opposed to more democracy and increasing the number of House Representatives as they are doing most everything in their power to truncate democratic representation. The Democrats would probably be less on board then they are for DC statehood which the Grand Old Party (GOP) opposes.

There are many institutionalized changes in the political and economic organization of American life that would benefit the interests of the People and society over the special interests of greed, corruption, and immorality, such as publicly financed campaign elections lasting only 60 days. Other kinds of structural reforms would ameliorate the contemporary and long-lasting problems that have been hurting democracy and immobilizing the legislative, executive, and judicial branches of government. Limiting or term limits for Supreme Court Justices to 10–12 years is a necessary reform of that institution for legal, political, and economic reasons that currently sees the highest court of the land at a historical low in respectability. The process of becoming a nominee should resurrect the American Bar Association vetting potential nominees not the ideological and financially based Federalist society. Other transforming changes ideally include the elimination of uber-capitalism, multibillionaires, mega monopolies, the electoral college, filibusters, upper chamber supermajorities, super Political Action Committees (PACs), *Citizens United*[7] as well as the "invisible" party primaries that precede the People casting their votes for select nominees during the overly long and financially costly marathon season of primaries and caucuses.[8] Open primaries rather than closed primaries would also reduce polarization and facilitate bipartisan majoritarianism. Not to mention the need to ameliorate the juridical issue of SCOTUS becoming a court of first resort, ignoring the coveted tradition of legal standing, and usurping the power of the executive and legislative bodies to make policy rather than settle law. All these necessary changes on behalf of a New Democracy seem like monumental challenges on so many levels especially because they will be resisted tooth and nail by the powers that be and by the rest of those people captured by the political status quo.

## Why Representative Democracy Needs to Change in the United States

The second sentence of the 14th Amendment reads:

> No State shall make or enforce any law which shall abridge the privileges or immunities of citizens of the United States; nor shall any State deprive any person of life, liberty, or property without due process of law; nor deny to any person within its jurisdiction the equal protection of the laws.

Unfortunately, as the historian Eric Foner demonstrated in *The Second Founding: How the Civil War and Reconstruction Remade the Constitution* (2019), the justices of the Supreme Court in a series of rulings culminating with Plessy v. Ferguson in 1896 had narrowed the scope of the 14th Amendment to the point that it was little different than it was before the Civil War. And despite Brown v. Board of Education of Topeka in 1954 and the passage by Congress of the Civil Rights Act of 1964 that prohibited discrimination on the basis of race, color, religion, sex, or national origin, we find ourselves once again thanks to an alt-right Supreme Court and the passage of ensuing discriminatory legislation in red states, returning to the pre-Civil War period unrestricted by federal intervention.

As Bouie wrote in another commentary, The Threat to Freedom Is Coming from the States, dated May 28, 2023, for *The New York Times*:

> Across the country, we are seeing sharp new limits on the rights and privileges of Americans. And despite a national mythology that ties the threat of tyranny to the machinations of a distant, central government, the actual threat to American freedom is coming from the states.
>
> It is states that have stripped tens of millions of American women of their right to bodily autonomy, with disastrous consequences for their lives and health. It is the states that have limited the right to travel freely if it means trying to obtain an abortion. It is states that have begun a crusade against the right to express one's gender and sexuality, under the pretext of "protecting children." It is states that are threatening to seize the children of parents who believe their kids need gender-affirming care. And it is the states that have begun to renege on the promise of free and fair elections.
>
> That it is states, and specifically state legislatures, that are the vanguard of a repressive turn in American life shouldn't be a surprise. Americans have a long history with various forms of subnational authoritarianism: state and local tyrannies that sustained themselves through exclusion, violence and the political security provided by the federal structure of the American political system.

In many respects, the history of American political life is the story of
the struggle to unravel those subnational units of oppression and establish
a universal and inviolable grant of political and civil rights, backed by the
force of the national government.

Viewed in this light, our time is one in which we face an organized
movement to undermine the grant of universal rights and elevate the rights
of states over those of people, in order to protect and secure traditional
patterns of domination and status. The only rights worth having, in this
world, are those that serve the larger purpose of hierarchy.[9]

With respect to voting rights in particular, one immediate strategy would be
to pass state democracy laws to protect and secure the voting rights of all
citizens. Five laws that every Democratic, if not Republican, controlled state
should adopt as soon as possible are: (1) Ban Voter Challenges; (2) Prevent
Long Voting Lines; (3) Limit the Role of Partisan Poll Watchers; (4) Strengthen
the Vote Counting and Election Certification Process; and (5) Require Courts
to Prioritize Protecting Voting Rights.[10]

In 2021 for the first time in its history the United States was added to
the Stockholm-based International Institute for Democracy and Electoral
Assistance's list of "backsliding democracies" alongside other nations like
Hungary and Poland.[11] In a related essay on this decline in US democracy,
Robert McChesney and John Nichols wrote an essay about the "local deserts"
in American journalism, To Protect and Extend Democracy, Recreate Local
News Media:

> The essence of the information crisis facing America is not the emergence
> and dominance of propaganda, baseless claims, and cynical conspiracy
> theorizing from unidentified and lavishly funded sources. The tsunami of
> misinformation, and the extent to which it now permeates our politics,
> results from the much larger problem, which is the collapse of local
> journalism as a viable institution in cities, villages, and towns across the
> nation.[12]

Meanwhile, without local journalistic news stories percolating up into
national stories, these news deserts and their audiences have become
competitive markets for various national news media silos who like Fox
News will cater to their needs. And with the simultaneous decline in
globalism and rise in nationalism, coupled with the public's loss of its sense of
higher purpose, the progressive agenda has become less legitimate and even
evil in Republican circles. At the same time, the damaging and outmoded
philosophy of neoliberalism has morphed into something more sinister with
the capture of the public sphere by alt-right news-entertainment and media
platforms spreading authoritarian and anti-democratic ideologies often built

on lies and disinformation and still grounded in the voodoo economics of trickle down.

McChesney and Nichols further opined that an "accurate explanation for the rise of American authoritarianism has many elements. Any campaign to purge fascism from the mainstream of American politics will, necessarily, require multiple interventions."[13] One of those interventions in the United States should have to deal with electoral politics and cognitive stupidity. Americans may not be stupider than their neighbors around the world. Nevertheless, cognitive stupidity according to some neuroscientists has become an existential threat to America.

This viewpoint has to do with the very "well-known psychological phenomenon that describes the tendency for individuals to overestimate their level of knowledge, or competence in a particular area."[14] By name the Dunning-Kruger effect is understood as a cognitive bias or a systemic tendency to engage in erroneous forms of thinking and judging. A "generic" contrarian is an illustration of where very high IQ persons may be liable for engaging in or supporting very ineffective or absurd things, such as when elites – local or global – buy into conspiracy theories about the elites running the world primarily because of their frustration of not actually being able to do so. Such as those Silicon Valley technology billionaires or Elon Musk who have provided money or platforms to Robert F. Kennedy, Jr., who has less than a zero chance of winning the Democratic nomination in 2024. For those that may not know, RFK, Jr., one of Bobbie Kennedy's 69-year-old sons holds views that are "a mishmash of right-wing fantasies mixed with remnants of" his progressive past including single-payer health care, his "Bitcoin boosterism, anti-vaccine conspiracy theories," and "assertions that Prozac causes mass shootings."[15] Or the socialist candidate for president in 2024 like Cornel West who has resigned himself to the political margins of irrelevancy by running on the Green Party with ballot access to only 15 states rather than like Bernie Sanders in 2016 and 2020 who chose to run as a Democrat because – win or lose his bid for the presidency – he would enhance the value of the Democratic ticket, be it Hillary Clinton or Joe Biden running as the candidate. West could have very well taken the higher ground in the 2024 presidential election.[16]

Dunning-Kruger also refers to one's "subjective ability" to judge oneself or others in contrast to the "objective reality" of the self or the other. Some definitions of these cognitive effects have been limited to the biases of people in specific areas with low skill competencies who give themselves overly positive assessments of their abilities in those areas. Other definitions have applied the effects to false self-evaluations on skill levels of all kinds.[17] According to these expansive definitions, stupidity is not necessarily about a lack of intelligence or knowledge as measured by traditional scores on tests, IQ or otherwise. In neuroscience, for example, stupidity also has to do with people's failures to effectively use their cognitive abilities. That is, a person with an "average" or even lower IQ and without expertise in anything can still be "smart." Conversely, a person with a "genius" IQ lacking what is referred to as "commonsense" or "street smarts" can still be "stupid."

In a post-truth America, science and anti-science, or facts and fictions, are often weighed the same. Worse yet, in some circles, anti-science, fictions, or fabricated truths are not only celebrated, but they are also cognitively acted upon. Fittingly, the Dunning-Kruger effect has become a real danger to US democracy and to its "tyranny of the minority" for four basic reasons. First, when people are unaware or ignorant of their own ignorance or "cognitive stupidity," then they are also likely to midjudge the intelligence, expertise, or competence of others. Second, some of the people suffering from cognitive stupidity in the United States are in positions of power who have been elected to govern our nation. Third, a far greater number of sufferers of cognitive stupidity do not have positions of power in America, but they still have the power to vote and to spread their stupid ideas online and offline. Fourth, not unlike the phenomena of "collective unconscious" or "collective intelligence" there are the phenomena of "collective ignorance" or "collective stupidity." Historically, these cognitive realities of paradoxical forces have always been in "equal" competition influencing mindsets, social practices, and legal codes.

At the personal level, take the numerous cases where people every day without any medical training provide health care advice to their families or friends based on internet searches where they came across a nutritionist from the world of "alternative" medicine who claims that there are herbal ingredients that have the power to cure cancer. While some of those folks are simply scam artists trying to sell phony cures, many of these "amateurs" believe that they have superior knowledge or understanding of health and physiology than do the biochemists and other physiologists. Consequently, there are desperately ill people mostly with little to lose who have trusted these self-proclaimed "experts" and have paid prematurely with their lives.

Applying the Dunning-Kruger effect to the world of contemporary US politics is even more disturbing because people are often attracted to confident leaders whether they are being real or phony in their words, beliefs, or deeds. Ergo, many "politicians are incentivized to be overconfident in their beliefs and opinions, and to overstate their expertise."[18] Take two examples from Trumpworld. While he was the 45th POTUS, without having any real understanding of what was causing COVID-19 or what causes cancer, Trump was routinely dismissing the opinions of professionals who had dedicated their lives to understanding these phenomena, failing to acknowledge his own ignorance of science, and recommending alternative remedies that were costing people their lives. One of the reasons that politicians like Trump have received as many votes as they have, was because the Make America Great Again (MAGA) base of QAnon and other conspiracy theory followers were suffering from the Dunning-Kruger effect. This was especially true in 2020 after his base and some 45 million other Republican voters should have known what the lying Tucker Carlson with 3.5 million viewers, the highest-rated cable news show in the business, was saying privately to his colleagues in text messages but not publicly to his huge audience: Trump was a "disaster," his behavior after he lost the election was "disgusting," and there was "no upside" to the former president.[19]

Likewise, by March 2023, more than two years after Trump led a failed insurrection, even before the primary season had begun the MAGA constituency and the Dunning-Kruger effect had already secured the GOP 2024 nomination for the two-time impeached and treasonous former president. And this was the case whether he was to be indicted or not for his myriad of crimes in New York, Washington, DC, Georgia, and elsewhere. Those voters' decisions were consistent with the political science research findings that people who know the least about politics are also the same people who are most confident of their political knowledge.[20] This all makes perfect sense because the less people know about something, the less ability they possess to know what they do not know. Conversely, the more we know about a subject, the more we become aware of how complicated things are, and how much more there is to learn about what we do not know.

Fortunately, the problems of cognitive stupidly and electoral politics are "fixable" conditions by becoming aware of the limitations of our own natural intelligence and of the US political system of democracy. We can account for these intellectual shortcomings, alter our reasoning and capabilities vis-à-vis the processes of introspection or self-discovery and political enlightenment, and transform the present democracy with all its shortcomings into a more representative democracy derived from an amended constitutional Bill of Economic Rights for all as part of a Fourth Founding of US democracy. Once again, all of this is a lot easier said than accomplished. Nevertheless, if the people have the "collective will" then a struggle for and a realization of a new democracy would be possible.

Journalist, Pulitzer Prize winning author, and clergyman Chris Hedges has written a scathing critique of US democracy that underscores the challenges facing us. He begins by claiming that "Our political class does not govern. It entertains. It plays its assigned role in our fictitious democracy, howling with outrage to constituents and selling them out."[21] Hedges continues:

> Governance exists. But it is not seen. It is certainly not democratic. It is done by the armies of lobbyists and corporate executives, from the fossil fuel industry, the arms industry, the pharmaceutical industry and Wall Street. Governance happens in secret. Corporations have seized the levers of power, including the media. Growing obscenely rich, the ruling oligarchs have deformed national institutions, including state and federal

legislatures and the courts, to serve their insatiable greed. They know what they are doing. They understand the depths of their own corruption. They know they are hated. They are prepared for that too. They have militarized police forces and have built a vast archipelago of prisons to keep the unemployed and underemployed in bondage. All the while, they pay little to no income tax and exploit sweatshop labor overseas. They lavishly bankroll the political clowns who speak in the vulgar and crude idiom of an enraged public or in the dulcet tones used to mollify the liberal class.

Donald Trump's seminal contribution to the political landscape is the license to say in public what political decorum once prohibited. His legacy is the degradation of political discourse to the monosyllabic tirades of Shakespeare's Caliban, which simultaneously scandalize and energize the kabuki theater that passes for government. This burlesque differs little from the German Reichstag…

H.G. Wells called the old guard, the good liberals, the ones who speak in measured words and embrace reason, the "inexplicit men." They say the right things and do nothing. They are as vital to the rise of tyranny as are the Christian fascists, a few of whom held the House hostage by blocking 14 rounds of voting to prevent Kevin McCarthy from becoming speaker. By the time McCarthy was elected on the 15th round, he had caved on nearly every demand made by the obstructionists, including permitting any of the 435 members of the House to force a vote for his removal at any time, thus guaranteeing political paralysis.[22]

Hedges further accuses these "political hacks" as being modern versions of Sinclair Lewis's slick con artist Elmer Gantry who cynically betrayed a gullible public to amass personal power and fortune. He argues that their "moral vacuity provides spectacle." Quoting once more from H.G. Wells, "a great material civilization, halted, paralyzed," concluding that it "happened in Ancient Rome. It happened in Weimar Germany. It is happening here."[23]

## The Constitutional Bill of Rights Depends on Economic Rights

Before confronting our broken status quo and taking on the establishment that sustains these conditions with a socially transformative democratic agenda, it is important to understand that the Constitutional Bill of Rights depends fundamentally on economic rights. As Franklin D. Roosevelt articulated in his last State of the Union address in 1944: "True individual freedom cannot exist without economic security and independence." More recently, Senator Sanders has repeatedly argued, "Economic rights are human rights, and true individual freedom cannot exist without those rights."[24] In other words, fundamental economic rights or human rights are necessary for individual rights.

A truly free or democratic society requires first and foremost that every man, woman, and child have economic rights – the right to quality health care, the right to good education, the right to secure, meaningful, and well-paying work, the right to decent and affordable housing, the right to live in a clean environment, and the right to security and dignity in old age. Without these basic economic or human rights, the Constitutional rights to freedom of religion, expression, and assembly, or to a free press, equal protection under the law, taxation without representation, and so on, are peripheral at best and hollow at worst especially for those without the currency to live the American dream.

The neglect and omission of economic rights eventually "came to haunt the United States, as unions grew weaker, corporations grew stronger, real wages became stagnant, and ordinary Americans became more and more alienated from a political process that was failing them."[25] Neither the Democrats nor the Republicans have done anything structural or substantial to alter the trending US relations of inequality, power, and distribution between the oligarchs and the people over the past three decades. In the meanwhile, the partisanship of the two major political parties has only been intensifying and the paralysis of the federal government has been ossifying. Even civil discourse and intermittent bipartisanism of yesteryears involving mostly agreement over international conflicts and wars is now something in the rearview mirror.

Marianne Williamson, the best-selling author, spiritual counselor, and unsuccessful presidential contender in a crowded 2020 Democratic field is the only 2024 challenger to Joe Biden for the nomination. In an interview with John Nichols immediately following her DC announcement on March 4, 2023, that she was running again, she explained the reasons why. This

> is about ending a 50-year aberrational chapter of American history and beginning a new one. Neoliberalism has devastated not only our economy – creating the greatest income inequality in 100 years – it has infected every aspect of our culture with injustice and despair. It's time for us to recognize that, cut the cord, and begin again.[26]

Williamson elucidates that because of her "experience with all kinds of personality types and all kinds of people" that she has "a deep understanding of what a sociopath is." It is simply someone that "does not care" and "because of that I recognize as deeply as I do that an economic system—namely hyper-capitalism, namely neoliberalism—has at its root a deep spiritual darkness. It does not care." She continues:

> It is a sociopathic economic system that prioritizes short-term profit maximization for these huge corporate entities. It is a destructive force.

And the political establishment, at its best right now, only tries to stave off its worst aspects. That's what corporatist Democrats do. They recognize the disease to some extent, and they try to help people survive it. But they refuse to challenge the underlying corporate forces that make the return of all the pain and all that trauma inevitable.[27]

Turning from the economic to the political, Williamson explains how her struggles are rooted in the Declaration of Independence and in Lincoln's concept "that government of the people, by the people, for the people, shall not perish from the earth." She argues further that at this historical moment the government is perishing. And that the people of the United States need to recognize that we are not a government functioning of the people, by the people, and for the people. We're not actually even functioning as a democracy:

> We are functioning as a government of the corporations, by the corporations, and for the corporations. And we are functioning as an oligarchy. As Louis Brandeis, the late Supreme Court justice said, you can have large amounts of money and power concentrated in the hands of a few or you can have democracy. You cannot have both. Election denialism, voter suppression, all the dangers of right-wing extremism are attacking democracy from without. But neoliberalism is eroding it from within.[28]

While the Democrats are still fighting on behalf of the rights of the first amendment, the Republicans are busy trying to censor the first amendment, to ban books and curricula around race, gender, and multicultural identity, to abolish girls and women's reproductive rights, and to marginally restrict the right to vote.[29] Where there is one functional or bipartisan understanding between the bought and paid for Democrats and the bought and paid for Republicans, this has been about their shared views that economic rights have nothing in common with civil rights, let alone human rights, and therefore, workers democratic rights are not worthy of universal protection. Nowhere is this more self-evident then around the limited rights of workers to organize and to participate in democratically operating workplaces. At the same time, Gallup reports that America's approval rate of and for unions is the highest it has been since 1965 and that labor activism is on the rise.[30] Yet out of 131.18 million full-time workers in the United States only a bit more than 222,000 people engaged in work stoppages in 2022.[31]

As David Feldman wrote on March 3, 2023 "because Americans don't strike, because we don't seize control of the economy's on/off switch, we are miserable." That is, "50% of US workers feel stressed out daily; 41% say their job is a constant source of worry; 22% say their job makes them sad; and 18% say it makes them angry."[32] Part of the problem has to do with a state of affairs where, for example, Biden who claims that he's the most pro-union president in US history is the same person whose "very first 2020 presidential campaign fundraiser was hosted by Steven Cozen, founder of the union-busting law firm Cozen O'Connor."[33] Likewise, the pro-union Democrats, as opposed to the anti-union Republicans, were also busy celebrating Biden's stewardship after he signed the congressional resolution on December 2, 2022, that forced railway workers to accept a new contract, averting a "catastrophic" nationwide strike. As part of Feldman's setting of the stage for his regular Office Hours show on Friday evenings, he opined:

> Perhaps if there had been a "catastrophic" nationwide railroad strike which resulted in a contract with paid sick leave and better scheduling, that "catastrophic" chemical spill in East Palestine, Ohio (as well as all those other "catastrophic" derailments this year), could have been averted. If you're on the side of labor, you recognize America needs a series of "catastrophic" nationwide strikes…
>
> "You mean like in France?" Yeah, precisely.
>
> France's life expectancy is close to 83 years old, while in America it's down to 77. [Its] retirement age is 62, and compared to America their healthcare is practically free.
>
> Every couple of days the French workers shut it all down [a bit of an exaggeration but you get his point] …I can assure you it's the best thing for worker efficiency. Based on GDP per hours worked, France has a [slightly] higher productivity rate than America.
>
> And with all those strikes, France's economy, despite a population of only 67 million, is still the seventh largest in the world.
>
> The dirty, dark secret Supply Siders don't want you to know is that a country can have an enormous GDP even when they share it with all their citizens.
>
> So yeah, a series of nationwide strikes just like France. In Paris, a strike is like bad weather, you learn to adjust.
>
> I know France has problems, but when it comes to important things like how long do you live? and do you want to keep on living? the French are better off than we are.
>
> Because nationwide strikes are good for your health [and not just because you don't have to work during strikes].
>
> Americans are warned a nationwide strike will cripple the economy. When nearly half of us can't come up with a thousand dollars for an emergency, it sounds like our economy is already crippled.[34]

Many other structural changes resulting from a series of nationwide walkouts would also be good for human dignity, the political economy, and American democracy. Don't take my word for it. Just ask those folks who were involved during 2023 in several major contract disputes, including 340,000

Teamsters at United Parcel Service, 150,000 screen writers and television actors, 140,000 autoworkers and 85,000 Kaiser Permanent workers.

Unfortunately, with or without Trumpism, neoliberalism through proxy remains the default or hegemonic setting for the GOP and for all but progressive Democrats. I am referring not only to the growing influence of "market radicals" on the political right but also to the oligarchic control of the political economy of global capitalism. Herein lies the ultimate challenge to the necessary constitutional-structural reforms that are called for as a means of moving our democratic system from a tyranny by the minority to a tyranny by the majority. As the historian of ideas, Quinn Slobodian demonstrates in *Crack Up Capitalism* (2023) that free marketeers during the age of ultracapitalism "are realizing their ultimate goal: an end to nation-states and the constraints of democracy."[35]

Slobodian follows the most radical libertarians – from Milton Friedman to Steve Bannon to billionaire Peter Thiel – around the globe as they have sought legal spaces, free ports, tax havens, and special economic zones that are always unencumbered by the restraints of oversight, regulation, and democratic government. Slobodian takes us from the past to the present as he warns us of coming threats to democracy worldwide. He literally leads us

> from Hong Kong in the 1970s to South Africa in the late days of apartheid, from the neo-Confederate South to the former frontier of the American West, from the medieval City of London to the gold vaults of right-wing billionaires, and finally into the world's oceans and war zones, charting the relentless quest for a blank slate where market competition is unfettered by democracy.[36]

Turning to the future of constitutionalism and democracy in America and the 2024 presidential election. When President Biden announced that he would seek a second term in office on April 19, 2023, he released a well-produced video whose message was that the struggle to defend and protect American democracy is far from over and that Biden-Harris are ready "to finish the job." The video made Biden's case for a second term by "emphasizing how Donald Trump and the Republican fascists and the MAGA movement are continuing their assaults on American democracy, personal freedom, civil rights, and a good society and that he is the leader best positioned to stop them."[37] Republicans responded to Biden's announcement with an AI-generated attack ad that depicted "a dystopian vision of the US if Biden is reelected. It also raises worrying questions about the place of deepfakes in political campaigning," wrote AI and robotics senior reporter, James Vincent, for The Verge.[38]

The ad contained a series of stylistic images imagining Biden's re-election in 2024. Sensing Biden's "weakness" and "incompetence," it "suggests this will lead to a series of crises, with images depicting explosions in Taiwan after a Chinese invasion and military deployments on what are presumably US streets."[39] The video also shows scenes of financial collapse, an "invasion" by hordes of brown people across the US-Mexico border, and domestic unrest with soldiers being deployed to enforce martial law in San Francisco (and presumably other "blue" cities as well).[40] It is not clear what tools were used to create the images, nor whether doing so would have violated any terms and conditions:

> A number of high-profile AI image generators like Midjourney and DALL-E limit the creation of overtly political images. However, most of the images in the ad are fairly generic and could likely be generated without falling foul of any system's filters.[41]

A small disclaimer in the top left of the frame reads "built entirely with AI imagery" and a caption underneath the YouTube says, "An AI-generated look into the country's possible future if Joe Biden is reelected in 2024."[42] The Republican National Committee told *Axios* that the ad was the first one of its kind put out by the Rpublican National Committee (RNC). Other questions raised by the ad are more complex and worrisome according to Vincent:

> Many experts have warned that AI generated deepfakes could be used to spread political misinformation, but what if that misinformation comes from politicians themselves? And how does one draw the line between misinformation and regular campaigning? For example, the RNC could have decided to make the ad about Biden's age and included AI-generated images of him in a wheelchair. Viewers might well mistake the pictures for real photographs, especially if the disclaimers are as small as they [were] in today's ad.[43]

As ominous as the Republican threat to American democracy and unfettered monopoly capitalism have been and continue to be, allow me before turning to "what is to be done" leave you with a few final thoughts on the economic perils of democratic versus authoritarian nation-states. First, think about the legally regulated versus self-regulated capital whether industrial, financial, or technical in nature. The legally regulated rarely impedes the "free" market and the self-regulated never impedes it. I can think of no better examples of this legal reality than that of white-collar and corporate offenses committed by economic elites. Moreover, think about how destructive an unregulated social media has been to the welfare of American democracy. As with most capitalist decisions they often boil down to their interests and profits trumping the well-being of the interests and resources of the people and ecosystems. Generally, profits tend to win out, and people tend to lose out. Now imagine how dangerous a more developed and unregulated Artificial Intelligence engaged in a global war of autocracies versus democracies could be.[44] The problem or question then becomes not unlike the arms race, which nations are going to regulate first, if at all?

## A Future of and by and for Ordinary Americans

The industrial revolution is being replaced by the technological revolution. "The robots are coming, artificial intelligence is expanding, yet no one is doing enough to make sure that workers benefit rather than losing out." Many people expect that the technological revolution will be as disruptive to our post-industrial society as the industrial revolution was to agrarian society. The tech revolution "could bring amazing opportunities and emancipation," or it could bring "new forms of exploitation, deeper inequalities, injustices and anger."[45] It depends on whether ordinary Americans and their representatives can seize "the power to shape a future that puts the benefits of social, political, and technological progress to work for the working class."[46] It also depends on whether workers can democratically share in the control or decision-making of their workplaces with the owners of those businesses. Presently, most people who perform the day-to-day work in large businesses have been excluded from any decision-making. Such power to make decisions about the nature of the work process or workplace have been in the hands of the wealthy owners, CEOs, and Wall Street investors.

Back in 2018, Senator Tammy Baldwin (D-WI) and her staff released a report that had determined:

- Companies with worker representatives on their boards created 9% more wealth for their shareholders than comparable companies without board-level worker representation.
- Communities that are home to companies with worker representation distribute income more equally and provide their citizens greater economic opportunity.
- Wages in countries that require worker representation on corporate boards are 18%–25% higher than wages in the United States.[47]

On March 3, 2019, Baldwin re-introduced S.915, the Reward Work Act, which in addition to requiring that one-third of the directors of each public company be elected by employees, promulgated regulations to direct national securities exchanges and issuers, and prohibited stock buybacks on the open market.[48] The bill never became law although polls found that the plan was popular with Democrats, Independents, and Republicans in every region of the country. Senator Sanders has also called for worker-elected board members to be as high as 45%, and he has continued to argue on behalf of making "it easier for workers to establish employee-owned businesses that can compete at the national and global levels." Sanders similarly maintains that the United States must "support small business owners and small farmers, who struggle to hold their own against multinational corporations that have rigged the playing field to favor one-size-fits-all conglomerates."[49]

In the context of the technological revolution, worker democracy, and social justice for all, Sanders in his latest book has laid out a five-part strategy – (1) Start Planning for Our Future, (2) Break 'Em Up!, (3) Tax the Robots, (4) Shorten the Workweek and Make Jobs More Flexible, and (5) Medicare for All, Free College Education, and Expanded Social Security Must Be Guaranteed – to transform the status quo from the prevailing economic and social relations that favor the interests of billionaires, multi-millionaires, and multinational corporations over the individual and collective interests of the American people.

Historically, building electoral majorities in the absence of bipartisanism have always been difficult to achieve let alone sustain in American politics. When successful, these have rarely survived more than a couple of decades. In part, this has been because majorities depend on the convergence of many factors including social timing, historical events, public sentiments, political talent, bringing people together in unlikely coalitions, and institution building.[50] In part, this has to do with the unresolved structural contradictions of the political economy of capitalist accumulation and its inequitable distribution of goods, services, and resources.[51]

### Start Planning for Our Future

The United States unlike the European countries does not have a history of engaging in social planning and policy design by analyzing data and forecasting economic changes that extend from technological development to climate change to migration patterns to social demands and so on. Should there be any hope for a fair distribution of the benefits from the technological revolution, then the pace, the direction, and the uses of technologies can no longer be left to market forces or to the monetization of technology alone. Planning need not be state controlled. Planning could result from the creation of a cabinet-level agency that focuses on the future of work, workers, and families. Whose charges would be informed by research projects, critical investments, and policy choices aiming toward the equitable distribution of the technological benefits across society. While responses to new technologies need not be anti-innovation or anti-automation or anti-displacement, the goal should be to leverage technology to build a sustainable economy that works to enhance the interests and lives of all peoples and communities, especially marginal ones.

*Break 'Em Up!*

Power over the future of the US economy should no longer yield to corporate monopolies, financial equities, and technology giants. The harmfulness of multinational capital accumulation needs to be reined in as soon as possible so as not to exacerbate the trending negative effects. Ergo, future law enforcement, congresses, and presidents will have to step up their anti-trust regulation game and prosecution of powerful corporate offenders, or our economic and political inequities will only continue to grow as they have for the past 50 years. The time is well past due for the US government to serve the people as trustbusters and regulators in the public rather than in the private interest.

Presently, companies like Amazon, Google, Uber, and Facebook are seen as having a disruptive impact on trade, politics, communications, and transportation, as playing grossly oversized roles in the basic functions of societies, and as being unelected, unaccountable, and self-serving planners of the economies by and for the wealthy. These corporate conglomerates have also become potential targets for anti-trust regulation by their captive legislative bodies. Moreover, setting standards regarding these firms alone will not be enough when billionaires like Jeff Bezos and Elon Musk are buying up companies like the *Washington Post* and Twitter, now known as X since July 2023. In the future, those firms that profit from using digital platforms, robots, and artificial intelligence may "grow exponentially faster than the market-dominating behemoths about which Americans are already justifiably concerned."[52]

To adjudicate the transformative technology trilemma, I would recommend the Collective Intelligence Project (CIP) as a prototype of what types of "think tanks" need to be pursued. The CIP is an incubator for new governance models that utilize transformative technology. The CIP focuses "on the research and development of *collective intelligence capabilities*: decision-making technologies, processes, and institutions that expand a group's capacity to construct and cooperate towards shared goals."[53] The CIP believes that by applying collective intelligence capabilities to advances in technology, there is a high likelihood of significantly altering societies for the betterment of humanity.

*Tax the Robots*

As workers continue to be replaced in several industries by robots, it is also time to adjust US tax and regulatory policies. This is particularly necessary for tax systems that were designed to tax labor rather than capital. In these systems since the vast majority of tax revenues are derived from labor, companies are incentivized to eliminate or reduce employees to avoid taxes.

Thus, unless automation and robots are taxed to offset the lost revenue from labor (or without taxing capital), multinational corporations will engage in a race to the bottom profiteering. Taxing robots already exists in South Korea. In the United States, taxing robots and automation has its share of opponents and lobbyists. Taxing robots also has the backing of Microsoft's Bill Gates and others.

In 2017 former San Francisco supervisor Jane Kim's Jobs of the Future initiative proposed a study to examine the sustainability of a statewide California payroll tax on employers who replace employees with a robot, algorithm, or other forms of automation.[54] In 2018 a *Harvard Law & Policy Review* article by Abbott and Bogenschneider made an excellent case for taxing automation. They argued among other things that automation should not be allowed to reduce taxes and that a taxing system should at a minimum be at least "neutral" between robots and human workers. Taxing robots and automation could provide funds for retraining displaced workers.

> This could be achieved through some combination of disallowing corporate tax deductions for automated workers, creating an "automation tax" which mirrors existing unemployment schemes, granting offsetting tax preferences for human workers, levying a corporate self-employed tax, and increasing the corporate tax rate.[55]

These law professors conclude that taxation is a critical component of automation policy: "It can benefit everyone, or it can benefit the select few at the expense of many."[56]

### Shorten the Workweek and Make Jobs More Flexible

Jeff Bezos owns Amazon, a trillion-dollar company made possible by automating and digital technology. While Bezos has racked up billions, his unionless and overworked warehousers have been collapsing on the job. It only stands to reason that since robots are doing more of the work that humans should be working less. In 2018, John McDonnel, the veteran UK Labour Party parliamentary led a successful drive to make a four-day workweek without a pay cut part of the party's national platform:

> With millions saying they would like to work shorter hours, and millions of others without a job or wanting more hours, it's essential that we consider how we address the problems in the labor market as well as preparing for the future challenges of automation.[57]

Adrian Harper, a researcher at the New Economics Foundation and editor of the report, *The Shorter Working Week: A Radical and Pragmatic*

*Proposal*, told the tech magazine *Gizmodo*: "It's just that the proceeds of automation should be shared evenly—in the form of working time reduction. Machines should liberate us from work, not subject us to this ever-increasing inequality."[58] German trade unions have gone so far as to successfully strike for a 28-hour workweek.

Even before the pandemic many workplaces and occupations in the United States had been shortening their workweeks and making jobs more flexible. More people than ever before are working from home one or more days a week, and many are having work meetings over zoom. Other people are already working four-day workweeks in such fields as law enforcement and nursing. Many people working in the "gig economy" would welcome stable work and shorter workweeks with benefits. It only stands to reason that since robots are doing more of the work that humans should be working less and enjoying their leisure time more.

Sanders references a 1930 essay, Economic Possibilities for Our Grandchildren, written by John Maynard Keynes whose 15-hour workweek by the 21st century based on his vision of economic and technological progress had fallen short. And then writes:

> But if we make the right choices and investments, we might get to the place where, as Keynes suggested, "for the first time since his creation, man will be faced with his real, his permanent problem – how to use his freedom from pressing economic cares, how to occupy the leisure, which science and compound interest will have won for him, to live wisely and agreeably and well."[59]

### *Medicare for All, Free College Education, and Expanded Social Security Must Be Guaranteed*

While most European states with much smaller Gross Domestic Products (GDPs) take care of their citizens' basic needs across society and provide more for health care, education, and retirement than the United States does, this does not need to be. During this transitional period from the former industrial economy to the new technology economy, not only could the US catch up with most other developed nations in the world that treat these basic needs as fundamental human rights, but we could also surpass all of them. If only we addressed our grossly obscene and inequitable systems of taxation where currently the top 1% of all Americans own more wealth than the bottom 92% and whose CEOs of major corporations earn 400 times more than what their employees make.

With some relatively minor changes in the tax codes and redistribution of a relatively small portion of that wealth, the United States could provide universal health care to all its citizens for less money than it currently spends on health care including what it does not spend to insure or under insure some 85 million people. The United States could once again provide "free" education to students at public colleges and universities as it did back in the 1950s and 1960s.

> By embracing Medicare for All, as well as plans to expand Social Security, we can ensure that working-class people – many of whom find themselves self-employed or working in the gig economy – will not be left in the lurch because they do not have a steady employer that provides health benefits and a pension.[60]

## Constitutionalism and the Missing Struggle for a New Democracy

There are two constitutional traditions in the United States of America: one derived from the federal constitution and the other derived from 50 state constitutions. The former tradition has been largely static, even stagnant, and has not been meaningfully amended since the voting age was lowered from age 21 to 18 in 1971. Comparatively, the state constitutional tradition has been a dynamic "history of change, revision and innovation."[61] During the 2022 midterm elections, for example, by way of referendums or initiatives and propositions, voters across the nation decided constitutional matters by general votes on abortion and health care, elections and voting, firearms, marijuana, minimum wage, and sports betting.[62] Specifically, voters in California, Michigan, and Vermont amended their state constitutions to effectively secure the right to an abortion; voters in Oregon amended their Constitution to give every resident a fundamental right to affordable health care; voters in Nevada amended their Constitution to allow open primaries and ranked-choice voting; and voters in Iowa amended their Constitution to affirm the right to keep and bear arms.

In contrast to the US Constitution and the convening of national conventions that are quite limited or restrictive when it comes to amendment or change, the state constitutions are far more flexible and directly assessable to the people. They have been "a forum for reconsidering, and ultimately revising or rejecting, a number of governing principles and institutions that were adopted by the federal convention of 1787."[63] In other words, while the federal constitution does not permit citizens to play a role in lawmaking beyond voting for representatives in Congress, many state constitutions require certain measures to be submitted to the people before they can take effect. Similarly, other state constitutions may allow for the enactment of some, or even all, statutes based on the outcome of a popular vote.

Positive rights provisions first appeared in the late 19th and early 20th centuries. Most notably during the late Reconstruction-Era conventions in Alabama, North Carolina, and South Carolina. These provisions were made for state and local governments to address the needs of the poor, disabled, or elderly. Next, Progressive-Era state constitutional conventions witnessed

Americans trying to place their social and economic rights directly into the structure of the political arrangements, such as limiting the maximum number of hours worked per week, establishing a minimum wage per hour, securing safe working conditions, and compensating for workplace injuries. During other periods in American history, government provisions were established for providing shelter for the homeless or compensation for victims of crime.[64]

In a moment of Depression-era radicalism, Nebraskan voters rejected bicameralism in favor of a unicameral legislature. In addition to being "sites of revision and experimentation," state constitutional conventions have also "served as forums for debating ideas, like the wisdom of a bicameral legislature, that are practically unheard of in national politics."[65] Similarly, a delegate to the Illinois constitutional convention of 1969 and 1970 in response to the US Supreme Court's decision in Reynolds v. Sims, which asked of the states that they make "honest and good faith efforts to construct districts, in both houses of the legislature, as nearly of equal population as practicable" stated: "With one-man-one vote there is absolutely no reason at all for having two houses of legislature. It is purely duplicative…running over the same track twice with different groups of people."[66]

As Jamelle Bouie has concluded, because "of their flexibility, because of the frequency and relative ease with which they change, state constitutions and state constitution-making are valuable forms for practicing democracy."[67] They also provide a model or a road map in both substance and procedure for the types of US Constitutional reforms necessary to make our tripartite system of federal government more representative of the people's interests. For example, with one person one vote and the elimination of the Electoral College, a case could be made for doing away with the Senate and a bicameral system of government while incorporating such customary or former tasks as the confirmation of justices and judges into the expanding duties of the House. Then the federal system of government would be like the unicameral state legislature in Nebraska, as well as the unicameral city councils, county boards, and school districts that operate throughout the United States.

Back in the day when the New Deal Republican George Norris was campaigning to change Nebraska's bicameral system into a unicameral system during the height of the Great Depression and it was voted up and down by nearly a half million people, 286,086 in favor and 193,152 against, he pointed out that the bicameral system of government had been modeled after the British Parliament. Where only the House of Commons had representatives elected by the people. Its upper body the House of Lords consisting of aristocratic members appointed by the king. Norris also emphasized that what was relevant is that the "constitutions of our various states are built upon the idea that there is but one class" of people. And "if this be true, there is no sense or reason in having the same thing done twice, especially if it is to be done by two bodies of men elected in the same way and having the same jurisdiction."[68]

## Transforming an Old Democratic Minority into a New Democratic Majority

The missing struggle for a "fourth founding" or fourth tier of American constitutional democracy is

> rooted not only in the language of our Constitution and laws, but also in our expanded national creed of liberty and justice for all not only in the actions of government, but also in the commitments of citizens, not only in the reinvention of federal structures, but also in the devolution of power to local governance.

The fourth tier would build on the "second" and "third" tiers of American democracy that in succession began with a functioning US Constitution in 1789. The "second founding" referring to the adoption of the Reconstruction amendments that abolished slavery, guaranteed equal protection under the law, and made Black male citizens eligible to vote in the period following the Civil War. The "third founding" referring to the passage of the Civil Rights Act of 1964 prohibiting discrimination based on race, color, religion, sex, or national origin in response to the civil rights movement following the Brown v. Board of Education (1954, 1955) decisions that overturned "separate but equal" and outlawed racial segregation. The contemporary "fourth founding" of American democracy refers to what needs to be done to build upon and rearrange the existing constitutional republic from indirect, unequal, and minority rule to majoritarian rule by direct vote on the adoptions of initiatives, referendums, amendments, and propositions.

The rest of this democratic vision revolves around an incorporation of the Final Report and Recommendations from *Our Common Purpose: Reinventing American Democracy for the 21st Century* by the Commission on the Practice of Democratic Citizenship, 2020. That Common Purpose emerges based on a rights-based representative government in which (1) elected leaders are constrained by constitutionalism, rules of law, the separation of powers, the free expression of people, and the legal protection and moral affirmation of the rights of individuals, and (2) those groups and parties that are not part of the electoral majorities cannot easily be disenfranchised or suffer loss of their rights. The Commission envisions a representative constitutional democracy dependent "on a virtuous cycle in which responsive political institutions foster a healthy civil culture of participation and responsibility." This culture – a combination of values, norms, and narratives – keeps our political institutions responsive and inclusive. "Institutions and culture interact in the realm of civil society: the ecosystem of associations and groups in which people practice habits of participation and self-rule and reinforce norms of mutual obligation."[69]

Although I generally agree with the strategies and recommendations for reinventing American Democracy for the 21st century, I continue to believe that both the Electoral College and privately funded elections are fundamentally anti-democratic and need to be abolished if a "government of the people, by the people, for the people" is ever to be achieved.

### Overview of Strategies and Recommendations

STRATEGY 1: Achieve Equality of Voice and Representation

RECOMMENDATION 1.1
Substantially enlarge the House of Representatives through federal legislation to make it and the Electoral College more representative of the nation's population.

RECOMMENDATION 1.2
Introduce ranked-choice voting in presidential, congressional, and state elections.

RECOMMENDATION 1.3
Amend or repeal and replace the 1967 law that mandates single-member districts for the House, so that states have the option to use multi-member districts on the condition that they adopt a non-winner-take-all election model.

RECOMMENDATION 1.4
Support adoption, through state legislation, of independent citizen-redistricting commissions in all fifty states. Complete nationwide adoption, through federal legislation, that requires fair congressional districts to be determined by state-established independent citizen-redistricting commissions; allows these commissions to meet criteria with non-winner-take-all models; and provides federal funding for these state processes, with the goal of establishing national consistency in procedures.

RECOMMENDATION 1.5
Amend the Constitution to authorize the regulation of election contributions and spending to eliminate undue influence of money in our political system, and to protect the rights of all Americans to free speech, political participation, and meaningful representation in government.

RECOMMENDATION 1.6
Pass strong campaign-finance disclosure laws in all fifty states that require full transparency for campaign donations, including from 501(c)(4) organizations and LLCs.

RECOMMENDATION 1.7
Pass "clean election laws" for federal, state, and local elections through mechanisms such as public matching donation systems and democracy vouchers, which amplify the power of small donors.

RECOMMENDATION 1.8
Establish, through federal legislation, eighteen year-terms for Supreme Court justices with appointments staggered such that one nomination comes up during each term of Congress. At the end of their term, justices will transition to an appeals court or, if they choose, to senior status for the remainder of their life tenure, which would allow them to determine how much time they spend hearing cases on appeals court.

STRATEGY 2: Empower Voters

RECOMMENDATION 2.1
Give people more choices about where and when they vote, with state-level legislation in all states that support the implementation of vote centers and early voting. During an emergency like COVID-19, officials must be prepared to act swiftly and adopt extraordinary measures to preserve ballot access and protect the fundamental right to vote.

RECOMMENDATION 2.2
Change federal election day to Veterans Day to honor the service of veterans and the sacrifices they have made in defense of our constitutional democracy, and to ensure that voting can occur on a day that many people have off from work. Align state election calendars with this new federal election day.

RECOMMENDATION 2.3
Establish, through state and federal legislation, same-day registration and universal automatic voter registration, with sufficient funding and training to ensure that all government agencies that have contact with citizens include such registration as part of their processes

RECOMMENDATION 2.4
Establish, through state legislation, the preregistration of sixteen- and seventeen-year-olds and provide educational opportunities for them to practice voting as part of the preregistration process.

RECOMMENDATION 2.5
Establish, through congressional legislation, that voting in federal elections be a requirement of citizenship, just as jury service is in the states. All eligible

voters would have to participate, in person or by mail, or submit a valid reason for nonparticipation. Eligible voters who do not do so would receive a citation and small fine. (Participation could, of course, include voting for "none of the above.")

## RECOMMENDATION 2.6
Establish, through state legislatures and/or offices of secretaries of state, paid voter orientation for voters participating in their first federal election, analogous to a combination of jury orientation and jury pay. Most states use short videos produced by the state judicial system to provide jurors with a nonpolitical orientation to their duty; first-time voters should receive a similar orientation to their duty.

## RECOMMENDATION 2.7
Restore federal and state voting rights to citizens with felony convictions immediately and automatically upon their release from prison, and ensure that those rights are also restored to those already living in the community.

STRATEGY 3: Ensure the Responsiveness of Government Institutions

## RECOMMENDATION 3.1
Adopt formats, processes, and technologies that are designed to encourage widespread participation by residents in official public hearings and meetings at local and state levels.

## RECOMMENDATION 3.2
Design structured and engaging mechanisms for every member of Congress to interact directly and regularly with a random sample of their constituents in an informed and substantive conversation about policy areas under consideration.

## RECOMMENDATION 3.3
Promote experimentation with citizens' assemblies to enable the public to interact directly with Congress as an institution on issues of Congress's choosing.

## RECOMMENDATION 3.4
Expand the breadth of participatory opportunities at municipal and state levels for citizens to shape decision-making, budgeting, and other policy-making processes.

STRATEGY 4: Dramatically Expand Civic Bridging Capacity

RECOMMENDATION 4.1
Establish a National Trust for Civic Infrastructure to scale up social, civic, and democratic infrastructure. Fund the Trust with a major nationwide investment campaign that bridges private enterprise and philanthropic seed funding. This might later be sustained through annual appropriations from Congress on the model of the National Endowment for Democracy.

RECOMMENDATION 4.2
Activate a range of funders to invest in the leadership capacity of the so-called civic one million: the catalytic leaders who drive civic renewal in communities around the country. Use this funding to encourage these leaders to support innovations in bridge-building and participatory constitutional democracy.

STRATEGY 5: Build Civic Information Architecture that Supports Common Purpose

RECOMMENDATION 5.1
Form a high-level working group to articulate and measure social media's civic obligations and incorporate those defined metrics in the Democratic Engagement Project, described in Recommendation 5.5.

RECOMMENDATION 5.2
Through state and/or federal legislation, subsidize innovation to reinvent the public functions that social media has displaced: for instance, with a tax on digital advertising that could be deployed in a public media fund that would support experimental approaches to public social media platforms as well as local and regional investigative journalism.

RECOMMENDATION 5.3
To supplement experiments with public media platforms (Recommendation 5.2), establish a public-interest mandate for for-profit social media platforms. Analogous to zoning requirements, this mandate would require such for-profit digital platform companies to support the development of designated public-friendly digital spaces on their own platforms.

RECOMMENDATION 5.4
Through federal legislation and regulation, require of digital platform companies: interoperability (like railroad-track gauges), data portability, and data openness sufficient to equip researchers to measure and evaluate democratic engagement in digital contexts.

RECOMMENDATION 5.5
Establish and fund the Democratic Engagement Project: a new data source and clearinghouse for research that supports social and civic infrastructure. The Project would conduct a focused, large-scale, systematic, and longitudinal study of individual and organizational democratic engagement, including the full integration of measurement and the evaluation of democratic engagement in digital contexts.

STRATEGY 6: Inspire a Culture of Commitment to American Constitutional Democracy and One Another

RECOMMENDATION 6.1
Establish a universal expectation of a year of national service and dramatically expand funding for service programs or fellowships that would offer young people paid service opportunities. Such opportunities should be made available not only in AmeriCorps or the military but also in local programs offered by municipal governments, local news outlets, and nonprofit organizations.

RECOMMENDATION 6.2
To coincide with the 250th anniversary of the Declaration of Independence, create a Telling Our Nation's Story initiative to engage communities throughout the country in direct, open-ended, and inclusive conversations about the complex and always evolving American story. Led by civil society organizations, these conversations will allow participants at all points along the political spectrum to explore both their feelings about and hopes for this country.

RECOMMENDATION 6.3
Launch a philanthropic initiative to support the growing civil society ecosystem of civic gatherings and rituals focused on the ethical, moral, and spiritual dimensions of our civic values.

RECOMMENDATION 6.4
Increase public and private funding for media campaigns and grassroots narratives about how to revitalize constitutional democracy and encourage a commitment to our constitutional democracy and one another.

RECOMMENDATION 6.5
Invest in civic educators and civic education for all ages and in all communities through curricula, ongoing program evaluations, professional development for teachers, and a federal award program that recognizes civic-learning achievements. These measures should encompass lifelong (K–12 and adult) civic-learning experiences with the full community in mind.

## Notes

1  Jamelle Bouie. 2023. Something's got to give. *The New York Times*. May 7. Sunday Opinion, p. 3.
2  Jill Lepore. 2023. How to stave off constitutional extinction. *The New York Times*. July 2. Sunday Opinion, pp. 6–7.
3  Ibid.
4  Danielle Allen. 2023. The House was supposed to grow with population. It didn't. Let's fix that. *Washington Post*. February 28. www.washingtonpost.com/opini ons/2023/02/28/danielle-allen-democracy-reform-congress-house-expansion/
5  Ibid.
6  Ibid.
7  As of April 23, 2023, nationwide support for a *Citizens United* Amendment included 22 states and more than 800 cities that have passed resolutions to overturn the disastrous anti-democratic decision that gave corporations the right to spend unlimited amounts of money to influence elections. While most Congressional Democrats in the House and Senate support the Amendment, all but a handful of Republicans oppose it. Source: Public Citizen.
8  Ronald Brownstein. 2023. Does Trump Stand a Real Change to Repeat 2016? The 'party decides" theory faces it biggest test. *The Atlantic*. March 2. www.thea tlantic.com/politics/archive/2023/03/will-it-matter-if-republican-leadership-uni tes-against-trump/673254/
9  Jamelle Bouie. 2023. The threat to freedom is coming from the states. *The New York Times*. May 28. Sunday Opinion, p. 3.
10  Marc Elias. 2023. Five voting laws needed to protect democracy. *Democracy Docket*. February 8. www.democracydocket.com/opinion/five-voting-laws-nee ded-to-protect-democracy/
11  The Guardian. 2021. U.S. added to the list of 'backsliding democracies" for the first time. *The Guardian*. November 22. www.theguardian.com/us-news/2021/ nov/22/us-list-backsliding-democracies-civil-libertiesinternational
12  Robert W. McChesney and John Nichols. 2021. The local journalism initiative: A proposal to protect and extend democracy. *Columbia Journalism Review*. November. 20. www.cjr.org/business_of_news/the-local-journalism-ini tiative.php
13  Ibid.
14  Bobby Azarian. 2023. A neuroscientist explains why stupidity is an existential threat to America. *RawStory*. February 20. www.rawstory.com/raw-investigates/ threat-of-stupidity/
15  Paul Krugman. 2023. The rich are Crazier than you and me. *The New York Times*. July 6. www.nytimes.com/2023/07/06/opinion/robert-kennedy-jr-silicon-valley.html
16  D.D. Guttenplan and Bhaskar Sunkara. 2023. Cornel Well should run as a democrat. *The Nation*. July 6. www.thenation.com/article/politics/cornel-west-democratic-primary. See also, Wen Stephenson. 2023. Cornel West: The Christian socialist running for president. *The Nation*. July 31. www.thenation.com/article/ activism/cornel-west-interview
17  Manda Raz and Pouria Pouryaha, eds. 2021. *Decision Making in Emergency Medicine: Bases, Errors and Solutions*. Gateway East, Singapore: Springer Nature.
18  Azarian. 2023.

19 Eric Lutz. 2023. Tucker Carlson doesn't think much of Donald Trump—Or his audience. *Vanity Fair*. March 8. www.vanityfair.com/news/2023/03/tucker-carl son-doesnt-think-much-of-donald-trump-or-his-audience

20 Ian G. Anson. 2018. Partisanship, political knowledge, and the Dunning-Kruger effect. *Political Psychology*, 39(5): 1173–1192. https://onlinelibrary.wiley.com/ doi/abs/10.1111/pops.12490

21 Chris Hedges. 2023. America's theater of the absurd: Our politics had become an endless carnival. *Salon*. January 10. www.salon.com/2023/01/10/americas-thea ter-of-the-absurd-our-has-become-an-endless-carnival/

22 Hedges. 2023. It is also worth noting that less than 10 months later, McCarthy was voted out as House Speaker for working with the Democrats to not shut the government down.

23 Ibid.

24 Bernie Sanders. 2023. *It's OK to be Angry About Capitalism*. New York: Crown, p. 12.

25 Ibid., p. 165.

26 John Nichols. 2023. Marianne Williamson: Anything is possible. *The Nation*. March 9. www.thenation.com/article/politics/marianne-williamson-2024-race/

27 Ibid.

28 Ibid.

29 The Editorial Board. 2023. Florida is trying to take away the American right to speak freely. *The New York Times*. March 4. www.nytimes.com/2023/03/04/ opinion/desantis-florida-free-speech-bill.html. In a similar vein, as of January 25, 2023, GOP state lawmakers in at least 32 states had pre-filed or introduced 150 restrictive voting bills making it harder to vote. See Brennan Center for Justice. *Voting Laws Roundup*. February 2023. www.brennancenter.org/our-work/resea rch-reports/voting-laws-roundup-february-2023

30 Justin McCarthy. 2022. U.S. approval of labor unions at highest point since 1965. *Gallup*. August 30. https://news.gallup.com/poll/398303/approval-labor-unions-highest-point-1965.aspx

31 Andrew Wallender. 2023. Starbucks, education strikes fuel 17-year high in work stoppages. *Bloomberg Law*. January 10. https://news.bloomberglaw.com/daily-labor-report/starbucks-education-strikes-fuel-17-year-high-in-work-stoppages

32 David Feldman. 2023. Workers STRIKE! Not missiles. *David Feldman Show*. March 3. https://davidfeldman.substack.com/p/workers-strike-not-missiles?

33 Ibid.

34 Ibid.

35 Quinn Slobodian. 2023. *Crack-Up Capitalism: Market Radicals and the Dream of a World Without Democracy*. New York: Metropolitan Books. Quoted from description. https://tertulia.com/book/crack-up-capitalism-market-radicals-and-the-dream-of-a-world-without-democracy-quinn-slobodian

36 Ibid.

37 Chauncey DeVega. 2023. Beware Joe Biden, Donald Trump has got his hands on AI. *Salon*. May 19. www.salon.com/2023/05/19/beware-joe-biden-donald-has-got-his-hands-on-ai/

38 James Vincent. 2023. Republicans respond to Biden reelection announcement with AI-generated attack ad. *The Verge*. April 25. www.theverge.com/2023/4/25/ 23697328/biden-reelection-rnc-ai-generated-attack-ad-deepfake

39 Ibid.

40 DeVega. 2023.
41 Vincent. 2023.
42 Ibid.
43 Ibid.
44 Personally, I happen to think that an unregulated AI would be "on the side" of autocracy over democracy simply because the former is more dependable and predictable than the latter.
45 Quoted in Sanders. 2023, p. 196.
46 Sanders. 2023, p. 197.
47 Tammy Baldwin. March 27, 2019. www.baldwin.senate.gov/news/press-releases/reward-work-act-2019
48 S.915 – Reward Work Act. 116th Congress (2019–2020). www.congress.gov/bill/116th-congress/senate-bill/915/text
49 Sanders. 2023, p. 206.
50 Timothy Shenk. 2022. *Realigners: Partisan Hacks, Political Visionaries, and the Struggle to Rule American Democracy*. New York: Farrar, Straus and Giroux.
51 Gregg Barak. 2017. *Unchecked Corporate Power: Why the Crimes of Multinational Corporations are Routinized Away and What We Can Do About It*. New York and London: Rutledge.
52 Sanders. 2023, p. 199.
53 The Collective Intelligence Project. 2023. Whitepaper. https://cip.org/whitepaper
54 Money Watch. 2017. A tax-the-robots push emerges in California. *CBS News*. September 6. www.cbsnews.com/news/a-tax-the-robots-push-emerges-in-california/
55 Ryan Abbott and Bret Bogenschneider. 2018. Should Robots pay taxes? Tax policy in the age of automation. *Harvard Law & Policy Review*, 12: 145. https://harvardlpr.com/wp-content/uploads/sites/20/2018/03/AbbottBogenschneider.pdf
56 Ibid., p. 175.
57 Dan Sabbagh. 2018. John McConnell shapes labour case for four-day week. *The Guardian*. November 8. www.theguardian.com/politics/2018/nov/09/john-mcdonnell-shapes-labour-case-for-four-day-week
58 Brian Merchant. 2019. The case for an automation-powered 4-day work week. *Gizmodo*. February 1. https://gizmodo.com/the-case-for-an-automation-powered-4-day-work-week-1832248913
59 Quoted in Sanders. 2023, p. 202.
60 Sanders. 2023, p. 203.
61 Jamelle Bouie. 2022. There is a way to break out of our constitutional stagnation. *The New York Times*. November 18. www.nytimes.com/2022/11/18/opinion/midterms-states-constitutions.html
62 NBC News. 2022. Ballot measure results 2022. *Decision 2022*. November 20. www.nbcnews.com/politics/2022-elections/ballot-measures
63 Quoted in Boule, 2022 from John J. Dinan, 2006. *The American State Constitutional Tradition*. Lawrence, KA: University Press of Kansas.
64 Gregg Barak. 1991. *Gimme Shelter: A Social History of Homelessness in Contemporary America*. New York: Prager.

65  Boule. 2022.
66  Ibid.
67  Ibid.
68  Nebraska Legislature Website. 2023. History of the Nebraska unicameral: The birth of a unicameral. Retrieved February 22. https://nebraskalegislature.gov/about/history_unicameral.php
69  Reinventing American Democracy for the 21st Century, p. 3.

# INDEX

For Product Safety Concerns and Information please contact our EU
representative  GPSR@taylorandfrancis.com
Taylor & Francis Verlag GmbH, Kaufingerstraße 24, 80331 München, Germany

www.ingramcontent.com/pod-product-compliance
Ingram Content Group UK Ltd.
Pitfield, Milton Keynes, MK11 3LW, UK
UKHW021450080625
459435UK00012B/446